This is an excellent book. Critical studies are gaining ground in the entrepreneurship field; and this edited volume provides a much needed overview that challenges our thinking on what constitutes entrepreneurship and why. The chapters highlight the value of critically reviewing well-known phenomena such as minority, ethnic, indigenous entrepreneurship, social entrepreneurship, gender and entrepreneurship. The editors have done a superb job in assembling such knowledgeable contributors. A must read for all of us interested in the contribution critical perspectives can make to entrepreneurship research.

Friederike Welter, *Institut für Mittelstandsforschung Bonn, and University of Siegen, Germany*

The coming of Essers, Dey, Tedmanson and Verduyn's excellent collection is in itself a manifesto for the strength of critical entrepreneurship studies. As contributions to this field, each and every chapter voices entrepreneurship as a social change activity capable of speaking back, explicitly or implicitly, to what the 'entrepreneur' of neoliberalism attempts to conceal. At the same time, each chapter articulates a whole other world of possibilities. A 'must read' to act upon!

Marta B. Calás, *Professor of Organization Studies and International Management, University of Massachusetts, USA*

Adopting a proactive stance for highlighting new critiques and contexts of entrepreneurship, this thought-provoking collection of critical narratives discusses entrepreneurship as a social change activity. With an interest in non-traditional entrepreneurial activities, this authoritative volume advances critical scholarship and fosters a new agenda for entrepreneurship research in the coming decade.

Denise Fletcher, *Professor of Entrepreneurship and Innovation, University of Luxembourg, Luxembourg*

Critical Perspectives on Entrepreneurship

Entrepreneurship is largely considered to be a positive force, driving venture creation and economic growth. *Critical Perspectives on Entrepreneurship* questions the accepted norms and dominant assumptions of scholarship on the matter, and reveals how they can actually obscure important questions of identity, ideology and inequality.

The book's distinguished authors and editors explore how entrepreneurship study can privilege certain forms of economic action, while labelling other, more collective forms of organisation and exchange as problematic. Demystifying the archetypal vision of the white, male entrepreneur, this book gives voice to other entrepreneurial subjectivities and engages with the tensions, paradoxes and ambiguities at the heart of the topic.

This challenging collection seeks to further the momentum for alternate analyses of the field, and to promote the growing voice of critical entrepreneurship studies. It is a useful tool for researchers, advanced students and policy-makers.

Caroline Essers is Associate Professor of Strategic Human Resource Management at Radboud University, the Netherlands.

Pascal Dey is Associate Professor in the People, Organizations and Society Department, Grenoble Ecole de Management, France, and Senior Lecturer at the Institute for Business Ethics, University of St Gallen, Switzerland.

Deirdre Tedmanson is Associate Professor and Associate Head of School in the School of Psychology, Social Work and Social Policy at the University of South Australia.

Karen Verduyn is Senior Lecturer at the Faculty of Economics and Business Administration at Vrije Universiteit Amsterdam, the Netherlands, and Programme Director of their M.Sc. in Entrepreneurship.

Routledge Rethinking Entrepreneurship Research
Edited by Alain Fayolle and Philippe Riot

The current focus on entrepreneurship as a purely market-based phenomenon and an unquestionably desirable economic and profitable activity leads to undervaluing and under-researching important issues in relation to power, ideology or phenomenology. New postures, new theoretical lenses and new approaches are needed to study entrepreneurship as a contextualised and socially embedded phenomenon. The objective of this series therefore is to adopt a critical and constructive posture towards the theories, methods, epistemologies, assumptions and beliefs which dominate mainstream thinking. It aims to provide a forum for scholarship which questions the prevailing assumptions and beliefs currently dominating entrepreneurship research and invites contributions from a wide range of different communities of scholars, which focus on novelty, diversity and critique.

Rethinking Entrepreneurship
Debating research orientations
Edited by Alain Fayolle and Philippe Riot

Family Entrepreneurship
Rethinking the research agenda
Kathleen Randerson, Cristina Bettinelli, Alain Fayolle and Giovanna Dossena

Challenging Entrepreneurship Research
Edited by Hans Landström, Annaleena Parankangas, Alain Fayolle and Philippe Riot

Critical Perspectives on Entrepreneurship
Challenging Dominant Discourses
Edited by Caroline Essers, Pascal Dey, Deirdre Tedmanson and Karen Verduyn

Critical Perspectives on Entrepreneurship

Challenging Dominant Discourses

Edited by Caroline Essers,
Pascal Dey, Deirdre Tedmanson
and Karen Verduyn

Routledge
Taylor & Francis Group

LONDON AND NEW YORK

First published 2017 by Routledge

2 Park Square, Milton Park, Abingdon, Oxfordshire OX14 4RN
52 Vanderbilt Avenue, New York, NY 10017

Routledge is an imprint of the Taylor & Francis Group, an informa business

First issued in paperback 2019

British Library Cataloguing in Publication Data
A catalogue record for this book is available from the British Library

Library of Congress Cataloging in Publication Data
A catalog record for this book has been requested

ISBN: 978-1-138-93887-8 (hbk)
ISBN: 978-0-367-87338-7 (pbk)

Typeset in Bembo
by Wearset Ltd, Boldon, Tyne and Wear

Contents

PART V
Deconstructing entrepreneurship 223

Contributors

Haya Al-Dajani is an Associate Professor (Reader) in Entrepreneurship at the Futures Entrepreneurship Centre, Plymouth Business School at Plymouth University in the UK. Her research focuses on the critical relationship between entrepreneurship and female empowerment in development contexts. Al-Dajani's work has been published in the *British Journal of Management, Gender, Work and Organisation, International Small Business Journal, Industrial Marketing Management,* the *International Journal of Entrepreneurial Behaviour Research* and the *International Journal of Gender and Entrepreneurship.*

Huriye Yeröz Aygören obtained her Ph.D. degree in management from Jönköping University, International Business School in Sweden. Her research concerns the intersectional analysis of identity, difference and diversity in the contexts of entrepreneurship. With her work, she seeks to contribute to a deeper understanding of diverse contexts and subject formation involved in entrepreneurial processes by combining the insights of entrepreneurship studies with social theories. Her research has been featured at various international conferences and in journals such as *Equality, Diversity and Inclusion: An International Journal* and the *European Journal of International Management.* She currently teaches at Isik University in Turkey.

Karin Berglund is Associate Professor and Centre Director for Stockholm School of Entrepreneurship at Stockholm University. She has a special interest in the expansion of conventional entrepreneurship to new contexts and to emerging forms of social entrepreneurships. Her overarching research interest lies in studying the emergence of these entrepreneurships as part of an enterprise culture fostered in neo-liberal societies, and analysing the effects they produce. She uses her mainly ethnographic studies to contribute to critical management, organisation and entrepreneurship studies.

Peter de Boer is an M.Sc. who has graduated *bene meritum* at the Radboud University Nijmegen's Institute for Management Research in the field of economic geography. He has specific interests in the fields of urban and regional economics, network theories, sustainable energy and entrepreneurship. In 2013 and 2014 he conducted extensive research on the significance of small-scale entrepreneurship in South East Asia, where he expanded his interest in and knowledge of the means of entrepreneuring and economic development in the so-called Global South. Currently he works for a private firm in the Netherlands as a consultant for European funding, such as ESF and ERDF.

Pascal Dey is Associate Professor at Grenoble Ecole de Management (People, Organizations and Society Department), and Senior Lecturer at the University of St Gallen (Institute for Business Ethics). His main research interests unfold at the intersection of (social) entrepreneurship, critical management studies, and the ethico-politics of organising. His most recent research investigates new ways of realigning entrepreneurship with society based on the work of Giorgio Agamben (destituent power), Michel Foucault (parrhesia) and theories of prefigurative praxis. His work has appeared in, among others, *Organization, Organization Studies, Entrepreneurship and Regional Development, International Journal of Entrepreneurial Behaviour and Research, Journal of Enterprising Communities* and *Journal of Business Ethics*.

Caroline Essers is Associate Professor of Strategic Human Resource Management at the Radboud University Nijmegen, Faculty of Management. Her research focuses on the social dynamics of entrepreneurship, such as the identity constructions of (female migrant) entrepreneurs and their networking. Her research on entrepreneurship uses diverse perspectives, such as postcolonial feminist theory, and social constructivist approaches, such as the narrative/life-story approach. Her work has been published in *Organization Studies, Organization, Human Relations, Gender, Work and Organization, British Journal of Management, Entrepreneurship and Regional Development*, and *International Journal of Entrepreneurial Behaviour and Research*. She is a board member of the Entrepreneurship Studies Network (a special interest group of the Institute for Small Business and Entrepreneurship), and an Associate Editor of *Gender, Work and Organization*.

Michelle Evans is Associate Professor in Leadership with the School of Management and Marketing at Charles Sturt University, Australia. As a leadership scholar, she investigates areas of Indigenous leadership, collective leadership, political leadership and Indigenous entrepreneurship. Her doctoral study focused on establishing a theoretical framework for the leadership work enacted by Aboriginal and Torres Strait Islander artists in Australia. This was followed by a Fulbright post-doctoral study replicating her doctoral research in the USA interviewing First Alaskan, Native Hawaiian and American Indian artists about the intersection of their artist practice and leadership. She is Director of Australia's only Indigenous entrepreneurship growth development programme. The MURRA Indigenous Business Master Classes engage established businesses in a six-day programme and have built a significant and influential alumni. She has published widely in journals, including *Public Administration Review and Leadership*, and she is currently working on her first sole-authored book project with Routledge publishers.

Gerard Hanlon is Professor of Organisational Sociology at the School of Business and Management, Queen Mary University of London. His recent work has concentrated on neo-liberalism, post-workerism and the changing nature of work and subjectivity, the shift from a real to a total subsumption of labour to capital, innovation and entrepreneurship. His most recent work dealing with entrepreneurship and Critical Management Studies has been published in *Sociology* (forthcoming 2017), *Human Relations* (forthcoming 2017), and as a book entitled *The Dark Side of Management: A Secret History of Management Knowledge* (2015, Routledge, London).

Miguel Imas lectures on organisational-social psychology at the Faculty of Business and Law, Kingston University, and is Associate Researcher at the London Multimedia Lab, LSE. He holds a B.Sc. and Ph.D. in Social Psychology from the LSE, and is and has been visiting professor at several universities in South America. He has undertaken extensive (visual) post-colonial ethnographic research in Latin America and Africa, where he has engaged with Indigenous as well as deprived communities and organisations. His research focuses on postcolonial and decolonial organisation studies, postcolonial feminism, critical management, and creativity and sustainability among disenfranchised communities and organisations. His most recent work was published by the University of Chicago Press/Intellect Ltd.

Trevor Jones is an Honorary Professor at the Centre for Research in Ethnic Minority Entrepreneurship (CREME), University of Birmingham. He is recognised as a pioneer in the field, and was responsible for the first systematic study of ethnic minority businesses in the UK. He is currently working on a wide variety of issues such as: new migrant entrepreneurs; the employment of migrant workers; and the historical development of ethnic minority business research in Europe. He has published extensively in journals such as *Work, Employment and Society*, *Entrepreneurship and Regional Development*, and *Ethnic and Racial Studies*.

Isaac Lyne is a UWS Ph.D. candidate writing on social enterprise and local economic development in Cambodia. Between 2009 and 2012, he coordinated a social enterprise project based at the Royal University of Phnom Penh funded by the British Council. He has also been a coordinator of the National Social Enterprise Conference of Cambodia since 2011. He has published articles in *Education, Knowledge and Economy* and the *International Journal for Management Research*, and he has also co-authored papers for EMES (European Research Network on social Enterprise).

Susan Marlow is Professor of Entrepreneurship at the University of Nottingham, UK, holder of the Queens Award for Enterprise and Fellow of the UK Institute of Small Business and Entrepreneurship. Her key research interests focus on the influence of gender on women's entrepreneurial activities, in which context she has published extensively in top-rated UK and US journals such as *International Small Business Journal, British Journal of Management, Journal of Business Venturing,* and *Entrepreneurship, Theory and Practice.*

Dorota Marsh is a senior lecturer at the University of Central Lancashire. Her research interest areas include the Eastern European transition and post-Communist economies. She is MBA programme leader at Lancashire Business School, and received the 'Excellence in Teaching Delivery and Intellectual Stimulation of Students' award.

Banu Özkazanç-Pan is an Assistant Professor of Management and a Fellow at the Entrepreneurship Center at the College of Management, University of Massachusetts-Boston. Her research interests include postcolonial, trans-national and feminist perspectives on entrepreneurship, identity formation in entrepreneurs, and investigating the possibilities for gender equity in entrepreneurial ecosystems. She has published her work in *Academy of Management Review, International Journal of Entrepreneurial Behaviour and Research, Equality, Diversity and Inclusion, New England Journal of Entrepreneurship, Scandinavian Journal of Management* and other outlets.

Monder Ram is Director of the Centre for Research in Ethnic Minority Entrepreneurship (CREME), University of Birmingham. He has extensive experience of working with and researching dynamics of ethnic minority entrepreneurship, employment relations in small firms and policy issues, which has been supported by grants from a full range of research funders, including research councils, government departments, regional and local agencies, and the private sector. He has published extensively in journals such as *Work, Employment and Society, Entrepreneurship and Regional Development,* and *Ethnic and Racial Studies.*

Annika Skoglund is Associate Senior Lecturer at Uppsala University and is currently involved in two ethnographic research projects that span different empirical and theoretical contexts. The first seeks to develop theory about climate social science and the second grapples with criticism of conventional entrepreneurship and the subsequent turn to 'alternative entrepreneurship'. She complements these theoretical curiosities with an advancement of audiovisual methods, specifically videography, for entrepreneurship and organisation studies.

Lothar Smith works as an assistant professor at the Radboud University Nijmegen's Institute for Management Research in the field of development geography. He has specific interests in the fields of international migration, transnationalism, developmental issues, globalisation and urbanity. He is a member of the Nijmegen Centre for Borders Research (NCBR), the Global–Local Divides and Connections (GLOCAL) group, and a visiting researcher at the African Centre for Migration and Society, University of Witwatersrand, South Africa. Recent publications include the co-edited *Gender, Remittances and Development in the Global South* (2015, Ashgate) and other publications regarding transnationalism. He also serves on the editorial board of the *African Human Mobility Review* (AHMR) and the academic advisory board of the African Studies Centre Leiden.

Deirdre Tedmanson is Associate Professor and Associate Head of School in the School of Psychology, Social Work and Social Policy at the University of South Australia. She is an active researcher with the University's Centre for Social Change, where her research focuses on Indigenous policy and governance issues; social development; critical management studies; social and emotional well-being and mental health; participatory action research; and the gendered and cultural dimensions of entrepreneurship. Deirdre is also an associate of the Centre for Aboriginal Economic Policy Research at the Australian National University, and has published widely including in *Organization; Gender, Work and Organization; Management Learning Journal; Culture and Organization; Journal of Management Inquiry;* and the *International Journal of Entrepreneurial Behaviour & Research.*

Annelies Thoelen holds M.A.s in Art History from the KU Leuven (Belgium) and in Cultural Management from the University of Antwerp (Belgium). She obtained her Ph.D. in Business Economics in 2015 from Hasselt University (Belgium), and is currently a lecturer at LUCA School of Arts, C-Mine (Belgium). Her main research interests include the creative industries, ethnic identity, branding strategies of creatives, symbolic value and qualitative research methods, in particular narrative, discursive and rhetoric analysis. Her work has been published in *Culture and Organization.*

Pete Thomas is Senior Lecturer at Lancaster University Management School. His research interests centre on organisational discourse, narrative and process, and employment relations. He has published in leading journals, including *Journal of Management Studies, Organization Studies* and *Business History.*

Karen Verduyn is a senior lecturer at the Faculty of Economics and Business Administration of VU University Amsterdam, and programme director of the Amsterdam (joint) M.Sc. in Entrepreneurship. Her research projects revolve around understanding the complexities of entrepreneurial everyday life. She has published in such journals as the *International Review of Entrepreneurship,* the *Journal of Enterprising Communities, Entrepreneurship and Regional Development, International Journal of Entrepreneurial Behaviour and Research,* and *Organization.* She is a board member of the Entrepreneurship Studies Network (a special interest group of the Institute for Small Business and Entrepreneurship), and the *International Journal of Entrepreneurship and Small Business.*

María Villares is a Research Fellow at the Center for Research in Ethnic Minority Entrepreneurship (CREME), University of Birmingham and Research Associate at the International Migration Institute (University of Oxford). Her research interests are in the areas of international migration, labour market incorporation of migrants, employment relations in small firms, and gender and intergenerational dynamics.

Alia Weston is an Assistant Professor at OCAD University in Toronto, Canada. She has expertise in the areas of design and business management. Her research is focused on understanding how people respond creatively to challenges in their social and organisational environments. In particular, she studies creative engagement and related practices such as innovation, entrepreneurship, art and design to explore how these can contribute to social transformation. Key themes in her research include exploring creative work practices within resource-constrained environments, and exploring how alternative business practices can contribute to solving key challenges in society. She has contributed to work in Africa and Latin America. In conjunction with her research, she runs practical workshops, in which participants engage with issues related to creative and sustainable work practices. The following animation gives an example of her work: https://vimeo.com/83479051.

Patrizia Zanoni is Professor of Organisation Studies in the Faculty of Business Economics at Hasselt University (Belgium) and a Research Fellow at the Faculty of Economics and Business at KU Leuven (Belgium). She leads the research centre SEIN – Identity, Diversity and Inequality Research. Drawing on various theoretical traditions including critical discourse analysis, Marxist theory and institutional theory, her research investigates how social identities (e.g. gender, ethnicity, age and disability) inform struggles over the generation and distribution of symbolic and economic value within and across organisations. Her work has appeared in *Organization, Organization Studies, Human Relations, Journal of Management Studies, Scandinavian Journal of Management, Journal of World Business, Culture and Organization British Journal of Sociology of Education, British Educational Research Journal,* and *Journal of Nursing Management,* as well as numerous chapters in edited volumes.

1 Critical entrepreneurship studies

A manifesto

Caroline Essers, Pascal Dey, Deirdre Tedmanson and Karen Verduyn

This edited collection on critical entrepreneurship studies aims to explore, and thereby expand our understanding of entrepreneurship by elaborating on this popular and widely invoked discourse using different critical perspectives. The reason to write (and read!) this book is at least twofold. First, even though entrepreneurship is a very diverse, multifaceted and contested phenomenon, and regardless of the fact that entrepreneurship research has become increasingly more hospitable towards alternative theoretical influences and methodological procedures, it is fairly uncontroversial to say that the majority of entrepreneurship research is still functionalist in nature (Perren and Jennings 2005). Research in this tradition is mainly interested in entrepreneurship as a purely market-based phenomenon: a 'special' trait or set of behaviours which drive venture creation and which precipitate economic growth. Hence, one reason why we deem this edited collection to be important relates to the observation that aside from a 'few exceptions, the extensive literature on entrepreneurship positions it as a positive economic activity' (Calas *et al.* 2009, p. 552). This focus on entrepreneurship as a 'desirable' economic activity, perceived unquestioningly as positive, obscures important questions about who can sensibly be considered an entrepreneur and who can not (Jones and Spicer 2009); how entrepreneurship works ideologically to conceal the true state of reality (Armstrong 2001; Costa and Saraiva 2012) or to make people do things they would not otherwise do (Dey and Lehner 2016); or how entrepreneurship fuels inequality and perpetuates unequal relations of power (Curran and Blackburn 2001; Kenny and Scriver 2012). Second, although critical approaches may still inhabit a marginal position in the broader academic discourse on entrepreneurship, we assert that critical research has gained noticeable traction over the past decade. Various contributions have been discussed at the influential and important platform of critical management studies conferences, as well as at the annual meetings of the Academy of Management.

In light of the ongoing dominance of functionalist approaches as well as recent signs of change towards more critical and nuanced perspectives, we offer this book as a collection of critical narratives which render visible diverse examples of non-traditional entrepreneurship as well as usually overshadowed aspects of 'traditional' entrepreneurship. The chapters in this book interrogate entrepreneurship from a range of differing perspectives. They each reveal how extant research has tended to privilege entrepreneurship as a distinct field of economic action and an exclusive activity for distinct groups of people, while at the same time illustrating examples of other, more collective and value-based forms of entrepreneurial organising and exchange. Accordingly, the book takes issue with and exposes some of the dominant ideologies, intellectual traditions and prevailing assumptions which bind entrepreneurship within the dictum of profit maximisation and wealth creation (Görling and Rehn 2008; Rindova *et al.* 2009). At the same time, the book assumes a proactive stance in seeking to position entrepreneurship as an activity, behaviour or process which can be linked to new ethical and political possibilities. Together, the chapters give voice to unheard stories, places and potentialities of entrepreneurship which are usually left out of existing research (Steyaert and Katz 2004). In this book, entrepreneurship is reconceptualised as a social change activity that moves against the grain of orthodoxy in order to realise spaces of freedom and otherness (Dey and Steyaert 2016; Hjorth 2004; Verduyn *et al.* 2014; Essers and Tedmanson 2014).

It is our explicit hope that this edited collection will further the momentum for alternate analyses of entrepreneurship within the field of critical scholarship. We have chosen to include illuminating chapters that aim to explore how political and socio-cultural factors influence entrepreneurial processes, identities and activities, and have sought to extend entrepreneurship research horizons by highlighting new critiques and contexts that challenge existing orthodoxies.

The book is divided into five thematic parts. In Part I, we contest the neoliberal aspects of entrepreneurship discourse by showing other meanings of entrepreneurship, including social entrepreneurship initiatives. In Chapter 2, Karin Berglund uses three examples of social entrepreneurship from the Swedish context – a green self-reliant community, a case of supporting women's entrepreneurship, and a project that combines artistry and entrepreneurship – as a vehicle to, through the concept of the precariat, discuss how social entrepreneurship may be political. Through the discussion of standing, the chapter addresses questions such as: Where is social entrepreneurship headed and what does it bring with it? Is social entrepreneurship a path toward sustainability in its ambition to criticise capitalism and non-sustainable society, and to offer more socially, environmentally and culturally sustainable solutions? Or does it indicate, rather – like the precariat – a fragmentation of society which contributes to political exclusion?

In Chapter 3, by drawing upon Gibson-Graham's work, Isaac Lyne illustrates the resistance to homogenising notions of 'community' conveyed by the discourse of social enterprise. He applies critical resource flow analysis to draw out meaningful claims on resources, the way resources come to be mobilised, and how 'surplus' is generated and distributed not only through social enterprise but also through religious festivities and non-monetary exchanges. In Chapter 4, Gerard Hanlon investigates the relationship between entrepreneurship and contemporary capitalism. Taking its cue from the work of Kirzner, Hanlon's contribution suggests that the essence of entrepreneurship is increasingly characterised by the capture of value and not, as common sense has it, creation, innovation and production. Specifically, Hanlon points out that entrepreneurship is increasingly engaged in the use of property rights as a means of capturing value produced beyond the corporation through 'free' labour and the enclosing of skills and knowledge developed elsewhere. In doing so, it encourages a society based in secrecy and mistrust. This contribution concludes that entrepreneurship plays an eminent ideological role in how it justifies a new regime of accumulation. This regime is more unequal; it appears to be increasingly located in rent as opposed to the search for profit-driven efficiencies within the production process and, somewhat unexpectedly, is characterised by capital's growing uninterest in the how or where of production.

In Part II, we aim to show how an ideological dichotomy has been constructed in what we perceive to be hegemonic entrepreneurship research, and between notions of entrepreneurship, economic development and self-employment. We focus here on entrepreneurship for self-employment in non-Western contexts. In Chapter 5, Alia Weston and Miguel Imas expand their theoretical ideas on the barefoot entrepreneurs (i.e. people who dwell at the margins of our society) by exploring them as a reflection of decolonial practices founded on art-resistance and socio-economic principles of a transformative humanistic kind. They discuss these ideas in order to give these entrepreneurs voice and a platform to engage with the ongoing struggles, lives and experiences of marginalised and forgotten communities. These disenfranchised communities have been deprived of a voice by neoliberal capitalist practices that invoke entrepreneurial activity. The entrepreneurial activity imposed by this economic system legitimises their exploitation and marginalisation, continuing to colonise their discourses, identities and daily lives. Critically in this chapter, they question this neoliberal practice in order to further decolonise and expose its exploitative nature. By decolonising, they seek two things: first, to reconstruct entrepreneurship as an emancipatory creative activity that build solidarity among all communities; and second, an entrepreneurship that redistributes economic power and helps communities on a sustainable path.

In Chapter 6, Deirdre Tedmanson and Michelle Evans explore how entrepreneurship research is largely bound by Western organisational discourses. The purpose is to call into question the hegemonic performativity of conventional discourse about heroic (white male) styles of leadership in entrepreneurship. Tedmanson and Evans explore Indigenous leadership subjectivities to reveal new ways in which order and leadership is enacted in cultural contexts through participation and inclusivity, rather than top-down command (Peredo and Anderson 2006; Spiller *et al.* 2011). The contradictions and tensions inherent in assumptions which idealise Western hierarchical understandings of power and authority are deconstructed. Using contemporary empirical research, relational forms of collective and collaborative leadership are explored in the context of Indigenous entrepreneurship in Australia. The chapter focuses on the social transformation occurring in the development of Indigenous entrepreneurship driven by community connectedness rather than by any simplistic reproduction of 'homo-economicus' (Evans 2012; Tedmanson *et al.* 2012). Writing from an Indigenous worldview and standpoint (Foley 2008; Moreton-Robinson 2003), the authors explore leadership as the creation of a 'space of belonging' and critically analyse how the co-creation of entrepreneurial effort strengthens Indigenous community efficacy (Tedmanson 2014; Evans 2012).

Part II ends with Peter de Boer and Lothar Smith's contribution (Chapter 7), in which they explore the role of the so-called Warung restaurants. The fundamental question they ask is whether these restaurants, characteristic of the informal economy, support the endeavours of cities aspiring to be part of the global economy. Basing their findings on research conducted among owners and customers in the city of Yogyakarta as well as various government agencies concerned with their existence, they conclude that these Warungs are strongly intertwined with the formal economy. Fundamentally they are an efficient way of providing the lowest classes of the city with an affordable, decent meal. However, in a more subtle manner these Warungs also provide a certain social fabric to the city; they are places that give meaning to the lives of the urban poor. Hence, this case also shows the importance of (informal) small business ownership, an economic activity often seen as 'marginalised' and less 'real' entrepreneurially in mainstream entrepreneurship literature.

In Part III, we demonstrate how traditional entrepreneurship research furthers an archetype of the white, Christian entrepreneur – which marginalises 'Other' ethnic entrepreneurs. The contributors critically discuss how 'Other' entrepreneurs construct their entrepreneurial identities in relation to their ethnic identities, and how this challenges public discourses about ethnic minorities. In Chapter 8, Jones, Ram and Villares draw particular attention to the importance of context when examining ethnic minority businesses. They problematise prevailing tendencies to view entrepreneurship as an unfettered route to social mobility for ethnic minority and immigrant groups. They argue that the conceptualisation of ethnic minority entrepreneurship needs to recognise the diverse economic and social relationships in which firms are embedded. This signifies a weakening of ethnicity as an explanatory factor implied for the anatomy of immigrant and ethnic minority enterprise. Ethnic minority entrepreneurs do not necessarily opt for entrepreneurship because they essentially have more entrepreneurial 'genes' than other ethnicities, but start businesses for a variety of reasons. Their surrounding structures have an impact on their motivations and possibilities, and it is important to scrutinise these surroundings when theorising ethnic minority entrepreneurship – seeing it in a less essentialist way – and to analyse how different groups of ethnic minority entrepreneurs seek agency through these structures to enterprise. In Chapter 9, while drawing on De Clercq and Voronov (2009), Thoelen and Zanoni investigate the narrative use of ethnic minority identity for constructing legitimacy through 'fitting in' and 'standing out'. By doing so they aim to bridge individual and organisational levels of inquiry to understand how ethnic minority entrepreneurs' identities may be used as an asset for business achievement. Based on in-depth interviews with ethnic entrepreneurs in the creative industries, they identify four types of use of the ethnic minority background: the 'ethnic' creative strategy, the 'hybrid' creative strategy, the 'heroic' creative strategy and the 'neutral' creative strategy. The study contributes to the stream of literature approaching ethnic minority entrepreneurs as agents instead of structural 'dopes', by highlighting the heterogeneous ways in which ethnic minority identity and background can be deployed for business strategies and how they construct these identities in relation to the public discourse on ethnic minority entrepreneurs. The objective of the final chapter of this section (Chapter 10) is to scrutinise a particular group of entrepreneurs, namely migrant female entrepreneurs with a Turkish or Moroccan background (a group usually and typically excluded in not only popular discourse but also in mainstream entrepreneurship literature) within a typical Western society, one that firmly ascribes to individualism. Verduyn and Essers combine the stories of female ethnic entrepreneurs with Dutch institutional stories to see on what premises these women, and these institutions, base their stories, and if and how they show overlap or contrast. Since centre–margin positionalities are central to our investigations, deconstruction analysis is used as an inspirational source for the analysis. It reveals that the institutional stories resonate strongly with the hegemonic, positive discourse on entrepreneurship, whereas these women's stories are more ambivalent, and in many ways resist the institution's point of view.

Part IV discusses the way entrepreneurship is traditionally constructed around discourses of a masculine, male subject. Using various feminist lenses, the authors explicate how gender and entrepreneur*ing* come together to generate different experiences of entrepreneur*ship*. In Chapter 11, Marlow and Al-Dajani argue how an important facet of the feminist critique of contemporary entrepreneurship has been the increasing focus of the influence of gender upon women's experiences of business ownership; analyses of how women have been excluded from the dominant entrepreneurial discourse, or are positioned in deficit and lack as entrepreneurial subject beings (Ahl 2006; Ahl and Marlow 2012). Indeed, feminist theory has emerged as a convincing theoretical critique to expose the limiting gendered bias within the current entrepreneurial project (Calas *et al.* 2009). Yet this stance in and of itself is now recognised as constrained by presumptions of gender as generic and also in being premised upon a US/European-centric stance (Al-Dajani and Marlow 2010). To advance feminist critiques of entrepreneurship, the chapter argues that it is now imperative to develop analyses which recognise how institutional influences arising from differing cultures, contexts and locations

(Welter 2011) influence women's entrepreneurial activities. Following this, Banu Ozkazanc-Pan, in Chapter 12, explores how many entrepreneurship advocates herald the potential of enterprise to bring empowerment to women, particularly in non-Western and 'Third World' contexts. This is also the case in nations that are in the midst of transition from state-controlled to neoliberal economic arrangements. Within this context, both national and supranational organisations have collectively advocated for an increase in women's entrepreneurship as a means to boost GPD, increase women's employment and provide income to women. Using the exemplar of Turkey, a transition middle-income economy, Ozkazanc-Pan suggests that advocating for women's entrepreneurship without the necessary structural and socio-cultural shifts cannot yield empowerment. Through a postcolonial feminist lens, she suggests that meaningful social change with regard to women's empowerment can only take place through entrepreneurship that is culturally contextualised across differences of ethnicity, religiosity and class. In the final chapter of Part IV (Chapter 13), Huriye Aygören further elaborates on how entrepreneurship has become a favoured instrument wherever there is poverty, unemployment and other socio-economic issues. However, it is only recently that entrepreneurship scholars have started to discuss whether entrepreneurship may be a means towards emancipation and social change, or may rather bracket inequalities and lead to societal exclusion especially for those disadvantaged groups. Hence, little focus is given to ongoing processes which bring about different societal outcomes. Aygören puts forward the view that these questions might be powerfully tackled by combining the insights of feminist organisational studies with Bourdieusian cultural sociology on social inequalities. Analysing the life stories of migrant women entrepreneurs with a Turkish background living and working in Sweden, she contributes to discussions of inequality, examining the impact of capital development processes in maintaining and transforming market and non-market conditions and positions of (in)equality via women's access and take-up of particular subject positions in the context of entrepreneurship. Her focus on life stories reflects her interest in opening and complicating the category of entrepreneur subject and subject formation in intersectional contexts.

By applying techniques from deconstruction and critical discourse analysis, the authors in in the final part of this book 'unveil' the many taken-for-granted assumptions embedded in the field of entrepreneurship. In Chapter 14, Marsh and Thomas examine the process of transformation in Poland from a communist regime to a neoliberal economy. They focus on the discursive formation of the neoliberal project and the move from a simple 'imaginary' to a fully operationalised social formation. In their approach to transformation they understand it not as a purely objective process that automatically produces a particular outcome, but as a strategy for achieving and stabilising a new 'fix' between a regime of capital accumulation and a regime of political regulation (Jessop 2004, cited in Fairclough 2007, p. 52). Drawing upon critical discourse analysis (CDA) (Chouliaraki and Fairclough 1999; Fairclough

2003, 2005), they explore the ways in which discursive resources are articulated together in order to bring about social change. They examine how these discursive resources have played a part, not only in concealing the social cost of neoliberal transformation, but also in naturalising and legitimising policies. They analyse how a discourse of enterprise (Platforma Obywatelska 2001; Rokita and Kawalec 2005) has been fostered and promoted in Poland, seen as a necessary step away from the past and its planned economy and state intervention. Their analysis of the nodal discourse of entrepreneurship goes beyond its importance as a tool of disciplining individuals as they also demonstrate its role in legitimisation of the self-reproduction of the former ruling class via a deliberate way of orchestrating the expropriation of the common. Meanwhile, in Chapter 15, Annika Skoglund elaborates on the concept of 'ecopreneurship', which is supposed to provide answers to ecological problems by the enhancement of sustainable development. Ecopreneurship thus brings policy discourse closer to everyday engagement with the green environment. In the form of non-profit or profit ventures, ecopreneurship is recognised as an important step towards the establishment of an eco-economy. Uncritically, ecopreneurs thus propose to bring us all closer to a full inclusion in the social-ecological system. However, we know very little about the basic assumptions that underpin such an inclusion. What qualities are embraced as sustainable and which practices are promoted to erase those qualities deemed unsustainable? Such oppositional issues are investigated by a deconstruction of the ecological reasoning that may be found within examples of ecopreneurship, ranging from academic literature to various ventures. Skoglund pays specific attention to how 'vulnerability' and 'compassion' are deployed, to unravel the function of counter-concepts, such as 'invincibility' and 'indifference'. This complements our understanding of how an alternative form of entrepreneurship emerges on the surface of oppositional categorisations of people. Such a deconstruction can also teach us how political subjectivity is inhibited and limited, in the complex adaptive system that ecopreneurship cultivates.

All the individual chapters in this book engage critically with the dominant discourse of entrepreneurship in order to challenge the inflated perception of entrepreneurship as an unequivocally positive economic activity (see also Calas *et al.* 2009). While each chapter summons a distinct set of theoretical premises and concepts to challenge common knowledge, and to rethink entrepreneurship in fresh and inspiring ways, together they are united by a critical and reflexive spirit which refuses to accept prevailing ideas and functionalist ideals (Grant and Perren 2002), economics (Sarasvathy and Venkataraman 2011), individual heroism (Williams and Nadin 2013), masculinities (Calas *et al.* 2009) and instrumental reason (Gibson-Graham 2006). This spirit allows the contributors to this book to unveil the uglier and more sombre side of entrepreneurship (Olaison and Sorenson 2014; Jones and Murtola 2012). Isaac Lyne's investigation, for example, questions whether social enterprise is always such a straight-forward, uncontested and ideology-free activity as Western common sense would lead us to believe. The key insight of Lyne's investigation is that social enterprise, just like any other form of entrepreneurship, is, first and foremost, a political event predicated on a distinct set of contingent socio-cultural relations which often create unanticipated (Dey and Marti 2016), and at times downright negative effects (Scott and Teasdale 2012). *In extremis*, social enterprises set out to solve wicked problems, but – despite the best of intentions – can end up perpetuating rather than solving them (Edwards 2008). In a similar way, Gerard Hanlon notes that entrepreneurship is sometimes driven more by the capture of value produced by others than by creation and innovation, thus operating as a key ideological justification of a new form of capital accumulation (Jones and Murtola 2012).

The rose-tinted view of entrepreneurship as a panacea for all (Tedmanson *et al.* 2012) is further challenged by those chapters which look more closely at how entrepreneurship is enacted in the context of marginalised groups. Specifically, they explore how self-employment either empowers the most vulnerable and needy people in society, or, as Karin Berglund's investigation suggests, advances a new class of precarious workers. In this age of individualism and neoliberalism, we believe it is especially important to study the often forgotten entrepreneurial subjectivities and communities, to give voice and an international platform to entrepreneurs who are struggling against colonised, ethnocentric and phallocentric practices and norms. It is important to share such stories, and to start a broader discussion of how entrepreneurship may possibly become an emancipatory activity that redistributes economic power and helps communities grow sustainably. As Alia Weston and Miguel Imas show us in their discussion of barefoot entrepreneurs, this speaking back by community-based entrepreneurs reflects more than just a form of survival for the poor and the marginalised; it is often fundamentally liberationist in orientation.

This book shows how the heroic, white masculine style of leadership in entrepreneurship still prevails, but it also brings to the fore that there are other interesting models of entrepreneurial leadership. Banu Ozkazanc-Pan discusses feminist entrepreneurship from a postcolonial perspective, while Huriye Aygören details the particular struggles of resistance and power within immigrant women's experiences as entrepreneurs. In their analysis of ethnic minority entrepreneurs 'fitting in' and 'standing out' in the creative industries, Annelies Thoelen and Patrizia Zanoni show how being 'othered' can also be converted from deficit to attribute. Similarly, Peter de Boer and Lothar Smith's dynamic discussion reveals the vibrancy of micro-enterprise in Indonesia as an example of entrepreneurship which challenges the dominant large-scale capitalist trends in major urban centres.

Through the stories we have carefully selected, we also demonstrate how 'Other' entrepreneurs in Western contexts construct their multiple identities, intertwining their ethnic identities with their entrepreneurial ones, and how this actually challenges public discourses on ethnic minorities whose outlook is often pejorative. In their critical analysis of Indigenous community-based entrepreneurship in Australia, Tedmanson and Evans reveal how organisation, order and leadership are enacted through participation, reciprocity and inclusivity, whereas Trevor Jones, Monder Ram and Maria Villares elaborate that it is not so much their specific 'ethnicity' that urges or 'pushes' ethnic minorities into entrepreneurial careers, but rather their surrounding structures. This makes the phenomenon of migrant entrepreneurship less an individual choice made by 'Them', but rather a latent potentiality of society which should not be exoticised and played down as a topic, which is often the case in mainstream entrepreneurship scholarship. It is much more interesting to see how migrants are working increasingly in what may be deemed 'sophisticated' sectors such as the creative industries, and less in 'lower end markets'. Yet, as Annelies Thoelen and Patrizia Zanoni sophisticatedly show, they are still considered outsiders by their stakeholders, and they have to both 'fit in' and 'stand out' if they want to gain entrepreneurial legitimacy. Doing so, they may be seen as very agentic entrepreneurs.

Susan Marlow and Haya Al-Dajani, and Karen Verduyn and Caroline Essers sexplore how entrepreneurship is traditionally constructed as a masculine, male subject, which still excludes many women from the dominant entrepreneurship discourse, or at least puts them in the 'second-best' box. We need to go beyond this already accepted theoretical dichotomy of gender and entrepreneurship; it is time we specifically study how different cultures, contexts and locations impact upon the way women can be(come) entrepreneurs. This is particularly important today, as policy makers seem to have found the 'egg of Columbus' by propounding entrepreneurship as 'the' recipe for the empowerment of women in the Third World. However, without provision of the necessary structural and socio-cultural conditions, this egg may be an empty shell with not much to offer these women, or, even worse, lead to their further structural exclusion.

The conjunction of entrepreneurship and the emergence of neoliberalism in Poland is traced by Dorota Marsh and Pete Thomas who help us to understand how the 'homo sovieticus' has been replaced by the 'homo entrepreneurus', a development that is giving rise to a new capitalist class that has come to appropriate the nation's productive capacity. Similarly, deconstruction has been employed by Skoglund to nuance the popularised and heroised image of the 'ecopreneur', ironically brought to life to erase some of 'regular' entrepreneurship's downsides (such as depleting biodiversity).

So where does this leave critical entrepreneurship studies? Does it stop with this book? Are we 'there' yet? Our answer would be an authoritative 'NO'. Although the contributors to this book have provided us with many fresh and thought-provoking insights, we are convinced that we still have a long way to go. Critical engagement with entrepreneurship must become an unending endeavour, not least because mainstream renditions of entrepreneurship, the main target of this book, will not simply cease to exist. This implies that we must become relentless and persistent in undoing what is taken for granted about entrepreneurship, and the theoretico-ideological assumptions upon which they are based (Dey 2007). In light of this, we see this collection as a beginning, a first step in what will hopefully become a continuous and growing movement which looks to a more communal sense of the economic rather than a purely individualistic nihilism (Tedmanson *et al.* 2015).

The task in front of us is, we believe, three-fold: to invite new theorising; to enquire into new topics; and to turn CES into a transnational, racially aware, postcolonial, ground-up and communally generative movement.

First, having attempted to collect timely and important contributions in CES, we are acutely aware that this book does not offer an exhaustive account of critical scholarship. Embracing recent calls to be more imaginative, daring and caring in our research (Steyaert *et al.* 2011), critical scholarship going forward must not only multiply CES (more of the same), but uncover and embrace critical theories and concepts which have hitherto remained outside of entrepreneurship studies. This may involve, for instance, composition studies, contemporary French pragmatism, actor network theory (and after), new materialism, to name but a few. Consideration of such new theoretical vistas permits us to recompose entrepreneurship from the rubble of critique, and to establish new links and connections which have not yet been made.

Second, since Routledge approached us to write this book, the world has changed tremendously, often unfortunately in ways less favourable to the publics with whom we engage. Many refugees have left their countries seeking better lives in Europe, Australia, across Asia, the UK and elsewhere. Such changes and developments in our societies call for a renewed critical scholarship which considers the topic of entrepreneurship within this context of major political, economic and social upheaval. We invite and encourage critical scholars to research how these new migrants on the one hand may use entrepreneurship to socially and economically integrate (or resist integration) into our societies. At the same time, the darker sides of such entrepreneurial activities need highlighting. We seek to further explore how the formal and informal economy intersects, and how this may give meaning to the lives of the urban poor. We argue that it is important to demonstrate the importance of (informal) small businesses and micro-enterprises as a form of economic activity, challenging what is often seen as 'marginal' and less 'real' in mainstream entrepreneurship literature. In this book, many authors argue that the context in which entrepreneurial activities take place is crucial. It is the very nature of a particular context that it shapes people's entrepreneurship, their entrepreneurial identity and entrepreneurial behaviour. However, one book cannot cover all contexts. We encourage entrepreneurship scholars to divert from the mainstream path, and to explore the diverse contexts in which entrepreneurship takes place. Much more research needs to be done in the majority world – the so-called Third World – where entrepreneurship is being stimulated and carried out in ways that run counter to Western hegemonic thinking of entrepreneurship as something individualist, masculine and 'big'. Combining a consideration of context with an analysis of the behaviour of entrepreneurs, or looking at the interaction of structure and agency, is scholarship to be welcomed. This direction could be taken further; when exploring the context for entrepreneurs with a migrant background, the concept of translocational positionality, for example, could be used (Villares *et al.* forthcoming). Such a theoretical and analytical lens would enhance our understanding of the trajectories of migrant entrepreneurs. It would take into account dimensions such as gender and ethnicity in both time and space, while recognising the importance of connecting the resources and experiences at both the country of origin and destination, as well as these entrepreneurs' social positions in the ethnic economy, the labour market and within family structures (see also Villares *et al.* forthcoming). This is also true of transnationalist feminism, which aims to unsettle binary conceptions between 'Us' and 'Them', and further aims to emphasise power, identity and subjectivity for transnational populations across national borders (Kaplan and Grewal 2002). Applying such a conceptualisation to entrepreneurship would enable us to appreciate the entrepreneurship of migrant women as it is, moving away from images of the 'Other' such as being uneducated, illiterate and passive women, to that of educated, competent, active and socially aware women. Furthermore, ongoing study of postcolonial feminism in relation to entrepreneurship is much needed in CES research. How does Indigenous communitarian feminism operate and how do Indigenous communities across the world enact emancipatory practices in community and organisation?

Third, we believe there is a need to coordinate our collective critical endeavours, thus finding ways of transforming our individual research endeavours into larger, more impactful, while still distinct, movements. Following Derrida,

> [W]e must join forces to exert pressure and organize ripostes, and we must do so on an international scale and according to new modalities, though always while analyzing and discussing the very foundations of our responsibility, its discourses, its heritage, and its axioms.
>
> (Derrida 2003, p. 126)

We have been fortunate enough to have witnessed the beginning of such events; the biannual Critical Management Studies Conference, as well as other conferences, have served as spaces of inspiration for us where tentative and 'dangerous' ideas (Steyaert and Dey 2010) can be shared in a collegial environment. We are excited about being part of and contributing to prospective CES events, and curious as to what the future holds in store for critical scholarship on entrepreneurship.

References

Ahl, H. (2006), Why research on women entrepreneurs needs new directions. *Entrepreneurship Theory and Practice*, **30**(5), pp. 595–623.

Ahl, H. and Marlow, S. (2012), Gender and entrepreneurship research: Employing feminist theory to escape the dead end. *Organization*, **19**(5), pp. 543–562.

Al-Dajani, H. and Marlow, S. (2010), The impact of women's home-based enterprise on marriage dynamics: Evidence from Jordan. *International Small Business Journal*, **28**(5), pp. 470–487.

Armstrong P. (2001), Science, enterprise and profit: Ideology in the knowledge-driven economy. *Economy and Society*, **30**, pp. 524–552.

Calas, M., Smircich, L. and Bourne, K. (2009), Extending the boundaries: Reframing 'entrepreneurship as social change' through feminist perspectives. *Academy of Management Review*, **34**(3), pp. 552–569.

Chouliaraki L. and Fairclough, N. (1999), *Discourse in Late Modernity*. Edinburgh: Edinburgh University Press.

Costa, A.S.M. and Saraiva, L.A.S. (2012), Hegemonic discourses on entrepreneurship as an ideological mechanism for the reproduction of capital. *Organization*, **19**(5), pp. 587–614.

Curran, J. and Blackburn, R.A. (2001), *Researching the Small Enterprise*. London: Sage.

De Clercq, D. and Voronov, M. (2009), The role of cultural and symbolic capital in entrepreneurs' ability to meet expectations about conformity and innovation. *Journal of Small Business Management*, **47**(3), pp. 398–420.

Dey, P. (2007), *On the Name of Social Entrepreneurship: Business School Teaching, Research, and Development Aid*. Unpublished doctoral dissertation, University of Basel, Switzerland.

Dey, P. and Lehner, O. (2016), Registering ideology in the creation of social entrepreneurs: Intermediary organizations, 'ideal subjects', and the promise of enjoyment. *Journal of Business Ethics,* doi: 10.1007/s10551-016-3112-z.

Dey, P., and Marti, L. (2016), Studying crowdfunding through extreme cases: Cursory reflections on the social value creation process of a potato salad project. In O. Lehner (ed.), *Routledge Handbook of Social and Sustainable Finance*. New York: Routledge, pp. 325–341.

Dey, P. and Steyaert, C. (2016), Rethinking the space of ethics in social entrepreneurship: Power, subjectivity, and practices of concrete freedom. *Journal of Business Ethics*, **133**(4), pp. 627–641.

Derrida, J. (2003), Autoimmunity: Real and symbolic suicides. In G. Borradori (ed.), *Philosophy in a Time of Terror: Dialogues with Jürgen Habermas and Jacques Derrida*. Chicago, IL: University of Chicago Press.

Edwards, M. (2008), *Just Another Emperor? The Myths and Realities of Philanthrocapitalism*. New York: Demos.

Essers, C. and Tedmanson, D. (2014), Upsetting 'others' in the Netherlands: Narratives of Muslim Turkish migrant businesswomen at the crossroads of ethnicity, gender and religion. *Gender, Work and Organization*, **21**(4), pp. 353–367.

Evans, M. (2012), *Be: Longing – Enacting Indigenous Arts Leadership*. Unpublished Ph.D. thesis, Melbourne University.

Fairclough, N. (2003), *Analyzing Discourse*. London: Routledge.

Fairclough, N. (2005), Critical discourse analysis in transdisciplinary research. In R. Wodak and P. Chilton (eds), *A New Agenda in (Critical) Discourse Analysis: Theory, Methodology and Interdisciplinarity*. Amsterdam: John Benjamins Publishing, pp. 53–70.

Fairclough, N. (2007), *Language and Globalization*. London: Routledge.

Fairclough, N. (2013), *Critical Discourse Analysis: The Critical Study of Language*. London: Routledge.

Foley, D. (2008), Does culture and social capital impact on the networking attributes of Indigenous entrepreneurs? *Journal of Enterprising Communities: People and Places in the Global Economy*, **32**(3), pp. 204–224.

Gibson-Graham, J.K. (2006), *A Postcapitalist Politics*. Minneapolis: University of Minnesota Press.

Görling, S. and Rehn, A. (2008), Accidental ventures: A materialist reading of opportunity and entrepreneurial potential. *Scandinavian Journal of Management*, **24**(2), pp. 94–102.

Grant, P. and Perren, L. (2002), Small business and entrepreneurial research, meta-theories, paradigms and prejudices. *International Small Business Journal*, **20**, pp. 185–211.

Hjorth, D. (2004), Creating space for play/invention – concepts of space and organisational entrepreneurship. *Entrepreneurship and Regional Development*, **16**(5), pp. 413–432.

Hyndman, J. (2004). Mind the gap: Bridging feminist and political geography through geopolitics. *Political Geography*, **23**, pp. 307–322.

Jessop, B. (2004), Critical semiotic analysis and cultural political economy. *Critical Discourse Studies*, **1**(1), pp. 1–16.

Jones, C. and Murtola, A.M. (2012), Entrepreneurship and expropriation. *Organization*, **19**(5), pp. 635–655.

Kaplan, C. and Grewal, I. (2002), Transnational practices and interdisciplinary feminist scholarship: Refiguring women's and gender studies. In R. Weigman (ed.), *Women's Studies on its Own*. Durham, NC: Duke University Press, pp. 66–81.

Kenny, K. and Scriver, S. (2012), Dangerously empty? Hegemony and the construction of the Irish entrepreneur. *Organization*, **19**(5), pp. 615–633.

Moreton-Robinson, A. (2003), I still call Australia home: Indigenous belonging and place in a white postcolonizing society. In S. Ahmed, C. Castaneda and A.M. Fortier (eds), *Uprootings/Regroundings: Questions of Home and Migration*. New York: Berg, pp. 23–40.

Olaison, L. and Sorensen, B.M. (2014), The abject of entrepreneurship: Failure, fiasco, fraud. *International Journal of Entrepreneurial Behaviour & Research*, **20**(2), pp. 193–211.

Peredo, A.M. and Anderson, R.B. (2006), Indigenous entrepreneurship research: Themes and variations. In C.S. Galbraith and C.H. Stiles (eds), *Developmental Entrepreneurship: Adversity, Risk, and Isolation*. Oxford: Elsevier, pp. 253–273.

Perren, L. and Jennings, P. (2005), Government discourses on entrepreneurship: Issues of legitimization, subjugation, and power. *Entrepreneurship: Theory and Practice*, **29**(2), pp. 173–184.

Platforma Obywatelska (2001), *Program Platformy Obywatelskiej*. Warszawa. Available at www.platforma.org.

Rindova, V., Barry, D. and Ketchen, D.J. (2009), Entrepreneuring as emancipation. *Academy of Management Review*, **(34)**3, pp. 477–491.

Rokita, J. and Kawalec, S. (2005), *Państwo dla obywateli. Plan rządzenia 2005–2009*. Warszawa: Instytut Pastwa i Administracji.

Sarasvathy, S.D. and Venkataraman, S. (2011), Entrepreneurship as method: Open questions for an entrepreneurial future. *Entrepreneurship Theory and Practice*, **35**(1), pp. 113–135.

Scott, D. and Teasdale, S. (2012), Whose failure? Learning from the financial collapse of a social enterprise in 'Steeltown'. *Voluntary Sector Review*, **3**(2), pp. 139–155.

Spiller, C., Erakovic, L., Henare, M. and Pio, E. (2011), Relational well-being and wealth: Māori businesses and an ethic of care. *Journal of Business Ethics*, **98**(1), pp. 153–169.

Steyaert, C. and Dey, P. (2010), Nine verbs to keep the social entrepreneurship research agenda 'dangerous'. *The Journal of Social Entrepreneurship*, **1**(2), pp. 231–254.

Steyaert, C. and Katz, J. (2004), Reclaiming the space of entrepreneurship in society: Geographical, discursive and social dimensions. *Entrepreneurship & Regional Development*, **16**, pp. 179–196.

Steyaert, C., Hjorth, D. and Gartner, W.B. (2011), Six memos for a curious and imaginative future scholarship in entrepreneurship studies. *Entrepreneurship & Regional Development: An International Journal*, **23**(1–2), pp. 1–7.

Tedmanson, D., Verduyn, K., Essers, C. and Gartner, W. (2012), Critical perspectives in entrepreneurship research. *Organization*, **19**(5), pp. 531–541.

Tedmanson, D. (2014), Indigenous social entrepreneurship: Resistance and renewal'. In S. Grant and H. Douglas, *Social Innovation and Social Enterprise: Context and Theories*. Sydney: Palgrave Macmillan.

Tedmanson, D., Essers, C., Dey, P. and Verduyn, K. (2015), An *un*common wealth: Transforming the commons with purpose, for people and not for profit! *Journal of Management Inquiry*, **24**(4), pp. 439–444.

Verduyn, K., Dey, P., Tedmanson, D. and Essers, C. (2014), Emancipation and/or oppression? Conceptualizing dimensions. *International Journal of Entrepreneurial Behaviour & Research*, **20**, 98–107.

Villares, M., Ram, M. and Jones, T. (forthcoming), Female immigrant global entrepreneurship: From invisibility to empowerment? In K. Lewis (ed.), *Handbook of Female Global Entrepreneurship*. London: Routledge.

Welter, F. (2011), Contextualizing entrepreneurship – conceptual challenges and ways forward. *Entrepreneurship Theory and Practice*, **35**(1), pp. 165–184.

Williams, C.C. and Nadin, S.J. (2013), Beyond the entrepreneur as a heroic figurehead of capitalism: Re-representing the lived practices of entrepreneurs. *Entrepreneurship and Regional Development*, **25**(7–8), pp. 552–568.

Part I

Contesting neoliberal aspects of traditional entrepreneurship approaches

2 Social entrepreneurs

Precious and precarious

Karin Berglund

Introduction

Social entrepreneurship has certainly gained incredible traction during the past few decades, presenting solutions for tackling all kinds of social issues. From Ashoka – the pre-eminent social entrepreneurship incubator – we learn that 'social entrepreneurs are individuals with innovative solutions to society's most pressing social problems' (Ashoka 2015). The Schwab Foundation further describes how social entrepreneurs 'pursue poverty alleviation goals with entrepreneurial zeal, business methods and the courage to innovate and overcome traditional practices' (Skoll World Forum 2015), and *Forbes* presents social entrepreneurs as today's disruptors but tomorrow's saviours (Carlyle *et al.* 2015). Social entrepreneurs are certainly depicted as precious, since they take care of societal needs in innovative ways. The preciousness of social entrepreneurship is not only emphasised in the support and media discourse, but is also recognised in the expanding government and policy discourse (Nicholls 2010), as well as in academic discourse that has increased dramatically over the past two decades.[1] However, the romantic image of the precious social entrepreneur not only ignores the fact that social enterprises may fail, but it also neglects the fact that the very conditions under which social entrepreneurs operate are often arduous and precarious.

The precarious life of social entrepreneurs has also been highlighted in the emergent critical academic discourse on social entrepreneurship. Dey and Steyaert (2010, p. 85) point to how social entrepreneurship is storied through a 'messianistic script of harmonious social change', which says little about the hardships of the mundane everyday life of social entrepreneurs. Indeed, precious stories are hard to resist, since they offer hope as to how the alarming crisis of today can be manoeuvred. A study of three popular autobiographies of US social entrepreneurs gives a good illustration of how the 'messianistic script' is voiced as a desire for meaningful work (Dempsey and Sanders 2010). This meaningfulness is, however, also found to be coupled with unpaid or underpaid work and a tendency to sacrifice close relationships in favour of helping the people targeted in the social enterprise (Dempsey and Sanders 2010). The higher calling at the heart of social entrepreneurship discourse fosters a more moral entrepreneur (Berglund and Skoglund 2016). While this figure is regarded as highly precious in today's society, with its recurrent crises, social entrepreneurs may need to live a precarious life in many ways.

Critical scholars have argued in a number of ways that the glossy precious side of the story also entails a darker side of precariousness. Social entrepreneurship discourse reconstructs the entrepreneurial hero as a hard-working individual who needs to make substantial sacrifices (Dempsey and Sanders 2010). The 'little narratives' of social entrepreneurs' everyday toil to make social innovations work, containing both adversities and meaningfulness, often fade away and cease to resound (Dey and Steyaert 2010). Indeed, these stories are easily filtered through either the messianistic acclaimed stories that depoliticise efforts to initiate social change, and counter-narratives that critique the assumptions made in the messianistic narrative (ibid.). Once everyday work is accounted for, dilemmas unfold as integrated in social entrepreneuring (Berglund and Schwartz 2013). Social entrepreneurs not only have to figure out innovative business models and make ends meet, but are also involved in identity struggles to understand the difference between what they do and what kind of social change is actually achieved through their operations (ibid.).

Following the emergent critical discourse on social entrepreneurship, it is not social entrepreneurs' activities per se that appear to be the problem but rather that their activity is held up as a superior (and individual) solution to tackle all kinds of problems against the background of a progressive neoliberal society that undermines collective and political action (e.g. Barinaga 2014; Berglund and Skoglund 2016; Dey 2014). With neoliberal life comes an expectation for individuals to be active, flexible and to take responsibility (Lemke 2001). This undoubtedly opens up the construction of myriad creative solutions through which complex problems may be tackled, be they social, ecologic or economic. While neoliberal society, at best, offers its citizens the freedom to create opportunities and solve societal problems, it also compels us all to live this freedom in an entrepreneurial spirit. This tension is of interest in this contribution that seeks to unravel how social entrepreneurship is linked to both precious and precarious career trajectories.

This chapter presents three themes of precariousness that are interpreted through my experiences from four ethnographically studied cases of social entrepreneurship. What the cases have in common is that all are based in the Swedish context, they have been studied over a longer time period (between four and 13 years), and they have spurred me to reflect upon problematic aspects of social entrepreneurship. In parallel with the neoliberalisation of society, these problematic aspects have become more evident over time.

While the social entrepreneurs in question have told me about the meaningful work they pursue, I have also been introduced to their daily industrious work through which more troublesome aspects have been made visible. The four cases will be used as a vehicle to give voice to 'little narratives' with the aim of highlighting ambivalences and paradoxes in juggling preciousness and precariousness. In addition to this, I am interested in the potential political and collective mobilisation that takes place, and that may develop, as social forms of entrepreneurship advance in contemporary society. In order to accomplish these tasks I will engage with Guy Standing's (2013) ideas on how the neoliberalisation of society has given rise to a new precarious class: 'the precariat'.

Standing's discussion of the unfolding precariat represents a 'counter-narrative' (Dey and Steyaert 2010) to precious stories of all kinds of entrepreneurs, since it portrays entrepreneurship as an engine of capitalist production and exploitation fuelling inequality, social injustice and insecurity whereby people of all kinds may enter precarious situations. Standing depicts how people may slip into precariousness without noticing, finding themselves between jobs, taking insecure employment or short-term contracts, and are often poorly paid for their work in comparison to the workforce who enjoys the forms of employment security that were established under industrial citizenship. This is how the precariat takes form as a new class, which Standing (2013) describes as dangerous because it increasingly inhabits a life parallel to the welfare state and involves extremist tendencies. In addition, the precariat class consists of several layers of more or less vulnerable groups, which complicates a collective mobilisation. In due course this may lead to democratic disruptions and societal decline. If social stability is not reached, these groups may instead undermine one another in what Standing views as a 'Politics of Inferno'. Following Standing, 'the precariat hovers on the borderline, exposed to circumstances that could turn them from strugglers into deviants and loose cannons prone to listen to populist politicians and demagogues' (2011, p. 132). To avoid this scenario the various groups of the precariat need to become aware of one another so that they may join forces to mobilise a 'Politics of Paradise' to re-create just and equal structures to provide all citizens with social stability. As in all class struggles this requires recognition of each other as part of a class and a collective work to move from layered identities (more or less precarious groups) to multiple and parallel identities, all of which have universal rights.

What Standing does not take into account is how entrepreneurship takes on new social forms which seek to combat the very problems that conventional entrepreneurship brings about and how social forms of entrepreneurship seek to rescue people who are in precarious situations. Standing's theory of the precariat however creates a fruitful 'precarious counter-force' to the preciousness of social entrepreneurship that serves the purpose of this chapter; to unravel the links between preciousness and precariousness of social entrepreneurship.

Indeed, precious social entrepreneurship and the precariat class are related in as yet unknown ways, as they seem to tell two different, contradictory stories of the present. While social entrepreneurship tells the story of forming new collective solutions, the precariat tells a story of how collective solutions elude. Where social entrepreneurship is described as a vehicle for creating social change and for precipitating new societal structures, the precariat depicts the negative consequences of scattered groups where individuals in precarious situations are required to learn to secure themselves. While social entrepreneurs are seen to collectively care for and empower people in precarious situations, the precariat tells the story of a dangerous and disempowered class on the run.

Before turning to my encounters with social entrepreneurs and the three themes of precariousness and preciousness revealed through my analysis, the ideas of the precariat will be further developed in the next section. To end the chapter I will return to the discussion about how social entrepreneurship and the precariat may be linked. Through this exercise, I will investigate how the missing piece of the puzzle (social entrepreneurship) may fit into Standing's discussion of the precariat class, and how the missing piece of the puzzle (precariousness) may fit with the messianistic story of social entrepreneurship. My hopes are to thus contribute to a more nuanced story of social entrepreneurship and to open up opportunities for new questions and avenues for critical research on social entrepreneurship.

The precariat: social entrepreneurs on the move?

In his book *The Precariat: The New Dangerous Class* (2011), Guy Standing describes how the labour market's conditions have changed during a – historically speaking – relatively short period of time. In a society that promotes competition and individual responsibility, all collective actions, demands and solutions that could inhibit market forces are removed. While the market permeates every nook and cranny of everyday life, this creates a situation where democracy and public deliberation are undermined. It is in this terrain that the precariat takes shape as a new class, which may be dangerous to society, since it tears apart social ties. For this reason, Standing suggests moving from the emerging 'Politics of Inferno' towards a 'Politics of Paradise'. Despite the pervasiveness he associates with the individualised and neoliberal society, a Politics of Paradise remains a desired end-state. Standing thus relates the Politics of Pardise to the combating of growing inequality and insecurity, stigmatisation of particular groups, and blurring boundaries between labour, work, play and leisure time (where everything tends to become labour). Through proposals to introduce a basic income for all citizens, treating jobs as instrumental (and not as the only way to meaningfulness), allowing the existence of parallel identities and placing universality as an overarching principle for government, Standing writes optimistically about how the established path may be rerouted from 'Inferno' to 'Paradise'.

To be in a precarious situation is to be in an unstable situation. This situation is characterised by the expectation to be flexible and adaptable to the changes occurring in the (labour) market, which leads to insecure conditions of employment, short-term jobs, and often poorly paid work. These are depicted as consequences of a transformation from a welfare society to a neoliberal society, which rests on the idea of a free market with its emphasis on both privatisation and deregulation (Harvey 2005). What Standing points to is the implication this transformation has for (un)employment. If people used to refer to (un)employment as a result of economic and structural factors, in a neoliberal society this is rather a matter of individual responsibility, emphasising the ability of the individual to keep her or his position as employable (Standing 2013, pp. 72–73; see also Cremin 2010).

Standing describes how people nowadays are working increasingly hard, and may also hold several jobs to secure a living, since the return from each job is both low and uncertain; how working life nowadays involves 'work for work' to find a new or better job or to become part of the 'salariat' who can still enjoy stable full-time employment. Thus, the seven forms of labour security[2] that were developed during industrialisation have been subjected to cutbacks (2013, p. 22). Belonging to the precariat therefore means being exposed to the strains that follow by taking part in working life at one moment, but standing outside it at the next. Securing a work-life identity may be difficult in this situation, which is why the individual suffers from the lack of the kind of development that one gains through social security, work and lifestyle (ibid., p. 31). Instead, insecurity is followed by the four discouraging states of wrath, anomie, worry and alienation. While wrath, anomie and worry appear to occur simultaneously, they all lead to alienation. As if this was not enough, insecurity is said to bring about hopelessness and passivity (p. 36), as well as fewer marriages and later childbearing (p. 101). In addition, precarious work situations are depicted as entailing a feeling of work as instrumental to survival, which is why people opportunistically take what they can get to avoid the insecurity that follows from being, for example, generous and thoughtful.

The precarious class is indeed described as victim of a time when global transformation has increased the commodification of everything from labour to education. When Standing rhetorically poses the question: 'Who ends up in the precariat?' the answer is 'all actually' (2013, p. 93). For different reasons, ranging from illness, the choice of a 'wrong' occupation that is not valued by the market, accidents or some other misfortune, one is either pushed into the precariat, or sees it as a path towards something better. More specifically, however, the discussion of the precariat may well relate to 'all', but the consequences of insecurity revolve mainly around women (and the feminisation of work), migrants, immigrants, young people, criminals or any other socially vulnerable group: in many respects the audience that social entrepreneurs typically listen to, and want to support.

Among the categories that overlap with the precariat are the self-employed (remember: Standing does not speak of social entrepreneurs, but in his conceptualisation of the precariat they could fall into both the category of the self-employed or the rebel). Standing points to the difficulties of separating the precariat from self-employment at a time when the boundaries between services and service work are collapsing (2013, p. 30), spanning the divide between being on the one hand their own and, on the other, a subcontractor. This is similar to how boundaries between work and private life are blurred when employees are defined in terms of 'entreployees' (Pongratz and Voss 2003) stressing salaried employees' ability to be flexible, 'deliver' tasks and generally carry out work in an entrepreneurial manner. According to Standing, who only mentions conventional entrepreneurship in passing and mainly in relation to large corporations, the precariat are seen as vulnerable in relation to their own engagement in entrepreneurial endeavours, as they are limited by their ignorance of legal aspects (2013, p. 187).

Even if Standing acknowledges that there may be a double identity to those of the precariat, as victim/hero, that it is possible to relate to precarious situations either as a 'smiler' or a 'mourner', and the potential for primitive rebels to be shaped in this terrain, the picture painted is mainly that of the exposed individual (see e.g. Standing 2013, pp. 10–12): an alienated individual who no longer acts according to her or his convictions, but who may even act *against* them (p. 37). Typically, alienation is seen to be followed by a well-developed ability to listen to others and perform tasks on the orders of others. Individuals of the precariat are thereby seen to have few trustful relationships, at least in relation to work (p. 39).

But the precariat is far from homogeneous (p. 27), because not everyone has reason to perceive her- or himself as being in a precarious situation, and because those who do perceive themselves to be in this situation may simultaneously compete for work with others in precarious situations. Standing makes a comparison to previous class battles and argues that this one does not provide a clear arena with a lucid description of how protests can be expressed. Rather, those being part of the precariat may know little about each other and may therefore view one another as competitors, or even enemies, rather than as combatants of a class that should raise their voices. This undermines the potentiality of a collective mobilisation, since '[t]he precariat hovers on the borderline, exposed to circumstances that could turn them from strugglers into deviants and loose cannons prone to listen to populist politicians and demagogues' (p. 197). This is why Standing describes the precariat as fighting an invisible civil war, where any one party can accuse the other of his or her own condition (p. 43), which leads to the Politics of Inferno. This trajectory may actually be easier to take than directing criticism against that which shapes the precariat's insecurity and vulnerability; that is to say the dismantling and lack of social and economic structures, which would entail a political mobilisation to shape a Politics of Paradise.

Hence, the precariat runs the risk of falling into permanent political exclusion, which according to Standing leads to the demise of democratic society. Could it be that the insecure individuals of the precariat are also attracted by the emerging social forms of entrepreneurship – as a way to create a better world for others in the same situation while securing their own livelihoods? This would mean that social entrepreneurship could be a means for political mobilisation that Standing believes is conspicuously absent.

The emergence of social entrepreneurship in Sweden

It is almost 13 years since I started to research alternative forms of entrepreneurship, such as social entrepreneurship, that have emerged during the past two decades. When I began my studies of this phenomenon, Sweden had just recovered from the financial crisis during the 1990s when the interest rate soared to 500 per cent in 1992, Abba, the music phenomenon, were celebrating their thirtieth anniversary with 'The Tribute' concert, Percy Barnevik, former CEO of ABB, was in public disgrace having sullied his reputation through his generous pension agreement, and the Swedish Social Democrats remained in office following the general election. At this time, a project entitled 'Diversity in Entrepreneurship' (DiE) was started up in a small town in the middle of Sweden with the aim of creating a more diverse stock of entrepreneurs in this region. It also sought to develop an understanding of entrepreneurship that extended the idea of 'just' starting up a business. Specifically, the scope of the project was very broad, ranging from assuming an entrepreneurial identity (Berglund 2006), taking initiatives in one's own life, organising an unfulfilled need by a particular social group to take part in creatively reorganising the public sector, to both perceiving, exposing and taking action against social, political and economic contradictions and the oppressive elements that these contradictions bring about (Berglund 2007; Berglund and Johansson 2007).

Today, the interest rate is lower than ever and there is speculation as to when it will hit zero, Abba have opened their interactive museum in Stockholm and Percy Barnevik has (partly) been rehabilitated through his initiative to co-found the organisation 'Hand in Hand' which aims to fight poverty with grassroots social entrepreneurship. After almost a decade under a centre-right government, Sweden has also, like many other (Western) nations, undergone a shift of political rule, from the Scandinavian welfare society to a neoliberal focus on entrepreneurialism (Baccaro and Howell 2011). Markets have been deregulated, which has opened up opportunities for publicly owned companies to be privatised and for the publicly organised welfare state to be exposed to private sector competition (Ahl *et al.* 2014). In addition, this transformation has led to the emergence of an abundance of alternative forms of entrepreneurship which address social gaps and initiate processes of social change in Swedish society (Berglund *et al.* 2012). This change has been followed by an increased focus on the role of the individual in re-creating societal structures in order to secure her- and himself and society (Berglund and Skoglund 2016).

Over the years, I have witnessed how the 'social' has become an increasingly popular adjective used to describe the kinds of entrepreneurial initiatives that are taken in the betterment of the world, and also to define these entrepreneurs as some kinds of new saviours. Similar to the introductory examples from Ashoka and the Schwab Foundation, the new breed of entrepreneurs are described as having messianistic tendencies. Social entrepreneurs not only provide jobs for themselves and for others, but they also solve social problems that have emerged, sometimes in the backwater of a withdrawing welfare state which relies on entrepreneurs to manage not only the private market but also the expanding public market. The longitudinal character of the ethnographies presented here, along with the variation of social missions, has given rise to both surprises and reflections on my part as well as on the part of the social entrepreneurs I have encountered. The stories presented here are based on my interpretation of these surprises and reflections.

The purpose of linking precariousness and preciousness will be achieved through three themes that have emerged over the years and from my encounters with different social entrepreneurs. These themes exemplify how social entrepreneurs may be seen on the one hand as experts in the compensation for the ongoing welfare retrenchments in the advanced liberal society and, on the other, as a critical response to its shortcomings.

Encounters with social entrepreneurs

My encounters with social entrepreneurs will be described below from the following three aspects of the precariat. First, I suggest that they move from the precariousness situation of unemployment to the precariousness situation of having to be sustained through entrepreneurship. Second, I will illustrate how the efforts of social entrepreneurs are not a one-way road to running one's own company, but rather that this may involve moving between self-employment, employment and being an employer, not in order to secure an income, as in necessity entrepreneurship, but to secure the process of social change initiated. Third, these movements allow for parallel identities to be referred to interchangeably. These identities have fallen outside the norm of the Western world's male entrepreneur and may be a useful resource to 'play with' when moving between different organisational contexts. In this movement reflections are spurred on the connectedness among the diverse groups of the precariat, which brings about a sense of affinity and belonging, which in turn creates conditions for the political collective action required in the mobilisation of a class.

To begin my story, I will return to 2003 and the small town in a region situated in central Sweden where the DiE project was about to be launched. At that time, the terms 'social' and 'entrepreneurship' had not yet been connected, at least not in local discourse, but that was no obstacle to the unfolding of social entrepreneurship in lived reality.

From one kind of precariousness to another

I will never forget the group of women from ethnic minorities in the DiE project, whom I met for the first time in 2003. Some were reluctant about the whole idea of why they should become entrepreneurs in the first place, and expressed their doubts vociferously. Others revealed their doubts more through their facial expressions. I particularly came to think about one conversation we had in the grand town hall, splendidly decorated and with an atmosphere which radiated power from the past, when they told me that all they had ever wanted was a job. Their argumentation went something like this: I just want a job! I don't want to be an entrepreneur and start my own business and all that, but I want a job! Is that so hard to understand? I am so happy that I have been able to come here and start up a decent life, and now I really want to give something back and contribute to the community. But not as an entrepreneur, I want to work with what I am trained to do and practise my profession. I know there are jobs available out there! But we don't get asked. At the time, the link between entrepreneurship and social change was new to me and I remember that I was a little surprised when the women did not see the possibilities they (in my view) were offered in the project. However, I also recall how impressed I was by their belief in the Swedish welfare society and their will to challenge the obstacles they had faced.

In my first encounters with these immigrant women, they talked openly about the precarious situation, about suffering economically, socially and privately from being cut off from the labour market, having their hands full taking care of children and family. This implied that they could never relax, as they were always on their toes looking for work or another opportunity that might lead to work (e.g. education) while trying to make ends meet. Finding a job was described as important, not only because of the obvious economic security it could provide them with, but also because it would offer them the chance to give some structure to their life, as well as a sense of community and belonging. However, at this point of time, when the project was about to be launched, they made it clear that they did not view entrepreneurship as a possible trajectory. Entrepreneurship was simply not an option.

Despite the scepticism expressed, many immigrant women were curious and started to attend project meetings. As they began to learn about entrepreneurship, its connection to creativity and its importance for building an equal society, I could follow how their curiosity to the way in which entrepreneurship could be used as a means to bring about social change increased over the three years A significant turning point came when they learned that entrepreneurship was male coded, which led to a critical discussion ending with the following question and response: 'Why could we not become entrepreneurs? We certainly have no shortage of ideas!' No sooner said than done; they began to initiate various kinds of entrepreneurial activities, spanning from starting businesses to hosting a multicultural café and opening second-hand shops selling products from foreign cultures. Before long they were ready to set up their own organisation, the 'Network of Entrepreneurs from Ethic Minorities' (Neem). From Neem they began to carry out several projects with the aim of opening up for entrepreneurship to become an opportunity for immigrant women. They also initiated a public debate on micro-finance in Sweden, pointing to the need to make it possible to start small even for those who owned nothing and were trapped in a cycle of state aid. In 2009 they started to cooperate with a local bank to offer micro-credit to women in general and immigrant women in particular. This was followed by the introduction of the Micro Credit Institute.

Looking back, I can see that, during the initial stage of organising Neem, many of these women started to engage in a kind of entrepreneurship that was yet to be recognised as 'social'. The social element of entrepreneurship, which incrementally unfolded was articulated in terms of their collective action to mobilise both themselves and like-minded women; in this case, other immigrant women who could see that they could benefit from a broader view of entrepreneurship. This certainly opened up new opportunities for action, but not in the 'business-as-usual' way. Rather than starting with the idea of setting up their own business, the focus in entrepreneurship was on empowering others to start thinking of themselves in terms of their entrepreneurial capacity as both individuals and as a collective of ethnic women. Through collective supervision they encouraged each other to formulate entrepreneurial ideas. Only then did the need to make credit applications and assess their ideas in more formal contexts, such as at the bank or for an external stakeholder, arise.

During this process, the women started to assume an entrepreneurial identity that deviated from the norm of the Western self-made man, but which opened up a space where they became portrayed (e.g. in local newspapers) and seen (e.g. in different municipal contexts) as engaged, active and motivated women with a lot of ideas blurring the boundaries between business and politics. They emphasised the need to take immigrant women seriously in politics (mainly locally but also nationally and internationally), in conjunction with their idea of providing support to all kinds of businesses, not least those that later came to be seen as social enterprises. When they started to point to the need to implement a micro-credit system in Sweden, this was met with both dismay and indignation by authorities asking 'Why would Sweden need such a system? A democratic society based on solidarity with well-functioning banks and business support?' The 'ifs and buts' of a micro-credit system became a hot political topic, since it not only addressed 'business-as-usual' aspects of business loans, but also exposed the way in which the prevailing system only included certain individuals while perpetually excluding others.

When I look back at this process, I can see a shift from a wish to find employment, where the women expressed their precariousness, to a situation where they saw their possibilities to develop opportunities for self-employment, where precariousness still prevailed but was silenced. This shows how the attribute 'entrepreneurial' was embraced; emphasising individuals' potential to take social matters into their own hands (Berglund and Skoglund 2016). The women no longer returned to their beliefs in getting a job through the employment office, but pointed more to their ability to take care of themselves by starting up their own business. Thus, state security was successively abandoned as part of welfare state retrenchment and thriving entrepreneurialism. In this shift the women in Neem moved from one state of precariousness to another. In the first 'unemployment stage' they felt cut off from the community and found themselves to be in a precarious situation, economically, socially and privately. In the second 'entrepreneurial stage' they regained a sense of meaningfulness and agency in relation to their entrepreneurial life where they empowered both themselves and others. This involved not only starting a social enterprise, but also pursuing political goals through mobilising the group via collective initiatives of social entrepreneurship.

Securing social change through moving between employment and social entrepreneurship

Another encounter has been with Kia Mohebi, an exuberant woman who started the social enterprise 'Inspons' (inspons.se) where people are invited to conduct their own fundraising to support a social mission in which they are engaged. Through challenging oneself with a physical exercise-related project, such as a race, competition or some form of adventure, they invite their friends to support them by donating money to a good cause. The purpose of Inspons is to increase support for charitable causes by encouraging a healthier and more active life. This entrepreneurial initiative has gained a lot of attention, and in 2012 Kia was nominated as 'Innovator of the Year' at the local business gala *Guldstänk* [roughly, 'A Sprinkling of Gold']. In an interview with Mälardalen University, she describes how

> Inspons can be an easy way to find like-minded adventurers who want to make the world a better place, under one roof. We strive together with the charities for a healthy giving, because we think health is just as important as the life you save.
>
> (Mälardalen University 2013)

One example of a 'like-minded adventurer' is a father who, together with his son, runs in different races all year round to raise money for the Swedish National Association for Disabled Children and Young People. While the father is running he pushes his son, who was born with a severe congenital brain injury, in front of him in a specially designed running stroller. The donations go to the project 'An Active Life For All' which aims to make it possible for disabled children and teenagers to take part in sports. In the summer of 2014, the father posted a comment on Facebook stating that they had reached their goal of raising 100,000 SEK, with a large thank you to Inspons.

One of my first encounters with Kia was at a social entrepreneurship conference, when she cycled on to the stage in her cycling kit and told her story of how she came up with the idea of starting a social enterprise. In a more recent encounter we met at the university incubator where she had been offered a full-time position. When I asked her about her social entrepreneurship she told me it was too hard to make ends meet and to put dinner on the table. She also told me about having to learn how to do 'business as usual' and grow a thicker skin, because it was difficult to balance trying to put together a business model that not only works economically but also embraces virtues of 'doing good'. In particular, she emphasised how many people expected *her* to take the moral high ground. Sometimes this gave her legitimacy, but it also put her in a corner as she felt that it made it more difficult to charge for 'the doing-good' services. So when she had the opportunity to apply for a job, which she was offered, at the university incubator, she said yes. However, despite the fact that she had seen the tensions of social entrepreneurship and that she had been offered full-time and secure employment, there was never any question of leaving the social enterprise she had established perhaps not so much to make a living, or to secure herself from unemployment, but more to secure her contributions to social change. In addition, Kia stresses the need to also do 'business as usual', not to paint oneself into a corner as the do-gooder who abstains from making money. When I invited her to share her experiences from social entrepreneurship as a guest lecturer in one of my classes on social entrepreneurship, she emphasised to the students that there is no conflict between doing good for society at large and being kind to yourself. This involves earning a livelihood in a sensible way as much as setting boundaries to what she should do and to be able to say no to that which is contrary to her social mission.

As in many other encounters, this story tells us how, once a social mission is initiated, social entrepreneurs often seem to have difficulties with leaving it behind (cf. Berglund and Schwartz 2013; Dempsey and Sanders 2010). Sometimes they can make a living out of the social mission and sometimes not, which is why they need to combine their venture with various kinds of paid employment. One example of such a 'combiner' is Camilla Gustafsson, who views paid employment as one way to fund her social enterprise which is geared towards improving the lives of children in West Africa. Camilla tells of how her tough experience of growing up with a father who had alcohol problems left its mark on her, and she describes movingly how she oscillated between being a good student and an absent student and how, one day, she finally had to drag herself into the bathroom, and brushing her teeth, facing herself in the mirror and looking herself straight in the eye while posing the question: 'Who do you want to be, Camilla? Who do you really want to be?' She then talked about how she has striven ever since to become the person she wanted to be and how she started the non-profit organisation 'The Free Project' which aims to change and improve the lives of orphans in the village of Karimenga in northern Ghana. When she was invited recently to talk about her project in a morning programme on Swedish television, she spoke enthusiastically about how she started to build the orphanage and secured access to basic needs, such as electricity through solar cell panels. During her next trip she built a school and drilled for water, explaining that the children were otherwise directed to a dirty river to fetch water that might make them sick. To illustrate this, she has brought a bottle of floodwater to the TV pro-gramme[3] so that everyone could understand the conditions under which the children had to live. In her upcoming third trip she plans to organise a self-sufficiency project, based on developing a chicken farm, keeping bees and cultivating the land.

To finance the project, which she stresses is 100 per cent voluntary work, she works as a receptionist between her excursions to Ghana. In addition to saving part of her salary, she lectures about her experiences, collaborates with companies and organises concerts and exhibitions, but she also relies on private donations. After a lecture in a course on entrepreneurial learning to teachers in primary school in May 2014 she organised a photographic exhibition from her work in Ghana. In her lecture she emphasised that the entire surplus was to be donated to the Free Project. When I invited Camilla to lecture on her social engagement and thoughts about entrepreneurship to students in entrepreneur-ship courses, she has always stressed that the fees she received would go in full and directly to the Free Project. She also usually invites seminar participants to contribute in some way and her invitations have, as far as I have seen, been met with a great response. 'Because seeing that it is possible to make a differ-ence really inspires you to continue', Camilla ended her lecture.

Both Kia and Camilla illustrate that social entrepreneurship is neither a straight path nor a one-way road to preciousness (meaningfulness) or precari-ousness (troublesome life). While Standing (2013) speaks about how the pre-carious class may have to move between jobs to secure their living, this is seldom the case in the stories related by the social entrepreneurs I have encountered. Instead, they stress how they have committed themselves to pursue social change, which may require different means. What remains is their desire to hold on to their vision and conviction that it is possible to change the situation for someone else. The reward, the meaningfulness this offers them, can never be measured in money, which is not a contradiction to earning a good salary.

Growing parallel identities

The final encounter is with the organisation 'Sisters in Business', which – similar to Neem – aims to support entrepreneurship among people in general, but in particular among vulnerable groups, and, more generally, groups which do not correspond to the norm of the male Western entrepreneurial hero who conquers the world and survives in a Darwinian mode (Ogbor 2000). In contrast to Neem, Sisters was not planned through a project, but rather arose by chance when an entrepreneur started to sublet parts of an apartment as office space. The apartment unexpectedly became a waterhole for would-be entrepreneurs and people in general who wanted to develop their ideas. A culture took shape where social entrepreneurship was nurtured through embracing diversity that was knitted together with friendly support and recognition for how their businesses could bring about social change. New opportunities were formulated through dialoguing, sharing experiences and solving problems. This was recognised as something new; not least their emphasis on creating an environment that was hospitable to all kinds of people, and in particular to those who did not find a place in any other community and who thus often struggled with themselves and their ideas.

In Sisters, a place (and space) was mobilised that attracted people who did not view themselves as entrepreneurs from the start but who slowly began to recognise their entrepreneurial potential. They not only offered the physical place (the apartment) but also a space of possibility where wishes and dreams could be expressed and enacted. Schoolteachers, app developers, mothers on parental leave, women politicians and students all started to contact them, sometimes on their blog, at other times through visits or at some of the breakfast meetings, inspiration seminars, dinners and events that Sisters arranged. Backed by this network, social entrepreneurship was nurtured and linked to the advantage of cooperating, not only to sell and buy one another's products and services, but also to engage in activities for the common good. Apart from engaging in various cooperation projects with the municipality, with regard to including 'othered' groups and their entrepreneurial potential, Sisters have geared themselves towards the advancement of the common good. For example, they have been involved in the 'innovation system' where they, together with other publicly funded organisations such as the local university, the state-owned business support institution, the municipal science park along with associations catering to the interest of the private sector, seek to support entrepreneurship and innovation in the county. Through this engagement they have tried to ensure that policy definitions, projects and activities remain open to all individuals and ideas pointing to the need to discard the gut feeling to reject an idea, because it could very well be that idea which is innovative.

In line with some of the social entrepreneurs I have encountered during my research, some of whom I have described above, Sisters manage to keep different identities 'in flux'. They refer to themselves not only as social entrepreneurs and innovators, but variously as employees, voluntary workers, enthusiasts and visionaries with a political commitment to take action and move boundaries that exclude particular groups and their ideas. In addition, they stress diversity through describing the identities of young people, women, immigrants in general and immigrant women in particular, often emphasising their countries of birth. These multiple identities are referred to in parallel and may be linked to Standing's hope for a Politics of Paradise to rescue identities:

> Turning to the political side of identity, modern neo-fascism is vehemently against acceptance of others' identity and culture. Neo-liberals also oppose the idea of identity on the grounds that individuals in a market society have no common identity. They presume a common personhood, a melting pot of folk, as implicit in the US and French

constitutions. Both postures are unhelpful, to put it mildly. *It would be better to assert that we can and do have multiple identities, and we need to construct institutions and policies to defend and enhance them.* The precariat is most exposed to a crisis of identity. It must not desert multiculturalism or the legitimation of multiple identities. However, it must do more, in that it must have its interests represented in all identity structures and institutions. This is not a plea for a new form of corporatism. It is a call for the precariat to become a class-for-itself.

(Standing 2011, p. 237, emphasis added)

Standing talks about the necessity for the precariat to become a class for itself which does not build on unity but on multiplicity. His idea is to recognise common features of precariousness without denying the multiplicity of identities and their specific relations to the precariat to be recognised. It is the ensuring of multiple identities that may be discerned in all of the cases narrated here. These social entrepreneurs refer to themselves as socially and politically engaged *and* as entrepreneurs with an interest in developing business, as business owners *and* employees *and* voluntary workers, as Swedes *and* immigrants, as men *and* women, as young *and* old, as publicly employed *and* privately employed. The examples of social entrepreneurship provided here do indeed involve the mobilisation of people from one kind of preciousness to another. However, in their recognition and appreciation of a diversity of identities (and occupations) among themselves and among others, and a common will to bring about social change, an awareness of a class whose defining feature is multiplicity (not unity) could arise. Even if social entrepreneurs tend to silence precariousness, or avoid referring to themselves as part of the precariat, they are certainly aware of their insecurity and inequality. On some occasions the social entrepreneurs I have followed have reflected upon the difficulties of pursuing social change and making a living from it, but often end up comparing their situation with those whom they wish to help and mention that they should stop whining about their life. The recognition of injustice seem to spur their social attempts to change and to get to grips with some of its consequences in various ways; not only through their social entrepreneurial action, but also in their coupling of entrepreneurial action to contexts where political issues are realigned with the government of the state. In that sense, social entrepreneurship may be understood not only as a means through which individual entrepreneurial actors have turned into experts in the provision of welfare, but also in how they return to political authorities with questions, opinions, demands, requests and requirements. Neem's engagement with micro-credit, which involved several public institutions, Camilla's efforts to use art and media to make children's situation in Africa politically recognised, and Sisters in Business's work with the innovation system in the county are but a few examples. These examples show how social entrepreneurs try to solve acute short-term problems, but also how they seek to redirect problems that need a more long-term and universal solution.

Social entrepreneurship and the precariat: one and the same?

The messianistic stories related by social entrepreneurs (where preciousness is absent) and the counter-narrative of the precariat (where social entrepreneurship is absent) are contradictory; yet there are obvious links. Social entrepreneurs are individuals with ambitions to take care of people who find themselves in precarious situations and remove them from insecurity, often through embracing the logic of entrepreneurship itself. In that sense precariousness is sought after, since it is the very market where social entrepreneurs operate. But in their ambitions to get to grips with precariousness, social entrepreneurs may also put themselves in the same situation; because when social entrepreneurs seek to create a more stable situation (secure and empowering) for themselves and for others, by holding on to visions of social change, they move between employment, self-employment and being an employer, acknowledging and appreciating a diversity of identities, and progress from a pronounced situation of the precariousness of unemployment to a silenced situation of the precariousness of entrepreneurial life. Thus, precariousness as described by Standing prevails, but its bleak backdrop does not appear to fit the stories of social entrepreneurs. What does fit their stories, however, is the meaningfulness of what they do for others.

By discussing Standing (2011, 2013) and his notion of precariat as an emerging class, it is possible to adopt a more critical stance that adds to the emerging critical discourse of social entrepreneurship. The need to be flexible, to adjust and to self-secure is emphasised as significant for both the precariat and social entrepreneurs. These qualities are also stressed as important for the entrepreneurial life called for in neoliberal society. However, whereas Standing (2013) presents insecurity as suggestive of feelings of fear and 'unknown unknowns' (i.e. things people don't even know that they don't know them), social entrepreneurship alludes to the hope of 'potential opportunities'. There are also differences between Standing's portrayal of the precariat's sense of insecurity and powerlessness and social entrepreneurs' descriptions of how they passionately embrace meaningfulness in their move from one stage of precariousness to another.

In this chapter I have used the precariat as a lever to downplay preciousness and listen to the 'little narratives' of social entrepreneurs (Dey and Steyaert 2010) in order to also pay attention to how precariousness is voiced. My intention has not been to provide rich and detailed stories of one social entrepreneur's everyday lives, but to retell how stories of social entrepreneurs have changed over time. I have sought to reflect upon how precious (meaningful) and precarious (troublesome) sides of social entrepreneurship are played out over time and in different contexts. The three themes identified in my analysis all tell about both meaningfulness and a troublesome life and how these are juggled in social entrepreneurial life. While the first theme shows how social entrepreneurs manage economic and social security by moving from one kind of precariousness to another, the second theme tells about how economic security is stabilised through moving between employment and entrepreneurship, and the third theme shows how social entrepreneurs seeks to redirect questions of social security to political authorities by creating new collectives through which political demands may be reclaimed.

Hence, in the little narratives there is no 'either/or' trajectory, but one that contains both meaning and problems. This has led me to reflect on the backdrop against which social entrepreneurial life unfolds. The principle of universality rests, according to Standing (2011, p. 11), on an ethos of solidarity that can retain political stability. To follow this principle politics could leave utilitarian values behind and start concentrating on life in general. But when public social issues are to be resolved by private entrepreneurial initiative, how can the principle of universality be realised? In short, how might the principle of universality underpinning a Politics of Paradise be integrated into social entrepreneurship?

While these broad questions should not leave any researcher in this field unaffected, I have opened up for debate the following three more precise questions: Will the precious stories of social entrepreneurship run the risk of further scaling and expanding precariousness? Could the more critical discourse of social entrepreneurship, inter alia developed in this book, help social entrepreneurs continue with what they do, and at the same time help them figure out how individual social entrepreneurial activities could be collectively mobilised? Further, and to respond to Standing's fear of political exclusion, could social entrepreneurs, through their undertakings, return some of their responsibility to political authorities?

From my encounters with social entrepreneurs, the critical entrepreneurship discourse could open up for them to tell stories of *both* preciousness *and* precariousness that better capture the experiences, dilemmas, struggles and meaningfulness they face in their everyday lives, *without* veiling ways in which universal principles can be realigned with political authorities.

On the one hand, the examples provided in this chapter show how social entrepreneurship, as a political activity, has been extended to new social categories. On the other hand, it is impossible to see how, from their various initiatives, they can follow the principle of universality to bring about social change through turning a Politics of Inferno into a Politics of Paradise. Social entrepreneurship as a messianistic story that offers hope to solve all kinds of social problems certainly has its limits, as does the view of the precariat as too dystrophic, since it neglects the collective mobilisation that actually proceeds through social entrepreneurship. In discussing the endeavours of social entrepreneurs through the lens of the precariat I hope to have shown the limits of the two discourses, bringing some nuances to both the messianistic social entrepreneurship narrative describing social entrepreneurs as precious, and the hopeless counter-narrative of the precariat class where all of us will soon be in a precarious situation.

Now I cross my fingers and cherish the hope that the critical discourse on social entrepreneurship will find a meaningful life outside academia to increase the reflection on both preciousness and precariousness in the little narratives told by social entrepreneurs. This may destabilise the glossy discourse and open up for the political potential of social entrepreneurship to raise awareness of how they may be part of the same precarious class whereby collective initiatives can be made.

Notes

1 The topic 'social entrepreneurship' has gained incredible traction in academia during the past few decades, presenting solutions for tackling all kinds of social issues. Searching Web of Science for articles on social entrepreneurship during the period prior to the millennium (1945–1999) renders 176 hits for articles including social entrepreneurship, while the subsequent period (2000–2015) illustrates a dramatic increase to 3,306 articles.
2 The following seven forms of labour security are highlighted by Standing (2013): (1) Labour market security. (2) Employment security. (3) Job security. (4) Work security. (5) Skill reproduction security. (6) Income security. (7) Representation security. See Standing (2011, p. 10) for a detailed description of each of the forms.
3 Available at www.tv4.se/nyhetsmorgon/artiklar/så-kan-du-hjälpa-föräldralösa-barn-i-ghana-54256df1c459486f4800001b.

References

Ahl, H., Berglund, K., Pettersson, K. and Tillmar, M. (2014), From feminism to FemInc.ism: On the uneasy relationship between feminism, entrepreneurship and the Nordic welfare state. *International Entrepreneurship and Management Journal*, pp. 1–24.

Ashoka (2015), What is the social entrepreneur? Available at https://www.ashoka. org/social_entrepreneur (accessed 25 May 2016).

Baccaro, L. and Howell, C. (2011), A common neoliberal trajectory the transformation of industrial relations in advanced capitalism. *Politics and Society*, **39**(4), pp. 521–563.

Barinaga, E. (2014), Microfinance in a developed welfare state: A hybrid technology for the government of the outcast. *Geoforum*, **51**, pp. 27–36.

Berglund, K. (2006), Discursive diversity in fashioning entrepreneurial identity. In Hjorth, D. and Steyaert, C. (eds) *Entrepreneurship as Social Change – A Third Movements in Entrepreneurship Book*, Cheltenham, and Northampton, MA: Edward Elgar, pp. 231–250.

Berglund, K. (2007/2012), *Jakten på Entreprenörer – om öppningar och låsningar i Entreprenörskapsdiskursen* [The Hunt for Entrepreneurs – Openings and Lockings in Entrepreneurship Discourse], Stockholm: Santérus Academic Press.

Berglund, K. (2013), Fighting against all odds: Entrepreneurship education as employability training. *Ephemera*, **13**(4), pp. 717–735.

Berglund, K. and Johansson, A.W. (2007), The entrepreneurship discourse – Outlined from diverse constructions of entrepreneurship on the academic scene. *Journal of Enterprising Communities: People and Places in the Global Economy*, **1**(1), pp. 77–102.

Berglund, K. and Schwartz, B. (2013), Holding on to the anomaly of social entrepreneurship dilemmas in starting up and running a Fair-Trade enterprise. *Journal of Social Entrepreneurship*, **4**(3), pp. 237–255.

Berglund, K. and Skoglund, A. (2016), Social entrepreneurship: To defend society from itself. In Fayolle, Al. and Riot, P. (eds) *Rethinking Entrepreneurship: Debating Research Orientations*, New York: Routledge, pp. 57–77.

Berglund, K., Johannisson, B. and Schwartz, B. (eds) (2012), *Societal Entrepreneurship: Positioning, Penetrating, Promoting*, Cheltenham: Edward Elgar.

Carlyle, E., Sinha, P. and Toma, G. (2015), Social Entrepreneurs. *Forbes*. Available at www.forbes.com/30under30/#/social-entrepreneurs (accessed 25 May 2016).

Cremin, C. (2010), Never employable enough: The (im)possibility of satisfying the boss's desire. *Organization* **17**(2), pp. 131–149.

Dempsey, S.E. and Sanders, M.L. (2010), Meaningful work? Nonprofit marketization and work/life imbalance in popular autobiographies of social entrepreneurship. *Organization*, **17**(4), pp. 437–459.

Dey, P. (2014), Governing the social through 'social entrepreneurship': A Foucauldian view of the 'art of governing' in advanced liberalism. In Douglas, H. and Grant, S. (eds) *Social Innovation and Social Entrepreneurship: Context and Theories*, Prahran, Victoria: Tilde Publishing, pp. 55–72.

Dey, P. and Steyaert, C. (2010), The politics of narrating social entrepreneurship. *Journal of Enterprising Communities: People and Places in the Global Economy*, **4**(1), pp. 85–108.

Harvey, D. (2005), *A Brief History of Neoliberalism*, Oxford: Oxford University Press.

Lemke, T. (2001), 'The birth of bio-politics': Michel Foucault's lecture at the Collège de France on neo-liberal governmentality. *Economy and Society*, **30**(2), pp. 190–207.

Mälardalen University (2013), Respons på Inspons: Mdh-alumn nominerad till Årets Innovatör 2012. Available at www.mdh.se/respons-pa-inspons-1.36865 (accessed 25 May 2016).

Nicholls, A. (2010), The legitimacy of social entrepreneurship: Reflexive isomorphism in a pre-paradigmatic field. *Entrepreneurship Theory and Practice*, **34**(4), pp. 611–633.

Ogbor, J.O. (2000), Mythicizing and reification in entrepreneurial discourse. In Godwyn, M. and Gittell, J.H. (eds) *Sociology of Organizations: Structures and Relationships*, London: Sage, pp. 457–469.

Pongratz, H.J. and Günter Voss, G.G. (2003), From employee to 'entreployee': Towards a 'self-entrepreneurial' work force? *Concepts and Transformation*, **8**(3), pp. 239–254.

Schwab Foundation (2015), What is a social entrepreneur? Available at www.schwab-found.org/content/what-social-entrepreneur (accessed 25 May 2016).

Skoll World Forum (2015), What is social entrepreneurship? Available at http://archive.skoll.org/about/what-is-social-entrepreneurship (accessed 25 May 2016).

Standing, G. (2011), *The Precariat: The New Dangerous Class*, London: A&C Black.

Standing, G. (2013), *Prekariatet: den nya farliga klassen* [The Precariat: The New Dangerous Class], Göteborg: Daidalos.

TV4 (2014), Så kan du hjälpa föräldralösa barn I Ghana. Available at www.tv4.se/nyhetsmorgon/artiklar/så-kan-du-hjälpa-föräldralösa-barn-i-ghana-54256df1c459486f4800001b/ (accessed 25 May 2016).

3 Social enterprise and the everydayness of precarious Indigenous Cambodian villagers

Challenging ethnocentric epistemologies

Isaac Lyne

Introduction

Social enterprises are commonly expressed as 'businesses with social goals' (Harding 2004), which mostly reinvest their surpluses to improve their outreach (DTI 2002). Social enterprise is actually not a new practice, but instead a 'new language' that reinvigorated old organisational forms in the late 1980s as a way to tackle social exclusion through market strategies (Defourny and Nyssens 2010). Social enterprises are evaluated in positive terms (Hervieux *et al.* 2010). They empower communities by putting them in control of asset management and solutions to their problems (Gunn and Durkin 2010), and mobilising and strengthening social reciprocity or 'social capital' (Kay 2006). The process of social entrepreneurship, which is involved in implementing social enterprises and their subsequent successes (Haugh 2005), also makes social enterprises agile or innovative.[1] They fill gaps in the provision of social goods and services left by the public or private sector (Galera and Borzaga 2009), essentially compensating for 'government and market failures' (Koch 2010).

Social enterprises are also viewed as 'wealth-creation engines' in their own right, evidenced by the generation of substantial revenues, employment and the societal conditions needed for stronger markets (Harding 2004; Dees 2008). In the Developing World context the United Nations Global Compact applies this logic by promoting social enterprise development as a way of generating conducive socio-economic conditions for business at the 'bottom of the pyramid' (BoP), the win–win scenario in which corporations can more easily enter markets and boost the economy (Power *et al.* 2012). While many now see social enterprises offering 'hope' for sustainable development (Seelos and Mair 2009), this chapter adopts a more critical perspective by suggesting that understandings of this in the Developing World are hampered due to their distinct focus on Western epistemologies. At stake here is the recognition that interest in social enterprises first emerged in response to Western welfare problems and may be considered as a Western-centric welfare discourse (Hackett 2009).

Purporting that particular manifestations of social enterprises are conditioned, at least in part, by the cultural context in which they are enacted (Peredo and McLean 2006), this chapter seeks to unveil the ethnocentrism inherent in dominant renditions of social enterprise by zooming in on a United Nations project geared towards promoting entrepreneurial activity in and, ultimately, the livelihood of Indigenous Cambodian forested communities. Fundamentally, this research explores the everydayness of social enterprises in two adjacent villages, in Rovieng District, which lies to the south of Preah Vihear Province in northern Cambodia. The central research question guiding this research is: How do social enterprises emerge, survive and/or succeed in Preah Vihear? In addressing this question, the investigation unveils the narrowness of Western understandings of social enterprise by raising sensitivity for the cultural contingency of social entrepreneurial projects and practices.

The remainder of this chapter is structured as follows. An outline of the United Nations project in question is followed by a discussion of the situated context of the study, relating to Indigenous minorities in Preah Vihear. The data collection and writing process is followed by an analysis of findings that contrast institutional logics with local ones and then look critically at conceptual matters related to social enterprises, including social capital, community participation and surplus distribution. Contextual constraints upon innovation are also identified before a concluding discussion about the meaning of social enterprise from a village point of view. The chapter seeks to make a critical contribution to debates about social enterprise by showing how value-free, managerialist approaches which are identifiable in the Western discourses (Curtis 2008; Dey and Steyaert 2010) once again conflict with the specificity of the Developing World context. In this case, the chapter calls for a wider reading of the customary transactions within diverse economies to make sense of incentives for social enterprise development.

The United Nations 'Creative Industries Support Program' (CISP) in Cambodia

This Creative Industries Support Program (CISP) in Cambodia ran from 2008 to 2012, funded with US$3.3 million from the Spanish government. It was implemented by four different United Nations agencies with participation from four Ministries of Cambodia.[2] Programme documents claim that CISP was aimed at enhancing 'cultural entrepreneurship' but upon close inspection much of this is oriented towards social enterprise development. Somewhat commensurately with social enterprise, CISP objectives included mobilising 'social capital' and the participation of Indigenous communities as a way to ensure the equitable development of creative industries (MDG-F 2008, pp. 8–14). Most specifically, CISP was focused on the development of niche products as a way to instil resilience into Indigenous minorities' cultures whose way of life is being increasingly impacted by the market economy (pp. 29–30). The specific case in which I an take interest is a value chain programme for Oleoresin which is tapped (by 'resin producers') from dipterocarp trees. Oleoresin has a domestic and international market for boat caulking and boat sealant and an international market paint/varnish and perfumery/ cosmetics (Andaya-Milani 2011). In accordance with CISP objectives, Oleoresin was a focus of attention in Preah Vihear Province because it is a traditional product of the Kuy Indigenous minority peoples.

The situated context: Kuy minorities in Rovieng District, Preah Vihear

Kuy Indigenous peoples mainly reside in the rural north of Cambodia (as well as parts of Laos and Thailand). They traditionally mix rice farming with livelihoods derived from the forest. Spiritual beliefs are Animist mixed with Buddhism. More importance is traditionally attached to local spirits (Ah'ret, in the Kuy language) than among the wider Khmer Buddhist population as well as to places of spiritual significance – particularly burial forests – where spirits are known to reside (Keating 2012; Swift 2013).

The Kuy in Preah Vihear live with a legacy of turmoil. Inevitably they suffered with the rest of the Cambodians after the Maoist Khmer Rouge overran the country, forcing most of the population into collective labour in rice collectives, rubber plantations or irrigation works and around 20 per cent of the national population died within four years (1975–1979) from starvation, disease and executions (Henderson 2007). In Rovieng, Kuy minorities were mistrusted by Khmer Rouge cadre and treated harshly (Swift 2013). The ousting of the Khmer Rouge from power in 1979 by the Vietnamese-backed 'Kampuchea People's Republic' did nothing to improve their fortunes. Rather, Preah Vihear became a resistance stronghold and site for continual insurgency by the Khmer Rouge aligned with Royalist and Nationalist factions during 18 subsequent years of civil war (Bekaert 1993; Sorenson 1993).

Despite relative peace since the demobilisation of the Khmer Rouge in the late 1990s, Kuy minorities continue to be impacted by events beyond their control. Land grabbing (the expropriation of land, often violently, under circumstances of legal ambiguity) along with RGC-issued concessions for industrial agriculture, forestry and mining (which frequently amount to land grabbing) and deforestation has increasingly excluded Kuy minorities from access to natural resources and sites of spiritual significance (Keating 2012). Conflicts have proliferated (CCHR 2014) and companies have obtained security 'on loan' from RGC armed forces who have killed several and beaten many Kuy people accessing concession areas (Keating 2013, pp. 313–314). Stating that the way of life for Kuy minorities is 'impacted by the market economy' thus seems restrained. Most pertinently to the following text, on account of producers' exclusion from resources the quantity of Oleoresin that producers can tap has reportedly halved, from 20 to 40 average litres per day in just four years between 2005 and 2009 (ILO 2010, p. 19).

Data collection and analysis

Data collection between January and April 2011 began with three interviews: the UN–CISP coordinator; the director of a consultancy company hired to train Resin Producer Associations (RPAs) on marketing and finally the director of a local non-governmental organisation (NGO) recruited to the CISP Oleoresin programme. The objective at this point was to find out more about CISP and to gain insight into their perception of the reasons for an Oleoresin intervention. Twelve qualitative interviews were subsequently undertaken with members of two RPAs located in adjacent villages. From this point onward they appear as RPA-1 and RPA-2. The main beneft gained from a comparison of two RPAs as opposed to a study of just one is that each RPA emerged under different circumstances and there are different insights to be drawn. RPA-1 emerged autonomously and preceded the CISP intervention, while RPA-2 was formed purely in response to the procured interventions of CISP, initially being encouraged by the NGO and then encouraged further to cooperate by the consultant company in training. In each instance six interviews (five members plus the respective RPA leader) took place. This was followed by a group discussion with four interviewees (two members of RPA-2, one member of RPA-1 and also the leader of RPA-1). The FGD objective was to see how responses differ in a group context and also to see what issues emerge as matters of importance during discussions among villagers which are not elucidated in a single-person interview.

All interviewees were Kuy Indigenous minority villagers. Kuy minorities generally speak Khmer, which Swift (2013) puts down to their assimilation into wider Khmer culture in response to discrimination. A Kuy assistant was recruited for my interviews but all interviews were conducted in Khmer language, allowing me to engage at an elementary conversational level while taking notes from the translations given. Interviews tended to last between 90 minutes and two hours. Interviews for RPA leaders were shorter. All interviews were recorded and stored as electronic files. Interview notes were typed up and critical moments were revisited in recordings to gain an accurate translation from a native Khmer speaker. Responses to each question were entered into a spreadsheet for the purpose of drawing out general trends. The analysis was synthesised with literature on social enterprise alongside literature on Cambodia and Kuy minority experiences in order to develop a case study narrative.

This research was initially undertaken as part of a broader comparative study of three different types of social enterprises in northern Cambodia (Lyne *et al.* 2013). This steered the outcomes as far as Western-centric debates and definitions surrounding social enterprise tended to take precedence. In part this was driven by the desire for outputs useful to the British Council which administrated the initiative Development in Higher Education Partnerships (DeLPHE) funding the research. Upon reflection, more questions in the interview schedule derived from literature on Cambodian culture would give greater nuance to social enterprise from a grassroots village perspective.

Findings

Official and local logics of CISP

The analysis revealed a clear disjuncture between the various promoters of the resin project of CISP (e.g. coordinator, consultants, NGOs), and how the two RPAs on the ground received the project. As to the former, the CISP coordinator asserted that protecting natural forestry resources and negotiating and managing access to NTFPs are critical issues for Indigenous peoples because these resources have supported the livelihoods of Kuy minorities for generations. The organisation of resin producers into coherent and responsible associations was paramount to this objective. The emphasis on social capital and community participation in CISP documents was readily apparent in his reasoning. The local NGO director also saw the remit as helping villagers to get organised to incentivise good forest management. The consultant concurred that community organising is important but from his perspective the most important activity was resin marketing. In his view better marketing would enable villagers to leverage pressure for ensuring resin quality which in turn would build reputation in the locality and generate a better bargaining position with wholesalers. It was proposed that the RPAs would collaborate across villages on a 'resin market' to start dealing directly with wholesalers who would be brought into the area. He referred to this setup as a social enterprise. Among the three promoters of the CISP project, he was the only one to frame the desired outcome of CISP using the specific terminology of social enterprise.

In contradiction to the official CISP logic, implied in the assumptions and sensitivities of the project document, there are differences in outlook between the two resin associations in Rovieng. All but one of the RPA-1 members, unsurprisingly, said that their first priority as an RPA member is to improve their income. However, there are critical differences between members of the two associations in terms of how they sensed this was to be achieved. In RPA-1 (which emerged organically, pre-dating the CISP intervention) most members joined to promote forestry protection. This was viewed as the best way to secure and perhaps improve their income. RPA-1 members recognised villagers' participation in the destruction of their own livelihoods. Largely due to their increasing exclusion from natural resources, villagers have been compelled to generate more cash income by cutting down trees to sell timber on the black market, sometimes taking up with illegal logging operations. It was stated that the RPA-1 should promote better behaviour among villagers to ensure good relations with outside officials so that they are not

Figure 3.1 Felled dipterocarp trees in Rovieng District (April 2011).
Source: Photograph by author.

banned from the forest. To this end RPA-1 has, with the encouragement of the local NGO, become part of a 'Community Forestry organixation' which under 2002 Law on Forestry provides limited user rights on 'state public land' for subsistence purposes.

The RPA-2 membership (excluding a younger member) in contrast joined solely because they thought they could somehow *sell more resin without much thought for conservation at all*. This reflected on the origins of RPA-2 in response to the procured consultant services. While the leader had concerns with conservation, there was less agreement among other members about the necessity to change behaviour. There was also a profound lack of agreement about whether cutting trees is unethical given that powerful people outside of the village (including the military) do it on a much larger scale. Two members said they were dissatisfied with the RPA-2 because they were not selling any more resin at all and that this justified cutting trees if they had no other way of making money. Two members also complained about the teaching, stating that more quality control in the group would just mean that they would not make money. It seems that the training was fraught with contradictions in the eyes of these respondents and the understanding of it was unclear.

Community participation and social capital

The leader of the self-formed RPA-1 was elected. According to members he had good relations with forestry officials and was generally viewed by others as a 'leading person' who was trusted to make decisions. There was a view among members that '*special people*' should not make decisions alone and that attending meetings was important. But it was also generally asserted that the leader should determine what decisions need to be made and call people to a meeting when he feels it is necessary to do so. One member said that everybody must be able to participate but sometimes it can be a burden, so it should be limited. In summary, because members were clear on their objectives, having formed the association among themselves without instigation from outside, there was a strong sense of ownership. Rather than being wholly participatory, RPA-1 in this instance lends support to 'stewardship' theories on social enterprise governance; i.e. participation in decisions is limited for better efficiency and leadership is exercised by the manager/entrepreneur who is also part of the community that the enterprise serves (Mason *et al.* 2007, pp. 290–291), although inertia among members perhaps had much to do with the model they adopted.

The RPA-2 leader was not elected. He was chosen by lottery following the consultant training. He had also lived in the village for only ten months. It did not seem imperative among members that he had a standing in the village. Two RPA-2 members actually pointed to the Village Chief rather than to the association leader when I asked who they thought were the most important members, even though the Village Chief is not an actual member of the RPA-2. There was reportedly very low attendance at meetings. Three members expressed the view that participation in the RPA's affairs was not necessary and that instead the leader should take care of matters on his own and communicate with the NGO and forestry officials. It was clear that RPA-2 was not living up to the CISP objective of promoting greater participation among communities in the management of their resources and affairs. In part this may have been the anticipated outcome of the RPA-2 having been directly constituted through a programme focused on resin marketing. When villagers failed to make more money, their participation rapidly declined. The inertia of members was much higher than in RPA-1 and social capital, or bridging ties across different members of the community, was hard to envisage. Instead some members saw their chances for security hinging on relations with the Village Chief, although this was true in both villages in different ways. This underlines another contingency in the understanding of how a social enterprise is likely to operate, which is the prevalence of patron–client relationships.

Constraints upon innovation: patron–client bonds

The trainer sent by the consultant company expressed frustration that no members of either RPA were willing (in accordance with the consultant's recommendations) to develop a resin storage system with a view to bringing traders into the area. It transpired that RPA members sell liquid resin directly to the Village Chief, who in turn deals with all outside wholesalers. Some come to his house where the resin is stored. Otherwise he has connections in Phnom Tbeng Meanchey, the main town in Preah Vihear Province. None of the members interviewed in either RPA, including leaders, would countenance any other system than selling their resin to the Village Chief who has the sole monopoly on the middleman position. All RPA members in different ways are heavily invested, as individuals, in patron–client relations with the Village Chief. More widely in Southeast Asian studies, patron–client relationships are a norm of reciprocity whereby villagers with limited options try to gain subsistence guarantees from personal (dyadic) relationships with more powerful actors. There are implied obligations on the part of the patron; for instance, it is anticipated that a legitimate patron will be 'generous' – regardless of whether or not their minimal obligations are met in practice (Scott 1977). This reality is widely observed in studies of Cambodian villages, where familial relations with patrons are deeply personal and carefully guarded (Ledgerwood 2007).

This anticipation of patron relations as insurance is deeply embedded among villagers whose livelihoods are precarious. Village Chiefs are not selected by vote; they are appointed directly by the Romoneiy Commune Chief. This is the case in all Cambodian villages; the Village Chief connects the village to community-level politics which is overwhelmingly dominated by the ruling Cambodian People's Party (although opposition parties are represented) (Hughes 2007). In the north of Cambodia powerful actors notoriously continue to extract rents from land titling as a privilege and in some instances elite actors are known to mobilise violence to press their claims upon resources (Diepart and Dupuis 2014). Under such circumstances, and no doubt in large part also due to past traumatic experiences set out earlier, maintaining a connection to a patron figure makes a lot of sense. The inequality of benefits from resin collection thus resonates with value chain studies elsewhere in Cambodia showing how the disproportionate sacrifice of surplus in return for 'protection' amounts to rational economic behaviour on the part of precarious villagers (Thavat 2010). This all calls into question the extent to which social enterprise may be considered as a market-based innovation that meets people's social needs, as is generally asserted to be the case in literature. First of all this underlines how markets themselves are always contextual. The supply-and-demand crowd always come with local norms and customs and also laws enforced by different means, as Polanyi (1957, pp. 266–267) is well known for pointing out. Moreover, patrons have a tendency to thwart changes that are not in their own interest or to make sure that any changes serve their own interests or those of their most valuable supporters, as Matthews (2007) illustrates in a study of village-based financial institutions in Cambodia. The propensity for the types of 'social innovations' to which social enterprises are in general deemed to be central (Defourny and Nyssens 2013) must therefore be placed within some quite rigid limitations, in consideration of the way these RPAs work in practice.

This also calls into question some of the assumptions about who should stand to benefit from social enterprises. As a general rule Western literature leans towards the notion that a social enterprise must be 'not for profit' (Defourny and Nyssens, 2010) but in this instance it seems pertinent to ask what it is that surplus is *being used for*. As Scott (1977) illustrates, patron–client relationships in pre-capitalist society have traditionally provided the most basic type of social insurance available to peasantry. Arguably in this instance, with villagers caught between the customary economy typified by subsistence and trade in non-monetary goods, and the advancing capitalist economy, insurance payments made by allowing the Village Chief to appropriate their surplus in value form are deemed to have social effects, or, in the language of social enterprise, deemed to be meeting important social needs. Beyond the questions about non-profit essentialism raised by patron–client relationships, it can also be asserted that the situated context (described earlier in this chapter) renders the non-profit orientation questionable more widely still. These are matters that I turn to next in consideration of debates about the distribution of surplus and equity within the social enterprise itself.

Social enterprise and community solidarity: using surplus for social goals?

Both RPA leaders and two members of RPA-1 expressed the view that the use of monetary surpluses (from resin collection) for community development *might* be desirable. It was seen as a good idea, for instance, if some money is invested into the construction of a well, concrete latrines and better timber for construction. RPA-1's leader and one other member also said a saving programme might be one way to achieve this goal. However, on the whole the notion of a social enterprise that reinvests its surpluses into social objectives instead of redistributing them to members (DTI 2002) was seen as implausible. Those who said it was a good idea were less optimistic when I asked if it was actually a possibility. All other RPA members (notably all of those in RPA-2) stressed that resin income is the property of members and their families alone. Money was needed for daily life. With less land accessible to farm and graze animals, and declining access to forestry which provides salvaged wood for fuel, different types of food and materials that could be traded 'for other items', there are more things they must pay for nowadays with cash. Several villagers not only stated that it was impractical to reinvest surplus income into village development, but also that they could not imagine this as the reason for an RPA at all. They felt it was the Village Chief's job to leverage resources through the Commune Council officials or that NGOs should provide such infrastructure.

If one clings to the view that social enterprises are a means by which communities gain control over their resources and solutions to their problems (Gunn and Durkin 2010), then the views of RPA members about the use of surplus become problematic. However, it makes sense to look beyond the reinvestment of surplus to understand a social enterprise contextually in this instance. Uncertain futures make villagers' lack of incentive to invest surplus in this way understandable. What they build today could be taken away tomorrow by the next land concession signed off by the RGC. This calls into question Western-centric views of social enterprise because the notion that a community-based social enterprise *could* actually put a village community in ultimate control of its resources in northern Cambodia is dubious. This intersection of a customary and a capitalist economy is always a problematic place for villagers to be because an increasing circulation of cash does not, per se, raise the quality of life (cf. James *et al.* 2012, pp. 247–248) and in some conditions even worsens it. However, under these conditions of uncertainty, it seems reasonable enough that villagers deem the distribution of monetary income as a means for the day-to-day survival of a household as *social in itself.*

In addition to a lack of appetite for channelling monetary surplus beyond the household, there is also little appetite in either RPA for any talk of equity vis-à-vis the disadvantaged. This constrains the type of solidarity viewed by some writers as the raison d'être for, and the identity politics of, social enterprise development (Hulgård *et al.* 2010). Every respondent said that those who work the hardest should get the most money. When I probed this they insisted it was regardless of someone's disability. This is despite the fact that RPA membership included amputees and that Preah Vihear is one of five provinces that collectively account for more than 60 per cent of national landmine contamination (Landmine and Cluster Munition Monitor 2016). Four respondents (three in RPA-1 which was otherwise the more social RPA) expressed that the badly disadvantaged, including the disabled, should go to an NGO – the RPA should bear no responsibility for them. An elderly respondent expressed it in the strongest terms: 'nobody owes anything to anybody else. If they are disabled, they need to be smarter. They have to think more how to get money.' Following the situated context written earlier, it is evident that past experiences and trauma, including forced collective labour during the Khmer Rouge era and conflicts up until the late 1990s, put social solidarity in a particular context. This concurs essentially with others who also find that damaged trust and undermined relationships beyond the household are, in different ways, an enduring legacy of the Khmer Rouge era and the subsequent conflicts (Zucker 2011).

Concluding discussion: a different way of seeing social enterprise?

At the outset of this chapter I asked the question: How do social enterprises emerge, survive and/or succeed in Preah Vihear? The short answer would seem to be: autonomously and organically with their own self-determined objectives. The obvious lesson is that the assumption that social enterprise development in one village could mobilise the type of social capital found in another village has proved to be flawed. CISP documents recognise that each group engages needs to find its own way to mobilise community participation because one size cannot fit all, but there is still an overriding emphasis on the development of models that can be widely replicated (MDG-F 2011, p. 14). This emphasis is similar to that placed on replicable models in social enterprise consultancy literature (Alter 2007, p. 49). But the problem more precisely here is that the value-free managerialist approach (Dey and Steyaert 2010) which seems the easiest to replicate turns out to also be the least reflective or dialogical (Ridley-Duff and Bull 2011).

A compounding issue is that the two RPAs mobilised with different routes in mind towards objectives that are similar, but not entirely the same. The purpose of RPA-1 was not wealth creation as such; rather, it was continued subsistence. The notion of social enterprises being wealth-creation engines in their own right that lay down the conditions for business at the 'bottom of the pyramid' might make sense to outsiders looking inward, who see potential for value chain improvement and better benefits from the resin industry at large. But it is not seen that way from the RPA-1 village looking outward. Rather, the reasoning is the conservation/protection of the wealth they already have. Moreover, in this instance, where the RPA-1 was proving relatively sustainable, the notion of social enterprise as a value chain improvement comes up against deeply guarded practices of patronage which were arguably underappreciated in the delivery of the CISP project. In a sense, so too underappreciated was the temporal nature of being in time for Indigenous Kuy minorities. Past experiences, current problems and an increasingly uncertain future all constrain the potential for commercial social enterprise development but render the seeking of security within specific relationships perfectly intelligible.

A final point I turn towards is to the undisputed credit of the CISP project design. Oleoresin was targeted as a traditional product of Kuy communities and the objective was to preserve their way of life. This was the clearer objective of the CISP coordinator; far more important it seemed were the developing markets per se. From this point a better answer is given, I feel, to the research question I asked: whether the notion of 'emerging and thriving' is removed altogether from the usual reading of 'markets'. For sure, resin collection is a source of income, but it is also part of the customary economy. RPA-1 members were clear about this. They were reliant upon access to the forest not only for resin but also for a range of NTFPs which provide not just subsistence but also access to products (not always strictly legal ones) that can be traded for other goods. To this, a further material issue may be added. Access to forestry has traditionally sustained the Animist spiritual practices of Kuy minorities, providing both materials for rituals and sites where such rituals take place. As Keating (2012, 2013) describes in depth, the exclusion of Kuy communities from forestry resources and therefore from their spiritual beliefs and practices has been fundamentally damaging to village solidarity. In RPA-1 this emerged more strongly in comments lamenting selfishness and lack of friendliness. It was elaborated more in the group discussion when I asked how social life had changed. There were fewer ceremonies, people were busier earning money, but overridingly, their rights of access to sites of particular significance were forbidden. The RPA-1 leader expressed the view that keeping access to some spiritual sites open was tied up in forest conservation objectives. It was therefore relevant to the RPA-1, although he was also clear that the main incentive was to safeguard resin collection. Perhaps too many objectives would be deemed confusing, but, even so, RPA-1 might come closer to a reading of social enterprise when it is interconnectedly (with household survival) a means of preserving customary practices from one generation to the next.

In this sense, outside of normal ways of framing social enterprise, it could be taken into consideration that spiritualist practices are in themselves also one part of an economy when 'economies' are broadly and diversely understood (Gibson-Graham *et al.* 2013). Spiritual practices which involve both 'reciprocal exchanges' and exchanges without such rigid equivalences may be counted as non-capitalist and non-monetary transactions with economic value nonetheless. What this shows is that perhaps the contribution that RPA-1, as a better organised and more recognisable social enterprise than RPA-2, survives and thrives by keeping a diverse economy (which is inclusive of a range of capitalist, alternative and non-capitalist economic practices of exchange and labour, and thus both customary and modern) in motion. The contribution is restorative more than innovative, in that it maintains the plausibility of practices that are preconditional to village solidarity and well-being.

Notes

1 This chapter is focused on social enterprise, as opposed to social entrepreneurship. The latter is a broad topic that encompasses a range of contexts; it is attributed, for instance, to the actions of policy makers and civic activists as far as it involves the mobilising of resources in different combinations in pursuit of a social effect. However, related to social enterprise specifically, Ridley-Duff and Bull express that 'social enterprises (form) are the product of social entrepreneurship (process)' (2011, p. 78).

2 Participating agencies were: the United Nations Development Programme; the United Nations Science and Cultural Organization; the International Labour Organization and the Food and Agriculture Organization. Participating Government Ministries were the Ministries of: Culture and Fine Arts; Industry, Mines and Energy; Commerce; and Agriculture, Forestry and Fisheries (MDG-F 2011).

48 I. Lyne

References

Alter, K. (2007), *Social Enterprise Typology*, Wilmington, DE: Virtue Venures LLC.

Andaya-Milani, N. (2011), Dipterocarpus resin in the international market: A market scan. In *Forum on Sustainable and Pro-poor Oleoresin Industry Development in Cambodia*, 23 September, Phnom Penh, Cambodia, pp. 51–61.

Beckert, J. (1999), Agency, entrepreneurs, and institutional change: The role of strategic choice and institutionalized practices in organizations. *Organization Studies*, **20**(5), pp. 777-779.

Bekaert, J. (1993), The return of the Khmer Rouge. *Southeast Asian Affairs*, pp. 130–143.

CCHR (2014), Ponlok Khmer NGO threatened of closure in Preah Vihear Province. Cambodian Center for Human Rights. Available at http://cchrcambodia.org/index_old.php?url=media/media.php&p=alert_detail.php&alid=50&id=5 (accessed 25 May 2016).

Curtis, T. (2008), Finding that grit makes a pearl: A critical re-reading of research into social enterprise. *International Journal of Entrepreneurial Behaviour and Research*, **14**(5), pp. 276–290.

Dees, J.G. (2008), Philanthropy and enterprise: Harnessing the power of business and social entrepreneurship for development. *Innovations: Technology, Governance, Globalization*, **3**(3), pp. 119–132.

Defourny, J. and Nyssens, M. (2010), Conceptions of social enterprise and social entrepreneurship in Europe and the United States: Convergences and divergences. *Journal of Social Entrepreneurship*, **1**(1), pp. 32–53.

Defourny, J. and Nyssens, M. (2013), Social innovation, social economy and social enterprise: What can the European debate tell US? In F. Moulaert, D. MacCallum, A. Mehmood and A. Hamdouch (eds), *The International Handbook on Social Innovation: Collective Action, Social Learning and Transdisciplinary Research*, Cheltenham: Edward Elgar, pp. 40–53.

Dey, P. and Steyaert, C. (2010), The politics of narrating social entrepreneurship. *Journal of Enterprising Communities: People and Places in the Global Economy*, **4**(1), pp. 85–108.

Diepart, J.C. and Dupuis, D. (2014), The peasants in turmoil: Khmer Rouge, state formation and the control of land in northwest Cambodia. *The Journal of Peasant Studies*, **41**(4), pp. 445–468.

DTI (2002), *Social Enterprise: A Strategy for Success*, Department of Trade and Industry, London: HMSO.

Galera, G. and Borzaga, C. (2009), Social enterprise: An international overview of its conceptual evolution and legal implementation. *Social Enterprise Journal*, **5**(3), pp. 210–228.

Gibson-Graham, J.K., Cameron, J. and Healy, S. (2013), *Take Back the Economy: An Ethical Guide for Transforming Our Communities*, Minneapolis: University of Minnesota Press.

Gunn, R. and Durkin, C. (2010), *Social Entrepreneurship: A Skills Approach*, Bristol: Policy Press.

Hackett, M. (2009), 'Social enterprise' in a global financial crisis: Is there a developing-world voice? In *Australasian Political Studies Association Conference (2009: Sydney, Australia) APSA 2009*, Macquarie University, pp. 1–16.

Harding, R. (2004), Social enterprise: The new economic engine? *Business Strategy Review*, **15**(4), pp. 39–43.

Hardt, M. and Negri, N. (2000), *Empire*. Cambridge, MA: Harvard University Press.

Haugh, H. (2005), A research agenda for social entrepreneurship. *Social Enterprise Journal*, **1**(1), pp. 1–12.

Henderson, J.C. (2007), Communism, heritage and tourism in East Asia. *International Journal of Heritage Studies*, **13**(3), pp. 240–254.

Hervieux, C., Gedajlovic, E. and Turcotte, M.B. (2010), The legitimization of social entrepreneurship. *Journal of Enterprising Communities: People and Places in the Global Economy*, **4**(1), pp. 37–67.

Hughes, C. (2007), The Seila Program in Cambodia. In J. Manor (ed.), *Aid that Works: Successful Development in Fragile States*, Washington, DC: World Bank Publications, pp. 85–121.

Hughes, C. (2009), Reconstructing legitimate political authority through elections? In J. Öjendal and M. Lilja (eds), *Beyond Democracy in Cambodia: Political Reconstruction in a Post-conflict Society*, Denmark: Nordic Institute of Asian Studies.

Hulgård, L., Defourny, J. and Pestoff, V. (2010), *Social Enterprise, Social Entrepreneurship, Social Economy, Solidarity Economy: An EMES Reader on the 'SE Field'*, Liege: EMES European Research Network.

ILO (2010), *Operationalizing Gender Aspects in the Creative Industries Support Programme*, Phnom Penh: International Labour Organization.

James, P., Nadarajah, Y., Haive, K. and Stead, V. (2012), *Sustainable Communities, Sustainable Development: Other Paths for Papua New Guinea*, Honolulu: University of Hawai'i Press.

Kay, A. (2006), Social capital, the social economy and community development. *Community Development Journal*, **41**(2), pp. 160–173.

Keating, N.B. (2012), Spirits of the forest: Cambodia's Kuy people practice spirit-based conservation. *Anthropology Faculty Publications*, Paper 1. Available at http://digitalcommons.brockport.edu/ant_facpub/1/ (accessed 25 May 2016).

Keating, N.B. (2013), Kuy alterities: The struggle to conceptualise and claim Indigenous land rights in neoliberal Cambodia. *Asia Pacific Viewpoint*, **54**(3), pp. 309–322.

Koch, J.L. (2010), Social entrepreneurship as a bottom-up model of socio-economic development. *Development Outreach*, **12**(1), pp. 16–18.

Landmine and Cluster Munition Monitor (2016), *Archives 1997–2014: Cambodia*. Available at http://archives.the-monitor.org/index.php/publications/display?url=lm/2003/cambodia.html (accessed 25 May 2016).

Ledgerwood, J. (2007), *Understanding Cambodia: Social Hierarchy, Patron–Client Relationships and Power*, Northern Illinois University: Department of Anthropology and Center for Southeast Asian Studies.

Lyne, I., Ngin, C. and Santoyo-Rio, E. (2013), Understanding Social Enterprise, Social Economy and Local Social Entrepreneurship in the Context of Rural Cambodia. Paper presented to the Fourth EMES International Research Conference on Social Enterprise, Liege.

Mason, C., Kirkbride, J. and Bryde, D. (2007), From stakeholders to institutions: The changing face of social enterprise governance theory. *Management Decision*, **45**(2), pp. 284–301.

Matthews, B. (2007), Literacy and internal control of community finance institutions in rural Cambodia. In M. Chen, R. Jhabvala, R. Kanbur and C. Richards (eds), *Membership-based Organizations of the Poor*, London: Routledge, pp. 138–154.

MDG–F (2008), *Creative Industries Support Programme Document: Cambodia*, Phnom Penh: Millenium Development Goal Fund, Country Thematic Window for Culture and Development.

MDG–F (2011), *Joint Programmes Information: Creative Industries Support Programme*, Millenium Development Goal Achievement Fund, Available at www.mdgfund. org/sites/default/files/Cambodia%20Joint%20Programmes%20Fact%20Sheet.pdf (accessed 25 May 2016).

Peredo, A.M. and McLean, M. (2006), Social entrepreneurship: A critical review of the concept. *Journal of World Business*, **41**(1), pp. 56–65.

Polanyi, K. (1957), The economy as instituted process. in K. Polanyi, C.M. Arensberg and H.W. Pearson (eds), *Trade and Market in the Early Empires*, Glencoe: Free Press, pp. 243–270.

Power, G., Wilson, B., Brandenburg, M., Melia-Teevan, K. and Lai, J. (2012), *A Framework for Action: Social Enterprise and Impact Investing*. United Nations Global Compact Office, June 2012. Available at www.unglobalcompact.org/docs/issues_ doc/development/Framework_Social_Enterprise_Impact_Investing.pdf (accessed 25 May 2016).

Ridley-Duff, R. and Bull, M. (2011), *Understanding Social Enterprise: Theory and Practice*, London: Sage.

Scott, J.C. (1977), *The Moral Economy of the Peasant: Rebellion and Subsistence in Southeast Asia*, New Haven, CT: Yale University Press.

Seelos, C. and Mair, J. (2009), Hope for sustainable development: How social entrepreneurs make it happen. In R. Ziegler (ed.), *An Introduction to Social Entrepreneurship: Voices, Preconditions, Contexts*, Cheltenham: Edward Elgar, pp. 228–246.

Sorenson, M.E. (1993), *The United Nations Peace Action Plan. Case Study – Cambodia. A Curriculum for Secondary School Students*, New York: United Nations Association of the United States of America.

Swift, P. (2013), Changing ethnic identities among the Kuy in Cambodia: Assimilation, reassertion and the making of Indigenous identity. *Asia Pacific Viewpoint*, **54**(3), pp. 296–308.

Thavat, M. (2010), *Aiding Trade: Case Studies in Agricultural Value Chain Development in Cambodia*. Doctor of Philosophy thesis, Australian National University.

Zucker, E.M. (2011), Trust and distrust in a highland Khmer community after thirty years of war. In J. Marston (ed.), *Anthropology and Community in Cambodia: Reflections on the Work of May Ebihara*, Caulfield, Victoria: Monash University Press, pp. 79–104.

4 Reasons to be fearful

The 'Google Model of Production',
entrepreneurship, corporate power
and the concentration of dispersed
knowledge

Gerard Hanlon

Introduction

Much recent entrepreneur scholarship prioritises the creative, innovative, strategic and liberating role of entrepreneurship in society. This chapter argues that this position is simply wrong. Rather than distance entrepreneurship from exploitative value capture, what follows makes such a proposition central to the 'new' economy – to the 'Google Model of Production' (Marazzi 2011, p. 51). In making this argument, the chapter rethinks the classic entrepreneurship theory of Mises, Hayek, Schumpeter, etc. against recent changes in the economy. As such, the chapter centralises tensions between creativity beyond the organisation and growing corporate tendencies to entrepreneurially capture value that it did not create. In so doing this entrepreneurship also limits society's innovative potential because corporations use property rights to make the virtually limitless scarce and the inclusive exclusive. Such actions are acts of class struggle from above.

Creating and innovating continues within the Google Model (e.g. Wikipedia or Linux) but, because it prioritises entrepreneurial capture to make limited what is dispersed and to close the potentially open, innovation is shackled. Rather than kill entrepreneurship as creativity in the manner of Schumpeter, the chapter argues that creativity and large corporate entrepreneurship not only co-exist but are co-constitutive to argue that the market concentrates dispersed knowledge.

What follows examines this emerging model. The first section outlines the model's contours; the second analyses the different entrepreneurial traditions that provide ways of understanding the model; the third provides a way of supplementing our understanding of this transition through the use of Workerism and post-Workerism with their emphasis on 'free labour' and the rise of immaterial labour and products; the subsequent section examines how entrepreneurial profit seeks to make immaterial goods rivals and excludable despite the fact that this limits innovation and productivity; the chapter then returns to the Google Model and pulls these changes together before it concludes.

The Google Model of Production

As suggested above, this model of production places entrepreneurial value capture and the concentration of dispersed knowledge at its centre. Indeed, its central features are the accessing of free or subsidised labour, the increased capacity of corporations to capture dispersed knowledge, and the use of property rights and market dominance to restrict access to services and products thereby limiting the potential for innovation and productivity. Many of these methods of capture are commonplace in management scholarship (e.g. strategic acquisition: Eliasson 2005; Pénin et al. 2011), the capturing of 'free' labour through the use of data generated by users of Facebook or Google (Soar 2011), the capturing of 'subsidised' labour (e.g. growth of internships: Perlin 2011), the use of contracts to 'lock in' creative labour as new forms of 'indentured' work (Stahl 2010), the capturing of customer knowledge from labourers/consumers/users (e.g. crowdsourcing: Eliasson 2003; Oliveira and von Hippel 2010; Pénin et al. 2011), the increasing use of laws to extend or renegotiate property rights in favour of value capturing corporate actors (Perelman 2002; Samuelson 1999; Trosow 2010; Pénin et al. 2011), or the use of technological and other fixes to lock customers into using a host of other services (Economist 2012a). The chapter argues that examining any one phenomenon on its own is less informative than analysing them together because together they represent a shift in economic, social and organisational life which foregrounds entrepreneurial capture.

The digital economy is important to these changes even if many of the industries engaged in some or all of them are long established. For example, Lego and Proctor and Gamble avail of user communities and crowdsourcing but they are hardly new (Pénin et al. 2011), and three-quarters of all US or European corporations with sales over US$250 million allegedly practise open innovation (Ettlinger 2014). Nevertheless, new technologies enable companies to access labour and knowledge, and this is a central element of the change – every time you click on Google your free labour reveals information about your preferences which is then used to target advertising and reap rewards. Often unbeknownst to the consumer/user, this information is further used to identify the results of their future searches more thoroughly. Thus, as a believer in climate change you search the topic, your previous searches have revealed your beliefs and enable Google to prioritise links reinforcing your views, thereby making you comfortable and 'locking' you into Google as your preferred search engine. The 'free gift' Google provides enables it to access free labour and dispersed knowledge (e.g. beliefs about climate change) to then concentrate knowledge (e.g. by limiting access to potentially uncomfortable knowledge) and to better individualise, target and sell advertising (Lanier 2011; Pariser 2011). By so doing, Google 'locks in' customers to allow it to learn more, target further advertising, and claim quasi-monopoly royalties in a virtuous circle of capture. In addition, the model operates on the basis of content Google does not create but which is of interest to its (now) labourers/consumers/users. Free or subsidised labour is provided in two senses. First, the user is working for free by providing knowledge to Google because he or she is a mine of information to be accessed, stored and packaged for profit. Second, the information searched is often created elsewhere and provided for free (e.g. news media content: Pariser 2011).

The model is located in openness, lock-in and free labour. It engages users and their dispersed knowledge through the provision of free services, cash prizes, stimulation, piquing interest, venture capital – like relations between large firms and smaller innovative ones (Chesbrough 2006; West 2003; Ettlinger 2014; Afuah and Tucci 2012). Second, it simultaneously uses property rights to secure value capture (Pénin *et al.* 2011; Ettlinger 2014). For example, Google claims that:

> By submitting, posting or displaying content on or through Google services which are intended to be available to the members of the public, you grant Google a worldwide, non-exclusive, royalty-free license to reproduce, adapt, modify, publish and distribute such Content on Google services for the purpose of displaying, distributing and promoting Google services. Google reserves the right to syndicate Content submitted, posted or displayed by you on or through Google services and use that Content in connection with any service offered by Google.
>
> (Google 2013)

Equally, property rights are important to online stores such as iTunes wherein you do not own the music you download. Instead you have the right to use it under licence but cannot sell on 'your' music second-hand as you could a traditional collection. Such property arrangements enable iTunes to achieve 'lock-in' because you cannot simply take 'your' music with you. You have to stay engaged with iTunes, thereby enabling it to gather more dispersed knowledge from your downloading habits – your free labour.

Again, it is important to stress that these processes are not simply about internet companies. Proctor and Gamble solicited 10,000 ideas about product and technological innovation from external sources and sought to source 50 per cent of its innovation from outside the organisation (Ettlinger 2014). Budget airlines make one check in online, self-service supermarkets make one collect one's own food, bag and pay for it via self-service machines, and the mining company Goldcorp ran a competition to find the most likely location for the largest gold deposits on its estate (Afuah and Tucci 2012). Here again, labour is freely provided or subsidised.

This free labour is tied to another economic area – namely dispersed knowledge or knowledge created within and beyond the organisation. New technologies and capacities enable firms to tap into and concentrate dispersed knowledge in increasingly sophisticated ways. Many argue that the market now has an ever greater ability to access and distribute knowledge

(Chesbrough 2003, 2006; Eliasson and Eliasson 2003; Eliasson 2005). In addition, organisations realise they cannot simply rely on their ability to hire genius; they must use the market to capture and concentrate knowledge via open innovation (Chesbrough 2006), the strategic acquisition and the market power of the 'extended firm' (Eliasson 2005). In an environment of dispersed knowledge, the capacity of senior management to scan the market for value capture becomes an increasingly important competitive strategy (Eliasson 1990; Eliasson and Eliasson 2003). One sees this knowledge capture through crowdsourcing, user communities, strategic acquisition, or the use of 'free' and 'subsidised' labour. As we will see, this accessing, concentrating, and privatising of knowledge creates new forms of value restriction and exploitation.

Transitioning to the Google Model: entrepreneurship and transformation

The entrepreneurship literature influenced by Mises and Hayek, and relatedly Schumpeter and Knight, examines many of these issues. For example, Hayek's emphasis on knowledge (see Chesbrough 2003, 2006; Eliasson 1998; Kirzner 1973a), Schumpeter on innovation (see Eliasson and Eliasson 2003; Chesbrough 2003, 2006), or Mises on entrepreneurship (see Kirzner 1973a; Foss *et al.* 2007; Klein 2008) have all influenced debates in these fields. Contemporary scholars generally stress the subjective, the necessity of transition, the increase in innovation, creativity, democratisation, value creation, and the meritocratic nature of these changes. The transformation is seen as liberating, wherein the accessing and use of dispersed knowledge through the market, new business strategies and new forms of organisation are beneficial. In these different analyses, either directly or indirectly, innovation and creativity are democratised, unleashed, and thereby progressive.

However, a tension within the entrepreneurship tradition exists concerning whether entrepreneurship is rooted in discovery (as Hayek and Kirzner argue) or judgement or imagination (as Mises and Knights suggest: see Klein 2008; Foss *et al.* 2007). Methodologically, this tension focuses on whether opportunities are objective (i.e. out there waiting to be discovered: Kirzner 1973; Shane 2003) or subjective and based in the entrepreneur's reading of markets (Klein 2008; Eliasson 1990). One question then is whether or not entrepreneurs capture existing value or, through their judgement/ imagination, generate new value when the new form, product or service is consumed.[1] This tension highlights the tracing of value to a number of points – what might be called imagining, creating or capturing. Crudely, the first two imply a direct generation of value through entrepreneurship, whereas the latter implies capturing value created elsewhere. This chapter argues that the Google Model increasingly emphasises capturing value already there. A key feature of this is also the concentration of dispersed knowledge.

Knowledge and market equilibrium are central here. For example, Schumpeter (1983) posited the entrepreneur as a value-creating innovative rule breaker who put together resources in new combinations and broke through the staleness of market equilibrium. In so doing, the entrepreneur disrupts equilibrium, transforms the economy and ushers in a new stage of capitalist growth. Here the quest for knowledge, information and new projects pressures the market and creates disequilibrium (Dahmén 1984). The entrepreneur drives forth new desires, affects and innovations, and through their actions shows others a new way of organising economies. In this vision, the entrepreneur is an iconoclast even within the corporation. However, Schumpeter (1943, p. 134) feared the very organisational form created by these innovative entrepreneurs. He suggested that large organisations with their procedures, regulations, internal focus and research laboratories expropriate entrepreneurial creators of wealth and innovation. In short, corporations would create un-entrepreneurial management in behemoth organisations which would lack the necessary qualities to transform and develop economies. Because of its very success in delivering a new fantastically productive organisational form – the large corporation – entrepreneurship would be made redundant. This form would stifle transformation in favour of equilibrium and steady growth. At the heart of Schumpeter's work (1943) is the fear that knowledge would be made routine and concentrated in the large firm. He argued that entrepreneurs had to make decisions based on partial knowledge of an infinite number of combinations; hence knowledge was dispersed for him or her. However, for the rational 'static man' of management, knowledge could be corralled in the routine of corporations (Swedberg 2007).

In contrast to Schumpeter's idea that the entrepreneur breaks equilibrium, one of Hayek's (and Austrian economics generally) criticisms of mainstream economics is the role it gives to market equilibrium. Hayek (1948, pp. 33–56) understands knowledge differently. He argues that the processional nature of economics is denied in equilibrium, people are made passive and individual decision making is underplayed (Hayek 1948, pp. 94–99; Kirzner 1973, pp. 30–43; 1979; Chiles *et al.* 2007, 2010). Hayek's contention is that markets are dynamic, futures unknowable and people possess incomplete knowledge. In this world, we exhibit subjectivity, agency, spontaneity and ingenuity to survive and the entrepreneur represents the pinnacle of this (Hayek 1945, 1948; Eliasson 1990). Furthermore, this incompleteness means that we cannot reach equilibrium although we can move towards it (Hayek 1948, p. 100).

These core building blocks are found in Hayek and Mises (Foss and Klein 2010; Chiles *et al.* 2007, 2010 – Knight's work on risk and uncertainty is also important: see Foss *et al.* 2007; Klein 2010). The lack of certain knowledge and the need to anticipate the future implies that human judgement becomes central to action (Mises 1996; Foss *et al.* 2007). Unlike Schumpeter (1943, 1983), Mises (1996, p. 252) argues that we are all, to a greater or lesser degree, entrepreneurs because of this uncertainty. We are all entrepreneurs because we must reflect on and anticipate the future – entrepreneurship can only be avoided in death. Mises extends entrepreneurship to the population. This enshrines (entrepreneurial) knowledge at the heart of social relations by suggesting it drives development within marketplaces *and* organisations, thereby making this social relation the primary relation in life. Because of these attributes, entrepreneurship is both central to capitalist progress and different to the management. Management primarily entails 'subordinated entrepreneurial duties' (Mises 1996, p. 304) – although in practice within a living economy it is difficult to disentangle the two roles (Mises 1996, p. 306; Metcalfe 2006). Disentanglement becomes even more problematic with the rise of corporate capitalism so that some contemporary entrepreneurship scholars argue that senior management takes on the entrepreneurial role. Management assumes this role because its subjective view, tacit knowledge, lack of continuity within or between different management teams and the importance of strategic acquisition grow in an 'experimentally organized economy' (Eliasson 2005). Contra Schumpeter, corporate senior management act entrepreneurially because their subjective view, intuition and tacit knowledge are ever more important to the post-Fordist economy (Eliasson 1990, 2005; Eliasson and Eliasson 2003). Here corporate senior management must act entrepreneurially because they can only ever know a small part of the market. Their knowledge, like that of everyone else, is incomplete; hence they have to imagine futures and not rely on routine – they act as 'proxy entrepreneurs' (Foss *et al.* 2007, p. 1894). This entrepreneurial function entails searching for profit through allocating resources and anticipating future consumer needs. From such anticipation, profits or losses ensue which 'thereby shifts the ownership of the means of production from the hands of the less efficient into those of the more efficient' (Mises 1996, p. 299). If not methodologically, in practice the lines between entrepreneurship and senior management blur now more than ever.

For Mises, anticipation is the central component of entrepreneurship, whereas for Schumpeter it was innovation – the combining of the old and the new in composite forms (see Eliasson and Eliasson 2003, p. 12). Thus the future of the economy is located in the subjective strategic actions of the function – as such, and unlike Schumpeter, senior management become entrepreneurial through anticipation and the ability to match existing or new routines to this anticipation (Beckert 1999; Metcalfe 2006; Foss *et al.* 2007). Thus the economy continuously transforms and develops through what I call the 'entrepreneurial function of senior management'. Indeed, in a society located in possessive individualism and characterised by ever more dispersed knowledge, one person, organisation or state can only know a small portion of the value opportunities within society and hence entrepreneurship increases. Schumpeter's belief in equilibrium meant that knowledge could be concentrated, leading him to forecast the demise of entrepreneurs and the rise of corporations. However, in Mises' vision, Schumpeter's 'invincible corporation' (Eliasson 2005, p. 432) can no longer survive on routine innovation or 'subordinated entrepreneurial duties' and hence the necessary shift of corporations towards an entrepreneurial corporate senior management founded in areas of value capture such as open innovation or strategic acquisition.

Thus the subjective imagination of entrepreneurs, who stand or fall by the actually realised value from their anticipated future, is transferred to the behemoth corporation (Eliasson 1990; Eliasson and Eliasson 2003). Today, this corporate entrepreneurial capture dominates the economy.

Building on Mises, Kirzner's work is central to entrepreneurship as opportunity–discovery (Klein 2008, p. 176). Kirzner makes alertness to existing opportunity the entrepreneurial driver (Kirzner 1973; Shane 2003; Klein 2008). He believes that entrepreneurship is price taking or an 'arbitrage theory of profit' (Kirzner 1973, p. 85). In contrast to Knight/Mises, who argue that entrepreneurs imagine opportunities (Klein 2010), or to Schumpeter, who argues that entrepreneurs innovatively combine resources in new ways (Schumpeter 1983; Beckert 1999), Kirzner's function sees entrepreneurs as alert to markets and as allocating resources via price differentials. Entrepreneurs are market makers who coordinate transactions and look for undervalued resources (Burczak 2002; Ricketts 2006, p. 48; Metcalfe 2006). Here, entrepreneurship guides capitalism by adding to everyone's market knowledge – it disperses knowledge and thus lowers inefficiency. In this process, Kirzner prioritises capturing existing value. This is the central entrepreneurial form of the Google Model of Production.

As noted above, Hayek's theory of knowledge (1945, 1948) implies that people act in different ways and with variable abilities to access knowledge. Hence equilibrium is never achieved but when the plans of individuals come together there may be a tendency towards it. Entrepreneurs are central because through spotting and exploiting variability in markets they spread knowledge (Hayek 1948, p. 45) – in this sense both Kirzner and Hayek see competition as the capturing of price differentials and opportunities (Klein 2008). This makes position and prior subjective experience fundamental because both enable some people in some situations to see an opportunity they may not see in a different situation, or, indeed, in the same situation if they have a different set of prior experiences (Shane 2000, 2003; Eliasson 1990, 2005). Knowledge in this framework is about vision, spirit, affect and, importantly, 'alertness to information rather than its possession' (Kirzner 1973, p. 68).

This entrepreneurship is not creative; rather it is about capture (Burczak 2002; Alvarez and Barney 2007). Kirzner comments:

> I view the entrepreneur not as a source of innovative ideas ex nihilo but as being *alert* to the opportunities that exist *already* and are waiting to be noticed. In economic development, too, the entrepreneur is to be seen as *responding* to opportunities rather than *creating* them; as *capturing* profit opportunities *rather than* generating them.
>
> (Kirzner 1973, p. 74, emphasis added)

Following Mises (1996), Kirzner's entrepreneur is the ethical inheritor of all wealth (Burczak 2002). This wealth is then used to pay (or increasingly not pay) others their market price via transaction coordination (e.g. capitalists, landowners,or workers). Building on Locke and Mises, Kirzner (1973b) argues that entrepreneurs display initiative and it is this human will – this imagining of profit to be captured and realised – that creates products and not what flows afterwards through labour or capitalist risk – entrepreneurial activity is the key to wealth generation (Burczak 2002).

In Kirzner's vision of entrepreneurship, the Earl of Southampton derives the value from Hamlet, the Pope the Sistine Chapel, and Facebook the sociality of its users because these entrepreneurs were alert to see the (potential) value of what was there and hence allocated resource to it. They were the first to imagine the real existing opportunity (created by others) and with this vision they generated these 'whole products entirely on [their] own' (Kirzner 1973a, p. 10). As such, entrepreneurs are entitled not to a portion of the value but to the whole of it (Mises (1996, p. 297) makes a similar point).

Two features emerge from Kirzner's description of entrepreneurship (see Kirzner 1973, pp. 52–62). First, entrepreneurs are interested in arbitrage and are alert to undervalued resources rather than a Schumpeterian organisation of production and innovation per se. Second, entrepreneurial profits disperse knowledge throughout the market and are therefore short-lived because the very act of gaining entrepreneurial profit spreads knowledge of existing opportunities (Mises 1996, p. 296). Hence others enter markets. This second point creates a tendency to seek protection via property rights, or indeed illegitimate actions, so as to maintain the delivery of arbitrage rents (Alvarez and Barney 2004, p. 622; Metcalfe 2006). Historically this search for property right protection and monopoly has been stifled innovation, a tendency towards unproductive or destructive processes, and rent seeking (Baumol 1990; Hayek 1948; Perelman 2002). However, these negative tendencies are denied by Kirzner and Mises, who only see 'good' entrepreneurship (Foss *et al.* 2007, p. 1897).

We need to reaffirm Kirzner as the theorist of entrepreneurship in the Google Model. However as we will see, his is a flawed vision because it sees only 'good' entrepreneurship and it prioritises capture. When accompanied by corporate market dominance and property rights, this capture stifles the potential for innovation and productivity, concentrates the use of dispersed knowledge (contra Hayek), and encourages an emphasis on capturing royalties. This tendency is exacerbated because of the rise of new technologies of digitalisation and immaterial labour.

The 'transformed economy'

For our purposes, the economy was transformed in two important ways and both are related to particular forms of property – namely the growth of immaterial products and services (Hardt 2010; Hardt and Negri 2000). This transformation is generating new forms of production within which entrepreneurial capture is central. One way of broadening our understanding of transformation as capture is to build the workerist and post-workerist traditions which assert that when technology replaced labour in the factory, labour and knowledge generation took place in other forms – as leisure, as education, as ordinary life (Böhm and Land 2012); that is, as 'free' labour.

First qualitative shift: towards immaterial labour in post-Fordism

The first qualitative shift concerns where value is entrepreneurially captured. Increasingly, value and opportunity are captured from outside the firm (Prahalad and Ramswamy 2002, 2004; Baldwin and von Hippel 2010; Lucas 1988). This has occurred because of the rise of mass intellectuality and the development of what is called the 'general intellect' (Marx 1973, pp. 706–708). That is, knowledge is now located in science and technology, routines, procedures, etc. within the organisation but it is also increasingly located in creativity, innovation and our sociality beyond the organisation, and that it is from here that value is captured. The general intellect grew because efficiency in the factory meant that labour was replaced by fixed capital. Obviously such a reduction led to the development of free time – unemployment, underemployment, leisure, education, and so on. Free time then enabled labour to transform itself into a different subjectivity. This renewed (and renewing) subjectivity returns to production as an enhanced value-generating form. Marx asserted that this enhanced subjectivity becomes the centre of value generation because free time was a chimera as individuals were ever more in the service of capitalist valorisation – in short, all life becomes work. In this rendition labour becomes a new form of fixed capital because knowledge, science and technology are embedded in labour's being (i.e. in the social individual: Marx 1973, pp. 704–712)[2] or, in Hayek's terms, knowledge becomes more and more dispersed.

While Marx located this shift in science and technology (although Vercellone (2007) qualifies this criticism), recent theorists argue that the general intellect should include communication, desire, affect, language and emotion (Virno 2004; Marazzi 2008). These sources of value develop outside of what we traditionally think of as the workplace. They are produced at school, play, work, home, funerals, and they are put to work and give rise to explosive productivity increases. For example, volunteers translated Facebook from English to French in a few days and English to Spanish in two weeks (Afuah and Tucci 2012). In short, work and the possibility of value capture take place increasingly within and without the traditional workspace (Marazzi 2007, p. 29). It is this capacity to integrate users as intermediary customers/producers (Priem 2007), who add to the value chain and who enable the concentration of dispersed knowledge, that is a key competitive advantage.

We have entered a 'social factory' where all of life is seemingly put to work in ways that are different to the factory or office (Ryan 1991, p. 208; Fleming 2009). Today, many industries operate on the basis of this capturing of value outside the traditional workspace (e.g. social media sites, IKEA, Lego or the supermarket: Lucas 1988; Prahalad and Ramaswamy 2002; Pasquinelli 2008). For example, Oliveira and von Hippel (2010) suggest that 44 per cent of computerised retail banking innovations were autonomously developed and implemented by labourers/consumers/users before the banks introduced them; corporations use free open-source labour to gain a competitive advantage (West 2003; Lerner and Tirole 2005); companies use competition and collaborative-based crowdsourcing (Afuah and Tucci 2012) and access civil society to develop new market possibilities (Hanlon 2008). Here, users' 'most urgent needs' (Mises 1996, p. 290) are either satisfied or incubated autonomously and often by a non-profit orientation before any entrepreneurial action discovers them. In this process free or subsidised labour aids value extraction by acting as an enhancer of the distribution services of firms like Google or IBM to the ultimate customer/end user – the advertising agency, the data-mining company or the corporate client (Priem 2007). As with an Amazon or a Wal-Mart, distribution is ultimately about concentration.

Increasingly, productive labour is formed in the 'general intellect' or through dispersed knowledge rather than within the firm (e.g. YouTube is simply a platform made valuable through the material posted by users who do not work for YouTube nor post products made by YouTube but who seek general social contact that is 'immeasurable and invisible': Lucas 1988, p. 38), and obviously English, French and Spanish are open communal systems. Here, individuals have posted something of their subjectivity and this dispersed knowledge is captured, concentrated and commoditised in order to extract value via advertising. Equally, programming skills are often garnered outside the firm as a form of fun (Lerner and Tirole 2002), social and communicative skills enable hospitality industries (Warhurst and Nickson 2007) and the value of a brand is co-created (Arvidsson 2005). Today's economy is about the outright capture of free or subsidised labour and knowledge, and this 'Google Model' of production is generating new economic processes (Marazzi 2011, p. 56).[3]

This production system increasingly revolves around capturing undervalued resources, esources developed by (often unpaid or subsidised) labour and then captured by corporations in a 'finders-keepers' capitalism (see Burczak 2002). In one sense, although volunteer translators in collaborative crowdsourcing may have fun and/or gain reputational benefits and/or feel altruistic, they are also put to work. These labourers/consumers/users are akin to Kirzner's (1973, p. 62) employee – more productive but not entrepreneurially alert and therefore allowing value to be captured by others. Today, corporations behave increasingly like entrepreneurs whose alertness 'captures the opportunities he perceives' (Kirzner 1973, pp. 61–62).

Immaterial labour is immersed in the sociality of the general intellect (e.g. language, affect, etc.), which new technologies enable organisations to capture and concentrate. Central to this is market dominance and the vulnerability of labourers/consumers/users. Here, strategic acquisitions, the enforcing of strict contracts, achieving 'lock-in', or using or purchasing patents and other forms of property rights enable large corporations to achieve a quasi-monopoly from which to capture royalties (The Economist 2012a, 2012b). Knowledge is dispersed, so the giant corporation need not create or innovate. It merely uses its invincibility to capture and concentrate dispersed knowledge.

For example, the music industry's response to digitalisation has been twofold (Stahl 2010). One reaction is locking new artists into 'option' contracts wherein companies periodically exercise their option to renew or drop the artist depending on whether or not they show promise. Thus they access labour's creativity while offloading any responsibility for labour's development, thereby 'keeping their costs to their initial employer artificially low' (Stahl 2010, p. 338). Such contracts also prevent artists from offering their services to other companies. This restriction of artists' rights to freely sell their labour is akin to a new form of indenture. Second, firms responded by enforcing new '360' deals. Having realised that artists had property rights to revenues generated from merchandising, touring, producing music for films, etc., corporations used their power to capture this value. These rights were both a source of revenue and made artists somewhat independent of corporations; thus capital extended its contractual rights to these 'new' areas (Stahl 2010). This is market power enabling entrepreneurial capture and it is an increasing form of the new economy (Marazzi 2011; Ettlinger 2014). Importantly however, innovation has not stopped rather large corporations using entrepreneurial capture to corral it in ways that are contrary to Schumpeter's 'invincible corporation'. But neither is this Eliasson's (2005, p. 432) world of innovation as the undermining of the corporate behemoth. In fact it seems to be increasing dependency and vulnerability through raiding a growing creativity. Thus the corporation can pick off creativity and innovation in a manner akin to IBM or Google which both embraced open-source and restrictive property rights to capture innovation and thereby gain a competitive edge while maintaining closed innovation systems themselves (West 2003). Thus, although these corporations may have added value to the open-source system, they ensure any value slippage goes to them.

Second qualitative shift: towards the immaterial product in post-Fordism

The second change concerns the growth of two contrasting forms of property: the material and the immaterial. Again, this is something of a methodological makeshift as obviously this chapter is both material and immaterial (i.e. paper, ink, the virtual and ideas). The material is characterised by scarcity and, as a rival good, is not reproducible (i.e. if I am using a pen, you cannot use it). In contrast, the immaterial is characterised by being easily reproducible and virtually limitless – it is possible that this chapter could be read simultaneously by hundreds of individuals, so scarcity is not an issue (or at least not in the way it traditionally was – obviously resources are used and our attention capabilities are limited: see Pasquinelli 2008). This is important because it means that a variety of readers could contemporaneously make use of this work in different and innovative ways, thereby increasing its productive potential. Shane (2000, 2003) observes that the greater the number of people and the greater the variety of backgrounds of people accessing an opportunity, the greater the potential for entrepreneurship and innovation – open-source software is an example of this creativity. Indeed, one could argue that Google's decision to make its Android operating system open source or open innovation as a competitive strategy implicitly acknowledges the greater innovative capacity of openness (Ettlinger 2014).[4]

However, there is still the issue of property rights and excludability. Ownership of the rights to this chapter limits access and hence lessens its productive and innovative capacity. This is a real tension in the emerging immaterial economy. For example, publishing, music, social media, film, television, academia and education, scientific and medical knowledge, design, telecommunications, or art and literature – all have a strong footing in the immaterial or 'intellectual history' as Lucas defines it (1988, p. 38). Much of what these industries produce is reproducible at little cost and is thus simultaneously open to multiple uses by different people, thereby increasing opportunities for productivity and innovation through widening the net of use. That they are not open limits this potential innovative productivity (Hardt 2010, p. 349).

One example of this tension is the growth of, and conflict around, intellectual property rights; for example, the dispute about medicine and HIV in India wherein the pharmaceutical company Novartis challenged Indian generic medicine manufacturers by seeking to extend its patent of the drug Gilvec to sell it at Western prices. This was disputed in India's courts because some groups protested that Norvartis engaged in the monopoly capitalist process of 'ever-greening' – that is, making minor modifications to a drug in order to extend its patent and capture rents (Reid-Henry 2011). Another example is the initially successful, but ultimately failed, attempt to patent Basmati rice by the firm Rice Tec Inc. (US Patent No. 5663, 484). This legal manoeuvre occurred despite the fact that the rice had been farmed and developed through the dispersed knowledge of farmers in the Greater Punjab – a case of litigation and other legal attempts to concentrate knowledge being more important than creativity (Perelman 2002; Ettlinger 2014). Such disputes are increasing as intellectual property applications rise – since the 1980s the number of patents granted by the US state has doubled – not so much a growth in knowledge as a privatising of it (Marazzi 2008, p. 123). These (immaterial) knowledge-based patents have as their object products that, once developed, are cheap to reproduce. Potentially these restrictive rights limit rather than enhance overall productivity and innovation because some of the individuals who could use these products and see new opportunities within them are denied access.

Of course, intellectual property rights have had a chequered history (Perelman 2002). Hayek (1948, pp. 113–114) was sceptical about the relationship between innovation and property rights. The (recent) emergence of users as an important source of innovation and the growth of openness suggests that privatising this knowledge weakens rather than strengthens innovation because it lessens the number of users. In so doing, it limits the different potential uses of products which necessarily increase as user numbers grow. Profit and innovation and entrepreneurship and innovation are at odds in this scenario.

This view conflicts with much of entrepreneurship theory, which argues that innovation needs intellectual property rights protection because innovation is driven by the profit motive (Romer 1990b, p. 72; Aghion *et al.* 2005, p. 702; Shane 2002). For example, corporations engaging in open innovation have been encouraged to address property rights early on. Pénin *et al.* (2011, p. 24) suggest that firms using crowdsourcing need to create legal forms wherein all the ideas put forward by participants belong to the corporation rather than the labourer/consumer/user (even if left unused). This form of capture limits an idea's potential and is about casting as wide a proprietary and speculative net as possible. It is the power to concentrate knowledge's use; indeed, the knowledge itself often remains out there (e.g. in the capture of crowdsourcing the individual providing the knowledge still 'knows' but he or she cannot use this knowledge).

This returns us to the short-lived nature of entrepreneurial profit. Short-termism arises out of the function's role in dispersing knowledge. Property rights are used to extend the life of entrepreneurial profits by restricting action based on the spread of this knowledge (hence Hayek's unease). This does two things: it enables a 'super' profit because entrepreneurial profit is higher than 'normal' profit, and it redistributes wealth and production in particular ways and to particular groups. One outcome of this short-termism is a tendency to limit access to knowledge or concentrating rather than dispersing it; that is, being 'willing to sabotage the innovative effects of others' (Metcalfe 2006, p. 77). This creates scarcity by restricting knowledge's dispersal and hence halts the spread of productivity and innovation. Today, corporate entrepreneurial alertness seeks monopoly and concentrates knowledge deemed valuable. This tendency towards monopoly via scarcity becomes an increasing tension because the costs of reproducibility have lessened, thereby making wider access, and thus productivity and innovation, increasingly possible. But also today more innovation comes from beyond rather than within the organisation which subsequently captures and concentrates it (Oliveira and von Hippel 2010; Ettlinger 2014). This extra-corporate creativity is linked to the general intellect which both grows and enables corporations to overcome the entrepreneurial ossification predicted by Schumpeter through the capture of value which organisations recognise but do not generate (Chesbrough 2003, 2006). Thus we are witnessing a burgeoning of creativity *and* capture wherein capture nevertheless limits the benefits of our creative possibility to those groups which often do not create even as creativity itself increases. In so doing, it concentrates corporate power and wealth and allows capital further inroads into making all labour productive of value (Harvie 2005, p. 133).

Why is this so? Because for immaterial products property rights turn potentially limitless products into quasi-immovable resources and create a quasi-monopoly on use, thereby limiting productivity and innovation. This is different to the past where often only one person could use a product such as a hammer at any one time regardless of property rights. But there is no equivalent reason why this chapter is not available to anyone with a modem (Pariser 2011; Lanier 2011). Property rights and entrepreneurial capture act as fetters on innovation and productivity because they make goods rival and excludable when they do not have to be so. Furthermore, they do this despite the fact that today creativity often comes from labourers/consumers/users (Oliveira and von Hippel 2010; Hardt 2010; Hyde 2012). These twin changes – to production based in labour created beyond the firm and products that are increasingly immaterial – are important if we are to understand the Google Model. They relate explicitly to the issue of capture at the heart of Kirzner's entrepreneurial action which, despite his contention, is class based and favours the asset-rich (Burczak 2002).

Conclusion

As we have seen, labour and products are increasingly communicative so that today more of labour's knowledge and skill stems from the general intellect, dispersed knowledge or 'external effects' (Lucas 1988) – from the outside of traditional production. As noted above, one sees this in Facebook where the product is based on the subjectivities of labourers/consumers/users and is created in their free time. This is the social factory, where all we know and are and potentially are and know are put into production. However, Facebook is hampered by its ownership – to make use of Facebook one has to join (albeit for free) which means that only members can access your profile which in turn locks you in and limits the use of the service; i.e. people from MySpace (remember MySpace?) cannot access it. Here we see the dual aspect of the model, namely the rise of the immaterial, based on free labour, and easy reproducibility and of property rights which hinder use, productivity and innovation.

There is one further element; namely, production processes appear not to be of interest to the owner. Facebook's platform does not create the product which people seek – the product is created in dispersed locations, outside work, inside work, and it uses skills developed in the social factory, not in work. However, it is not only social media; land and gentrification (see Harvey 2002), journalism (Pariser 2011), open-source code (Lerner and Tirole 2005) or banking (Baldwin and von Hippel 2010) are, for example, similar. Open-source programmers write, edit, review and consume the product they create and which others consume. Today, where products are created or how appears to be of less interest to the corporation accessing them. Corporations are less concerned about the production process because, from their perspective, it is characterised by free labour waiting to be captured. This is quite different to the past and indicates a shift in society wherein it is becoming totally subsumed to capital (Hardt and Negri 2000). Today, management and self-management, organisation and self-organisation, and paid, subsidised and free labour extend capital as a social relation to all areas of life by 'compelling it [labour] to perform surplus-labour or spurring on the productive power of labour to produce relative surplus-value' (Marx 2000, p. 93). The dispersed nature of knowledge has led to increased innovation which corporations are simultaneously capturing, concentrating *and* limiting via property rights. In this process, life is potentially put to work for capture as quasi-monopoly royalties by capital.

This chapter has argued that we are witnessing an important moment within contemporary capitalism to suggest that an emerging tendency may guide us towards the future (Marx 1988). Obviously, that future is not here now. For example, large capitalist organisations still innovate in a productivist model (Oliveira and von Hippel 2010). Nevertheless, changes are occurring which suggest a society that is quite different to 30 or 40 years ago. This is the point. What is presented merely hints at some of the exploitative and monopolistic contours of this new future.[5]

These issues return us to Kirzner. His entrepreneurs are entitled to the full product because they see the opportunity to capture the value already there. This describes one tendency of post-Fordism. Firms rely increasingly on free labour, entrepreneurial capture of value, stay alert to opportunities and concentrate on dispersed knowledge, thereby limiting innovation and production. What we are witnessing is the corporate imposition of artificial scarcity enabling market dominance to 're-create' the capabilities of immovable property and generate royalties. As corporations increasingly extract value from free and subsidised labour and use property rights to limit the dispersal of knowledge to take royalties, they embrace Kirzner's entrepreneurial vision of capture. This analysis is in sharp contrast with much entrepreneurship and innovation literature which prioritises the creative, innovative, strategic and liberating role of entrepreneurship and seeks to distance itself from Kirzner. Despite entrepreneurship studies seemingly moving away from Kirzner, the entrepreneurial society actually has capture, the concentration of knowledge, enforced scarcity and property rights at its heart. This puts it in direct conflict with innovation and productivity in ways that contradict entrepreneurship theory. Entrepreneurship and property rights are the problem, not the solution.

Notes

1 Alvarez and Barney (2006) use the term 'creation' rather than 'imagination'. Klein (2008, p. 181) criticises this terminology because he argues that products have to be consumed for the act to be entrepreneurial; hence he suggests that 'imagination' is a better term to understand entrepreneurship.

2 Coming from a different theoretical register, human capital theorists and endogenous growth theorists highlight similar tendencies within capitalism which make

human capital and knowledge the decisive factor in economic development (see Becker 1962a, 1962b; Schultz 1962; Lucas 1988; Romer 1990a, 1990/b). Lucas (1988) divides what Marx called 'general intellect' into the internal and external effects of human capital wherein internal individual effects are achieved via education, learning by doing, etc., whereas external effects are developed from general social contact among (more or less) skilled human capital. Accessing both of these effects is central, in his view, to economic development. He also argues that external effects are invisible and immeasurable – which begs the question: Who then owns them or the value derived from them and on what basis would we make such allocations?

3 The international division of labour upon which this is predicated must be borne in mind (Caffentis 2011). Indeed, financialisation in this mode is also a mystifying process in the Marxist sense; i.e. it hides where and how value is produced (I would like to thank Matteo Mandarini for this observation).

4 Shane, however, supports property rights (Shane 2002) as a way of securing this innovation. In contrast, this chapter accepts his views on exposure but disagrees on the issue of property rights.

5 It is important at this stage to highlight that the chapter is not claiming that these occurrences are global or applicable to all sectors of the economy. This is only one, albeit important, tendency in the global economy and it is itself umbilically tied to the international division of labour and the rising (tightly managed and controlled) productive capacities, and global supply chains, of the BRIC economies and others (see Caffentis 2011).

References

Afuah, A. and Tucci, C.L. (2012), Studying the origins of social entrepreneurship: Compassion and the role of embedded agency. *Academy of Management Review*, **38**, pp. 460–462.

Aghion, P., Bloom, N., Blundell, R., Griffith, R. and Howitt, P. (2005), Competition and innovation: An inverted-U relationship. *Quarterly Journal of Economics*, **120**, pp. 701–728.

Alvarez, S.A. and Barney, J.B. (2004), Organizing rent generation and appropriation: Toward a theory oft he entrepreneurial firm. *Journal of Business Venturuing*, **19**(5), pp. 621–635.

Alvarez, S.A. and Barney, J.B. (2007), Discovery and creation: Alternative theories of entrepreneurial action. *Strategic Entrepreneurship Journal*, **1**(1–2), pp. 11–26.

Arvidsson, A. (2005), Brands: A critical perspective. *Journal of Consumer Behaviour*, **5**(2), pp. 235–258.

Baldwin, C. and von Hippel, E. (2010), Modelling a Paradign Shift: From Producer Innovation to User and Open Collaborative Innovation. MIT Sloan School of Management Working Chapter #4764–09 and Harvard Business School Finance Working Chapter #10–038. Available at http://ssrn.com/abstract=1502864 (accessed 25 May 2016).

Baumol, W. (1990), Entrepreneurship: Productive, unproductive and destructive. *Journal of Political Economy*, **98**(5), pp. 893–921.

Becker, G. (1962a), Investment in human capital – A theoretical analysis. *Journal of Political Economy*, **70**(5), pp. 9–49.

Becker, G. (1962b), Irrational behaviour and economic theory. *Journal of Political Economy*, **70**(1), pp. 1–13.

Beckert, J. (1999), Agency, entrepreneurs, and institutional change: The role of strategic choice and institutionalized practices in organizations. *Organization Studies,* **20**(5), pp. 777–779.

Benkler, Y. (2002), Coase's penguin, or, Linux and 'the nature of the firm'. *Yale Law Review,* **112**(3), pp. 369–446.

Böhm, S. and Land, C. (2012), The new 'hidden abode': Reflections on value and labour in the new economy. *The Sociological Review,* **60**(2), pp. 217–240.

Burczak, T. (2002), A critique of Kirzner's finders-keepers defense of profit. *The Review of Austrian Economics,* **15**(1), pp. 75–90.

Caffentis, G. (2011), A critique of cognitive capitalism. In P. Micheals and E. Bulut (eds), *Cognitive Capitalism, Education and Digital Labor,* New York: Peter Land International.

Chesbrough, H. (2003), The era of open innovation. *Sloan Management Review,* **44**(3), pp. 35–41.

Chesbrough, H. (2006), Open innovation: A new paradigm for understanding industrial innovation. in H. Chesbrough, W. Vanhaverbeke and J. West (eds), *Open Innovation: Researching A New Paradigm,* Oxford: Oxford University Press.

Chiles, T., Bluedorn, A. and Gupta, V. (2007), Beyond creative destruction and entrepreneurial discovery: A radical Austrian approach to entrepreneurship. *Organization Studies,* **28**(4), pp. 467–493.

Chiles, T., Vultee, D., Gupta, V., Greening, D. and Tuggle, C. (2010), The philosophical foundations of a radical approach to entrepreneurship. *Journal of Management Inquiry,* **19**(2), pp. 138–164.

Costea, B., Crump, N. and Amiridis, K. (2008), Managerialism, the therapeutic habitus and the self in contemporary organizing. *Human Relations,* **61**(5), pp. 661–685.

Dahmén, E. (1984), Schumpeterian dynamics – Some methodological notes. *Journal of Economic Behaviour and Organizations,* **5**, pp. 25–34.

Economist, The (2012a), Battle of the internet giants – Survival of the fittest. 1 December.

Economist, The (2012b), Another Game of Thrones: Google, Apple, Facebook and Amazon are at each others' throats in all sorts of ways. 1 December.

Eliasson, G. (1990), 'The firm as a competent team. *Journal of Economic Behaviour and Organization,* **13**, pp. 275–298.

Eliasson, G. (1998), From plan to markets. *Journal of Economic Behaviour and Organization,* **34**(1), pp. 49–68.

Eliasson, G. (2005), The nature of economic change and management in a new knowledge based information economy. *Information, Economics and Policy,* **17**, pp. 428–456.

Eliasson, G. and Eliasson, A. (2003), The theory of the firm and the markets for strategic acquisition. Available at www.snee.org/filer/papers/177.pdf (accessed 25 May 2016).

Ettlinger, N. (2014), The openness paradigm. *New Left Review,* **89**, pp. 89–100.

Fleming, P. (2009), *Authenticity and the Cultural Politics of Work: New Forms of Informal Control,* Oxford: Oxford University Press.

Foss N. and Klein, P. (2010), Alertness, action and the antecedents of entrepreneurship. *The Journal of Private Enterprise,* **25**(2), pp. 145–164.

Foss, K, Foss, N. and Klein, P. (2007), Original and derived judgement: An entrepreneurial theory of economic organization. *Organization Studies,* **28**(12), pp. 1893–1912.

Google (2013), *Google Terms of Service*. Available at www.google.com/apps/intl/en/terms/user_terms.html (accessed 25 May 2016).

Hanlon, G. (2008), A re-theorization of corporate social responsibility: On the denial of politics. In A. Crane *et al.* (eds), *Oxford Handbook of CSR*, Oxford: Oxford University Press.

Hardt, M. (2010), The common in Communism. *Rethinking Marxism*, **22**(3), pp. 346–356.

Hardt, M. and Negri, N. (2000), *Empire*. Cambridge, MA: Harvard University Press.

Harvey, D. (2002), The art of rent: Globalization, monopoly and the commodification of culture. *Socialist Register*, **38**, pp. 93–110.

Harvie, D. (2005), All labour produces value for capital and we all struggle against value. *The Commoner*, **10**, pp. 132–171.

Hayek, F. (1945), The use of knowledge in society. *American Economic Review*, **35**(5), pp. 519–530.

Hayek, F. (1948), *Individualism and Economic Order*, London: Chicago University Press.

Hyde, L. (2012), *Common as Air – Revolution, Art and Ownership*, London: Union Books.

Kirzner, I.M. (1973a), *Competition and Entrepreneurship*, Chicago, IL: University of Chicago Press.

Kirzner, I.M. (1973b), Producer, entrepreneur and the right to property. Paper presented at the Symposium on the Origins and Development of Property Rights, January. Institute of Humane Studies, San Francisco, CA.

Kirzner, I.M. (1997), Entrepreneurial discovery and the competitive market process: An Austrian approach. *Journal of Economic Literature*, **35**(1), pp. 60–85.

Klein, P. (2008), Opportunity, discovery, entrepreneurial action and economic organization. *Strategic Entrepreneurship Journal*, **2**, pp. 175–190.

Lanier, J. (2011), *You Are Not a Gadget*, London: Penguin.

Lerner, J. and Tirole, J. (2002), Some simple economics of open source. *Journal of Industrial Economics,* **52**(2), pp. 197–234.

Lerner, J. and Tirole, J. (2005), The scope of open source licensing. *Journal of Law, Economics and Organization*, **21**(1), pp. 20–56.

Lucas, R. (1988), On the mechanics of economic development. *Journal of Monetary Economics*, **22**, pp. 3–42.

Marazzi, C. (2007), Rules for the incommensurable. *SubStance*, **36**(1), pp. 11–36.

Marazzi, C. (2008), *Capital and Language – From the New Economy to the War Economy*, Los Angeles, CA: Semiotext(e).

Marazzi, C. (2011), *The Violence of Financial Capitalism*, Los Angeles, CA: Semiotext(e).

Marx, K. (1973), *Grundrisse*, Harmondsworth: Penguin.

Marx, K. (1981), *Capital Vol. 3*, Harmondsworth: Penguin.

Marx, K. (1988), *Economic and Philosophical Manuscripts of 1844*, New York: Prometheus Books.

Metcalfe, J.S. (2006), Entrepreneurship: An evolutionary perspective. In M. Casson *et al.* (eds), *The Oxford Handbook of Entrepreneurship*, Oxford: Oxford University Press.

Mises von, L. (1996), *Human Action – A Treatise on Economics*, Indianapolis: Liberty Fund.

Negri, A. (1991), *Marx Beyond Marx: Lessons On the Grundrisse*, New York: Autonomedia.

Oliveira, P. and von Hippel, E. (2010), Users as service innovators: The case of banking services. MIT Sloan Research Paper No. 4748–09. Available at http://ssrn.com/abstract=1460751 (accessed 25 May 2016).

O'Mahoney, S. (2003), Guarding the commons: How community managed software projects protect their work. *Research Policy*, **32**, pp. 1179–1198.

Pariser, E. (2011), *The Filter Bubble – What the Internet is Hiding From You*, London: Viking Press.

Pasquinelli, M. (2008), *Animal Spirits – A Bestiary of the Commons*, Rotterdam: NAi Publishers.

Pénin, J., Hussler, C. and Burger-Helmchen, T. (2011), New shapes and new stakes: A portrait of open innovation as a promising phenomenon. *Journal of Innovation Economics*, **1**(7), pp. 11–29.

Perelman, M. (2002), *Steal This Idea – Intellectual Property Rights and the Corporate Confiscation of Creativity*, New York: Palgrave.

Perlin, R (2011), *Intern Nation – How to Earn Nothing and Learn Little in the Brave New Economy*, London: Verso.

Prahalad, C.K. and Ramaswamy, V. (2002), The co-creation connection. *Strategy and Business*, **27**, pp. 1–12.

Prahalad, C.K. and Ramaswamy, V. (2004), Co-creation experiences: The next practice in value creation. *Journal of Interactive Marketing*, **18**(3), pp. 5–14.

Priem (2007), A consumer perspective on value creation. *The Academy of Management Review*, **32**(1), 219–235.

Reid-Henry, S. (2011), Novartis vs India: The court will decide. *New Internationalist*, 29 November.

Ricketts, M. (2006), Theories of entrepreneurship: Historical development and critical assessment. In M. Casson *et al.* (eds), *The Oxford Handbook of Entrepreneurship*, Oxford: Oxford University Press.

Romer, P.M. (1990a), Endogenous technological change. *Journal of Political Economy*, **98**(5), p. 2.

Romer, P.M. (1990b), The problem of development: A conference of the institute for the study of free enterprise systems. *Journal of Political Economy*, **98**(5), pp. 71–102.

Ryan, M. (1991), Epilogue. In A. Negri, *Marx Beyond Marx – Lessons on the Grundrisse*, New York: Autonomedia.

Samuelson, P. (1999), Intellectual property and the digital economy: Why the anti-circumvention regulations need to be revised. *Berkeley Technology Law Journal*, **14**, pp. 519–566.

Schultz, T. (1962), Reflections on investment in man. *Journal of Political Economy*, **70**(5.2), pp. 1–8.

Schumpeter, J. (1943), *Capitalism, Socialism and Democracy*, London: Allen & Unwin.

Schumpeter, J. (1983), *The Theory of Economic Development*, New Brunswick, NJ: Transaction Books.

Shane, S. (2000), Prior knowledge and the discovery of entrepreneurial opportunities. *Organization Science*, **11**(4), pp. 448–469.

Shane, S. (2002), Selling university technology: Patterns from MIT. *Management Science*, **48**(1), pp. 122–137.

Shane, S. (2003), *A General Theory of Entrepreneurship: The Individual–Opportunity Nexus*, Cheltenham: Edward Elgar.

Smith, A. (1981), *An Inquiry into the Nature and Causes of the Wealth of Nations*, Vol. 1, Indianapolis: Liberty Fund.

Soar, D. (2011), It knows. *London Review of Books*, **33**(19), pp. 3–6.

Stahl, M. (2010), Primitive accumulation, the social common, and the contractual lockdown of recording artists at the threshold of digitalization. *ephemera: theory and politics in organization*, **10**(3/4), pp. 337–355.

Swedberg, R. (2007), Rebuilding Schumpeter's theory of entrepreneurship. Paper presented at the Conference on Marshall, Schumpeter and Social Science, 17–18 March, Hototsubahsi University, Japan.

Taylor, F.W. (1919), *The Principles of Scientific Management*, New York: Harper and Brothers.

Trosow, S.E. (2010), The copyright policy paradox: Overcoming competing agendas in the digital labor movement. *ephemera: theory and politics in organization*, **10**(3/4), pp. 319–336.

Vercellone, C. (2007), From formal subsumption to the general intellect: Elements for a Marxist reading of the thesis of cognitive capitalism. *Historical Materialism*, **15**, pp. 13–36.

Virno, P. (2004), *The Grammar of the Multitude*, New York: Semiotext(e).

Warhurst, C. and Nickson, D. (2007), Employee experience of aesthetic labour in retail and hospitality. *Work, Employment and Society*, **21**(1), pp. 103–120.

West, J. (2003), How open is open enough? Melding proprietary and open source platform strategies. *Research Policy*, **32**, pp. 1259–1285.

Part II

Locating new forms of Indigenous and community-based entrepreneurship

5 Towards a barefoot community-based entrepreneuring

Alia Weston and J. Miguel Imas

Across a filthy, rubbish-filled creek we enter the slum's heaving residential area, treading carefully to ensure we do not step in human sewage.... The few hours I spend touring Mumbai's teeming Dharavi slum are uncomfortable and upsetting, teetering on voyeuristic. They are also among the most uplifting of my life. Instead of a neighbourhood characterised by misery, I find a bustling and enterprising place, packed with small-scale industries defying their circumstances to flourish amidst the squalor. Rather than pity, I am inspired by man's alchemic ability to thrive when the chips are down.

(Crerar in Roy 2011, p. 223)

Introduction

In this chapter, we revisit our theoretical ideas on the barefoot entrepreneurs (Imas *et al.* 2012) (i.e. people who dwell at the margins of our neoliberal societies) in order to continue to challenge and critically question entrepreneurial capitalism. Views such as Piketty's (2014) highlight the negative aspects of capitalism that have contributed to create poverty and unequal conditions around the world, damaging equally the eco-systems where many barefoot communities live and work. This invites further questions on the role played by entrepreneurship in sustaining this destruction (Klein 2014). There is, therefore, the need to question the supremacy of this grand discourse and equally to provide alternatives to it. This is the humble task we attempt here by supporting a barefoot community-based entrepreneurial discourse that can address the imbalances produced by traditional entrepreneurial acts, giving more prominence to the barefoot entrepreneurial acts to those who dwell at the margins.

We posit our discussion under three critical conceptual ideas based on Frantz Fanon's postcolonial humanistic thinking (1963); J.M. Imas and Alia Weston's (2016) organsparkZ art-activism; and the barefoot and solidarity economics of Manfred Max-Neef (1992) and Luis Razeto (2015). These diverse ideas contribute to understanding the importance barefoot entrepreneuring has for more peripheral communities suffering from this destruction as well as positioning the concept at the intersection of postcolonial, economics and art-creative interventions of a critical kind.

We start by critically reflecting upon issues around our capitalist system that creates the conditions for entrepreneurship. Once we spell out the problems and potential alternatives on how the economy should work, we move to revisit the notion of barefoot entrepreneurs, suggesting that it reflects more than just scattered survival tactics and practices of the poor or marginal. We argue that their activities can be conceptualised under principles that challenge the economic and entrepreneurial status quo, and attempt to transform their precarious situation. We subsequently provide two case examples on how these principles can guide a critical barefoot entrepreneurial agenda. These cases are part of our own research programme on marginal barefoot communities, where both of us have conducted postcolonial ethnographic research. That is, we emphasise also the importance of having a methodology that engages and participates with the barefoot entrepreneurial communities to co-create a space for this essential research. We conclude by reflecting on our ideas and on the importance that barefoot entrepreneuring has for the field of critical entrepreneurship.

Community-based barefoot entrepreneuring

Our main concern here is with expanding the experiences and understanding of barefoot entrepreneurs. In order to do this, we need first to identify alternative economic practices that seek to challenge the exploitative practices of the capitalist system upon which mainstream entrepreneurship is constructed.

Capitalism possesses a variety of interpretations, including free-market (and its extreme form of neoliberalism), social democratic and state-led capitalism (see e.g. Hall and Soskice 2001). For us however, capitalism essentially refers to a particular system of socio-economic relationships in which people engage in a private labour market and where relationships are based on monetary exchange. This is what primarily informs the way entrepreneurship is conceptualised and practised as a way of creating economic wealth. This is also the system where entrepreneurship thrives, rewarding those who are successful in the system.

This system has both positive and negative impacts upon society (Martin 2009). Yet, the precarious conditions caused by negative impacts (such as inequality and poverty) have, increasingly, generated calls to construct alternative ways of thinking that can challenge the way it perpetuates socio-economic relationships (e.g. Polanyi 1944/1968; Barber *et al.* 2012; Gibson-Graham and Cameron 2007; Martin 2009; Wolff 2013). These alternative approaches have formed the basis of collective engagement and an array of social movements around the world (Santos 2006; Santos and Rodríguez-Garavito 2006) that seek to dismantle not only its primacy but also its principles.

For instance, Martin (2009) proposes three approaches for challenging capitalism which may be broadly associated with different types of social/organisational engagement, the kind upon which barefoot entrepreneurs construct their relationships. The first approach, *challenging the foundations of capitalism*, may be associated with collective social engagement attempts to highlight discontent and create momentum towards changing government policy. Webster (2004) refers to different types of collective action that seeks to challenge and change capitalist practices. He emphasises the role of social movements and social mobilisation as mechanisms employed to overthrow the system. Social mobilisation signifies a subtler attempt to work with the socio-economic system and initiate reform from the inside. Challenges such as these often emerge in the form of (sometimes violent) mass movements bringing large numbers of protestors together who seek to confront the negative effects of dominant economic policies (Martin 2009). In this first approach, we see political entrepreneurial activities that attempt to move from the notion of the 'individual' to the idea of the collective, seeking not material but political reward in the sense of attempting to change the socio-economic status quo.

The second approach focuses on *creating alternative collective engagement* at a local community level. What these approaches do is to provide an alternative system of social relationships which are separate from the social relationships in a capitalist system and therefore subvert the system (Martin 2009; Barber *et al.* 2012). Approaches in this category include practices which are already employed in society but are not the dominant form of engagement. Examples are cooperative exchange schemes; local money systems; workers' control of production; community control of social services; and the free distribution of goods/services to the most needy (Martin 2009). In other contexts, particularly the Third World, there are many people who engage in alternative, informal work practices because they cannot afford to engage in the formal economic system (see e.g. Hart 1973). Teruelle (2012) points out that it may seem impossible to live outside of a capitalist system of social relationships. However, there are a number of successful social movements which illustrate otherwise. Examples include the Zapatista Army of National Liberation, the Brazilian Landless Peasants Movement (*Movimento dos Trabalhadores Rurais Sem-Terra*), the Occupy Movement, the San Francisco-based Retort group and the Anti-Capitalist Convergence (Teruelle 2012). This second alternative economic approach is what to some extent barefoot entrepreneurs attempt to create, namely a system outside the entrepreneurial capitalist system that seeks to alter our capitalist society and construct a communitarian alternative.

The third approach, but not the last, since these do not reflect a hierarchy, is *creating alternative belief systems*. The communal practices in this category are based on principles and values of socio-economic engagement that are conceptualised in a fundamentally different way from those associated with capitalism (Narotzky 2012). This approach is emphasised in the work of theorists who offer alternative ways of conceptualising economic and social engagement; for example, the concept of 'barefoot economics' in Latin America (Max-Neef 1991, 1992, 1995) as well as solidarity economics (Allard *et al.* 2008) and our own 'barefoot entrepreneurs' in the South (Imas *et al.* 2012).

To Narotzky (2012), this third approach forms part of an intellectual tradition that conceptualises creative processes of social innovation. Social innovation here points to the kind of economic and entrepreneurial engagement which facilitates change in societies. In addition, we argue that Martin's third approach (2009) would also encompass the advancement (not creation) of Indigenous perspectives. For example, the Sumak Kawsay movement is based on a philosophy that relates to the ancestral notion of harmonic good life, *bien vivir*, originating from Andean communities in Latin America (Misoczky 2011). This Indigenous approach has undergone a resurgence in recent years, and reflects a move in our contemporary society to engage with socio-economic practices that are based on alternative belief systems to capitalism.

We wish to note that there may be overlaps between approaches two and three where, for example, informal workers engage communally in ways that are based on alternative belief systems. However, the categories do have different emphases and it is the third approach upon which we further advance our representation of barefoot entrepreneurship. A note of caution is necessary here. It is not our intention to debate the purity of what is (or is not) an alternative belief system (Gibson-Graham and Cameron 2007). Our aim is, instead, to offer a way of explaining the everyday engagements of marginalised communities that are based on a local barefoot existence, whose socio-organisational practices challenge the values and principles of mainstream entrepreneurship embedded in the capitalist system. We consider this approach to be built on a (postcolonial) transformative humanistic approach, a barefoot economics and finally on an organsparkZ art-intervention. These three offer, beyond pure interpretation and conceptual representation, a challenge to our way of conceiving entrepreneurship. Next we will look separately at these three key ideas, although we regard them as one interrelated concept.

Transformative humanism

Fanon's concept of transformative humanism explains how people creatively organise together to change their circumstances for the ultimate benefit of their communities. In his work, Fanon argues for a 'new humanism' (Fanon 1963, p. 9; 1967/2008, p. 246) which emerges out of a struggle for liberation. Fanon's humanism may be seen as a 'revolutionary' form of humanism that positions people – including those who are marginalised – as having the potential to freely use their creativity to engage with and change the world (Gibson 2011; Hardt and Negri 2001; Pithouse 2003). He does not promote humanism as a militant form of engagement, but as an opportunity to start a movement that works to transform deep-seated traditions. He accepts that this is not easy but every person has the potential to engage in productive self-actualisation (Pithouse 2003).

Humanism as a theoretical concept is highly contested. Despite support for the concept by key radical thinkers (see e.g. Marx 1983; Sartre 1987), the anti-humanistic critiques (see e.g. Heidegger 2001; Foucault 1973) still position it as an unfashionable concept because it has been presented as a key aspect of modernity and colonialism (Pithouse 2003).[1] This may be one reason why Fanon has been referred to so little in organisational research (Ibarra-Colado 2006). However, despite the links with colonialism, Fanon did not oppose humanism as a concept and instead remained committed to it as a way of conveying the (postcolonial) lived experiences of humanity (Pithouse 2003). In African contexts, the concept of *Ubuntu* (and associated terms such as *Unhu*) has been described as 'African humanism' because it encompasses the way in which people place great importance on social/communal relationships, concern for others and meaningful cooperation in society (Mabovula 2011; Letseka 2000). Madlingozi (2007) refers to human-centred engagement and stresses that fundamental change is possible through sustained collective action. A related concept is 'revolutionary *Ubuntu*' which defends the rights of all people no matter their background and acknowledges the importance of communal engagements. This resonates with Fanon's humanism because it reflects the way in which marginalised individuals come together to engage communally in a struggle for social transformation (Alkimat 2009; Gibson 2011).

We take these ideas of transformative humanism to explain how marginalised people are able to creatively actualise social transformation by working together in their communities and transforming deep-seated traditions such as capitalism. In this case it is not simply a transformative subversion of capitalism, but a transformation based on principles and values that are fundamentally different to capitalism. Whereas capitalism emphasises the private creation of wealth, a humanistic perspective emphasises fundamentally different values such as creative self-actualisation, meaningful communal relationships and liberation. By extension, this perspective also encompasses an alternative view of entrepreneurship that is not focused on rewarding those who are successful in the system. Instead it reflects humanistic entrepreneurial engagements that are rooted in transformation of and by the community. This perspective recognises the potential that those who are marginalised have to entrepreneurially transform deep-seated traditions and create meaningful change.

Barefoot economics = solidarity economics

Barefoot economics is at the centre of our barefoot community-based entrepreneuring and the central idea in our original paper. Max-Neef's theory helps us to contemplate a different economic language, one that reflects upon the economic experiences of the poor and marginal. This is strongly associated with the sociological work conducted by Wacquant (2001, 2007) on the marginal and dispossessed that constructs his or her existence in the shanty town of the urban landscape. It is also reflected in the distributive and solidarity economics of another Chilean economist Luis Razeto (2015). Their theoretical ideas help us to conceptualise what it is like to dwell at the periphery of the capitalist centre, therefore helping us to apply a different rationale to understand the entrepreneurial activities of these agents.

To begin with, we highlight the issue of wealth creation. In this socio-economic space, wealth reflects something different to the capitalist credo that the individual will triumph *à la* Richard Branson. In the Branson model of entrepreneurship we find the hero grabbing all the potential wealth out of an artefact creation that suddenly becomes an economic and financial sensation. In this image the individual assumes mythical proportions, asking the community to 'imitate' his formula of success. Max-Neef's eco-community economics, in contrast, prioritises social issues such as the protection of all members of the community. The value in wealth creation comes first and foremost from taking care of those who live with us, presenting us with a more encompassing way of understanding entrepreneurial actions as part of community support and solidarity with each other.

Distribution, solidarity and collaboration are central for a barefoot community-based entrepreneurship. In solidarity with each other, we found an economy driven by the desire to sustain life rather than the purity of the creation of wealth that benefits only individuals (Miller 2010). Here relationships, in economic terms, are defined as part of a process of reorganising that implies interdependency and survival of community life. Cooperation and mutuality, individual and collective well-being; economic and social justice and ecological health, robust democracies, diversity and pluralism are the values promoted to eradicate the community destruction supported by capitalism and entrepreneurial ideologies (Razeto 2015). Wealth, maximisation of one individual positioned as a consequence of his (emphasising the masculine here) economic success are superseded by principles and values that identify those successes with a common process in which the hero is the community itself. Here the focus is on cooperation, participation and the desire to construct a slower but more sustainable future together, despite the challenges faced by these communities. A barefoot economics enables us to establish alternative types of socio-economic relationships and to define economic entrepreneurial activities in a different language, the language spoken by the marginalised.

In our view, this invites a different creative entrepreneurial process, one that is fundamentally motivated by the need to alter the ideological aspect of entrepreneurship deeply entrenched in neoliberalism (as an expression of the most extreme form of capitalism). In addition, by advancing this alternative view of entrepreneurship we seek to reclaim the notion of entrepreneurship and to legitimise the daily subsistence work that marginalised communities conduct on a daily basis. Here we refer to the communities that dwell in precarity and poverty, such as those described in the kukiya-favela organisation of the dispossessed (Imas and Weston 2012) or in Wacquant's sociology of the favela dwellers (2007). Furthermore, it could also give legitimacy to those who try to propose alternative readings of the economy as well as to those who work to construct more critical and postcolonial readings of entrepreneurship.

Max-Neef theorises that despite poverty, self-sufficiency is possible and effective through grassroots community mobilisation (Max-Neef, 1992). Barefoot and solidarity economics give us a base to theorise an alternative system of socio-economic relationships that are not tied to a capitalist system of relationships. In fact, Max-Neef's theoretical legacy for entrepreneurship is to accept the language of the dispossessed, the marginal and the poor, and under their terms to reflect, pass judgement and construct a more sustainable social and economic alternative life.

organsparkZ communities

Our third key element in constructing the basis for a community-based entrepreneurship invites us to explore ante/creative practices (Imas 2015) of what Imas and Weston (2016) identify as organsparkZ. 'organsparkZ' is a concept that Imas and Weston decapitalise on purpose to emphasise the issue of people living in precarity, and highlight the kind of creativity employed by disenfranchised communities. These communities express their innovative tactics (De Certeau 1984) in order to question the capitalist society and their condition of marginality. Fundamentally, they build their ante/creativity in a way that reflects the ante/narrative organisation theory described by Boje (2008) in which he critically questions the lineal and Western narrative of a well-rehearsed and plotted theory of organisation that imposes one way of reading concepts, theories, models and processes that prescribe the organisation of society. The ante/creativity approach invites us, instead, to explore the epistemology and ontology of socio-organisational engagement in a dialogical, critical and nonlinear manner. Through the organsparkZ concept they also incorporate Chantal Mouffe's (2007) agonistic approach that critically dissents from the normative political and economic discourses, and aims to give voice and space for action to all those who are silenced (i.e. the barefoot entrepreneurs' communities). Finally, they strongly associate their concept with the work of Kester's dialogical art (2011) and Bishop's participatory aesthetics (2012) in which both authors seek a more politically and socially involved understanding of art with the potential for social change.

organsparkZ reflects upon the unplanned, spontaneous and intuitively collective activities that the dispossessed and marginal have at their disposal, defying and resisting their conditions of marginality, and in the process reconceptualising through art their identities, drawing different territorial lines of their communities and creating visual and aesthetic ways that subvert the representations imposed from the outside capitalist system. Three key ideas then determine their subversion and ante/creative practices. One is art-space as a process of social engagement and transformation that emanates from within the community. Art acts as a catalyst to engage the community in order to fight the impositions of the capitalist system. Communities strive for social transformation of their territories and well-being. Second is the notion of dialogical-imagination that builds from Kester's dialogical art, but fundamentally reflects

Bakhtin's (1981) notion of dialogue as a co-participative act. It is the collective imagination of the community which enacts a fluid network of thoughts and activities, invoking changes in society. All are part of a movement that seeks transformation as part of a collective creative process. Finally, the third idea refers to an everyday encroached resistance (Bayat 2000) that is unobtrusive, protracted and pervasively used by disenfranchised communities in order to improve their lives.

The significance of organsparkZ to construct a barefoot community-based entrepreneurship lies in the potential of an ante/creative entrepreneurship as a way of emancipating and transforming not only the condition of the marginal but equally society from below rather than above. Via creative acts expressed in art, the community 'sells' a socially transformative fluid idea that attempts to indicate and sign a different discourse for the capitalist society. It defiantly shows resilience through creativity of a social kind, rather than seeking material wealth.

Thus, the three key conceptual ideas we have highlighted here provide a more socially encompassing discourse to interpret and reflect upon barefoot community-based entrepreneurs. These ideas do not exhaust how we should interpret all the ante/creative and spontaneous acts these communities present, but have a more critical appreciation of the resilience and potential for social transformation that communities possess. The most relevant contribution our community-based entrepreneurial perspective makes to this critical compendium of thoughts on entrepreneurship is an alternative language of entrepreneurship. We advance a distinctively different language on how to read entrepreneurial activities in spaces and places where the dominant, colonial and legitimised notion of entrepreneurship does not count and does not apply. Next, we engage with some examples to illustrate our more discursive account of a barefoot community-based entrepreneurship.

Barefoot community-based entrepreneuring examples

To illustrate our conceptual idea of barefoot community-based entrepreneuring, we present two cases. These cases are part of our postcolonial and critical research agenda in marginal communities of Latin America and Africa. To engage and build these cases, we employed, methodologically, critical postcolonial ethnographic methods of engagement. These methods invite us to construct a dialogue with participant communities, allowing the voices of the marginal to speak to us (e.g. Imas and Weston 2012). This methodological point is extremely relevant, as otherwise we would not have a story to share that reflects the language and reality of those who live in precarity and at the margins of society.

One of the cases refers to the occupation of factories by unemployed workers in Argentina. Their movement, known as *Fábricas Recuperadas* (occupied factories), emerged during the demise of a neoliberal capitalist setting in 2001. The second case is based on creative community initiatives which emerged in Zimbabwe during a parallel period of economic and political crisis in the post–2000 decade. Both are good examples of how community-based barefoot entrepreneurial experiences defy a given economic situation. We narrate how these examples illustrate the ways in which barefoot entrepreneurial ante/creative experiences can transform a community by emancipating and empowering them. These experiences have influenced similar experiences in places as far away as Greece and Spain, both badly affected by the global financial crisis, where people face precarious conditions.

The *fábrica*: a barefoot entrepreneurial occupation

The idea that the discourse of entrepreneurism may be equated to 'occupation' would certainly raise the eyebrows of business and managerialist elites. These elites have always considered entrepreneurship a neoliberal panacea to solve economic downturns or create wealth (e.g. Druker 2014; Mezias and Boyle 2002). For instance, as the recent financial crisis in Europe has demonstrated, one favourite dictum of business elites is to stimulate economic activity and the creation of jobs through 'entrepreneurial' policies. What then can communities, which find themselves at the periphery of these initiatives, do to overcome their sense of helplessness? How can those communities attempt to change the status quo and, rather than relying on private and state entrepreneurial-driven initiatives, generate their own solutions? How can those communities construct with dignity a way out of their precarious state?

The *fábrica recuperada* movement created by unemployed workers (see e.g. Kosmala and Imas 2012) following the financial crisis in Argentina exemplifies this barefoot community-based alternative. The movement was born as a result of neoliberal policies introduced by the government of Menem in Argentina in the 1990s. These policies created the conditions for the collapse of the financial market that caused bankruptcy and mass layoffs (Imas 2010). Deprived of state welfare policies and support, many of these workers and their communities faced a grim future.

> You know, these people were taken their money, closing the factory and walking away. There was nothing for us there. No compensation, no support, no prospects.... Our bank accounts were not allowing us to get our money out. There was nothing. So, what were we to do? How were we to feed our families?
>
> (Jose)

As workers, their families and communities understood that the state and the private sector were not going to alleviate their pain and suffering. As a result, these workers had to demonstrate resilience, creativity and the will to alter their predicament and precarious state. One of the key actions they took was to occupy the bankrupt and abandon businesses in order to make them sustainable again. While the market preachers consider that the best option is to recoup one's 'capital' and abandon unprofitable businesses, the workers thought differently. These disenfranchised individuals had to affect the performativity of an economic system which had primarily destroyed their lives. The movement involved factory workers co-opting their former places of employment in order to continue to use these spaces, both socially and as a form of gainful employment. This resulted in radically transformed relationships of socio-economic engagement which emerged on the edge of the market system (Narotzky 2012).

> When the *patrones* [owners] left, we did not know how to run the business. [None of us] have a proper business education. We were machine operators. Even the older one here, Pedro, he didn't know how or what to do. How were we going to sell our products? We didn't have clients, as everything was collapsing. We didn't have the government here to support us, as we were bankrupt and what we were doing was illegal. But, you know, we had to do something.
>
> (Arturo)

Several organisations which went bankrupt began to regroup and organise themselves, supporting one another and establishing alternative ways to the capitalist system that relies primarily on borrowing money as a way of supporting and creating 'business'.

> [H]ere, there was nothing, we didn't have the money. From where? But *compañeros* [comrades] from other businesses began to let us tools if necessary. We exchange parts of our machinery with other factories in order to keep printing. We shared transport. Activist students joined us to give us advice on how to reposit our work. What was unbelievable was that everyone cooperated. At least, everyone, lower and middle class felt we had to do something together as help from the state or abroad was not going to materialise.
>
> (Jacinto)

What the capitalist system equally lacked at that stage was the involvement of the community to support businesses. In the traditional sense, it is the costumers who keep a market or a business afloat. In this case, as the *fábricas* did not have the legality to sell their products, it was the community that gave them the support to do so. Humanism is embodied in the risk that people took in their own lives to support their communities. This is exemplified with the risk of potential jail sentences, since they were helping entrepreneurial initiatives that were regarded as illegal.

> Look, it was really, really tense. The police came to throw us out of here. They arrived one evening with a van to take us out and lock the *fábrica*.

Our neighbours came to tell us so we could barricade ourselves and keep the gates fully crossed. Our families arrived and what was so beautiful was to see the community standing out, outside blocking the police access to the gates.... We did have a problem, *compañeros* were getting us orders, but we could not take our prints out as the police was there. Then, our next-door neighbour suggested us to take the prints through his home. What? So, the hole there above our heads there, is from where we started to move our work we have been paid to produce so we could keep going.... It was beautiful and now we invite the community here, children, old people to come and share with us the *fábrica*.

(Roque)

The *fábrica* came to represent a symbol of resistance, of community, of participation. The boundaries between the factory and community became blurred as a growing integration of work and ideas flowed between them.

Look, we have an art room, we have a space for theatre, for music, we have the local schools visiting us to learn about our old machines [chuckles]; about what it takes to print a book, a comic, or else. ... We are here to learn and grow together as a community not as a business alone.

(Rogelio)

This example illustrates several things: first, that a transformative humanistic philosophy is alive in the community, especially for those who suffer at the hands of capitalist policies. They raise a revolutionary spirit to confront their precarious condition. It also reflects an economy based on solidarity, as otherwise they would have not been able to overcome what the market dictates in this situation. Solidarity implies the construction of a different economic language that allows them to challenge their alternative condition of being unemployed and penniless. Finally, they show the kind of ante/creative resilience described in organsparkZ activities, as otherwise these workers, families and communities could not have survived. They had to act ante/creatively, looking for solutions, from occupying the space (of the factory) to the way they creatively resist the impositions of the government and financial institutions in a neoliberally led society. Collectively, participatively, they engage in constructing alternative socio-economic relationships that can challenge the established and legitimised status quo, showing the kind of solidarity entrepreneurship required to sustain community existence.

Putting words into action: barefoot entrepreneurial resistance

Zimbabwe experienced a parallel economic collapse during the post-2000 period, precipitated by economic and political uncertainty. In this case the economic collapse was not purely due to neoliberal policies, but was pre-empted by a complex interplay of factors (Hammar *et al.* 2003). These included a failed economic structural adjustment in the 1990s, agrarian land reform, declines in agricultural and industrial production, and economic hyperinflation (Mlambo 2008; Raftopoulos 2009). The economic collapse led to harsh conditions, and people's livelihoods were similarly decimated as the capitalist economic system crumbled around them. Traditional ways of working could not be sustained and people looked for alternative ways to survive (Imas and Weston 2012).

With widespread unemployment, people engaged creatively in entrepreneurial resistance, and found alternative ways of organising. As the capitalist economic system collapsed, formal work opportunities became scarce. Instead, people worked with what they had in their immediate communities and entrepreneurially created work opportunities for themselves in informal economic spaces. Similar to the Argentine experience, this resulted in radically transformed relationships of socio-economic engagement which emerged on the edge of the market system (Narotzky 2012). In Zimbabwe, informal work practices gained cultural acceptance as the primary way for people to work (Jones 2010; Parsons 2007). The following quote highlights the emergence of an alternative economy:

> [I]t's gotten so bad that it's forced people to actually wake up ... to the situ[ation] ... you know, when people say 'OK, you need to hustle because there's no work'.... You know, so you find people in the street but it's more like ... we've formalised the informal sector.
>
> (Tendai)

Work practices became rooted in people's immediate barefoot experiences, and systems of exchange evolved to meet whatever needs people had. The following quote, highlighting the casual act of bartering, illustrates a revival of the social economy:

> Even bartering is better. So if you want some [thing that I have]; I give you a small parcel ... and you give me a little bit of diesel.
>
> (Ezekiel)

Acts like bartering may have appeared to be simple, isolated instances of exchanges, but the engagements surrounding these acts went much deeper than a casual exchange of goods. They point to the ways in which social and economic relationships had shifted in society. This shift formed a movement towards a more pronounced social and community way of working. Many community organisations sprang up with people working entrepreneurially in solidarity with one another. The following quote by Jiri exemplifies how a community collaborated with artistic forms of expression, such as poetry, to construct alternative forms of social-organisational engagement to resist their precarity:

You know they call it Madud, a lowly rated area ... I and other youths in this area decided to sit around and see the areas that we can concentrate on in order to expose our area to success. As you can see in this area, most of our youngsters have got nothing to do and they end up resorting to drugs, teenage sex, because they have got nothing to do. So to fill that emptiness we have decided to form a group which is called hidden voices. Currently we are concentrating on poetry but we have got a vision to grow bigger.

(Jiri)

Jiri's quote exemplifies the barefoot community engagements of a group of dispossessed youth who decided to work together to improve their community. Here their entrepreneurial focus is on advancing communal transformation rather than individual gain.

On another side of town, another community was similarly engaging with creative forms of expression such as poetry, spoken work and music. This community performed together in order to address their challenges. In this way they worked entrepreneurially to find solutions to challenges.

It's love ... because without that, there would not be a reason to actually live.

[For us, it's a] passion for words and at the same time a passion about causes. So it's using words to support certain causes. With 'Heroes' what we do is, we get together every month, we get people to perform ... you know, people looking at it like stress relief ... like putting your energy out there and then hopefully the people in the crowd get a chance to analyse and hopefully go away with something from it. They might come up with solutions.

(Tendai)

Their resilience within the conditions imposed upon them was based on ante/creative organsparkZ activities. Collectively they used creativity as a way to actively defy and resist their conditions of marginality and to make changes in their community.

I think that's, like, the first step in actually initiating change, you know ... so yeah, we get together and try and present it in a more creative way, like it's more palatable. So, I mean, you can have, like, pictures there with war and scars and what have you, and it actually shuts you off more than it gets you interested. So if you kinda, like, portray it in a more creative way, it draws people in. And when you're left with them, hopefully they've drawn a message from it. So yeah, this is what we do.

(Tendai)

In addition to creative performance, Tendai also highlighted youth workshops, which were a parallel focus of their entrepreneurial community engagements. These youth workshops further emphasise the transformative focus of their ante/creativity. Here creative forms of communication are used to support youth in affecting organsparkZ creative change in their own communities. But more than this, these community workshops illustrate Fanon's deeply humanistic form of resistance. Spoken word used for the purposes of education and liberation reflects transformative creative engagements which are of benefit for the wider community.

> So what we do is go out to schools and hold workshops. And the thing with these workshops is, like, we believe that the spoken word has the means to educate and liberate.... And we try to inspire something in the youth's minds so that they try and take control of it. You know, cos it's your community.... Try and take it to them and show them how they can effect change. For me, I think that's the most powerful side right now, cos it takes away that bitterness ... it's more of the education and interaction and less of the entertainment. So it's, putting those words into action which ... I think is of value.
>
> (Tendai)

The example of creative community organisation from Zimbabwe demonstrates in a number of ways how people engage in barefoot community-based entrepreneurship activities. First, the example illustrates how people resisted conditions of precarity which were precipitated by the collapse of a capitalist economy. Creative resistance is embodied in entrepreneurial engagements which are focused on alternative forms of exchange that lead to community transformation. The example illustrates an alternative economy based on social, humanistic exchange, and that is facilitated by creative communication (poetry, the spoken word and music). Here the revolutionary spirit of resistance is founded on passion and humanistic 'love' and compassion for the community. Finally, ante/creative organsparkZ activities enabled communities to survive the challenging conditions. Ante/creative forms of communication enabled a language for the community to find solutions to their challenges and effect transformation. Ultimately, similar to the case of the Argentine *fábricas*, the Zimbabwean example shows how collective engagements constructed alternative socio-economic relationships that were rooted in the local everyday (i.e. barefoot solidarity) experiences and struggles of communities. These similarly catalysed entrepreneurial engagements that create change and mutual transformation.

Concluding remarks

> They exist without permission. They are hated, hunted and persecuted. They live in quiet desperation amongst the filth. And yet they are capable of bringing entire civilisation to their knees.
>
> (Banksy 2005, p. 83)

In this chapter we have focused on theorising the everyday practices of communities who entrepreneurially organise and create more sustainable grassroots engagement as an alternative to entrepreneurial capitalism. We argue that these engagements are based on an alternative set of values and principles that are positioned at the intersection of postcolonial, solidarity and barefoot economics and art-creative interventions of a critical kind. We illustrate this with two examples from Argentina and Zimbabwe. In both cases, barefoot communal-based entrepreneurial practices are initiated by disenfranchised communities and sustained by an ongoing struggle for emancipation against a system of wealth creation that does not provide equally for them. The communities exemplify barefoot engagements through their alternative ante/creative, participative and transformative practices that are rooted in their local conditions of precarity, falling outside of the dominant economic system. These communities typify self-sufficient grassroots mobilisation of an ante/creative kind, resisting from the margins the attempts to subdue them by the failings of the capitalist system.

Thus, challenging the destructive nature of the capitalist entrepreneurial system (Harvey 2007) is something, as our quote from Banksy reflects, a capacity that marginal communities possess and must exercise in order to replace the entrepreneurship discourse, striving for the 'occupation' and 'alteration' of what we praise in our societies as the material success of a few. This will allow for the relocation of resources, the respect of the environment and the emancipation of the disenfranchised. That is the message of a barefoot-community-based entrepreneurship and our 'small' contribution to this volume.

Note

1 We acknowledge the continued debate on 'humanism'. For an extended discussion, see Pithouse (2003).

References

Alkimat, A. (ed.) (2009), *Revolutionary Ubuntu: The Shack Dwellers and Poor People of South Africa*. Available at www.eblackstudies.org/ebooks/ubuntu.pdf (accessed 25 May 2016).

Allard, J., Davidson, C. and Matthaei, J. (2008), *Solidarity Economy: Building Alternatives for People and Planet*, Chicago, IL: ChangeMaker Publications.

Bakhtin, M.M. (1981), *Dialogic Imagination: Four Essays*, Austin: University of Texas Press.

Banksy (2005), *Wall and Piece*, London: Century.

Barber, P.G., Leach, B. and Lem, W. (eds) (2012), *Confronting Capital: Critique and Engagement in Anthropology*, New York: Routledge.

Bayat, A. (2000), From 'dangerous classes' to 'quiet rebels': Politics of the urban subaltern in the Global South. *International Sociology*, **15**(3), pp. 533–557.

Bishop, C. (2012), *Artificial Hells: Participatory Art and the Politics of Spectatorship*, London: Verso.

Boje, D. (2008), *Storytelling Organizations*, London: Sage.

De Certeau, M. (1984), *The Practice of Everyday Life*, Berkeley: University of California Press.

Druker, P.F. (2014), *Innovation and Entrepreneurship: Practice and Principles*, London: Routledge.

Fanon, F. (1963), *The Wretched of the Earth*, New York: Grove Press.

Fanon, F. (1967/2008), *Black Skin White Masks*, London: Pluto Books.

Foucault, M. (1973), *The Order of Things: An Archaeology of the Human Sciences*, New York: Vintage.

Gibson, N.C. (2011), *Fanonian Practices in South Africa: From Steve Biko to Abhlali baseMjondolo*, New York: Palgrave Macmillan.

Gibson-Graham, J.K. and Cameron, J. (2007), Community enterprises: Imagining and enacting alternatives to capitalism. *Social Alternatives*, **26**(1), pp. 20–25.

Hall, P.A. and Soskice, D. (2001), An introduction to varieties of capitalism. In P.A. Hall and D. Soskice (eds), *Varieties of Capitalism – The Institutional Foundations of Comparative Advantage*, Oxford: Oxford University Press, pp. 1–70.

Hammar, A., Raftopoulos, B. and Jensen, S. (eds) (2003), *Zimbabwe's Unfinished Business: Rethinking Land, State and Nation in the Context of Crisis*, Harare: Weaver Press.

Hardt, M. and Negri, A. (2001), *Empire*, Cambridge, MA: Harvard University Press.

Hart, K. (1973), Informal income opportunities and urban employment in Ghana. *The Journal of Modern African Studies*, **11**(1), pp. 61–89.

Harvey, D. (2007), Neoliberalism as creative destruction. *The ANNALS of the American Academy of Political and Social Science*, **610**(1), pp. 21–44.

Heidegger, M. (2001), *Basic Writings*, San Francisco, CA: Harper.

Ibarra-Colado, E. (2006), Organization studies and epistemic coloniality in Latin America: Thinking otherness from the margins. *Organization*, **13**(4), pp. 463–488.

Imas, J.M. (2010), Dirty management: The legacy of Chile and Argentina. In E. Guedes and A. Farias (eds), *International Management and International Relations: A Critical Perspective from Latin America*, London: Routledge, pp. 185–200.

Imas, J.M. (2015), *Marginality: Entrepreneurial Ante/Creativity of the Precariat*, Mexico: Feria Internacional del Libro, CDMX.

Imas, J.M. and Weston, A. (2012), From Harare to Rio de Janeiro: Kukiya-favela organization narrative of the excluded. *Organization*, **19**(2), pp. 205–227.

Imas, J.M. and Weston, A. (2016), Organsparkz communities of art/spaces, imaginations, & resistances. In K. Kosmala and J.M. Imas (eds), *Precarious Spaces: The Arts, Social & Organisational Change*, London: Intellect Press, pp. 131–151.

Imas, J.M., Wilson, N. and Weston, A. (2012), Barefoot entrepreneurs. *Organization*, **19**(5), pp. 563–585.

Jones, J.L. (2010), 'Nothing is straight in Zimbabwe': The rise of the kukiya-kiya economy 2000–2008. *Journal of Southern African Studies*, **36**(2), pp. 285–299.

Kester, G.H. (2011), *The One and the Many: Contemporary Collaborative Art in a Global Context*, Durham, NC: Duke University Press.

Klein, N. (2014), *This Changes Everything: Capitalism vs. the Climate*, Canada: Vintage.

Kosmala, K. and Imas, M. (2012), Narrating a story of Buenos Aires' Fabricas Recuperadas. *International Journal of Management and Business*, **3**(1), pp. 103–114.

Letseka, M. (2000), Africana philosophy and educational discourse. In P. Higgs, N.C.G. Vakalisa, T.V. Mda and N.T. Assie-Lumumba (eds), *African Voices in Education*, Lansdowne: Juta, pp. 179–193.

Mabovula, N.N. (2011), The erosion of African communal values: A reappraisal of the African Ubuntu philosophy. *Inkanyiso: Journal of Humanities and Social Sciences*, **3**(1), pp. 38–47.

Madlingozi, T. (2007), Good victims, bad victims: Apartheid beneficiaries, victims and the struggle for social justice. In W. Le Roux and K. Van Marle (eds), *Law, Memory and Apartheid: Ten Years after AZAPO v President of South Africa*, Pretoria: Pretoria University Law Press, pp. 107–126.

Martin, B. (2009), Nonviolent strategy against capitalism. *Social Alternatives*, **28**(1), pp. 42–46.

Marx, K. (1983), *The Portable Karl Marx*, New York: Penguin.

Max-Neef, A.M. (1991), *Human Scale Development: Conception, Application and Further Reflections*, New York: The Apex Press.

Max-Neef, A.M. (1992), *From the Outside Looking In: Experiences in Barefoot Economics*, London: Zed Books.

Max-Neef, A.M. (1995), Economic growth and quality of life: A threshold hypothesis. *Ecological Economics*, **15**(2), pp. 115–118.

Mezias, S. and Boyle, A. (2002), *The Organizational Dynamics of Creative Destruction: Entrepreneurship and the Creation of New Industries*, New York: Palgrave Macmillan.

Miller, E. (2010), Solidarity economy: Key concepts and issues. In E. Kawano, T. Masterson and J. Teller-Ellsberg (eds), *Solidarity Economy I: Building Alternatives for People and Planet*, Amherst, MA: Center for Popular Economics, pp. 25–41.

Misoczky, M.C. (2011), World visions in dispute in contemporary Latin America: Development x harmonic life. *Organization*, **18**(3), pp. 345–363.

Mlambo, A. (2008), Historical antecedents to Operation Murambatsvina. In M.T. Vambe (ed.), *The Hidden Dimensions of Operation Murambatsvina in Zimbabwe*, Harare: Weaver Press, pp. 9–24.

Mouffe, C. (2007), Artistic activism and agonistic spaces. *Art & Research*, **1**(2): pp. 1–5.

Narotzky, S. (2012), Alternatives to expanded accumulation and the anthropological imagination: Turning necessity into a challenge to capitalism. In P.G. Barber, B. Leach and W. Lem (eds), *Confronting Capital: Critique and Engagement in Anthropology*, New York: Routledge, pp. 239–252.

Parsons, R.W.K. (2007), After Mugabe goes: The economic and political reconstruction of Zimbabwe. *South African Journal of Economics*, **75**(4), 599–615.

Piketty, T. (2014), *Capital in the Twenty-first Century*, London: The Belknap Press of Harvard University Press.

Pithouse, R. (2003), That the tool never possess the man: Taking Fanon's humanism seriously. *Politikon: South African Journal of Political Studies*, **30**(1), pp. 107–131.

Polanyi, K. (1944/1968), *The Great Transformation*, Boston, MA: Beacon Press.

Raftopoulos, B. (2009), The crisis in Zimbabwe, 1998–2008. In B. Raftopoulos and A. Mlambo (eds), *Becoming Zimbabwe: A History from the Pre-colonial Period to 2008*, Harare: Weaver Press, pp. 201–232.

Razeto, L. (2015), *Tópicos de Economía Comprensiva*, Santiago: Ediciones Universitas Nueva Civilización.

Roy, A. (2011), Slumdog cities: Rethinking subaltern urbanis. *International Journal of Urban and Regional Research*, **35**(2), pp. 223–238.

Santos, B.S. (2006), *Another Production is Possible: Beyond the Capitalist Canon*, London: Verso.

Santos, B.S. and Rodríguez-Garavito, C.A. (2006), Introduction: Expanding the economic canon and searching for alternatives to neoliberal globalization. In B.S.

Santos (ed.), *Another Production is Possible: Beyond the Capitalist Canon*, London: Verso, pp. 33–67.

Sartre, J.P. (1987), *Existentialism is a Humanism*, London: Methuen.

Teruelle, R. (2012), Reconciled to the belief: Investigating the need for hope. *Social Alternatives*, **31**(2), pp. 45–48.

Wacquant, L. (2001), *Los Parias Urbanos*, Buenos Aires: Manantial.

Wacquant, L. (2007), Territorial stigmatization in the age of advanced marginality. *Thesis Eleven*, **91**(1), pp. 66–77.

Webster, N. (2004), Understanding the evolving diversities and originalities in rural social movements in an age of globalization. *Civil Society and Social Movements Programme: Paper Number 7*, Geneva: UNRISD. pp. 1–25.

Wolff, R. (2013), *Capitalism Hits the Fan: The Global Economic Meltdown and What to Do About It*, Northampton, MA: Interlink Publishing.

6 Challenging leadership in discourses of Indigenous entrepreneurship in Australia

Deirdre Tedmanson and Michelle Evans

Introduction

Entrepreneurship research is largely bound by Western organisational discourses which perpetuate a racialised hierarchy and privilege non-Indigenous ways of being. The small and distinct field of Indigenous entrepreneurship research, now in its third decade, although emergent, contributes greatly by critically investigating cultural values from the inside for profit firm structures (Dana 2015). The purpose of this chapter is to call into question the hegemonic performativity of much conventional discourse about heroic (white male) styles of leadership in entrepreneurship. In so doing, we place Indigenous[1] leadership subjectivities at the centre of our analysis to reveal how Indigenous entrepreneurial leadership is enacted in a cultural context through participation and inclusivity (Montgomery *et al.* 2012; Spiller *et al.* 2011).

The contradictions and tensions inherent in assumptions which idealise Western hierarchical understandings of power and authority that dominate research accounts of entrepreneurship are deconstructed in this chapter. Through our focused analysis of the contextual (Welter 2011) we argue that entrepreneurship occurs within a cultural context and that leadership assumes many forms within these diverse contexts. Therefore, relational forms of collective and collaborative leadership are explored within the context of Indigenous entrepreneurship in Australia, using contemporary empirical research.

This chapter focuses on the social transformation occurring in Australia through the growth of Indigenous entrepreneurship driven by community connectedness to collective goals such as independent Indigenous economic development, rather than any simplistic reproduction of 'homo-economicus' (Evans 2012; Tedmanson *et al.* 2012). Asserting the importance of writing from an Indigenous worldview (Foley 2008; Moreton-Robinson 2003) we explore entrepreneurial leadership as the creation of a 'space of belonging' and critically analyse how the co-creation of entrepreneurial effort strengthens Indigenous community efficacy (Evans 2012; Tedmanson 2014).

Two studies are offered: one uses action research with Indigenous communities in Australia and the other focuses on stories of innovation in the Indigenous arts sector. The chapter chronicles how diverse narratives of entrepreneurship from the voices of Indigenous leaders can help us to think afresh about the entrepreneurial leadership involved (Evans 2012; Evans and Sinclair 2015; Banerjee and Tedmanson 2010). The chapter explores how collaborative action in entrepreneurship is building social capital and enabling well-being beyond the individual entrepreneur (Tedmanson and Guerin 2011). Using case study examples from Australia, we focus in our chapter on crafting new understandings of leadership (Evans 2012) in discourses of Indigenous entrepreneurship.

First, we will discuss the area of Indigenous entrepreneurship; then we will draw out specific examples of Indigenous entrepreneurship and discuss these examples within the context of diversity, social capital, social entrepreneurship and social change; next, we will discuss the literature on Indigenous leadership as it applies to entrepreneurship. We argue here that recognition of both leadership and entrepreneurial success is often largely culturally determined and racially loaded (Dana and Anderson 2007; Grant 2008; Tedmanson 2014; Evans and Sinclair 2015).

We aim to show how perceptions of both leadership and entrepreneurship are culturally determined, as are perceptions of what constitutes success, and that as a result recognition of the outstanding capacities of many Indigenous leaders is often lacking.

Finally, this chapter aims to focus on solidarity, on the small but powerful, creative sites, practices and stories of localised Indigenous agency and resilience. In doing so, it demonstrates a new perspective of entrepreneurship as an expression of the contemporary relevance of Indigenous wisdom and the strength and sustainability of Indigenous cultural agency.

Indigenous entrepreneurship

Interest in Indigenous entrepreneurship as a field for research is increasing. However, we believe it is imperative that the rich diversity of contexts within which Indigenous entrepreneurship takes place is understood and acknowledged as relevant to our understanding of the nature of Indigenous entrepreneurship. A contextualised approach to studying Indigenous entrepreneurship avoids the damage of simplistic or essentialising notions of Indigenous identity and aspirations. There are many complex factors which influence, limit and/ or facilitate the choices available to Indigenous communities and Indigenous entrepreneurs. Numerous accounts of organisational issues and Indigenous peoples tend to simplify or essentialise Indigenous interests. Such proscriptive definitions of what 'Indigenous people are, think, do or say, obscure the hybridity and complex intersectionality of the contemporary lived experience of many Indigenous peoples' (Tedmanson 2011, p. 65).

Indigenous entrepreneurship has both local and global dimensions. Across the world and within nation states, Indigenous peoples' experiences of colonisation, invasion, dispossession and ongoing systemic racisms share common features but are also culturally, linguistically and politically diverse. Since the

United Nations Declaration of the Rights of Indigenous Peoples in 2007, Indigenous entrepreneurship has become an area of increasing interest in the field of entrepreneurship studies but primarily within discussions of specific nation states and the context of the political economy in which Indigenous people live. Despite the diversity of contexts however, some common features emerge from grounded research.

While the study of ethnic minority entrepreneurs is concerned with the economic engagement of immigrant groups new to a particular area, and the diverse forms of social capital such groups may deploy to further their interests in their new homes (Light 2004), a focus on Indigenous entrepreneurs more often centres on how Indigenous communities (and individuals) with a deep and long-standing attachment to their ancestral lands engage in contemporary economic ventures (Tedmanson 2014; Tedmanson and Essers 2015). Conceptualisations of place-based, temporal and historic dimensions in the study of Indigenous entrepreneurship are at the forefront of the complexity of studying contextualised entrepreneurship (Welter 2011). However, this provides much challenge for researchers both methodologically and theoretically.

For example, Indigenous enterprise development and entrepreneurship may be viewed as part of a continuum of community-based development which aims to contribute to Indigenous political, social and economic self-determination (Peredo *et al.* 2004; Dana and Anderson 2007; Tedmanson 2014). Peredo and colleagues (2004, p. 1) explain how:

> The 'second wave' of Indigenous development, after direct economic assistance from outside, lies in Indigenous efforts to rebuild their 'nations' and improve their lot through entrepreneurial enterprise.

Indigenous entrepreneurship is often theorised as being characterised by a desire for a form of 'national building' development or an underlying and/or expressed desire on behalf of Indigenous communities to reclaim economic control over one's territory, with which there may be thousands of years of ancient connectedness. There may also be aspects of communal, customary or tribal responsibility involved, as well as forms of collective or community-based development aimed at strengthening culture and consolidating and sustaining intergenerational kinship connections.

Indigenous communities worldwide continue to survive against the harsh and often near genocidal legacies of past (and in some cases continuing) colonial oppressions. It is important therefore to understand entrepreneurship as part of a range of political and resistance strategies engaged in by peoples seeking to transform the oppressed and often marginalised status of their communities. The specific national histories of colonial or contemporary Western domination over Indigenous communities continue to exert a powerful contextual influence over Indigenous peoples' economic engagement (Banerjee and Tedmanson 2010).

Australia's Indigenous peoples continue to be the most 'displaced' and disadvantaged in the nation, living in the poorest conditions in the poorest urban areas or, for those in the 'remote' communities in the desert regions of central, northern and western Australia, in what are 'Third World' conditions, encircled by the colonising culture of a globalising First World nation, 'another country hidden within our borders' (Macklin 2008, p. 1).

The idea that 'outsider' experiences enrich and even advance entrepreneurs and leaders is a key idea we wish to link to the study of Indigenous entrepreneurial leadership (Sanders 2008; Sinclair and Wilson 2002). Research by Terjesen (2007) suggests that entrepreneurs are more likely to emerge from those groups which are displaced, deprived or marginalised, persecuted or discriminated against. The notion of the entrepreneur as a 'displaced' person has been explored by Shapero (1975), and others, such as Frederick and Foley (2006), argue that disadvantaged groups, whether Indigenous or non-Indigenous, will often seek to improve their economic and social positioning through engagement in entrepreneurial activities (see also Dana and Anderson 2007; Foley 2000, 2008; Banerjee and Tedmanson 2010; Sullivan and Margaritis 2000; Lee-Ross and Mitchell 2007; Tedmanson 2014).

Over-represented in the prison system, with high levels of unemployment, the lowest educational attainment, highest incidence of chronic disease, highest rates of infant mortality and a life expectancy some 20 years less than non-Indigenous 'white' Australians, Indigenous peoples in Australia endure the cumulative, intergenerational effects of invasion and the violence of ongoing structural racisms.

Creating value through cultural knowledges

Like Indigenous cultures in Latin America, Africa, Canada, New Zealand and other areas of the South Pacific region, Australia's Indigenous peoples face not only the continuing impact of the colonial past in the neo-colonial present, but also the effects of globalisation which has brought greater inequalities in wealth distribution, increased surveillance by governments and corporate incursions into Indigenous lands. This colonial continuum is a structural discursive context impacting upon the denigration of Indigenous knowledges – ways of being, seeing, doing, organising.

Normative values shape presumptions about the naturalness of individualism and competition at the heart of discourses about entrepreneurial activity (Steyaert and Katz 2004). In Australia, as elsewhere, the term 'entrepreneurship' has become an iconic mantra; a metaphor for innovative thinking and new ways of organising economic change across a broad range of settings, spaces and places; and is popularly couched in terms about risk, innovation, people, discovery, processes and opportunities (Gartner 2001).

Growth and development are portrayed in singular terms of wealth generation rather than more holistic considerations of the social, environmental or cultural benefits brought about by entrepreneurship. Most entrepreneurship research is informed by Western epistemologies, using Western methodologies to reproduce Western theoretical frames of reference (Escobar 2006; Ogbor 2000; Chakrabarty 2000).

Yet, despite this challenging context – or, we argue, more likely because of it – Indigenous entrepreneurship is on the rise in Australia as well as internationally. While neoliberal politics discursively positions Indigenous communities as cultural enclaves which are uneconomic, Indigenous communities are pushing back. Indigenous business leaders are emerging who defy the colonially derived logic of the dominant cultures which invaded their worlds to pursue local, national and international markets in innovative and creative ways, on their own terms and often on their own lands.

Rather than abandon traditional languages and customary ways, there are small-scale strategic enterprises emerging in which Indigenous entrepreneurs are adopting innovative approaches for the creative conversion of customary activities into market engagement. Creating value for the market from cultural knowledge and practices offers Indigenous entrepreneurs unique competitive advantages. These entrepreneurial approaches often embrace high-tech solutions to issues of distances between supply and demand – 'across both cultural and physical spaces' (Tedmanson 2014, p. 12). Many of these initiatives also have a social dimension to enterprise activity and aim to maintain and celebrate uniquely Indigenous languages, dance, art, music and cultural mores, reframing culture as an asset, not a deficit.

Lee-Ross and Mitchell (2007) have researched the nexus between customary cultural practices and entrepreneurship among Australia's Torres Strait Islander populations, and suggest that entrepreneurial activity among communities of the Torres Straits is both significant and primarily culturally driven. 'Traditional land-owning entrepreneurs of the Torres Straits do not alter traditional patterns of behaviour but rather optimise them within a modern economic environment' (Lee-Ross and Mitchell 2007, p. 202). In analysing responses to their research based on Hofstede's (1998) categorisations, Lee-Ross and Mitchell note that among the Indigenous entrepreneurs they surveyed, 'community pride' and 'kinship respect' are important motivators. This study reveals a strong resistance to 'foreign rules' and economic regulations being imposed from 'outside', where they conflicted with cultural or social norms (Lee-Ross and Mitchell 2007, p. 203).

Cultural survival, maintenance and resistance meant more to those questioned than adherence to external impositions of entrepreneurial 'outside' norms such as growth orientation and profit maximisation. Other motivations for entrepreneurial activity include a strong desire for increased economic independence of family and community (Lee-Ross and Mitchell 2007). Innovative practices incorporating Indigenous traditional environmental knowledge in land management and customary care for country are spawning community-based and family/kin entrepreneurship in rural and remote Australia.

Similar findings may also be found in action research conducted by Banerjee and Tedmanson (2010) with Indigenous communities in central Australia.

Maintenance of culture across the generations was a key feature of the aspirations of leaders fostering local enterprises. As one Indigenous leader in this study explained:

> [B]efore I die I want my kids and their kids to know their stories and *Tjukurpa*, to understand and have pride in their culture and be able to live off this land right way ... and make an income from it ... live independent, not like old days, mission gone, government not helping – the past is gone but we can make it live again new way to hand on down the generations.
>
> (Banerjee and Tedmanson 2010)

Australian Indigenous entrepreneurs are involved in diverse industry sectors, from mining, pastoral and tourism to professional services, construction and creative industries. Many are pursuing the sustainable use of traditional knowledge about country, wildlife and fisheries, along with activities that hybridise traditionally oriented aspects of culture with new technologies while at the same time maintaining customary lifestyles (Hindle and Moroz 2010; Banerjee and Tedmanson 2010).

For Indigenous academic Dennis Foley (2008, p. 207), an Indigenous entrepreneur is someone who:

> alters traditional patterns of behaviour by utilising their resources in the pursuit of self-determination and economic sustainability via entry into self-employment, forcing social change in the pursuit of opportunity beyond the cultural norms of their initial economic resources.

Foley (2008) also suggests that Indigenous entrepreneurs are motivated by a need to 'correct negative social perceptions and racial discrimination than by a need for wealth creation' (p. 207). Foley also argues that as shown in the research referred to above, a major motivator for Indigenous Australians to be entrepreneurial is to 'give their children a better future life than they themselves experienced' (p. 208).

Indigenous cultural entreprneurship

While Indigenous Australians are three times less likely to be self-employed than other Australians, there is a growing trend towards innovation in Indigenous arts and cultural tourism, with Indigenous entrepreneurs using the opportunities afforded by new media to reach out to increasingly receptive global audiences.

The motivation for this entrepreneurial creativity is partly about resistance to the structural racism endured by Indigenous Australians but also as a means for expressing the resilience of community and cultural identity. It exemplifies the engagement of entrepreneurial ventures in the pursuit of 'important social change' (Calas *et al.* 2009, p. 552).

Management of the Indigenous arts sector is changing as Indigenous controlled arts businesses emerge to take control of their own intellectual and artistic capital. One example is the Ernabella Arts Centre in the Anangu Pitjantjatjara Yunkunatyjara (APY) Lands of central Australia. This Arts Centre has become an icon of Indigenous social entrepreneurialism. Managed by an Indigenous board, it is exporting its work to Japan, Europe and the USA to provide remuneration to its collective of artists and to contribute to local community initiatives. Ernabella Arts is a focus for the local community, not only for its arts and traditional crafts enterprise activities but also for its centrality to social, cultural and community well-being.

Indigenous traditional owner, local leader and artist Minutjukur (2006, p. 2) describes this entrepreneurial activity as part of the 'good things we … have done':

> We want to talk about some of the good things that we … have done to make our community strong.… Our independently incorporated art centre, Ernabella Arts, is the oldest in Australia and has operated continuously for 58 years. It is known all around Australia and the world.

Indigenous entrepreneurs are also contributing to the emergence of a new cultural tourism sector with businesses increasingly operated and controlled by Indigenous communities, clans or family kinship groups. Indigenous cultural tourism as a commercial endeavour has a history of both 'white'/non-Indigenous control as well as a quest for self-determination:

> I want to bring tourists here, only a couple at a time, small numbers, but can show them my country and tell stories and involve family – pass on culture and leave something here for family … so people can stay on our homeland.
>
> (Elder cited in Tedmanson and Guerin 2011, p. 2)

It has been well documented that much Indigenous entrepreneurship is based on community-driven desire to act collectively to resist 'non-Indigenous' domination and further Indigenous well-being, epistemological perspectives and social goals, with 'profit subordinated to social outcomes' (Peredo and McLean 2006, p. 23; Peredo and Chrisman-James 2006; Banerjee and Tedmanson 2010).

However, this nonetheless meets the criteria for entrepreneurship, being strategic, purposeful and often also profitable. It is the aims and outcomes of Indigenous entrepreneurial endeavours which may vary rather than the nature of the activity in and of itself. As Nicholls (2008) argues, a social entrepreneur uses entrepreneurial concepts to create, organise and manage ventures which can assist social change – bringing a concept to market to address public or social needs rather than purely consumer ones. Indigenous entrepreneurs are often leaders who seek to make a positive impact on their communities.

In research by Banerjee and Tedmanson (2010), cultural maintenance, resistance and resilience meant more to those questioned than adherence to external impositions of 'outside' norms. Other motivations for what may more readily be classified as social enterprise activity have included a stated desire for the increased economic independence of one's own family and kin as well as the broader community (Tedmanson and Guerin 2011).

Innovative practices which incorporate Indigenous traditional environmental knowledge in land management and customary care for one's country are spawning community-based and family/kin enterprise activity in Australia. However, the creative arts sector remains the single most productive source of Indigenous entrepreneurial activity across the country. Over many decades, Indigenous artists and Indigenous arts leaders have emerged as the drivers of a unique form of Indigenous entrepreneurship in Australia.

Two studies in Indigenous leadership and entrepreneurship

Research into leadership, like much research about entrepreneurship, has been dominated by Western ways of thinking and is deeply permeated with assumptions about what it is to be a leader and how leadership takes place. Non-Indigenous stereotypes posit a 'white' hetero male normativity privileging conventional orthodox notions of what it is to be, do and embody 'leadership'. Leaders in this context share many of the characteristics normatively assumed to be those also of entrepreneurs – decisive, authoritative, risk taking and power seeking.

Yet, as Evans and Sinclair (2015, p. 1) point out, there is a diversity of 'embodied ways individuals enact leadership across country and community'. In their pivotal study on Indigenous leadership in creative arts in Australia, Evans and Sinclair (2015) identify new insights into the spatially and culturally rooted nature of Indigenous leaders of arts enterprises. This research is connected to, resonates and is synergistic with existing research into Indigenous entrepreneurship and Indigenous entrepreneurs (Foley 2000, 2008; Tedmanson 2014; Reveley and Down 2009; Lindsay 2005; Hindle and Moroz 2010; Dana and Anderson 2007; Peredo and McLean 2010, p. 23; Peredo and Chrisman-James 2006; Evans 2012; Evans and Sinclair 2015).

Much of this new research on Indigenous leadership in entrepreneurship emerges from the voices and perspectives of Indigenous leaders (Begay 1991; Calliou and Voyageur 2007; Foley 2007; Ottmann 2005; Kenny and Fraser 2012). As Evans and Sinclair (2015, p. 2) explain, their research features the voices of over 29 Australian Indigenous artists and creative arts managers for whom leadership 'is a foreign world, laden with notions of White individualism and imperialism'.

The idea of leadership as the demonstration of individual power and authority is alien to most Indigenous cultures which have traditionally been of a more collectivist and communal nature (Scott 2009). As Sinclair puts it (2007, p. 70):

Leaders and followers collude in the imagining of leadership as heroic feats that will fix problems and usher in a new era.

Or as Indigenous leader Lillian Holt puts it, 'leadership is a White male idea' (cited in Sinclair 2012, p. 16). To understand Indigenous leadership as something different from the heroic 'white male norm' is to consider the enactment of lead*ing* as a dynamic fluid concept which is embodied rather than assumed. To understand this subtler sense of what Henry and Wolf-gramm (2015) term 'relational leadership' from a standpoint of Indigenous epistemology, an explanation of how white privilege shapes discourse is needed.

'White privilege' refers here not to a racialised category of skin colour but rather to a 'set of locations that are historically, socially, politically, and cultur-ally produced and moreover, are intrinsically linked with unfolding relations of dominance' (Frankenburg 1997, p. 6). It acts as an 'invisible norm against which other races are judged in the construction of identity, representation, subjectivity, nationalism and law' (Moreton-Robinson 2003, p. vii).

Acknowledging white privilege means accepting a critical analysis of power which reveals to us how not only bodies but also minds are colonised through the assimilatory practices of the dominating political economy of First World nation states. Through the commodification of human inter-action and the at times direct but more often indirect actions of colonising nations to assimilate (or eradicate) Indigenous cultural traditions, neoliberal notions about heroic individualism are writ large on the public psyche (Mander and Tauli-Corpuz 2006). Power is thus inscribed through forms of Western governance, practices of knowledge/truth formation and new modes of social, economic and political subjectivity.

However, Indigenous leadership and entrepreneurship is a contextual response for agency as individuals and communities respond to the trauma of the past in the reality of the powerful structural processes of colonisation still ever present. Indigenous leadership and entrepreneurship moves fluidly through Indigenous practices that embed cultural knowledge and practices interrupting the Western dominant domains. These practices, namely leading and entrepreneuring, are problematic and comprise complex tensions, not the least that characterised by the binary tension between Indigenous and Western values (Nkomo 2011).

For Indigenous communities, daily life experience in a globalised world not only involves coping with the historical legacies of colonisation but having to do so from within a dominant culture paradigm which suggests that only Western ways of knowing and being, managing and organising – or leading – can deliver a viable economic future for Indigenous peoples. Indi-genous societies are thus dominated epistemologically as well as economically, creating complex challenges for Indigenous leaders and entrepreneurs within a broader political climate that is often antipathetic towards Indigenous holis-tic or environmentally aware values.

As Evans (2012, p. 97) reveals however, there is a resilience and quiet defiance in the highly effective leadership practices of an increasingly successful Indigenous arts sector in Australia. Drawing upon the power of traditional cultural knowledge and buoyed up by a deep connectedness to country and community, Indigenous entrepreneurial leaders are creating economic as well as social change.

> Indigenous artists … identified a tension between thinking about leadership as a primarily individual pursuit and the reality of community embedded Indigenous leadership. Leadership as they saw it is a delicate balance between self and community.

Indigenous leaders in this study spoke of 'responsibility' to community and of 'commitment' to see business ideas through; and/or not wishing to be perceived as or called 'leaders', since this term has such an individualised stigma and lacks the characteristic of humility which so many of the leaders interviewed conveyed. As one accomplished 'leader' stated (cited in Evans 2012, p. 98):

> Like I don't consider myself to be a leader at all … I don't ever want to be centre stage. I get the biggest buzz when I see somebody else come up and shine.

In a similar way the respondents to research conducted by the second author[2] of this chapter with colleagues (Banerjee and Tedmanson 2012) expressed the same reluctance about being 'the business manager' or 'boss' or being seen as an 'entrepreneur'. Most respondents spoke of simply 'wanting a better life for their children and community'. Others wanted to turn cultural assets into something profitable – in which they, their family and community could express pride in their Indigeneity (Banerjee and Tedmanson 2012, p. 153):

> When I meet my clients for the first time, their eyes nearly pop out of their head when they see that I'm Aboriginal. So many times I've been asked 'I wanted to see the manager' and then I tell them, I'm the owner of the company.

Indigenous leaders and entrepreneurs also share the common challenge of both direct and indirect racisms in their efforts to enact their agency. While Indigenous cultural tourism, arts and creative enterprise activity is a dominant area for leading entrepreneurs, many may also experience disillusionment at what becomes a form of double bind:

> [T]he problem is that while cultural knowledge is taken from Aboriginal communities to run tourism businesses, business knowledge is not

transferred back to these communities.... For me the cost of engaging (in business) with the white system is assimilation.

(Banerjee and Tedmanson 2012, p. 155)

Unsatisfactorily Aboriginal art is still defined geographically ... those trapped in the urban grid are said to possess no cultural authority, to be inauthentic. In the remote context Aboriginal people are said to be part of the natural order of things; indeed, in the colonial mind we were imagined to be an aspect of the natural environment like flora and fauna.

(Browning cited in Evans 2012, p. 48)

This challenging conjunction around 'authenticity' in the eyes of the dominant culture creates tensions for Indigenous leaders and limits their entrepreneurial engagement. Evans and Sinclair (2015) conceptualise four 'territories' here to explicate these complex tensions. The first of these relates to 'authorisation in a bicultural world'. While the notion of authorisation may be said to refer to the means through which a leader gains their support, for Indigenous leaders such authorisation is contingent upon community sanction/s rather than, for example, on legal rights to 'ownership' as is more commonplace in a Western context. From an Indigenous perspective, 'cultural authorisation occurs where individuals are granted permission, by community members, to do culturally appropriate work' (Evans and Sinclair 2015, p. 9).

Another demanding territory is that of 'identity and belonging' – having voice and agency within the context of one's own enterprise. Like the 'eye-popping' visibility of the Indigenous tour operator cited above, taking voice also means people being exposed, 'as they challenge stereotypes and help create fluid, hybrid identities for others to observe and take up' (Evans and Sinclair 2015, p. 12). The territory of 'practice' is in itself part experiential and part an embodied journey over the territory of knowledge – working between contexts to generate new and innovative ways of seeing and being in the world.

Perhaps the hardest of all territories to transverse of those which Evans and Sinclair identify however is that of the haunting 'history, colonisation and trauma' (2015, p. 14) which stains the contemporary worlds in which people seek to exercise their leadership, creativity and entrepreneur*ing* dreams. It is in the act of doing that these enduring contexts can be challenged and revisited upon with resistance.

As Ashcroft and colleagues (1995) argue, *post*colonial does not mean *after* colonialism; it begins when the colonisers arrive and doesn't finish when they go home. Indigenous societies are thus dominated epistemologically as well as economically, creating complex challenges for Indigenous leaders and managers within a broader political climate often antipathetic to Indigenous holistic and ecological values (Tedmanson 2011).

While 'territories' have mapped some of the key dilemma domains from an Indigenous leadership perspective and focused particularly on the intersectional challenges for leaders straddling the bicultural tightrope, a similar intersectionality can be seen to emerge from Indigenous entrepreneurship research (Altman 2001; Foley and O'Connor 2013; Tedmanson 2014; Tedmanson and Essers 2015; Reveley and Down 2009; Lindsay 2005; Dana and Anderson 2007; Peredo and McLean 2010; Peredo and Chrisman-James 2006).

Altman (2001) describes what he refers to as the 'hybrid economy' to depict the competing tensions in the Indigenous sphere among the market economy (mainly mining, tourism, arts, retail, commerce and pastoral industries), the state or public sector economy (federal and state agencies) and the customary economy (so-called Indigenous 'subsistence' activities occurring outside the market such as hunting, cultivating bush foods and fishing as well as other productive cultural and community or social enterprise activities).

Regulating this hybrid economy are also various government and non-governmental agencies and policies which 'govern' Indigenous community life. Indigenous entrepreneurs are thus constantly juggling between competing forces, working at the intersection of Indigenous identity and 'white control'. The liminal terrains of intersectionality and hybrid fusion are deeply etched with what still remains as perhaps the greatest challenge facing Indigenous leaders and entrepreneurs – the way Indigenous lives, lands and aspirations are continually shaped and surveyed by the discursive constructions of the dominant non-Indigenous culture.

Challenging discourses

Entrepreneurship in the West and mainstream discourse has become not only an often unrealistic, ideal-type of social construction but also an aggressive political ideology, promulgated to reproduce conservative assumptions about individualism, risk taking and economic rationalism (Tedmanson *et al.* 2012, p. 532). Such hegemonic discourses shape policies and perceptions to serve conservative political and economic ends when discussing hegemonic discourses of entrepreneurship as ideological mechanisms.

More recently, as is evident in this edited collection, authors have sought to express other entrepreneurial subjectivities than just those of the archetypical 'white' male entrepreneur (see e.g. Essers 2009a, 2009b; Essers and Benschop 2007, 2009; Özkazanç-Pan 2009; Down 2006, 2010; Calas *et al.* 2009; Jones and Spicer 2009). This newer research calls into question the embedded stereotypes and covert – sometimes overt – whiteness which has dominated much of the entrepreneurship literature.

At hand for the field of critical studies is not just new takes on the nature, extent and scope of entrepreneurship to expose and highlight the negative side of this discourse but also articulations which reveal the continuities, similarities and differences among discourses of entrepreneurship and discourses of leadership. As Evans (2012) and Evans and Sinclair (2015) reveal in their important work on Indigenous leadership, the field of leadership studies is also resplendent with the discourses of normative 'white male' heroism as the epitome of leadership (Sinclair 2007, 2012; Nkomo 2011). Such discourses portray others as always wanting 'against an unproblematised Western template' (Evans and Sinclair 2015, p. 3).

As we point out in our separate but deeply connected fields of research into entrepreneurship and leadership, the popular conceptualisation of 'leadership' as a performative, up-front, extravert, charismatic and linear/forward directional way of being is somewhat counter to many Indigenous cultures and an anathema not only culturally but also from the standpoint of both functionality and epistemology. Similarly, discourses which eulogise the all-powerful, strategic, obsessively single-minded, driven 'entrepreneur' – individually conjuring up his (or her) success by 'pulling themselves up by their bootstraps' – is not only inappropriate but often deeply antipathetic if not offensive to many Indigenous peoples whose raison d'être for entrepreneurship is likely to be more rooted in collective and communal experience.

Postcolonial or critical aalyses of such discourse (see e.g. Banerjee and Tedmanson 2010; Dana and Anderson 2007; Foley 2003, 2006; Lindsay 2005) point out the continuing effects of colonial oppression and how the unquestioned sovereignty of Western epistemological, economic, political and cultural representations continues to negate and silence Indigenous communities. As Hindle and Moroz (2010) suggest, Indigenous entrepreneurship often focuses on a wider range of stakeholders and social impacts than simply economic success defined in market terms alone (see also Dana and Anderson 2007; Hindle and Lansdowne 2005).

Hence, Indigenous entrepreneurship is often marginalised as a research field. Yet it is a field like leadership studies also, where interdisciplinary research among sociology, anthropology, psychology, development studies, political economy and organisational studies can arguably contribute more together than separately (Reveley and Down 2009).

Conclusion

In this chapter we have focused on two specific examples of Indigenous entrepreneurship and explored how their rich diversity builds on and reproduces social and cultural capital and, we argue, contributes to social change. We have also argued that Indigenous entrepreneurial success is often largely culturally determined and racially loaded (Dana and Anderson 2007; Grant 2008; Tedmanson 2014; Evans and Sinclair 2015).

We have explored how leadership and entrepreneurship are culturally determined, as are the conceptualisations of what constitutes success, and that as a result recognition of the outstanding capacities of many Indigenous leaders is often lacking. Finally, we wish to close this chapter by acknowledging with deep respect the resilience and agency of Indigenous cultural entrepreneurs, their wisdom and their strength.

Notes

1 Australia has two Indigenous peoples: Aboriginal and Torres Strait Islander peoples. We acknowledge that some Indigenous people, including participants in the two studies presented in this chapter, prefer to be referred to by their specific nation instead of by a general term such as 'Indigenous'. However, in an effort towards connecting this chapter with the broader international discourse of Indigenous entrepreneurship and leadership, we choose to use the word 'Indigenous'.
2 While having ancestry which interconnects with Aboriginality, the second author of this chapter respectfully identifies as a non-Indigenous researcher in this her specialist field of knowledge.

References

Altman, J.C. (2001), *Sustainable Development Options on Aboriginal Land: The Hybrid Economy in the Twenty-first Century*. Discussion Paper No. 226, Centre for Aboriginal Economic Policy Research, Canberra: Australian National University.

Armstrong, P. (2005), *Critique of Entrepreneurship: People and Policy*, Basingstoke: Palgrave Macmillan.

Ashcroft, B., Griffiths, G. and Tiffin, H. (1995), *The Post-colonial Studies Reader*, London: Routledge.

Banerjee, S.B. and Tedmanson, D. (2010), Grass burning under our feet: Indigenous enterprise development in a political economy of whiteness. *Management Learning*, **41**(2), pp. 147–165.

Begay, M.A. Jr. (1991), *Designing Native American Management and Leadership Training: Past Efforts, Present Endeavors and Future Options*, Cambridge, MA: Harvard University Press.

Calas, M., Smircich, L. and Bourne, K. (2009), Extending the boundaries: Reframing 'entrepreneurship as social change' through feminist perspectives. *Academy of Management Review*, **34**(3), pp. 552–569.

Calliou, B. and Voyageur, C. (2007), Aboriginal leadership development: Building capacity for success. *The Journal of Aboriginal Management*, **4**(1), pp. 1–8.

Chakrabarty, D. (2000), *Provincializing Europe: Postcolonial Thought and Historical Difference*, Princeton, NJ: Princeton University Press.

Dana, L.P. (2015), Indigenous entrepreneurship: An emerging field of research. *International Journal of Business and Globalisation*, **14**(2), pp. 158–169.

Dana, L.P. and Anderson, R. (2007), *International Handbook of Research on Indigenous Entrepreneurship*, Cheltenham: Edward Elgar.

Down, S. (2006), *Narratives of Enterprise. Crafting Entrepreneurial Self-identity in a Small Firm*, Cheltenham: Edward Elgar.

Escobar, A. (2006), Difference and conflict in the struggle over natural resources: A political ecology framework. *Development*, **49**, pp. 6–13.

Essers, C. (2009a), *New Directions in Postheroic Entrepreneurship: Narratives of Gender and Ethnicity*, Malmö: Liber AB.

Essers, C. (2009b), Reflections on the narrative approach; Dilemmas of power, emotions and social location while constructing life-stories. *Organization*, **16**(2), pp. 163–181.

Essers, C. and Benschop, Y. (2007), Enterprising identities: Female entrepreneurs of Moroccan and Turkish origin in the Netherlands. *Organization Studies*, **28**(1), pp. 49–69.

Evans, M. (2012), *Be:Longing: Enacting Indigenous Arts Leadership*, unpublished Ph.D. thesis, Melbourne Business School, The University of Melbourne.

Evans, M. and Sinclair, A. (2015), Navigating the territories of Indigenous leadership: Exploring the experiences and practices of Australian Indigenous arts leaders. *Leadership*, 1–21. DOI: 10.1177/1742715015574318.

Foley, D. (2000), *Successful Indigenous Australian Entrepreneurs: A Case Study Analysis*, Brisbane: Merino Lithographics.

Foley, D. (2008), Does culture and social capital impact on the networking attributes of Indigenous entrepreneurs? *Journal of Enterprising Communities: People and Places in the Global Economy*, **2**(3), pp. 204–224.

Foley, D and O'Connor, A. (2013), Social capital and the networking practices of Indigenous entrepreneurs. *Journal of Small Business Management*, **51**(2), pp. 276–296.

Frankenburg, R. (1997), *Displacing Whiteness*, London: Duke University Press.

Frederick, H. and Foley, D. (2006), Indigenous populations as disadvantaged entrepreneurs in Australia and New Zealand. *The International Indigenous Journal of Entrepreneurship, Advancement, Strategy and Education*, pp. 1–16.

Gartner, W.B. (2001), Is there an elephant in entrepreneurship? Blind assumptions in theory development. *Entrepreneurship Theory and Practice*, **25**(4), pp. 27–39.

Grant, S. (2008), Contextualising social enterprise in NZ. *Social Enterprise Journal*, **4**(1), pp. 9–23.

Henry, E. and Wolfgramm, R. (2015), Relational leadership: An Indigenous Maori perspective. *Leadership*, 1–17. DOI: 10.1177/1742715015616282.

Hindle, K. and Lansdowne, M. (2005), Brave spirits on new paths: Toward a globally relevant paradigm of Indigenous entrepreneurship research. *Journal of Small Business and Entrepreneurship. Special Issue on Indigenous Entrepreneurship*, **18**(2), pp. 131–141.

Hindle, K. and Moroz, P. (2010), Indigenous entrepreneurship as a research field: Developing a definitional framework from the emerging canon. *International Entrepreneurship and Management Journal*, **6**(4), pp. 357–385.

Hofstede, G. (1998), Identifying organizational subcultures: An empirical approach. *Journal of Management Studies*, **35**(1), pp. 1–12.

Jones, C. and Spicer, A. (2005), The sublime object of entrepreneurship. *Organization*, **12**(2), pp. 23–46.

Jones, C. and Spicer, A. (2009), *Unmasking the Entrepreneur*, London: Edward Elgar.

Kenny, C. and Fraser, T.N. (eds) (2012), *Living Indigenous Leadership: Native Narratives on Building Strong Communities*, Vancouver: UBC Press.

Lee-Ross, D. and Mitchell, B. (2007), Doing business In the Torres Straits: A study of the relationship between culture and the nature of Indigenous entrepreneurs. *Journal of Developmental Entrepreneurship*, **12**(2), p. 199.

Light, I. (2004), The ethnic ownership economy. In C.H. Stiles and C.S. Galbraith (eds), *Ethnic Entrepreneurship: Structure and Process*, Amsterdam: Elsevier Science, pp. 3–44.

Lindsay, N. (2005), Toward a cultural model of Indigenous entrepreneurial attitude. *Journal of the Academy of Marketing Science*, **5**(1), p. 17.

Macklin, J. (2008), *Closing the Gap – Building an Indigenous Future*. Address to the National Press Club, Canberra, 27 February. Available at http://jennymacklin.fahcsia.gov.au/node/751 (accessed 22 May 2011).

Mander, J. and Tauli-Corpuz, V. (2006), *Paradigm Wars: Indigenous Peoples Resistance to Globalization*, San Francisco, CA: Siera Club Books.

Martin, D.F. (2002), Reforming the welfare system in remote Aboriginal communities: An assessment of Noel Pearson's proposals. In T. Eardley and B. Bradbury (eds), *Competing Visions, Refereed Proceedings of the 2001 National Social Policy Conference.* SPRC Report 1/02, Social Policy Research Centre, Sydney: University of New South Wales, pp. 317–325.

Minutjukur, M. (2006), A letter to Australians. *New Matilda Magazine.* Available at www.newmatilda.com/home/articledetail.asp? ArticleID=1810 (accessed 20 January 2009).

Montgomery, N., Peredo, A.M. and Carlson, E. (2012), The Bop discourse as capitalist hegemony. *Academy of Management Annual Meeting Proceedings.*

Moreton-Robinson, A. (2003), I still call Australia home: Indigenous belonging and place in a white postcolonizing society. In S. Ahmed *et al.* (eds), *Uprootings/ Regroundings: Questions of Home and Migration*, Oxford: Berg.

Nicholls, A. (ed.) (2008), *Social Entrepreneurship: New Models of Sustainable Social Change*, Paperback Edition, Oxford: Oxford University Press.

Nkomo, S.M. (2011), A postcolonial and anti-colonial reading of 'African' leadership and management in organization studies: Tensions, contradictions and possibilities. *Organization*, **18**(3), 365–386.

Ogbor, J. (2000), Mythicising and reification in entrepreneurial discourse: Ideology – critique of entrepreneurial studies. *Journal of Management Studies*, **37**, pp. 605–635.

Ottmann, J. (2005), *First Nations Leadership Development within a Saskatchewan Context*, Ph.D. thesis, University of Saskatchewan, Canada.

Ozkazanc-Pan, B. (2009), *Globalization and Identity Formation: A Postcolonial Analysis of the International Entrepreneur,* Ph.D. thesis, University of Massachusetts-Amherst.

Pearson, C. and Helms, K. (2013), Indigenous social entrepreneurship: The Gumatj clan enterprise. *Journal of Entrepreneurship*, **22**, pp. 43–70.

Peredo, A.M. and Chrisman-James, J. (2006), Toward a theory of community-based enterprise. *Academy of Management Review*, **31**(2), pp. 309–328.

Peredo, A.M. and McLean, M. (2006), Social entrepreneurship: A critical review of the concept. *Journal of World Business*, **41**(1), pp. 56–65.

Peredo, A.M., Anderson, R., Galbraith, C., Honig, B. and Dana, L.P. (2004), Towards a theory of Indigenous entrepreneurship. *International Journal of Entrepreneurship and Small Business*, **1**(1), pp. 1–20.

Peredo, A.M. and McLean, M. (2010), Indigenous development and the cultural captivity of entrepreneurship, *Business & Society*, **52**(4), pp. 592–620.

Reveley, J. and Down, S. (2009), Stigmatization and self-presentation in Australian entrepreneurial identity formation. In D. Hjorth and C. Steyaert (eds), *The Politics Aesthetics of Entrepreneurship*, Cheltenham: Edward Elgar, pp. 162–179.

Sanders, W. (2008), Outsiders or insiders? Strategic choices for Australian Indigenous leadership. In P. t'Hart and J. Uhr (eds), *Public Leadership: Perspectives and Practices*, Canberra: ANU ePress, pp. 145–153.

Scott, J.C. (2009), *The Art of not Being Governed: An Anarchist History of Upland Southeast Asia*, New Haven, CT: Yale University Press.

Shapero, A. (1975), The displaced, uncomfortable entrepreneur. *Psychology Today*, pp. 83–88.

Sinclair, A. (2005), Body possibilities in leadership. *Leadership*, **1**, pp. 387–406.

Sinclair, A. (2007), *Leadership for the Disillusioned*, Sydney: Allen & Unwin.

Sinclair, A. (2011), Being leaders: Identities and identity work in leadership. In A. Bryman, D. Collinson and K. Grint, *The Sage Handbook of Leadership*, London: Sage, pp. 508–517.

Sinclair, A. and Wilson, V. (2002), *New Faces of Leadership*, Carlton: Melbourne University Press.

Spiller, C., Erakovic, L., Henare, M. and Pio, E. (2011), Wise up: Creating organizational wisdom through an ethic of Kaitiakitanga. *Journal of Business Ethics*, **104**(2), pp. 223–235.

Steyaert, C. and Katz, J. (2004), Reclaiming the space of entrepreneurship in society: Geographical, discursive social dimensions. *Entrepreneurship & Regional Development*, **16**(3), pp. 179–196.

Sullivan, A. and Margaritis, D. (2000), Public sector reform and Indigenous entrepreneurship. *International Journal of Entrepreneurial Behaviour and Research*, **6**(5), pp. 265–275.

Tedmanson, D. (2011), Empowering women, empowering cultures. In P. Werhane and M. Painter-Morland, *Leadership, Gender, and Organization*, Issues in Business Ethics, 27, Netherlands: Springer.

Tedmanson, D. (2014), Indigenous social entrepreneurship: Resistance and renewal. In S. Grant and H. Douglas, *Social Innovation and Social Enterprise: Context and Theories*, Sydney: Palgrave Macmillan.

Tedmanson, D. and Essers, C. (2015), Entrepreneurship and diversity. In R. Bendl, I. Bleijenbergh, E. Henttonen and A. Mills, *Oxford Handbook of Diversity in Organisations*, London: Oxford University Press.

Tedmanson, D. and Guerin, P. (2011), Enterprising social wellbeing: Social entrepreneurial and strengths based approaches to mental health and wellbeing in 'remote' Indigenous community contexts. *Australasian Psychiatry*, **19**(1), pp. 3–33.

Tedmanson, D., Verduyn, K., Essers, C. and Gartner, W. (2012), Critical perspectives in entrepreneurship research. *Organization*, **19**(5), pp. 531–541.

Terjesen, S. (2007), Note to instructors: Building a better rat trap. *Entrepreneurship Theory and Practice*, **31**(6), pp. 965–969.

Welter, F. (2011), Contextualizing entrepreneurship – conceptual challenges and ways forward. *Entrepreneurship Theory and Practice*, **35**(1), pp. 165–184.

Wolfgramm, R. and Henry, E. (2010), *Careers as Life Journeys Envisioning the Future, Present and Past*. Published proceedings from the Traditional Knowledge Conference, Ngā Pae o te Māramatanga Centre of Māori Research Excellence, Aotearoa, New Zealand.

7 Feeding the city

The importance of informal warung restaurants for Indonesia's urban economy

Peter de Boer and Lothar Smith

Introduction

Objective numbers may be difficult to provide, but there are estimated to be more than half a million warung restaurants in Indonesia. A warung is a small business providing typical Indonesian food and beverages at affordable prices. Fried rice and noodles can almost always be found, as well as snacks such as fruit, fried bananas, coffee, tea and soft drinks. In addition, other daily necessities like cosmetics and cigarettes are sold. Warungs are largely indistinguishable from each other. Despite some variations in the kind of food offered, and the origin of the entrepreneurs, warungs have a recognisable business presence throughout Indonesia. These restaurants are hallmarks of street life in all major Indonesian cities, and are a prime source for a daily meal for a large part of the Indonesian population, and for the working population in particular. To sustain their income it is crucial that warung owners maintain affordable prices for customers who are predominantly working poor or from the lower, poorer classes.

Our research focuses on the following questions: How can these warungs be typified, and what does their existence point to when looking at their position and role from the perspective of entrepreneurship studies? What is the significance of their role in an urban economy, particularly in relation to various global economy influences? Is their existence one that is sustainable in the long run, and can their approach be perceived as sufficiently dynamic to counter a prevailing perception among city planners that they are afforded little regard as exponents of an informal economy? The chronicles of warung businesses reflect practices that contain a plethora of meaning, values and relationships that question prominent perspectives of present-day entrepreneurship. These practices are experienced in the everydayness of the periphery of an economic system that promotes a discourse of entrepreneurship associated with capitalist economic development (Imas *et al.* 2012). The key question here is whether they can play an enduring role in emerging national economies, such as those of the so-called BRIC countries and their many 'plus list' variations (the original members: Brazil, Russia, India and China), which have a high potential of becoming the world's largest economies in this century. This requires an assessment of modern-day entrepreneurship, also entailing the role of informal economic activities. Beyond the economic impact we also argue that the informal economy deserves attention for remaining so prominent, sustainable and effective, and thus being still very much part of the mechanics of large towns and cities: part of the fabric of everyday city life. In this vein the persistence of an informal economy points to the strength of localities, the value of micro-economies and the importance of traditions, even as they mutate to new forms, for providing social spaces in the daily lives of people. Thus modes of informal entrepreneurship like warung restaurants, in our view, cannot be simply called upon to mutate to a more advanced and formal economic mode, or else be disbanded, as was done with the *becak* (three-wheeled bicycle) taxi in various cities in Indonesia (including Jakarta).

In the next section we develop the theoretical approach through which we discuss the case of the warung. In the section that follows we provide some brief insights into the methodology we have employed in our research. Subsequently we turn to the empirics of the situation in two sections: first, examining the nature of warungs with the research questions in mind about how these matter, and whether it is only in a (semi) informal modality that these enterprises can function, followed then by a section delving into the actual workings of a warung. Both sections inform the conclusions of this chapter, whereby we return to the key question whether and how warungs represent a sustainable and important dimension of globalising cities in the Global South. In our findings we emphasise that this is certainly not only a question of economics.

Theorising the warung

Warung activities may generally be seen as being characterised by a fairly low resource base that is especially labour-intensive, usually drawing upon strong family involvement. They are also characterised by their small-scale approach and the way they mould into and with the society around them. Warung may be typified as largely unregulated, despite being rather visible businesses in Indonesian city environments (Blunch *et al.* 2001). To understand the informal nature of the warung better we turn first to the concept of informal economy.

The concept of informal economy has two important characteristics: it is '[1] hidden from official observation and [2] is carried out for the purpose of creating a positive income effect' (Renooy 1990, p. 11). Most of the warung facilities are owned and run by families: everybody participates, unless he or she is working somewhere else. Warung entrepreneurs play flexibly with the rules of property: they can open a restaurant in any building available, but may also do so out on the street by erecting a structure over a piece of 'public' pavement under which they locate their mobile kitchen and place a few sets of tables and chairs. Thereby these pavements lose their function as walkways, pedestrians resorting to the road alongside to get past the warung. Yet most pedestrians do so without much bother or disdain. More important is that these warungs maintain certain normal safety rules and stick closely to certain hygiene guidelines. For the former they thus also cooperate with parking attendants to avoid serious traffic problems and ensure smooth access routes.

Warungs effectively rely on word of mouth to exist as a viable business. Yet, while this may hold true for most restaurants and perhaps any caterer, their role goes beyond the general value of word of mouth, as they are often quite an integral feature within the social networks of their customers, extending their role of providing a square meal, to involvement with their customers in all kinds of exchanges. Such a strong social relationship is understandable given that many customers frequent the same warung at least once a day. The warung economy is thus fundamentally *social* in nature, such that interests and stakes in the economy are always the product of relationships to others. Dense urban social networks (Glaeser 2012, p. 36) allow for very personal approaches between entrepreneurs and their customers (DeLanda 2006, p. 79).

The formal sector in Indonesia needs the informal warung sector and its attached social relations to enable growth, while employees and entrepreneurs need a safety net for shadowing economic activities to facilitate continuity in everyday economies. Technical maintenance that is performed by an acquaintance in a social network may be, for some, simply an image of poverty or underdevelopment, but it is much more one of entrepreneurial flexibility, adaptation and creativity (Dovey 2012). The chronicles of the warung businesses also join the *microstorias* of Imas and colleagues (2012) in which the authors recognise the idea of small-scale entrepreneurs at the margins as *the other*, as a subaltern voice of present-day entrepreneurs. Furthermore, due to social interaction and collaborative practices, entrepreneurs learn reciprocally from one another about changing markets and technologies (DeLanda 2006, p. 79). To allow this informal entrepreneurship and its unofficial actions to flourish, governments need to turn a 'blind eye' to the informal economy thriving within its purview.

Methodology

This chapter is based on fieldwork conducted in 2013 in two neighbourhoods, Gejayan/Colombo and Karangmalan, in the city of Yogyakarta, Indonesia. These neighbourhoods were typical for the city as a whole, being densely populated, and accommodating residents belonging to the lower and middle classes. In addition, in these neighbourhoods the distinction between what might be called private and public space was rather blurred, a concept to which the warung was well suited, as we argue below.

How were the warungs in this study selected? In essence warungs, fitting more specific labels such as warteg, padang, satay, warung makan and tahu pong, were chosen if they fulfilled the following key conditions:

- Their location was (semi-) permanent. The warung was either housed in a building or reconstructed on the same location daily.
- The warung sold typical Indonesian food and beverages such as nasi goring, mie and teh.
- The warung provided tables and chairs for a minimum of five and a maximum olf 40 guests.
- the warung was not a subordinate of a chain of restaurants.
- the warung owner had at minimum of one and a maximum of ten employees (including family members).
- The warung was not registered by a government agency.

Beyond methods such as transect walks and observations conducted in an exploratory phase (to determine the scale of warung activity in the neighbourhood) a key role was played by interviews. These interviews were conducted with 25 warung entrepreneurs, five warung employees and seven public officers. The latter category was approached to gain a better understanding of the relationships and intensity of contact between warung owners and government agencies not only from warung owners, but also from the perspective of the local government. Questions in those particular conversations thus also focused on existing policies and programmes targeting warungs, as well as factual practises of exchange.

Figure 7.1 (a) Stylised and (b) aerial view of the Jalan Gejayan/Colombo research area.

Source: Google Earth.

Embedding the warung: micro-scale everyday livelihoods, macro-scale city economics

The warung entrepreneurs are a unique kind of entrepreneur, responding directly to the everyday needs of Indonesia's urban society. First, their existence feeds the human 'engine' of the city, catering to an expansive working-class majority in the city of lower class citizens who demand nutritious and tasty food at an affordable price. Second, they ensure that a long heritage of rich Indonesian cuisine is preserved. Local culture stays intact because the warung restaurants quite effectively guard the fundaments of an Indonesian food culture, warding off external global fast food or ready-go food formulas. Third, alongside other institutes such as the kampong and religious institutes, they also provide a certain social cohesion in a society, functioning as a hub of exchange within neighbourhoods, and as occasions for important as well as more menial social exchange in social networks of urban dwellers, be this with friends, workmates, others from the same village of origin, etc.

Fuel for the city's human engine

The warung customers may be considered as the engine of Yogyakarta and many other Indonesian city economies. Tens of thousands of warung-like restaurants are to be found in Yogyakarta, and these small and micro-scaled enterprises together form a rich cultural, economic and social phenomenon. The warung sector is a highly comprehensive sector that functions in the shadow of the formal economy – providing a response to a demand that cannot, it appears, be effectively achieved through formal channels. This relates not only to the nature of what they provide, but also to some typical characteristics of these enterprises operating on the fringes of a mainstay economy: they are small-scale operations, basically depending on (underpaid) family labour; employees and owners are predominantly low or non-educated and the warung is unregistered, unmonitored and uncontrolled by the government. At the same time the warung business anticipates the demand from millions of low-paid labourers for low-priced lunches and dinners – a forgotten market in the formal industry and a needed activity feeding the millions of low-paid workers toiling in the formal economy of the city.

We assert that the social and cultural role played by the warung sector is invaluable. But when we consider the warung sector as the fuel for the engine of Yogyakarta its economic value also becomes apparent. The engine is Yogyakarta's working class; the fuel is the daily lunch and dinner provided by the local warung. Yogyakarta resides in the outer and producing end of the global factory. The focus on producing furniture, coconut oil, palm oil and textiles, and facilitating tourism makes Yogyakarta subordinate to more highly developed consumer markets. In this context, the prevalence of a large low-paid working class may be understood as a class that stands to benefit greatly from the provision of easily affordable, reliable, familiar and accessible food and beverages.

The affordability issue, given the marginal income generated, is exactly the crux of the position of the warung restaurant. Informal mechanisms eagerly appropriate any form of business that is left untouched by the formal industry. And why not? Surely an underused market offers possibilities for entrepreneurs to execute viable economic activities at the borders of the formal economy. For policy makers this is sufficient reason to keep their hands off and their gaze away from the informal economy – informal actors will self-regulate to manage themselves anyway. Moreover, the case of the warung is a matter of scale: while a single warung restaurant may be rather limited in terms of its economic significance to a local economy, this fails to give cognisance to the hundreds of thousands of people that find their occupation in informal Yogyakarta. A large part of the population of Yogyakarta work in small, similar enterprises (mechanics, vendors, cabbies and the like), and the accumulation of all of these enterprises results in a rather significant shadow economy which needs to be understood as a blessing, given the rapid urbanisation of Yogyakarta. Wherever people congregate, informal entrepreneurs open up tailor-made businesses catering to local needs, making Yogyakarta a place worth living in, also for the poor and underserviced. Indeed, in many cases informality has guided urbanisation to places where urban plans and formal industries had previously failed. In the same vein warungs can reveal the pattern of people's lives and consumption in ways that more technocratic planning cannot envisage.

The culture of food

The food sold in warungs is typically Indonesian and generally closely bound to the local cuisine. A padang restaurant restricts its menu with the typical food from Padang (a city in Sumatra, Indonesia), the warung Semarang mainly sells seafood originally from the harbour city Semarang (Central Java), and a warung Lombok sells very spicy dishes from the island of Lombok. Two things occur here: different localities are able to present their food 'heritage' to customers, and customers are able to consume distinctive Indonesian food. Both actions contribute to strengthening the Indonesian identity: if you live in Indonesia, you eat Indonesian. Indeed, a warung restaurant hardly ever sells Western-style food, which is limited usually to the sale of soft drinks.

It is clear that food plays an important cultural role in Indonesia. Warungs certainly function as an integral part of Indonesian city urban lifestyles. This food culture may be linked to a sense of hospitality but also to the importance of quality of taste and variation therein. Many Indonesians take foreigners to diminutive 'authentic'-looking places to experience local culture and enjoy tasty (local) food. Beyond the value of warungs as keepers of an Indonesian cuisine, warungs are also time saving (saving precious cooking time – with dishes requiring long preparation), affordable, easily accessible, and can generally guarantee safe health standards. The issues of time efficiency and easy access are of particular value, as these relate well to a fast-modernising (urban) Indonesia. In an era where a growing economy is accompanied by more jobs in the formal service industries, people need to resort to time-saving warungs to ensure that they get a square meal. The warung has always been recognised as being *murah* and *mudah* (cheap and easy). Perhaps the growing economy is even reinforcing their importance, as more and more Indonesians in the big cities of the country spend long periods of time away from their homes because of their jobs, but also the time required to get from home to work, and vice versa. As one regular visitor of a warung put it, 'five years ago I drove from my house to Malioboro [the commercial centre of Yogyakarta] in ten minutes. Now, this takes me 20 minutes!' (Yudi, personal communication (p.c.), 2013). The limited time available to the Indonesian is a reliable indicator in stipulating the importance of the 'fast food' offered by warung restaurants.

Warungs and formal institutions: indifferent, or incompatible?

The strong pace of urbanisation and the uprising of dozens of urban entrepreneurs are overwhelming political and legal institutions (Firman 2009). This rapid pace of change through urbanisation has a direct effect on the organisation and materiality of public infrastructure, but also impacts upon people's perception of what is considered relevant and desirable and what is not. For example, from a planning perspective there is generally a desire to distinguish between private and public space. The warung however demonstrates that in an informal, urban setting such distinctions are difficult, and perhaps less relevant, to make. Public space is managed on the spot, and is modified, reorganised and challenged by the people who use these spaces, making them their own space. Warungs illustrate how local entrepreneurs can transform a public space into an opportunity for private use which becomes a space that is beneficial to both public and private users.

In the case of warungs this is exemplified by their heterogeneity and how informal they are considered to be. Warungs using public pavements and sometimes even parts of a road for their business are likely to be considered by some parts of society as dissident, and this gradual encroachment as illegal or, at the very least, undesirable. On the other hand, those established in proper buildings are considered to be as permanent and proper as any formal store. Hence warung restaurants are not easily classified as informal businesses as there are many diverse examples of warungs in operation. Instead the prevalence of such a variety, and the fact that overall Indonesian society is largely accepting of all forms, and given that most are clearly informal in their nature, their popularity is a clear sign of a unique integration between informal and formal economic activities in cities. This calls for a renewed and more realistic view of the informal sector. In addition, we could argue that any disputable business (e.g. selling fireworks, soft drugs, alcohol or providing security) can move between a legal or illegal form depending on its location. The learning we gain here is that several types of businesses may be seen to comprise elements that may be typified as legal or illegal, informal or formal. Second, the prevalence of all kinds of forms of warung, also those impeding other activities in the same space, showcase a creative and adaptive entrepreneurial behaviour within what is otherwise a potential friction zone in the city of Yogyakarta. They are condoned by city officials, but also by the public since, as long as their presence does not become too much of a hindrance, even a danger, to others, they are valued and supported.

As one entrepreneur put it: Here, the kampong [village] road is so small [i.e. quiet], it is not really disturbing anything' (Ibu Istel, p.c., 26 July 2013). This entrepreneur is not merely opportunistic about her own situation but is also genuinely concerned for public safety, as shown by her critique of fellow warung entrepreneurs located on the Jalan Kaliurang road:

> That [i.e. Jalan Kaliurang] is different because it is a big road. So many vehicles, ranging from the small and bigger ones, go through that road. But with the way they are located the parking line (for mopeds and such) is interrupting the road.

Beyond possible issues over the actual location of warungs, in particular those with a 'pop-up' character (to use a fashionable term in heyday city planning), there are other characteristics exemplifying a particular situation in which warung entrepreneurs position themselves vis-à-vis the state. For one, as we will argue in more detail in the following section, resources and channels used, and procedures followed have a clear and formal character. Promotional activities, recruitment of employees, training procedures, financial administration; business forums, and quality improvement systems all express quite governable, even conventional modalities that any business would require, which poses questions to those seeking to qualify these entrepreneurs as being part of the informal economy.

Yet, with the exception of a few owners, warung entrepreneurs tend to ignore official registration and do not pay income tax. Even if the local government chose to forcibly impose official registration, the warung sector would always be reluctant to adhere to administrative edicts. Generally, warung owners are less than eager to become subject to regulations forced upon them from outside the sector. Warung entrepreneurs believe that they are able to manage their own sectors, and individual businesses are run quite well through informal self-regulation. Thus they prefer to keep the sector closed off to all possible external influences.

A particular example of such a warding-off approach concerns formal conditions of employment, i.e. the status of an employee. Indonesia has five different categories of employees [kategori pekerja]. Two of the most common are the 'regular employee' and the *pekerja keluarga*. The *pekerja keluarga* is known as the (unpaid) family worker. This categorisation is somewhat

Figure 7.2 Warung restaurants on the roadside of Jalan Persatuan, Yogyakarta.
Source: Photograph by Peter de Boer (June 2013).

blurred, as employees included in the *pekerja keluarga* are considered to be unpaid workers and hence are also excluded from the official social security system, which saves costs for the warung owner. For these entrepreneurs it is therefore financially attractive to hire family members, or else to be strategically vague about the status of any other employee, as a way to avoid needing to pay for social security costs. To understand how this is achieved it is necessary to grasp the way cities are administered. The most decentralised form of this is called *kelurahan*. This functions as an umbrella for neighbourhood representatives who take care of various matters in the neighbourhood through systems such as *gotong-royong*, which arranges mutual assistance of neighbours to each other (e.g. a joint bearing of financial burdens in case of the loss of family), and *siskamling*, where adult males of the neighbourhood take turns to operate a night watch system. The *kelurahan* representatives are generally the only direct contact that warung owners wish to have with the government. Yet these representatives are not responsible for tax collection, as this falls under the remit of the national Ministry of Commerce, which delegates the task of tax collection to city district councils. At least in the case of Yogyakarta, this council is not in direct contact with local warung owners. These owners consider it more than enough to communicate with the government through their representatives. From our research conversations with warung entrepreneurs it has become clear that many are not aware of where to turn to for advice or information on whatever particular issue they may be experiencing at the time. Thus they limit themselves to their representatives for complaints, requests and discussions, avoiding a potentially hostile world 'out there'.

It appears that a business environment has been created in which small entrepreneurs have sufficient opportunities to avoid costs, time and effort following formal registration of their warungs and thereupon payment of taxes. Many of these entrepreneurs are simply not aware of whether registration at the city's government offices is obligatory. At the same time the position of the representatives suggests that a direct and sufficient link to the government does exist. As these relationships are often also quite socially embedded, the net result is a misplaced responsibility with these representatives. Warung entrepreneurs are thereby able to remain operational in the informal sector, maintaining socially negotiated standards, while avoiding the costs, time and effort incurred with a formal registration. The factual response from the state to this approach of warung owners is equally problematic. For instance, the large-scale apprehension among warung owners to commit to government legislation has resulted in a refusal to invite these owners to take part in government training programmes. Yet these programmes may potentially reverse some of the perceptions and wariness of warung owners about the role and influence of the state, and provide them with new insights into the potential of higher levels of cooperation with various state agencies (Pak Ekonomi, p.c., 11 July 2013; Pak Sudharmono Hadi, p.c., 22 July 2013; Ibu Watik, p.c., 26 July 2013). Entrepreneurs at the margins need to play a more central role in the organisation and management if city policies and programmes are to work properly. This requires the municipality to give proper space to informal modes of entrepreneurship, thus recognising their potential through bottom-up mechanisms rather than top-down policies (Imas *et al.* 2012).

The overall consequence of this clash of interests is that innovation among warung owners remains limited. Most warungs remain in the hands of the same family, and these families generally know each other well. Yet, despite the continuity in ownership, or perhaps because of it, there is a general fear of losing out to the competition, and to that end knowledge shared within the sector is nominal. Beerepoot (2005) drew similar conclusions in his analysis of learning processes among subcontractors in the furniture manufacturing business of the Philippines. He argues that a limitation to local circulation of knowledge among small-scale entrepreneurs is decisive in any further direction taken with business. He argues that all entrepreneurs base their decisions on knowledge gained from monitoring activities of other local producers. This is a rather recognisable phenomenon that was certainly also evident among warung owners in Yogyakarta.

Doing business

With such healthy competition, attracting customers to warung restaurants is a constant and hard-fought battle. To create a competitive business, warung restaurants, like other kinds of business, will try to achieve a certain distinctiveness from other similar businesses. In the light of the warung being embedded in the informal economy, which assumes a lack of prospects for making substantial differences, it is valuable to see what the available differentiating processes of warung enterprises are, thereby questioning whether these also differ incrementally or more fundamentally from comparative formal practices.

From empirical fieldwork, it emerged that customers maintain six standards to help them choose which warung restaurant to visit. These six standards are: (1) products on offer, (2) overall pricing, (3) location, (4) quality of food, (5) customer friendliness, and (6) interior comfort and style. These criteria, it may be argued, closely resemble those used by hospitality businesses around the world. The question is whether this parallel should surprise us, as also poor businesses simply lose out in an informal context.

These criteria are understood in various ways, however. Thus two entrepreneurs argued how they felt there to be very little need to market themselves further, since they could rely on sufficient numbers already established. One of these two entrepreneurs argued that, whilst at first glance the competition from nearby warungs might seem fierce, her business specialised in dishes from Lombok, a speciality very few other warungs offered in the vicinity. The other warung owner argued that the quality of her sambal was renowned, drawing a steady number of customers to her warung. While such arguments may hold true, they do not seem to represent a very innovative or resilient business strategy. The main cause of their apparent apathy towards advertising their businesses in order to expand their income seemed to be a lacking knowledge of how to better differentiate their business from others nearby.

The warungs do little in terms of visual advertising. Such advertising is generally limited to typical advertising posters that indicate what dishes are offered as specialities. These posters are hung on the outside of the restaurant, not in the vicinity. It is fascinating that this is a common practice that may be perceived as uncreative and non-entrepreneurial. Yet this approach has a long history, having followed on from a general consensus among warung entrepreneurs to agree to, and abide by, a certain set of co-established 'golden rules', which includes norms on the scale and location of visual promotions. As warung entrepreneur Suti voiced clearly: 'No, we are not doing any advertisements. Just mouth-to-mouth' (p.c., 18 June 2013).

From the discussions with warung entrepreneurs it emerged that there are few who will go beyond the conventional borders of advertising. Of course exceptions do exist. Thus one warung owner (Adit, p.c., 18 June 2013) explained that he used Twitter and Facebook – modern social media – to draw attention to his warung restaurant. Another warung restaurant owner,

Yudi (p.c., 18 June 2013), used leaflets, gave a grand opening and offered bonuses to attract customers (students in particular) to his newly opened warung restaurant. While the second owner might be considered more tres-passing of existing conventions due to its physical nature, both remain excep-tions to the rule.

Instead, monitoring of prices of products of fellow warung entrepreneurs was conducted much more actively. Most warung owners indicated that they readily adjusted the prices of their products to distinguish themselves from competitors. Low prices, one owner argued, are essential for warungs 'because, with expensive ice tea, people will not come here' (Tria, p.c., 16 June 2013). Offering food and drinks at cheap prices, however, is never the primary selling point. Kona (p.c., 16 June 2013), owner of a padang res-taurant in Karangmalang, argues that she is proud to operate the best warung in the city. She bases this on her prime location, on the tasteful padang food she offers, and the very presence of chairs. The availability of seating for cus-tomers is indeed often an issue with warungs. Yet, beyond being tasty, the place is also 'one of the cheapest around', which pinpoints the essence of affordability. With margins on food sold being small, prices cannot drop to too low a level, as this would make the individual businesses, but also the sector as a whole, financially unviable.

Regarding possible variations in design and level of comfort of a warung, it is safe to conclude that warung restaurants generally lack originality. Many warung entrepreneurs described and praised the commodities offered in their restaurants: Ahmed argued how: Out of all this small restaurants, we have television and ventilator' (p.c., 16 June 2013). However, most warungs offered such 'commodities', albeit with varying degrees of quality and avail-ability. They generally included a set of chairs (as a substitute to perching on the ground), a ventilator and a television. More extras will not be found in the warung and, apart from the rare incidence of some plants, interior styles are quite bland. As a possible boon of instant recognition as a warung, most warung restaurants miss an individual and sophisticated business concept in catering to a specific audience. Of course this does not affect the overall quality of the warung restaurants.

It would be wrong however to conclude from the above comments that warung owners are indifferent about their businesses. Instead, they rely on the social role of their restaurants. Overall, warung entrepreneurs indicated that they cared about their customers and considered it crucial to listen and respond to complaints and suggestions, to thus be able to increase the quality of their warung. Particularly in the case of regular customers, such recogni-tion of the opinions of customers is important. Often these warungs are fre-quented by customers living in the same neighbourhood and over time these customers may become well acquainted with those working in the warung: 'My employees know them, almost all of them' (Tria, p.c., 16 June 2013). Interaction among entrepreneurs, employees and customers is thus also quite informal. This easy interaction also enables straightforward exchanges of opinions about food and beverages served, prompting in warung owners an awareness of the desires of their customers:

> The owner is aware of the desires of the customers in here. They always ask to the customers that come in here, what is the taste of the food, and what is the recommendation to the product ... so that is how they learn to make better and better food.
>
> (Employee Ibu Patni, p.c., 18 June 2013)

The importance attributed to the quality of food and service may be translated as generic processes of quality enhancement, packaged in an informal environment. Quality enhancement is thereby a process in which customers are given a clear voice in the quality, quantity, price and overall impression of the provided service or product. In that sense it may be argued that customers become family members, and that the customer hereby also has the chance to compensate for the loss of independence in making their own food at home. Entrepreneurs truly anticipate this by taking heed of the wishes of customers to further enhance the quality of their dishes and service provided. However personified and idiosyncratic this process may appear, this is actually about the standardisation of products and services and thus cannot be labelled as unofficial or uncontrolled. Instead, the warung restaurants have incrementally implemented certain levels of standardisation, as was also the case with the prior example of the kinds of advertisements allowed, and the way prices are regulated. Such consensus also shows that it would be a misunderstanding to think that informal practices operate without institutional norms. Indeed, such engrained norms may prove to be much more effective than those implemented by external government agencies. Whether these 'informal' institutions are also sufficiently sophisticated and encompassing to take all kinds of measures with which to deal with all kinds of external shifts impacting upon business, for instance, with regard to changing energy needs, shifting demographics of cities and the regulation of waste, is doubtful.

Conclusions

By exposing the position of the so-called informal position of warung entrepreneurs, we hope to have shed some light on how to perceive the spatiality of such economic activity within more overall urbanisation processes in cities of the Global South. We suggest that there are also lessons to be learned about the role of the informal economy for cities elsewhere. The city of Yogyakarta breathes informality: informality is everywhere. Hence, the ignorant and dismissive attitude of public authorities in Indonesia tends to be disappointing to many in the warung sector. An unambiguous willingness to improve socio-economic conditions among small entrepreneurs is both desired and, as we argue, desirable. The presence of many thousands of micro- and small entrepreneurs tells us a story of creativity, ingenuity and mutual benefit for consumer and warung owner/operator.

The key question of this chapter was to ask whether, and how, warungs represent a sustainable and important dimension of globalising cities in the Global South. Are they an old-fashioned element that represents a fading past, or are they part of the contemporary urban economy? As we have indicated, the answer to this question is certainly not only one to be developed from an economic angle only, even if this is a principal dimension of warung activity. What emerges from the way warung entrepreneurs go about their business, how they understand the institutional and social environment they are part of, is that they really do perceive their economic landscape as essentially both local and socially interconnected. Their economy is that of the mouths they feed, the neighbourhoods of which they are part, and the specific locality of the larger city within which their warung operates. The social and cultural values of warungs attest to this parochial focus and sensibility of warungs. Warungs not only provide affordable, traditional Indonesian meals for those on a lower income, preserving their time and budgets; they are also a gathering place, providing an occasion for exchange with other customers and/or the warung owner. Warung restaurants are an integral part of the social fabric of life in Yogyakarta for the working poor.

While we concur with Beerepoot (2005), on the basis of our own empirical insights, that warungs are not necessarily innovative forms of entrepreneurship, we add that such a conceptualisation of 'innovation' is less significant in our analysis of warungs. The business model of the warung owner we argue is 'sufficient'; not only does it provide a steady financial return, but by maintaining its small-scale and socially intensive approach it also maintains a certain cultural identity that appeals strongly to customers. The explicit choice to limit dealings with the state to neighbourhood representatives allows warung entrepreneurs to maintain their businesses' informal character. This in turn enables warungs to keep a certain distance from a steadily intruding global economy in the city around them, without however losing sight of the needs of their customers. Instead, the character of the warung may well be considered as a welcome breathing space, a necessary thread in the increasingly stretched social fabric, for their customers. Informal economies in this way represent not only economic but also culturally and socially sustaining alternative spaces.

References

Beerepoot, N. (2005), Collective learning by artisanal subcontractors in a Philippine furniture cluster. *Tijdschrift voor Economische en Sociale Geografie*, **96**(5), pp. 573–584, doi:10.1111/j.1467-9663.2005.00487.x.

Blunch, N., Canagarajah, S. and Raju, D. (2001), *Social Protection Discussion Paper Series*, Washington, DC.

DeLanda, M. (2006), *A New Philosophy of Society: Assemblage Theory and Social Complexity*, London and New York: Continuum Books.

Dovey, K. (2012), Informal urbanism and complex adaptive assemblage. *International Development Planning Review*, **34**(4), pp. 349–368, doi:10.3828/idpr.2012.23.

Firman, T. (2009), The continuity and change in mega-urbanization in Indonesia: A survey of Jakarta–Bandung Region (JBR) development. *Habitat International*, **33**(4), pp. 327–339, doi:10.1016/j.habitatint.2008.08.005.

Glaeser, E. (2012), *Triumph of the City*, London: Pan Macmillan.

Imas, J.M., Wilson, N. and Weston, A. (2012), Barefoot entrepreneurs. *Organization*, **19**(5), pp. 563–858, doi: 10.1177/1350508412459996.

Renooy, P.H. (1990), *The Informal Economy: Meaning, Measurement and Social Significance*, Doctoral dissertation, Universiteit van Amsterdam.

Part III

Critiquing the archetype of the white, Christian entrepreneur

8 Injecting reality into the migrant entrepreneurship agenda

Trevor Jones, Monder Ram and Mária Villares

Introduction

As the twenty-first century has gathered momentum, a detectable (if somewhat grudging) shift has been evident in the tone of research into business ownership by migrant-origin ethnic minorities. In this chapter we begin by outlining the initial domination of this research field by *supply-side* models, designed to explain the quite startling growth of business ownership among some of the most socio-economically disadvantaged sections of advanced capitalist society. We will argue that the generally uncritical celebration of migrant entrepreneurship (Centre for Entrepreneurs 2014) has been part and parcel of a broader neoliberal paradigm, described by one leading economist as 'the dominant economic view since the 1980s' (Chang 2014, p. 70). These views portray migrant entrepreneurship as embodying the domineering values of the free market, where migrants mobilise their ethnic resources to succeed against all odds.

This celebratory tendency was backed up by the escalating numbers of start-ups by migrant entrepreneurs, which became the reference as an alternative mode of labour and social incorporation in Western societies. In this chapter, we also highlight how this growth in the volume of migrant firms did not run in parallel to their quality, showing historical continuities in relation to the features of these new businesses, such as their distribution across sectors, size or the nature of employment relations. Supply-side accounts have explored the value of 'ethnic resources', which implied the mobilisation of ethnic solidarity ties, but without a crucial reflection on the over-romanticised repercussions of using co-ethnic and family labour force, as well as informal practices. We will also argue that this neoliberal paradigm was reinforced by the blindness of patriarchal relations in the celebrated small migrant firms, which hid the invisible work of women and children within the ethnic economy.

Often owing rather more to blind faith than to evidence-based analysis, the supply-side approach first came under serious challenge at the turn of the century from the nascent *mixed embeddedness* model (Kloosterman *et al.* 1999), an increasingly influential approach which is discussed in detail here. This approach shifted the focus from the characteristics of migrants and their over-played willingness to become entrepreneurs, to whether and how the opportunity structures allowed them to participate in this activity. It also underlined the mixed nature of migrant firms at the micro- (personal networks), meso- (market) and macro- (state) levels of analysis, opening the black box of how the opportunity structure shapes the drivers and dynamics of migrant entrepreneurship. The chapter ends with an account of a further critique, the *entrepreneurial transition* (Jones *et al.* 2012), which may be considered an outgrowth of mixed embeddedness, and in effect an attempt to graft an evolutionary time dimension on to it. Thinking of migrant entrepreneurship over time helps us reveal the underlying structures of social exclusion and inequality that explain why and how migrants enter the ethnic economy in replacement processes in a vacancy chain.

Despite the nuances brought by *mixed embeddedness* and the intergenerational aspects highlighted by the *entrepreneurial transition*, we argue that racialised, classed and gendered inequality processes have not been brought to the forefront of the analysis of migrant firms. Hence, in the final section of this chapter, we propose new emerging themes that may help shape the future of the field.

Ethnic resources and the supply of migrant firms

For over 40 years there has been a vigorous growth in this research field, initially launched in the USA by the seminal works of Bonacich (1973) and Light (1972); and, in parallel with migrant entrepreneurship itself, spreading seemingly inexorably to Europe, Australasia and virtually every conceivable nook and cranny of the advanced capitalist realm (see the works collected in Dana 2007). This quite startling expansion reflects the way in which the post-1970s age of post-industrialism has created a variety of new market opportunities for businesses owned by migrants from the less developed world (Sassen 1996). Here we note that this key factor of market demand was rarely examined in depth, being usually accepted uncritically as an increasingly favourable business environment for small independent firms (Piore and Sabel 1984).

During its first phase, much of the research literature emerging to examine these entrepreneurs tended to write about them almost as if they really *were* imperialist conquerors, pushing aside native businesses and cashing in on the competitive advantage conferred by ethnic communal social capital (Flap *et al.* 2000) to achieve impressive levels of upward mobility and self-enrichment (Soni *et al.* 1987). Given that many of these entrepreneurs hailed from the very countries most victimised by the colonialism of their now hosts (Virdee 2014), the irony of this could hardly be more painful. Commenting rather sardonically on the way that, in Britain, this celebratory attitude fed into the politics of the 1990s, Kundnani (2014, p. 52) observes, 'Asian millionaires were feted by leading politicians and glamorised in the media – the closest Britain had to the American "rags-to-riches" immigrant dream'. Prompted by critical commentators like Harvey (2005), we might see this triumphalist *boosterism* as very much part of a neoliberal agenda constructing small enterprise as the embodiment of the competitive and innovative virtues of the free market, with entrepreneurs portrayed virtually as conquering heroes (Shane 2008). While this mindset probably attains its extremes in the USA, it is also well established in the UK, where during the Thatcherite 1980s small firms were extolled by policy makers as 'rescuing the UK economy from industrial decline … providing employment, facilitating economic restructuring and providing alternative strategies for local government' (Dannreuther and Perren 2013, p. 59). For these authors, such a narrative sets up a smokescreen designed to blot out social tensions around class and operates to underpin a process of incorporation by which an oppositional proletariat is converted into a stakeholding petty bourgeoisie.

These 'success' narratives may also be the result of a magnified accomplishment in self-employment when compared to the highly exploitative working conditions of immigrant workers in paid employment. In the specific case of racialised migrants, the smokescreen effect is perhaps even more potent, with conspicuous entry into the self-employed middle class providing a magic wand by which racism can be wafted away (Virdee 2014). This discourse also perpetuated the culturalist deceit of an inherent entrepreneurial propensity of certain Asian-origin groups (Jones and Ram 2012). For a time in the late twentieth century, we were led to believe that the religious and cultural values of South and East Asia were effectively synonymous with entrepreneurial values, a claim whose credibility was undermined by its indiscriminate application to Indian Sikhs (Helweg 1986), Hindus (Lyon 1973) and Pakistani Muslims (Werbner 1984). Elsewhere we have referred to this approach as the 'fallacy of ethnic exceptionalism' (Jones and Ram 2007a), highlighting the tendency to present migrant-origin enterprise as operating in a kind of hermetically sealed bubble protected from the normal rules of engagement with the real world business environment. Moreover, the overlapping of ethnic resources with class resources has revealed the complexities of taking into account cultural/ethnic traits in isolation from other types of resources. For example, disentangling 'ethnic' resources reveals that we should not take them into account without understanding the 'class resources' entrepreneurs have. Pessar (1995) reveals how ethnic resources may have a multiplier or substitution effect of class resources: cultural resources are accumulated and mobilised depending on the class position of entrepreneurs, where those entrepreneurs with higher financial capital may have better chances to use ethnic capital (e.g. access to a co-ethnic labour force); or a substitution effect: when migrants have higher class resources they are less likely to mobilise ethnic resources and vice versa (Pessar 1995). Expanding the 'fallacy of ethnic exceptionalism' argument, Storti (2014) dismisses a scholarly overemphasis on 'the social embeddedness of entrepreneurial action' as little short of 'deterministic'.

Further reflecting its logical incoherence, there is a somewhat disturbing moral ambiguity pervading the ethnic resources perspective. At the same time as the entrepreneur's mobilisation of co-ethnic and family resources is por-trayed entirely positively as a celebration of mutual solidarity and collective loyalty (Werbner 1984), there are also grounds for seeing it as patriarchal exploitation as a means of cutting costs through the underpaid labour of family members (Brah 1996; Phizacklea 1988; Collins and Low 2010). This celebratory aspect of ethnic resources has led to a romanticised view of the use of family ties, where entrepreneurial families work in cooperation and harmony for a common good: the success of the business and their social integration into the hegemonic values of the societies of settlement. These views neglect the impact of patriarchy on the household-business sphere. We have argued elsewhere how when analysing migrant firms we ought to take into account the dynamics within the family in order to understand the entre-preneurial strategies and the nature of work and employment within the firm (Ram and Jones 2008). The gender-blindness (Morokvasic 1999) of migrant entrepreneurship literature has hidden the realities of women and children in male-controlled family businesses within the ethnic economy. The intensity of the activities of the majority of the migrant enterprises leads to the recourse of the family as a usual alternative, where husbands, brothers and fathers rip off the benefits of the invisible and unpaid work of women. As Phizacklea (1988, p. 18) puts it, 'ethnic business is predominantly male controlled and labour intensive. Men are bosses and women are either workers or can expect to control or give orders only to other women.' In a passage which could well apply to the successfully portrayed South Asian family firms in Britain, Phizacklea goes on to argue that 'those ethnic groups deemed to be more "successful" in the business world than others, are characterised by social structures which give easier access to female labour subordinated to patriarchal control mechanisms' (1988, p. 18). Therefore, understanding the 'black box' of ethnic-cultural resources should take into account how the access and mobilisation of resources is multi-layered and embedded in power relations.

Yet, even at the height of the neoliberal consensus, there were opposing voices such as Rainnie (1989) arguing that, while the widely touted small firm revival (Piore and Sabel 1984) had certainly thrown up a vast volume of new ventures, this numerical explosion was mostly occurring on the terms of an ever more powerful and exploitative corporate sector. To all intents and purposes, the migrant firm population explosion is an amplified version of this, with a truly enormous *quantitative* growth in regions like Northwestern Europe disguising the low *quality* of the typical labour-intensive family firm struggling to survive in overcrowded cut-throat markets (Jones *et al.* 2000; Ram and Jones 2008). Refreshingly, the long dominant perspectives are now under challenge from new, more balanced models which seek to move away from an obsession with the *supply* side (i.e. the generative processes which (allegedly) create the teeming hordes of migrant businesses) and spotlight the interplay with the *demand* side, the changing external context of markets and the institutions which regulate them (Kloosterman and Rath 2003).

Somewhat surprisingly, the impetus for this change has come not from North America, the pioneer origin of this entire field of study, where for a brief interlude interest bloomed in a novel *interactionist* perspective canvassed by Waldinger *et al.* (1990) before fizzling out and returning towards social capital-based studies (Rath 2000). Instead the new direction was first sign-posted in Europe, where the Dutch team of Kloosterman, Rath and their associates have been the pacesetters. In the following section we review the *Mixed Embeddedness* model, the Dutch team's exercise in matching supply and demand of migrant business; and we conclude with an account of the *Entre-preneurial Transition* model, our own equally radical view of migrant business as in effect a transient stage for immigrants striving to incorporate themselves into the economy of their adopted country (Jones *et al.* 2012).

Mixed embeddedness

First floated by Kloosterman *et al.* (1999), this model is most fully fleshed out by Kloosterman (2010) in a paper which underscores the 'mixed' nature of the migrant firm's provenance by representing it as rooted in no less than three spheres of influence in a manner which we have envisaged in Figure 8.1: (1) *microsphere* (personal social networks); (2) *mesosphere* (market); and (3) *macrosphere* (politico-legal regulation).

   Here, the absolutely vital dividing line lies between the microsphere and the outer two zones, an opposition between personal social capital on the one hand and the market and state on the other. Whether deliberately or not, Kloosterman reproduces the binary oppositions of social theory, *gemeinschaft/gesselschaft*, as proposed by Tonnies as long ago as the late nineteenth century (1974/1887). While the first of this pair (*gemeinschaft*) refers to face-to-face bonds between individuals based on the mutual trust created by kinship and friendship, the second (*gesselschaft*) is defined by anonymous calculative ration-ality, with exchanges based solely on monetary value. Within the latter, no one gives anything away 'if it be not in exchange for a gift or labour equivalent to that he considers at least equal to what he has given' (Tonnies 1974, p. 74).

   The *gemeinschaft/gesselschaft* dichotomy casts light on the academic dis-course in ethnic relations. Unquestionably, the rise and rise of modernity has

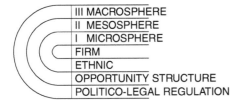

Figure 8.1 Kloosterman's 'Spheres of Influence'.

Source: Adapted from Jones *et al.* (2014).

massively expanded Tonnies' *gesselschaft* sphere at the expense of its more traditional counterpart, sometimes giving rise to a regretful 'sense of the passing of an allegedly organic world' (Delanty 2003, p. 15). Undoubtedly this sense of loss helps account for the popularity of Putnam's arguments about social networks (2000) as a means of personal empowerment in a world denuded of traditional bonds of solidarity. It is impossible to avoid the thought that many of the first-wave writers on migrant entrepreneurialism were governed by the supposition that newcomers from a pre-modern world would bring pre-modern *gemeinschaft* values with them; and that in the modern *gesselschaft*, where family and community values were assumed to be dead, the exclusive co-ethnic social capital of the migrants would grant matchless competitive advantage to their entrepreneurs through its informal provision of business resources. Perhaps part of the initial attraction of all this was that its view of business as based on intimate communal values served to soften the hard edges of competitive capitalism and even to illuminate the urban renewal possibilities of migrant business development in urban neighbourhoods of decline (Hall 1978).

Yet, with the increasing stridency of the neoliberal chorus from the 1980s onward, any illusions about 'cuddly capitalism' melted away to leave the migrant entrepreneurship agenda increasingly exposed as unbalanced, biased heavily towards the supply side with many of its assumptions about the almost inevitable entrepreneurialism of migrants unsustainable by empirical evidence (Jones and Ram 2013). It is precisely in outraged reaction to this excess of cultural determinism that the authors of mixed embeddedness insist on the vital need to place the migrant entrepreneur's personal social networks in the context of the larger political-economic context of the adopted country (Kloosterman *et al.* 1999). By no means do they wish to eliminate the microsphere from the analysis, and indeed Kloosterman (2010) waxes extremely enthusiastic about the way in which the very existence of many immigrant firms in Amsterdam is enabled solely by the uncosted inputs of finance and labour power contributed by their families and co-ethnics simply on the basis of mutual trust and solidarity.

The mesosphere

Even so, informal producer resources plus co-ethnic customer loyalty (Aldrich *et al.* 1981) can rarely support more than a handful of firms above basic survival level and Kloosterman's mesosphere (2010) attests to the migrant entrepreneur's need to seek market opportunities outside the womb-like protection of the *gemeinschaft*. At this point we can best appreciate the sheer realism of mixed embeddedness, its explicit recognition that the mesosphere is anything but a land of opportunity to be conquered by thrusting newcomers but instead a hostile environment where poorly resourced small-scale outsiders are pitched into vastly unequal competition with much larger, deeply entrenched incumbents. Not unexpectedly they tend to be excluded from the richest market potential, being mostly restricted to openings from which there is little demand from better-resourced native firms.

As Kloosterman (2010) demonstrates, these low-level residual markets fall into two categories according to whether they are declining or growing. In the declining sectors, typical activities are convenience retailing and clothing manufacture, obsolescent forms progressively abandoned by their original owners and picked up by the latest wave of incoming entrepreneurs. Although accurately described by Kloosterman as *vacancy chain opportunities*, we might perhaps use the term 'entrepreneurial scavenging' to capture the flavour of a rather desperate survival by means of the abandoned leavings of others. In effect this business consists of little more than making a living from leftovers.

Perhaps more closely capturing the sense of migrant business as called into being by historical change is Kloosterman's second category, *post-industrial low-skill opportunities* (2010). As outlined by writers like Sassen (1996), urban change is the key driving force here. In brief, post-industrial urbanism is characterised by a burgeoning professional labour force, a population of money-rich, time-poor individuals needing to buy in all manner of essential services. The crisis in the industrial sector, the increasing relevance of the service sector and a new division of labour explain the marginal position of migrants in Western societies, drawing a polarised urban landscape where sophisticated advanced companies share the cities with survival entrepreneurs settling in low-income areas (Sassen 1996; lund 2003). Among the entrepreneurial sectors growing as part of this are catering, personal services like hair and beauty, and taxi driving, all of which have been eagerly colonised by the immigrant self-employed. Understandably it is tempting to put a positive spin on this, identifying a new, small, business-friendly environment and enthusing with Collins *et al.* (1995, 17): 'The renewed growth of small business in industrial countries is a global phenomenon ... accompanied by the infusion of new ethnic owners.' More caustically, Scott (2012) refers to the type of work performed by these migrant opportunity seekers as 'servile activities', probably a more realistic assessment of their relative status in their adopted country. Servility of course is not a highly rewarded stance and the available research evidence on migrant entrepreneurs in catering (Jones and Ram 2007b) shows saturated markets, with new firms entering at an even faster rate than the break-neck growth in demand. In taxi driving, precarious returns are exacerbated by personal insecurity and physical danger (Kalra 2000), confirming a sense that these can only be described as pariah activities, absolutely indispensable for the larger society but punished rather than rewarded.

Going even further than Kloosterman's own pessimistic verdict on the prospects of those marooned in these sectors (2010), empirical findings on South Asian catering and clothing firms in Britain suggest that many of them fall so far short of profitability that they should not exist at all (Jones *et al.* 2006). In addition to their exposure to precarious market conditions, they must also operate under a constant legal shadow (Freeman and Ögelman 2000). That they manage to avoid extinction appears miraculous, a feat only achievable by the painful cost-cutting enabled by cutting regulatory corners; chiefly by using informal recruitment to bypass minimum wage and immigration legislation (Ram *et al.* 2006), as well as taking advantage of a gendered division of labour that positions women as a cheap and flexible labour force (Villares *et al.* forthcoming).

From a historical perspective, what is most striking about this entrepreneurial ghetto is its unshakable persistence over time. Dubbed 'sectoral inertia' by Sepulveda *et al.* (2011), the pattern of entrepreneurial segregation described by Kloosterman (2010) appears virtually unchanged whatever the fluctuations in the entrepreneurial personnel itself. One such fluctuation has been most conspicuously evident in twenty-first-century Northwestern Europe, where established flows of migrant labour from the Mediterranean basin, Maghreb, the Caribbean and South Asia have been partially replaced by economic migrants from post-Soviet Eastern Europe and asylum seekers from the war zones of the developing world. So geographically, demographically and socially variegated are these incomers that Vertovec (2007) has coined the phrase 'super-diversity' to capture the sheer complexity of this unprecedented multiculturalism. Yet, while many of these newcomers have set themselves up in self-employment, their novel provenance has been by no means matched by their business performance. On the contrary, the handful of studies hitherto directed at them in the UK (Jones *et al.* 2014; Sepulveda *et al.* 2011) have revealed a quite inordinate concentration in precisely the same low-level market entrapment that bedevilled their forerunners. According to Jones *et al.* (2014), over 60 per cent of East European entrepreneurs in the English East Midlands region are concentrated in these sectors as compared with only around 16 per cent for native owners. If anything, market exclusion is growing in intensity and, unhappily for believers in the liberating power of modern communications technology, it must be concluded that there is no evidence for any decisive advantage to be derived from the transnational connectivity now enjoyed by a great many migrant business owners (Jones *et al.* 2014).

Outside and above these marginalised market spaces lies the mainstream opportunity structure of the modern urban economy, the *post-industrial high-skills* sector according to Kloosterman (2010) or more graphically *cognitive-cultural* activities in Scott's terminology (2012). In contrast to the low-level sectors, with their relatively low demands on capital and skills and hence ease of business entry, the cognitive-cultural realm lies behind *high thresholds*, with technology- and capital-intensive activities demanding high-level educational qualifications and/or substantial financial investment from their prospective business owners. This rich mix of different forms of capital is then crucial in allowing such entrepreneurs to operate within this niche of the mainstream economy.

Although it goes without saying that the typically under-resourced migrant entrepreneur is automatically barred from these lush pastures, Kloosterman

(2010) nevertheless canvasses the idea that entry can be gained by immigrants willing and able to acquire the requisite human capital, a rationale whose feasibility is supported by the availability of universal secondary education in most of the host countries. Often this can be used as a launching pad to higher education, with fruitful entrepreneurial pay-off, as demonstrated by a highly encouraging study of Indian and Chinese graduate entrepreneurs in the UK (Mascarenhas-Keyes 2008). Similar support for this rationale is offered by findings on Turkish business consultants in the Netherlands (Rusinovic 2006), South Asian supply chain operators in the UK (Ram *et al.* 2011) and Asians in London's creative industries (Smallbone *et al.* 2005).

The macrosphere

What distinguishes mixed embeddedness most clearly from previous explanatory theories in this field is its identification of the politico-legal regulatory environment as a key influence on the supply of migrant entrepreneurs. In Figure 8.1 this sphere of influence appears as the 'macrosphere', the outermost zone whose outer location expresses its role as the ultimate set of control mechanisms. As laid out by Esping-Andersen (1990), there are significant international variations in regulatory regimes, with a particularly sharp divide between the deregulated neoliberal regimes of the USA, UK and Australasia on the one hand, and the relatively tightly regulated regimes of mainland Europe on the other. Picking up on the way in which immigration and labour laws affect opportunities for migrant entrepreneurs, Kloosterman *et al.* (1999) propose a marked contrast between the favourable environment of Anglo-America and the barriers imposed by mainland Europe (for example, stronger employment legislation). This contrast is confirmed by many of the contributors to a later international collection (Kloosterman and Rath 2003). Certainly at the time of the latter's publication, there were marked international leads and lags in the development of migrant business, with the UK's immigrant heritage entrepreneurial population discernibly larger than that in most of its European neighbours. Even so, given that the above collection does not contain any genuine cross-border comparisons, we would suggest this as a fruitful direction for future research.

Mixed embeddedness: some questions

As is only to be expected, mixed embeddedness is not without its flaws, often when apparently sound logic runs aground on the rocks of empirical reality. Immediately illustrative of this is the above argument about the advantages of deregulation for immigrant entrepreneurs, an assumption called into question by a UK study arguing that while weak regulation certainly encourages vast *quantities* of ethnic minority firms, the absence of any restriction on poorly equipped business entrants has negative effects on the *quality* of those firms. On a similar theme, a recent cross-border study of Pakistani entrepreneurs in

Britain, Denmark and Norway finds a better business performance in the highly regulated Scandinavian countries, largely due to better support from the state (Yassin 2014).

Similar tension between theory and practice arises from Kloosterman's apparent faith in human capital as a socio-economically propulsive force (2010). On the purely empirical level, Beckers and Blumberg (2013) use evidence from their Netherlands-based survey to question the effectiveness of the payoff from improved qualifications, while Ram *et al.* (2011) outline the painful personal costs endured by Asians in high-value supply chain firms.

One further respect in which this generally realistic model appears to pull its punches is its unwillingness to directly identify racism as the leading force excluding migrant entrepreneurs from mainstream markets. Certainly it is true that allegations of discrimination are frustratingly difficult to pin down and prove, not to mention legally sensitive. Even so there is now a growing body of qualitative evidence alleging discrimination by bank lenders (Alexander-Moore 1991; Jones *et al.* 1994) and customers (Ishaq *et al.* 2010) sufficiently robust to put the entire matter beyond question. We should also acknowledge the way in which the resource poverty handicapping the first generation of immigrant entrepreneurs in Europe results directly from their initial experience of labour market discrimination (Virdee 2014). Our feeling here is that the mixed embeddedness approach would be crucially enriched if racism were expressly foregrounded rather than hovering implicitly in the background as at present.

If the processes of a classed and racialised incorporation into the mainstream and ethnic economy ought to be conceptualised to advance the mixed embeddedness framework, gender should be brought to the forefront of the intersection between the meso- and macro-levels of analysis. As previously mentioned, one of the key omissions of understanding immigrant entrepreneurship critically is the neglect of the gendered character of migration, labour incorporation and gender dynamics within the firm and household. *Supply-side* accounts of immigrant entrepreneurship did not take into account systematically the role of gender dynamics. While the *mixed embeddedness* approach has balanced many shortcomings of previous accounts, it has failed to incorporate gendered processes of migration and employment, or to provide any insight into how the institutional framework impacts differently upon men and women in the countries of destination. For example, migration processes and patterns are also gender driven, as well as the demand for men or women in particular sectors of the economy, shaping the activities migrants can start up in terms of the financial, human and social capital they bring, but also what spaces of the market are available to them. In summary, the structural conditions that result in broader processes of racialised, classed and gendered inequalities should be taken into account.

The entrepreneurial transition

Taking realism on to a noticeably more apocalyptic path, we further propose that there is much highly suggestive evidence for migrant entrepreneurship as essentially a pathway rather than an end stage. Several decades ago, Bonacich and Modell (1980) advanced a historical view of Chinese and Japanese entrepreneurship in California as a kind of launching pad for the children of business families to enter professional employment. Implicitly this rationale gives rise to a three-stage intergenerational sequence: (1) the immigrant generation mainly engaged in low-level employment; (2) many of their American-born children striving for betterment through self-employment; (3) the children of these family firms propelled by accumulated business savings into higher education and thence to professional careers in law, education, administration, finance and (this being drawn from California) creative industries.

Harmonising with this, a more recent American study drawing from a large sample of Asian migrants shows that the acquisition of high-level human capital through education is far more likely to propel job seekers into professionalism than entrepreneurship (Nee and Sanders 2001). It would be difficult to miss the parallels here with recent trends in South Asian self-employment in the UK, where the reversal since the 1990s of a seemingly inexorable upward trend has been noted by several authors (Clark and Drinkwater 2000; Jones and Ram 2003; McEvoy and Hafeez 2006). Following on from this it was suggested that the very high educational success achieved by British-born Asians is being translated into two modes of career advancement:

1   diversification from low- to high-level self-employment;
2   a switch away from self-employment into professionalism, with the latter
    dwarfing the former quite substantially (Jones *et al.* 2012).

The emphasis is heavily on professionalism and, when we combine this with evidence that self-employment tends to be negatively correlated with educational credentials (Mascarenhas-Keyes 2008; Nee and Sanders 2001), the unavoidable conclusion is that human capital acquisition is a highly effective entrée into professional and white-collar employment for the native-born progeny of the immigrant generation. In this reading, the former's inordinately high concentration in self-employment (Campbell and Daly 1992) to be seen as a temporary abnormality, a short-term adjustment on the part of recently arrived newcomers with few recognised job market credentials and faced with a choice between low-skilled work for often discriminatory employers on the one hand; or creating work for themselves. Historically, this choice was given critical urgency by the deindustrialisation which began in the 1970s, with immigrants often disproportionately affected by a 'last-in-first-out' principle (Gaffikin and Morrissey 1992). Subsequent movement by the native-born generations towards professional and white-collar jobs might be seen almost as a 'normalisation' of the group's occupational structure, a trend enabled by the acquisition of personal resources making possible a more equal job competition than was available for the immigrant generation (Jones *et al.* 2012). This pattern resonates with accounts explaining the role of self-employment in the assimilation of migrants as a means of integration into the countries of destination: over generations, immigrant population will progressively access resources such as language skills and increasing levels of education, which will facilitate leaving those occupations and sectors overwhelmingly occupied by first-generation migrants (e.g. low-value self-employment) (Valdez 2006). In an effort of theoretical eclecticism, Chaudhary (2014) puts forward an alternative model where race and generation are integrated to analyse whether and how immigrants are retained in self-employment throughout generations. This *racialised incorporation* model (Chaudhary 2014, p. 9):

> sees both linear and nonlinear trajectories in socioeconomic incorporation (i.e., upward, downward, and stagnant) while simultaneously acknowledging the hierarchical nature of the socially constructed racialized categories into which groups are incorporated … allows researchers to simultaneously analyse the combined effects of race and generational status.

Chaudhary concludes that assimilation theories are helpful in understanding the incorporation of white immigrants, but cannot explain the racialised ways in which black, Asian and Hispanic migrants are incorporated into the US labour market, where the prestige of the sector brings nuances to these patterns.

In a similar fashion, the entrepreneurial transition approach, far from presenting this as a rigid formula, a master narrative with claims of historical inevitability and universal applicability, offers a flexible framework for researchers looking to make cross-border or historical comparisons. While departing from the thrust of mixed embeddedness in several respects, it is far from incompatible with that model, being on the contrary a direct response to the international variations flagged up by Kloosterman's macrosphere (2010). To a large degree these are variations in the historical evolution of migrant and ethnic minority entrepreneurship, with a highly mature core of origin in the USA and a process of outward diffusion producing less mature forms in geographically and culturally distant places. What is needed for a proper theoretical analysis of this is a coherent world-historical context based on a set of generic categories. These, it must be stressed, cannot be regarded as ironclad boxes but as something far more conditional and part of a tendency rather than of an inexorable march towards some kind of manifest destiny.

With this in mind, the proposed model must be carefully qualified in several respects, taking into account the differential impact of change upon specific ethnic communities. Immediately we can point to one conspicuous example in the UK of an immigrant-origin community – African-Caribbeans – whose employment history diverges significantly from the postulated sequence. Among scholars in the field, the glaring dissimilarities between this community and their South Asian fellow immigrants flared up as a controversial issue in the 1980s at a time when the sheer pace of the South Asian entrepreneurial explosion could hardly fail to be contrasted with the very limited and halting African-Caribbean business development (Ward 1987). Against this there were others who saw this rather moralising leaders-versus-laggards narrative as gratuitously divisive and suggested that, far from betraying failure, the low African-Caribbean self-employment rate was more indicative of a refusal to start-up firms in the stereotypical overcrowded immigrant markets (Jones *et al.* 1989; Ram and Jones 2008). Rather than betraying a lack of entrepreneurial spirit, their stance might be seen as more discriminating and selective (Ram and Jones 2008). Yet, whatever their motivations, it is unarguable that the African-Caribbean case does not conform to the thesis of business ownership as a necessary transition stage.

In spite of its deviation from the postulated sequence, we would argue that this African-Caribbean trend does not invalidate the model but rather confirms it – in the sense that we now have a coherent idea of what precisely is the norm from which it deviates. Arguably this applies equally to certain other ethnic communities whose deviation from the expected direction arises obviously from circumstances entirely external to the logic of the model itself. Exceptions to the rule they may be, an abstention which only serves to underline the existence of a rule. Immediately springing to mind here are the new migrants from Eastern Europe, whose unprecedented degree of mobility has been enabled by historically low air fares and who have been likened by Legrain (2007) to long-distance commuters; and portrayed by Favell (1998) as virtually transcending borders. Given the absence of even a long-term residential commitment to their country of destination, they can hardly be analysed in terms of intergenerational career paths in that country. By contrast, new migrant refugees from Africa and Southwest Asia are very likely to follow the proposed trajectory but at this infant stage any projections would be dangerously premature.

Equally uncertain is the future career path of that increasing proportion of the population classified as of 'mixed origin', usually the issue of unions between immigrants and native whites. Perhaps unsurprisingly there are no self-employment patterns sufficiently discernible to mark out this hybrid population as following any particularly distinctive labour market trajectory. To the extent that the link between ethnic origin and self-employment may be said to be weakened, or even erased, this appears to parallel the increasing tendency of young migrant-heritage business owners to reject the label 'ethnic' or 'immigrant' entrepreneur in favour of the pure identity of 'entrepreneur' (Ram *et al.* 2006). What this suggests is that, whether or not migrant enterprise itself is actually fading away, the label is being voluntarily abolished by its own bearers.

Less immediately apparent but equally resistant to classification are variations *within* the South Asian population, with the entrepreneurial transition evidently much more marked among the Indian-origin population than it is among Pakistanis or Bangladeshis (Ram and Jones 2008). Canvassing possible explanations, McEvoy (2013) enquires whether this is a time-lag effect, with Indians further advanced in the transition sequence; or whether the Islamic faith embracing a majority of the other two groups (Beckford *et al.* 2006) imposes a brake upon the cultural modernisation which is the essence of the transition. Muddying the waters still further, McEvoy (2013) also points out that Pakistani self-employment figures tend to be inflated by large numbers of taxi drivers whose self-employed status may be more legal than actual. Yet, even leaving such technicalities aside, we must still ask how far we are entitled to simply assume that traditional belief systems will simply wither away to leave the field open to the modernisation of the labour market. If tradition were to prove more obstinate than is customarily assumed, then we would have to revise many basic assumptions about developments in this field.

In its fundamentals, this last case lends itself to the description 'a known unknown'. While this phrase has been mercilessly mocked by political satirists, it is actually rather apt in the present instance, where there is acute awareness of profound changes afoot in the economic, cultural and demographic realms but a general inability to predict how far they might go. As well as uncertainties about specificities, there are also more overarching concerns, as captured in a recent newspaper article rather ominously entitled 'What might a world without work look like?' (Power 2013). In this piece the author is taking up a theme floated by Standing (2011), who highlights the way in which the latest phase of labour-saving technology eliminates not solely low-skill routine work but also higher level occupations, throwing even professional workers into a state of what he calls 'precarity'. In such a situation, where employment itself has been virtually abolished, it may well transpire that self-employment provides an urgently needed substitute livelihood for people irrespective of national or ethnic origin. Already it has been noted that the UK self-employment rate has risen to near-unprecedented levels and in all regions outside London this has arisen as partially compensation for the loss of jobs since 2008 (Clark 2014). Such an event is so extreme as to call into question Blanchflower's claim: 'self-employment: more may not be better' (2004). At the time of writing this was an admirably measured critique entirely endorsed by the present authors but entirely conditional upon the unproblematic availability of the employed work judged to be the superior alternative for most economically active adults. Ultimately of course cataclysmic shifts in the labour market serve to undermine any serious attempt at long-term projection.

Emerging themes

In this final section of the chapter we aim at proposing themes and approaches that may enhance the current knowledge on migrant entrepreneurship and, in particular, the theoretical developments of mixed embeddedness and the *Entrepreneurial Transition* perspectives.

The role of market regulations in comparative perspective

Understanding the role of market regulations for migrant entrepreneurship requires a genuine cross-country comparison, which is yet to take place. The advantages of market (de)regulation to enter entrepreneurial activities suggest that the Anglo liberal environment should lead to higher volume in entries, while a more highly regulated market (continental Europe, Scandinavian countries) would have a strong selection effect with only the better-equipped entrepreneurs entering this activity. Mixed welfare state models, such as the cases of Mediterranean or post-Soviet countries, would make interesting cases to study the intersection between market and state and its effects on migrant entrepreneurship. The impact of these aspects of the *macrosphere* in the mixed embeddedness model is yet to be analysed in a comparative manner.

Advancing the Entrepreneurial Transition model

The Entrepreneurial Transition model brings a new perspective on how migrants navigate the labour market throughout generations, looking at the dynamics of social inclusion and exclusion over time. However, this approach should also take into account the (1) gendered patterns of inclusion, and (2) the opportunities in high-value entrepreneurship.

Transitions in gender ideologies

The current Entrepreneurial Transition model accounts for a dynamic inter-generational perspective on immigrant entrepreneurship. However, it has certain limitations in incorporating shifts in gender ideologies and educational aspirations. Migration processes might have an impact on the availability of an unpaid labour force within the family and the business. Gender relations are not immutable within migrant families and it has been argued elsewhere how migration may also derive from changes in gender ideologies and aspirations for men and women in their countries of destination (Pessar 2005).

For example, the new roles in the productive sphere for women, access to higher education for the new generations of men and women, as well as exposure to more egalitarian values can shape the occupational aspirations for the children of migrants. These gendered processes may also impact upon the availability of a labour force for migrant entrepreneurs. It is essential to understand how entrepreneurs make their decisions about the education of their sons and daughters, their involvement in the business when growing up, as well as the opportunities available in paid employment for the children of migrants. The outcomes of these 'gender transitions' would also help us understand the (non-) reproduction of an unpaid labour force that would block or facilitate business turnover.

Diversification of sectors

We argue that it is also important to understand the types of industries where migrants are setting their businesses throughout generations. The Entrepreneurial Transition approach integrates how new generations transit from low- to high-value self-employment, but these 'high-value' activities have not been consistently analysed in relation to the relative weight, sectors, size and outcomes in relation to the previous generation's enterprises, and the strategies behind this mode of incorporation. More research is needed to understand which and how migrants enter into these high-value added sectors.

Conclusions

This chapter has outlined ways in which the migrant entrepreneurship narrative has striven to break away from neoliberal ideology, 'the dominant economic view since the 1980s' (Chang 2014, p. 70). Tenacious though this traditional supply-side mindset may be, we have attempted here to expose its lack of realism, its selectivity in concentrating either on sheer quantity of firms at the expense of quality (Barrett *et al.* 2003); or on an unrepresentative glamorous elite of high-flying success stories (Gidoomal 1997). These processes are confirmed by recent research on the effect of new migrants entering the ethnic economy in the UK, which shows that despite the changes in the composition of new migrants, there are significant historical continuities in the sectors they are incorporated into and their performance (Jones *et al.* 2014; Sepulveda *et al.* 2011).

Challenging this, both mixed embeddedness and the transition model are animated by an unromantic awareness of entrepreneurship as an extremely demanding livelihood (Scase and Goffee 1982), whose inherent hazards are inevitably magnified for racialised outsiders (Jones *et al.* 2014). Mixed embeddedness provides a lens for understanding the role of the state, markets and personal networks in the origin and proliferation of immigrant entrepreneurship, while the entrepreneurial transition perspective incorporates a generational dimension, situating low-value self-employment as a transitional category for newcomers. We propose new venues to advance this proposed model, through bringing a comparative perspective between different modes of regulation, and greater awareness of the role of gender ideologies and break-out strategies.

References

Aldrich, H., Cater, J., Jones, T. and McEvoy, D. (1981), Business development and self-segregation: Asian enterprise in three British cities. In C. Peach, V. Robinson and S. Smith (eds), *Ethnic Segregation in Cities*, London: Croom Helm.

Alexander-Moore, D. (1991), *The Black Cinderella*, London: Unity Books.

Ålund, A. (2003), Self-employment of non-privileged groups as integration strategy. *International Review of Sociology*, **13**(1), pp. 77–87.

Barrett, G., Jones, T. and McEvoy, D. (2003), The United Kingdom: Severely constrained entrepreneurialism. In R. Kloosterman and J. Rath (eds), *Immigrant Entrepreneurs: Venturing Abroad in the Age of Globalisation*, Oxford: Berg.

Beckers, P. and Blumberg, B.F. (2013), Immigrant entrepreneurship on the move: A longitudinal analysis of first-and second-generation immigrant entrepreneurship in the Netherlands. *Entrepreneurship & Regional Development*, **25**(7–8), pp. 654–691.

Beckford, J.A., Gale, R., Owen, D., Peach, C. and Weller, P. (2006), *Review of the Evidence Base on Faith Communities*, London: University of Warwick.

Blanchflower, D. (2004), Self-employment: More may not be better. *Swedish Economic Policy Review*, **11**, pp. 15–74.

Bonacich, E. (1973), A theory of middleman minorities. *American Sociological Review*, 38, pp. 583–594.

Bonacich, E. and Modell, R. (1980), *The Economic Basis of Ethnic Solidarity: Small Business in the Japanese American Community*, Berkeley: University of California Press.

Brah, A. (1996), *Cartographies of Diaspora: Contesting Identities*, London: Routledge.

Campbell, M. and Daly, M. (1992), Self-employment in the 1990s. *Employment Gazette*, June, pp. 269–292.

Centre for Entrepreneurs (2014), *Migrant Entrepreneurs: Building Our Businesses Creating Our Jobs*. Available at http://centreforentrepreneurs.org/wp-content/uploads/2015/11/MigrantEntrepreneursWEB.pdf (accessed 7 June 2016).

Chang, H.J. (2014), *Economics: The User's Guide*, London: Pelican.

Chaudhary, A.R. (2014), Racialized incorporation: The effects of race and generational status on self-employment and industry-sector prestige in the US. *International Migration Review*, **49**(2), pp. 318–354.

Clark, K. and Drinkwater, S. (2000), Pushed in or pulled out? Self-employment among ethnic minorities in England and Wales. *Labour Economics*, **7**, pp. 603–628.

Clark, T. (2014), Explosion in self-employment across UK hides real story behind upbeat job figures. *Guardian*, 6 May, p. 6.

Collins, J. and Low, A. (2010), Asian female immigrant entrepreneurs in small and medium-sized businesses in Australia. *Entrepreneurship and Regional Development*, **22**(1), pp. 97–111.

Collins, J., Gibson, K, Alcorso, C., Castles, S. and Tait, D. (1995), *Shop Full of Dreams – Ethnic Small Business in Australia Sydney*, Sydney and London: Pluto Press.

Dana, L.P. (ed.) (2007), *Handbook of Research on Ethnic Minority Entrepreneurship: A Co-evolutionary View on Resource Management*, London: Edward Elgar.

Dannreuther, C. and Perren, L. (2013), The entrepreneurial subject as a political signifier: Corpus analysis of forty years of Hansard. *International Small Business Journal*, **31**(6), pp. 603–628.

Delanty, G. (2003), *Community*, London: Routledge.

Esping-Andersen, G. (1990), *The Three Worlds of Welfare Capitalism*, Princeton, NJ: Princeton University Press.

Essers, C., Benschop, Y. and Doorewaard, H. (2010), Female ethnicity: Understanding Muslim migrant businesswomen in the Netherlands. *Gender, Work and Organization*, **17**(3), pp. 320–340.

Favell, A. (1998), To belong or not to belong: the post national question. In A. Favell and A. Geddes (eds), *The Politics of Belonging: Migrants and Minorities in Contemporary Europe*, Aldershot: Ashgate, pp. 209–227.

Flap, H., Kumcu, A. and Bulder, B. (2000), The social capital of ethnic entrepreneurs and their business success. In J. Rath (ed.), *Immigrant Businesses: The Economic, Political and Social Environment*, Basingstoke: Macmillan.

Freeman, G.P. and Ögelman, N. (2000), State regulatory regimes and immigrants' informal economic activity. In J. Rath (ed.), *Immigrant Businesses*, Basingstoke: Palgrave Macmillan, pp. 107–123.

Gaffikin, F. and Morrissey, M. (1992), *The New Unemployed: Joblessness and Poverty in the Market Economy*, London: Zed Books.

Gidoomal, R. (1997), *The UK Maharajahs: Inside the Asian Success Story*, London: Nicholas Brealey.

Hall, P. (1978), The inner cities dilemma. *New Society*, 3 February, pp. 223–225.

Harvey, D. (2005), *A Brief History of Neo-liberalism*, Oxford: Oxford University Press.

Helweg, A. (1986), *Sikhs in Britain*, Oxford: Oxford University Press.

Ishaq, M., Hussain, A. and Whittam, G. (2010), 'Racism: A barrier to entry? Experiences of small ethnic minority retail businesses. *International Small Business Journal*, **28**(4), pp. 362–377.

Jones, T. and Ram, M. (2003), South Asian businesses in retreat? The case of the UK. *Journal of Ethnic and Migration Studies*, **29**(3), pp. 485–500.

Jones, T. and Ram, M. (2007a), Re-embedding the ethnic business agenda. *Work, Employment and Society*, **21**(3), pp. 439–458.

Jones, T. and Ram, M. (2007b), Urban boosterism, tourism, and ethnic minority enterprise in Birmingham. In J. Rath (ed.), *Tourism, Ethnic Diversity, and the City*, London: Taylor and Francis, pp. 50–66.

Jones, T. and Ram, M. (2012), Revisiting ... ethnic minority businesses in the UK: A review of research and policy developments. *Environment and Planning C: Government and Policy*, **30**(6), pp. 944–950.

Jones, T., Mascarenhas-Keyes, S. and Ram, M. (2012), The ethnic entrepreneurial transition: Recent trends in British Indian self-employment. *Journal of Ethnic and Migration Studies*, **38**(1), pp. 93–109.

Jones, T., McEvoy, D. and Barrett, G. (1994), Labour intensive practices in the ethnic minority firm. in J. Atkinson and D. Storey (eds), *Employment, the Small Firm and the Labour Market*, London: Routledge, pp. 172–205.

Jones, T., McEvoy, D. and Barrett, G. (2000), The market as a decisive influence on ethnic minority business. In J. Rath (ed.), *Immigrant Businesses: The Economic, Political and Social Environment*, London: Macmillan, pp. 37–53.

Jones, T., Ram, M. and Edwards, P. (2006), Shades of grey in the informal economy. *International Journal of Sociology and Social Policy*, **26**(9/10), pp. 357–373.

Jones, T., Cater, J., de Silva, P. and McEvoy, D. (1989), *Ethnic Business and Community Needs*, Report to the CRE, Liverpool, Liverpool Polytechnic.

Jones, T., Ram, M., Edwards, P., Kiselinchev, A. and Muchenje, J. (2014), Mixed embeddedness and new migrant enterprise in the UK. *Entrepreneurship and Regional Development*, **26**(5–6), pp. 500–520.

Kalra, V. (2000), *From Textile Mills to Taxi Ranks*, Aldershot: Ashgate.

Kloosterman, R.C. (2010), Matching opportunities with resources: A framework for analysing (migrant) entrepreneurship from a mixed embeddedness perspective. *Entrepreneurship and Regional Development*, **22**(1), pp. 25–45.

Kloosterman, R. and Rath, J. (2003), *Immigrant Entrepreneurs: Venturing Abroad in the Age of Globalization*, New York: Berg/University of New York Press.

Kloosterman, R.C., van Leun, J. and Rath, J. (1999), Mixed embeddedness, (in)formal economic activities and immigrant business in the Netherlands. *International Journal of Urban and Regional Research*, **23**, pp. 252–266.

Koh, M. and Malecki, E. (2014), The emergence of ethnic entrepreneurs in Seoul, South Korea: Globalisation from below. *The Geographical Journal*, **182**, pp. 59–69.

Kundnani, A. (2014), *The End of Tolerance: Racism in 21st Century Britain*, London: Pluto Press.

Legrain, P. (2007), *Immigrants: Your Country Needs Them*, London: Little, Brown.

Light, I.H. (1972), *Ethnic Enterprise in America: Business and Welfare among Chinese, Japanese, and Blacks*, Berkeley: University of California Press.

Lyon, M. (1973), Ethnicity in Britain: The Gujarati tradition. *New Community*, **2**, pp. 1–11.

Mascarenhas-Keyes, S. (2008), *British Indian and Chinese Student, Graduate and Academic Entrepreneurship*, London: Department for Innovation, Universities and Skills.

McEvoy, D. (2013), Minority self-employment in the United Kingdom: Temporal and spatial trends. Paper presented at the Annual International Conference of the Royal Geographical Society, London.

McEvoy, D. and Hafeez, K. (2006), The changing face of ethnic minority entrepreneurship in Britain. Paper presented at the fourth Interdisciplinary European Conference on Entrepreneurship Research, Regensburg, Germany.

McEwan, C., Pollard, J. and Henry, N. (2005), The 'global' in the city economy: Multicultural economic development in Birmingham. *International Journal of Urban and Regional Research*, **29**(4), pp. 916–933.

Morokvasic, M. (1999), Beyond the hidden side: Immigrant and minority women in self-employment and business In Europe. Paper presented at the IOM Workshop on Women in Migration, Geneva.

Nee, V. and Sanders, J. (2001), Understanding the diversity of immigrant incorporation: A forms-of-capital model. *Ethnic and Racial Studies*, **24**(3), pp. 386–411.

Pessar, P. (1995), The elusive enclave: Ethnicity, class, and nationality among Latino entrepreneurs in greater Washington, DC. *Human Organization*, **54**(95), pp. 383–392.

Pessar, P. (2005), Women, gender, and international migration across and beyond the Americas: Inequalities and limited empowerment. In *Expert Group Meeting on International Migration and Development in Latin America and the Caribbean*, Mexico City: UN.

Phizacklea, A. (1988), Entrepreneurship, ethnicity and gender. In P. Bhachu and S. Westwood, *Enterprising Women: Ethnicity, Economy and Gender Relations*, London: Routledge, pp. 16–27.

Piketty, T. (2014), *Capital in the Twenty First Century*, Cambridge, MA: Harvard University Press.

Piore, M.J. and Sabel, C. (1984), *The Second Industrial Divide*, New York: Basic Books.

Power, N. (2013), What might a world without work look like? *Guardian*, 4 January, p. 34.

Putnam, R. (2000), *Bowling Alone: The Collapse and Revival of American Community*, New York: Simon and Schuster.

Rainnie, A. (1989), *Industrial Relations in Small Firms: Small isn't Beautiful*, London: Taylor & Francis.

Ram, M. and Jones, T. (2008), *Ethnic Minority Business in Britain*, Milton Keynes: Small Business Trust.

Ram, M., Patton, D. and Jones, T. (2006), Ethnic managerialism and its discontents: Policy implementation and 'ethnic minority businesses. *Policy Studies*, **27**(4), pp. 295–309.

Ram, M., Woldesenbet, K. and Jones, T. (2011), Raising the 'table stakes'? Ethnic minority business and supply chain relationships. *Work, Employment and Society*, **25**(2), pp. 310–325.

Rath, J. (2000), Immigrant businesses and their economic, politico-institutional and social environment. In J. Rath (ed.), *Immigrant Business: The Economic, Political and Social Environment*, Basingstoke: Macmillan.

Rusinovic, K. (2006), *Dynamic Entrepreneurship: First and Second Generation Immigrant Entrepreneurs in Dutch Cities*, Amsterdam: Amsterdam University Press.

Sassen, S. (1996), *Losing Control? Sovereignty in the Age of Globalization*, Berkeley, CA: Columbia University Press.

Scase, R. and Goffee, R. (1982), *The Entrepreneurial Middle Class*, London: Croom Helm.

Scott, A. (2012), *A World in Emergence: Cities and Regions in the 21st Century*, Cheltenham: Edward Elgar.

Sepulveda, L., Syrett, S. and Lyon, F. (2011), Population super-diversity and new migrant enterprise: The case of London. *Enterprise and Regional Development*, **23**(7/8), pp. 469–497.

Shane, S. (2008), *The Illusions of Enterprise: The Costly Myths that Entrepreneurs, Investors and Policy-Makers Live By*, New Haven, CT: Yale University Press.

Smallbone, D., Bertotti, M. and Ekanem, I. (2005), Diversification in ethnic minority business; The case of Asians in London's creative industries. *Journal of Small Business and Enterprise Development*, **12**(1), pp. 41–56.

Soni, S., Tricker, M. and Ward, R. (1987), *Ethnic Minority Business in Leicester*, Birmingham: Aston University.

Standing, G. (2011), *The Precariat: The New Dangerous Class*, London: Bloomsbury Academic.

Storti, L. (2014), Being an entrepreneur: Emergence and structuring of two immigrant entrepreneur groups. *Entrepreneurship and Regional Development*, **26**(7–8), pp. 521–545.

Tonnies, F. (1974/1887), *Community and Association*, London: Routledge and Kegan Paul.

Valdez, Z. (2006), Segmented assimilation among Mexicans in the Southwest. *The Sociological Quarterly*, **47**(3), pp. 397–424.

Vertovec, S. (2007), Super-diversity and its implications. *Ethnic and Racial Studies*, **30**(6), pp. 1024–1054.

Villares, M., Ram, M. and Jones, T. (forthcoming), Female immigrant global entrepreneurship: From invisibility to empowerment? In *Handbook of Female Global Entrepreneurship*, London: Routledge.

Virdee, S. (2014), *Racism, Class and the Racialized Outsider*, Basingstoke: Palgrave Macmillan.

Waldinger, R., Aldrich, H. and Ward, R. (1990), Opportunities, group characteristics and strategies. In R. Waldinger, H. Aldrich and D. Ward (eds), *Ethnic Entrepreneurs*, London: Sage.

Ward, R. (1987), Ethnic entrepreneurs in Britain and Europe. In R. Goffee and R. Scase (eds), *Entrepreneurs in Europe*, Beckenham: Croom Helm, pp. 83–104.

Werbner, P. (1984), Business on trust: Pakistani entrepreneurship in the Manchester garment trade. In R. Ward and R. Jenkins (eds), *Ethnic Communities in Business*, Cambridge: Cambridge University Press.

Yassin, N. (2014), A cross-national comparative study of immigrant entrepreneurship in the United Kingdom, Denmark, and Norway: A qualitative investigation of business start-up experiences. Unpublished Ph.D. thesis, University of Huddersfield.

9 Bringing strategy back

Ethnic minority entrepreneurs' construction of legitimacy by 'fitting in' and 'standing out' in the creative industries

Annelies Thoelen and Patrizia Zanoni

This chapter investigates the narrative strategies of ethnic minority entrepreneurs in the creative industries to acquire legitimacy in their professional field. Despite recent research in the stream of critical entrepreneurship studies that take up the ethnic minority entrepreneurs' own point of view (e.g. Essers and Benschop 2007, 2009; Essers *et al.* 2013; Pio 2005, 2007; Raghuram and Hardill 1998), we still see featuring in the bulk of ethnic minority entrepreneurship literature a paradigm that is overlooking the individual level, and which tends to focus on macro-structural characteristics constraining and/or enabling entrepreneurial actions of the *group* as a whole. This dominant paradigm typically studies the effects on ethnic minority businesses caused, on the one hand, by ethnic group features such as culture (e.g. Basu and Altinay 2002; Light and Bonacich 1988; Nwankwo 2005; Ram and Deakins 1996), ethnic networks (e.g. Chaganti and Greene 2002; Light 1972) and family bonds (e.g. Bagwell 2008; Ram 1992) or, on the other, by the host environments such as the formation of (ethnic) markets (e.g. Aldrich *et al.* 1985; Waldinger *et al.* 1990; Zhou 2004), specialisation in niches (e.g. Boyd 1998) and access to resources (e.g. Basu and Werbner 2001; Ram *et al.* 2003).

As a whole, the classical stream of ethnic minority entrepreneurship literature thus often highlights the perceived macro 'structural disadvantage' of ethnic minority entrepreneurs and their businesses (Brettell and Alstatt 2007). This omnipresent paradigm is critiqued by the research in critical entrepreneurship studies for deploying power on ethnic minority entrepreneurs by denying them agency as individuals, and representing them as almost 'non-subjects' (e.g. Essers and Benschop 2007). We state in this chapter, in line with this emerging stream, that the dominant paradigm indeed obscures 'individual' or 'personal' perspectives and identity constructions – needed to understand the experiences and heterogeneity of ethnic minority entrepreneurs – but we also aim to take this argument further by stating that the 'entrepreneurial' or 'business' actions are also obscured – needed to profoundly understand ethnic entrepreneurial business strategies and experiences.

The partisan nature of the dominant paradigm is namely co-highlighted by the stark contrast with the highly individualistic and agentic representation of majority entrepreneurs and their strategies present in mainstream entrepreneurship literature (Essers and Benschop 2007; Nicholson and Anderson 2005; Ogbor 2000). Here, (majority) entrepreneurs are understood as strong, heroic personalities, unconstrained risk-taking agents (Knight 1921) who spot opportunities, act, and create new value (Jones and Butler 1992; Schumpeter 1934) to build their own business success. Therefore, we aim in this chapter to stress that it is both the neglect of the individual identity and experiences (cf. Essers and Benschop 2007), together with a focus on ethnic entrepreneurial business strategies, which strongly reflects the ethnocentric vantage point, thus excluding powers of most current ethnic minority entrepreneurship research (Ogbor 2000).

In this chapter, in line with a structurationalist view (Giddens 1982, 1984), we thus understand ethnic minority entrepreneurs not only to be 'caught' in contexts that constrain and enable their actions in specific ways, but aim at taking up a 'agent-centred' approach, to develop a more heterogeneous image than is currently held of ethnic minority entrepreneurship by including the 'act of entrepreneurship' in our study. We therefore conceptualise ethnic minority entrepreneurs as entrepreneurial agents who – embedded as they are in specific social, economic and cultural contexts – possess the capability to not only actively construct their identities, yet also detect new demands, create opportunities, and envision successful business futures (cf. Werbner 1999). Our perspective contributes to the current literature by investigating how ethnic minority entrepreneurs narratively deploy their ethnic minority identity and experiences, with the specific goal of acquiring business legitimacy in their professional field. This means that the political nature of this chapter is an emancipatory one, accounting for ethnic minority entrepreneurs as full subjects, in agentic charge of both their identities and their business actions.

Ethnic entrepreneurs as strategic narrators crafting legitimacy

Taking issue with the overly deterministic group portrayals of ethnic minority entrepreneurs in most literature, this study aims to focus on their agency. In particular, we investigate how ethnic minority entrepreneurs narratively craft legitimacy, or 'credibility and the social process of acceptance and recognition by the strategic peers and other stakeholders constituting a field' (Aldrich and Fiol 1994; Baumann 2007; De Clercq and Voronov 2009; Deephouse 1999; Johnson *et al.* 2006; Suchman 1995). Legitimacy is considered key to businesses, as it allows access to quintessential resources needed for success (Minahan 2005; Wilson and Stokes 2004). Entrepreneurial narratives play a fundamental role in entrepreneurial legitimisation (Lounsbury and Glynn 2001) because they communicate and frame the entrepreneurs' specific personal and business intentions in a way that shows conformance to existing, socially constructed norms – thus becoming believable for others (Johnson *et al.* 2006). At the same time however, to acquire legitimacy entrepreneurs need to also demonstrate their innovativeness, or ability to break through those norms (Aldrich and Fiol 1994; De Clercq and Voronov 2009; Lounsbury and Glynn 2001).

Reflecting this double dynamic, legitimacy has been theorised as resulting from an entrepreneur's capacity to balance 'fitting in' and 'standing out' (De Clercq and Voronov 2009; Deephouse 1999). Drawing upon the work of Bourdieu (1986), De Clercq and Voronov (2009) argue that the cultural capital of entrepreneurs, or the capacity to access and mobilise institutions and cultural products of a society (De Clercq and Voronov 2009, pp. 404–405), enhances their ability to fit in. Namely, their objectified (material goods), institutionalised (formal certifications and credentials) and embodied (norms of behaviour) cultural capital demonstrates to social actors their understanding of and conformance with the sector's dominant norms and practices. At the same time, their symbolic capital, or 'the ability to manipulate symbolic resources, such as language, writing, and myth' (De Clercq and Voronov 2009, p. 406) bringing something original, new and different into the field enables them to stand out. We take up this theory, in line with a structurationalist view (Giddens 1982, 1984), meaning that we understand our ethnic minority creatives to be agents acting in a contextual structure. For their legitimacy narratives they namely use discursive material deriving from a common and shared context, which they agentically pick and use to construct their 'fitting in' and 'standing out' stories.

Ethnicity in legitimacy constructions of entrepreneurs in the creative industries

The idea that crafting legitimacy involves balancing 'conformity' and 'innovation' (De Clercq and Voronov 2009) vis-à-vis peers and stakeholders in the field offers a suitable lens to examine the specific narrative strategies of ethnic minority entrepreneurs. This is particularly the case in the creative industries, which include advertising, architecture, arts and antiques markets, crafts, design, fashion, film, music, performing arts, publishing, software and computer services, computer games and radio and TV (DCMS 2001). These industries offer a particularly suitable context for studying ethnic minority entrepreneurs' narrative crafting of legitimacy because they are often majority dominated, and entrepreneurs in these fields depend disproportionately on the perceptions and approval of others in the field for their success (Towse 2003). As creatives generally work through temporary collaborations including peers, clients, distributors and employees (Blair 2001; Delmestri *et al.* 2005; Jones 2002; Menger 1999), they need to continuously engage in narratives that legitimise their work and maintain social acceptance (Baumann 2007; Faulkner and Anderson 1987; Wilson and Stokes 2004).

As ethnic minority creative entrepreneurs are embedded in fields which are often dominated by ethnic majority stakeholders, they are thus, on the one hand, likely to deal with their minority background as a potential barrier to construct narratives signalling to others that they and their businesses 'fit in' in the field. In Western societies, ethnic minorities are often discursively constructed in highly negative terms as the culturally subordinate 'other' and are further associated with socio-economic disadvantage (Said 1978). On the other hand, an ethnic minority background may also provide these entrepreneurs with specific narrative opportunities to 'stand out' (Brandellero 2011; Mavrommatis 2006). In the creative industries diversity is also commonly portrayed as a source of authenticity, innovation and creativity (Florida 2002, 2005a, 2005b; Smallbone *et al.* 2005, 2010; NESTA 2006). Due to this 'double opportunity structure', ethnic minority entrepreneurs are called to discursive action to proactively construct their identities and entrepreneurial strategies, this both to avoid possible essentialisation due to imposing an unwanted identity by others, as well as to construct one's identity as a useful discursive resource for legitimacy.

Our analysis thus focuses on the narrative crafting of legitimacy, as this perspective allows us to highlight entrepreneurs' conscious and individual deployment of their ethnic identity in their business narratives. Therefore, we approach ethnic entrepreneurs here as active meaning makers who are able to narratively position themselves along the available discourses by selectively combining discursive elements to craft professional legitimacy (Brown and Coupland 2005; Brown 2006; Hytti 2003) and resist using discourses that might undermine their legitimacy (Johnson *et al.* 2006). Analytically, we rely on Riessman's (1993) narrative method to understand our texts as stories creating meaning, framing experiences and as produced through the interaction of two speakers.

The study

Our empirical study is based on 26 in-depth interviews with self-employed creatives active in Belgium and born in a country outside North America or the EU15 (or with at least one parent who was). Interested in discursive actions for constructing legitimacy, using agentically the discursive tools at hand, we purposely only recruited 'established' creative entrepreneurs for this research. We presumed that they had already achieved a certain degree of legitimacy when they won awards, prizes, received positive media coverage, had financial revenue through product sale and/or collaborated with significant peers.

Analysing the use of ethnicity in our respondents' narratives of legitimacy in terms of fitting in and standing out, we were able to identify four narrative strategies: (1) the use of one's own ethnic minority ethnicity as a source of creativity to stand out in the field; (2) the combination of one's own ethnic minority ethnicity and the ethnic majority culture to stand out in the field; (3) the use of minority ethnicity to construct a heroic story of entrepreneurship to fit into the field, and (4) the non-use of one's minority ethnicity in narratives of legitimacy. Four respondents mainly used the first strategy, nine the second, six the third and seven the fourth strategy. In the remainder of this chapter we illustrate each strategy through one exemplary narrative.

Crafting legitimacy via an 'ethnic' creative strategy

A first strategy is characterised by entrepreneurs' extensive use of their ethnic minority background in their creative production to stand out in their creative field. These respondents counterbalanced standing out through their ethnic background with fitting in through showing conformity to majority-dominated field norms concerning high-standard quality, aesthetics and entrepreneurship. To illustrate this strategy, we analyse the narrative of Fayza, a fashion designer with Moroccan roots, running her own label of fashionable headscarves (hijabs):

> You have the normal, traditional headscarf consisting of a piece of fabric.... There wasn't the ease of getting it on, and the different materials ... [It] isn't in fact comfortable to wear ... So [my type] is secured behind the ears.... It's more beautiful, you look younger too ... the other one is more grandmother-like.
>
> It's not because you wear a headscarf that you have to walk around like a frump.... That's also what I want ... big names like Dior, Chanel ... Yves Saint Laurent ... [their] style, also classy, that's want I want to achieve with my designs.... So I don't think that ... I should keep my prices very low.... No, I want to ... keep that high [standard].
>
> Designing exclusive headwear is something that doesn't exist yet. [So there is] no competition at all.... Since we have been to Paris [with the governmental fashion support agency] there has been more interest in accessory headscarves.
>
> Western ladies [are] wearing a beanie in the winter, together with a scarf, and that was something we couldn't.... Only a headscarf, that isn't so warm.... So I thought, I'm going to connect the two ... and then a small flower on the side and that's a success of course. It can be worn by both Western as Muslim ladies.... Those are things you as Western Muslim woman design and I think in the Arab world they are slowed down ... because they didn't get that Western [influence], and I've got both.
>
> People didn't take me seriously because I wear a headscarf ... [but] a Muslim woman is allowed to do everything. Studying, opening her own business ... Hadija, the wife of the prophet had a business, as the first woman in history. She had many men under her, and I look up to her.

In this text, Fayza deploys her minority culture as a source of inspiration for creating her unique product. She indicates her personal experience as a Muslim woman, unable to find fashionable and practical headscarves, as the origin of her enterprise. The strong emphasis on her cultural 'difference' allows her to claim a specific type of symbolic capital to stand out. As a Muslim woman wearing a headscarf herself, she argues that she is best placed to understand what kind of products Muslim women wearing headscarves want. Interestingly however, relying on this specific form of symbolic capital she risks being pinned down as a 'Muslim woman' and a 'typical' ethnic minority entrepreneur, an identity that is, in Western countries such as Belgium, often associated with subordination. To counter this possibility, Fayza stresses that her identity as a Muslim woman is compatible with an entrepreneurial one, referring to the wife of Mohammed who also owned a business.

Fayza's standing out is counterbalanced by fitting in via complying with the norms of her field which she constructs to be international and culturally diverse. In doing so, Fayza also deploys institutionalised, objectified and embodied cultural capital associated with her majority-dominated field. She draws on her institutionalised cultural capital she mentions to be acknowledged by the national government support agency for fashion, constructing to fit into the institutionalised high fashion industry of Belgium. Her objectified cultural capital emerges in her claim when narrating to have upgraded the traditional headscarf to a fashionable, elegant new product. By stating that she uses different fabrics, applies flowers, and wants women to look good and elegant, she presents herself as a creative entrepreneur who understands the quality and aesthetic norms of the fashion industry. Finally, Fayza's embodied cultural capital is enacted by constructing to behave as a real high fashion entrepreneur in making references to international upmarket brands such as Chanel, and in narrating to adopt their pricing strategy. In addition, the reference to the price of her products and the high standard underlines her understanding of the financial standards of the high fashion field, and stresses her behaviour as a high fashion entrepreneur.

Crafting legitimacy via a 'hybrid' creative strategy

In the second strategy, respondents construct a unique product by mixing their minority and majority cultures. They construct a standing out by claiming the ability to capture the best of two worlds in creative products, counterbalanced by fitting in through conformity with the aesthetic and symbolic norms of the field. Ethnic minority roots feature less prominently in this strategy, and are balanced with more Western elements. For illustration, we selected the narrative of Khalid, an interior designer, with roots in Algeria and Tunisia:

> My youth brought about a language deficit, as from Paris I was put in a [Dutch-speaking] Belgian [foster] family.... It all turned out bad.... I was obliged to start on an apprenticeship contract, to be able to stay here all together.... In the meanwhile ... I went travelling ... to Morocco....

There I found my roots again. So, only on my 17th I was for the first time confronted with the Arab world ... a world opened up for me, that wasn't known to me but felt very familiar.

[I] started working there ... in Marrakech ... where all the materials can be obtained, and where all the artisans – the best of the country – are.... I'm going one week back and one week forth. In Morocco I look at the things from a distance and vice versa.... I also always jump between these two worlds.... [T]hat's me, those two cultures, and I'm always seeking, and my misfortune is today my strength.

I just helped completing the design of the bridge of Nijmegen. And you have the architects of the Lange Wapper [bridge in Belgium] that call you ... [as] I don't have a degree [in designing], so I ... look at it from a totally different angle, and that's very important for society today.

[But] it's mainly Europeans that judge my work ... the Arabic world can't understand that.... I've made lots of chairs, of which they didn't understand us to be sitting on them.... It's innovative because I use [Moroccan] techniques of already 500 years old ... with a view from here, from there, so it's purified, and revisited.... There's always a solution in purification. Constantly purifying, purifying, purifying, and making sure you get back to the essence.

Khalid claims to stand out because he brings the best aesthetic elements and techniques of both his ethnic minority and majority background into his work. Namely, he constructs the incorporation of selected ancient traditional Moroccan techniques to make his work special and qualitative. Mentioning growing up in Belgium yet having found his roots again in Morocco, Khalid is claiming for himself the symbolic capital he needs to stand out in his field. This is further reflected in the construction of himself and his work as 'hybrid' and constantly jumping between two worlds both physically and mentally, especially when he states that he 'is' the two cultures.

To fit in, Khalid discursively deploys institutionalised, objectified and embodied cultural capital. For example, he draws upon his objectified and embodied cultural capital to fit in when claiming that his products are purified and 'essential', which is along contemporary aesthetic norms of Western design. To reinforce his conformity he mentions that, although all his work is produced in Morocco, the Arab world cannot understand it as it is made to meet the qualitative and aesthetic standards of the European context. When mentioning the cooperation with famous architects and designers, Khalid draws upon his institutionalised cultural capital to fit in. By doing so, he constructs himself as being a valued link in the chain, being called for advice on certain major and visible projects such as the Lange Wapper Bridge. Elsewhere in the interview, he also mentions that other established architects envy him for his freedom and creativity and are therefore eager to work with him.

Crafting legitimacy via a 'heroic' creative strategy

In this strategy, fitting in is constructed via a portrayal of the self as heroically overcoming difficulties – a common element in (majority) entrepreneurship narratives – that stems from one's minority background. This is counterbalanced with compliance to the dominant quality norms in the professional field, to construct 'stand out'. To illustrate this strategy we selected the interview of the Turkish-rooted Onat, founder and manager of Onat Publishing:

> You get a lot of rejection [of publishers]. Something every writer has to deal with ... [But] gradually ... I learned [from independent's feedback] that mine [my work] was good, yes. 'Strange that this wasn't picked up'.... Then I started to think. ... I came to the conclusion that I was considered to be an *allochtoon*! [pejorative term for a person with foreign roots]
>
> I have Turkish roots; I'm not going to deny that.... But I have no noteworthy differences with anybody else here.... Nevertheless publishers expect you to write on themes like migration, racism, ... My work apparently is similar to what Bret Easton Ellis is writing, that's a nice reference.... So my very first books were mainly a sort of coming of age with sex and drugs and rock'n roll – you could say that are quite Western themes – ... and that doesn't fit with them [the publishers]. They then can't sell me or something, you know.
>
> You have to know that literature, especially here, is very archaic. It's like this little elite world ... everyone knows everyone ... and *allochtoons* don't get in ... and in the end I thought: 'I'm going to do it all on my own'.... And that's the start of Onat Publishing.... I also publish others. Everyone is welcome if you are good.
>
> Not a lot of Belgian culture did filter through for us.... Someone who ... is interested in literature from Belgian parents, has a huge advantage.... For example: when I was 12, I went to the library by myself ... I found *Moby Dick* ... and said: 'Look mum, I've borrowed a book from the library!' ... and my mother said: '...did you steal that?!' ... They didn't know the concept of lending.... You know, I lagged behind a lot.

Onat associates his work with well-known Western writers and ideas. By stating that his work is similar to that of Bret Easton Ellis, he constructs his own work to stand out for its creativity and quality. Drawing upon his symbolic capital as a creative, he stresses that his work is of high quality, yet was never picked up by mainstream Belgian publishing due to its archaic and commercial logic. His emphasis on quality is supported by the statement that every writer, independent of his or her ethnic background, is welcome to approach Onat Publishing, as long as his or her work meets high-quality standards.

On the other hand, Onat uses his ethnic background to highlight his individual effort to acquire the cultural capital necessary to fit into the field. He extensively constructs, with anecdotes such as the *Moby Dick* story, how the lack of socialisation into the ethnic majority culture caused him to start out on his career as a writer with a structural cultural disadvantage. Precisely Onat's admission of this disadvantage proves his awareness of the dominant creative norms in the field. It also enables him to build a heroic narrative of acquiring this cultural capital himself through his individual efforts. By so doing, he stresses his agentic role, echoing a classical 'heroic' entrepreneurial narrative leading to success. By constructing himself as an emancipatory entrepreneur, overcoming the power-laden exclusion of his field, Onat thus enacts his embodied cultural capital to fit into his creative field. He constructs himself now as a publishing entrepreneur among all entrepreneurs, due to his own heroic efforts. At the same time, Onat forcefully rejects any association with other Muslim writers and expresses his disapproval for being pinned down as an '*allochthoon*' writer in a certain 'ethnic minority genre'. In this way, he resists the stigma associated with ethnic minorities and reaffirms his 'fitting in' in the majority genres and norms.

Crafting legitimacy via a non-ethnic creative strategy

Respondents using this last strategy are completely orientated towards the majority norms, values and culture. We see that discursive elements referring to a 'Western' culture are both used to stand out and to fit in, without any significant reference to an ethnic minority background. The narrative of Saida, a silversmith and flatware designer with roots in Palestine, is illustrative of this strategy:

> There aren't many people designing cutlery ... [it]'s something that needs to be very functional.... [My] objects ... are in the end daily objects with a ... I don't know really. Some say it's a twist ... sometimes it's a wink ... I'm just keeping the link with ... silversmithing. But actually I'm a designer ... for little productions, for larger productions, but there's always an exchange between craft [and] an industrial process.
>
> [I'm] almost always working on command ... I was lucky of course that ... Hermès and Puiforcat thought: 'OK, I believe in her, and I'll give her an order' ... what made a great difference was me becoming designer of the year. So that put me in the picture, and opened up the market in Belgium for me.
>
> Identity ... is really the theme 90 per cent of the people use in their work ... but I don't have that, far from it!... And still people really expect you to ... I've designed that waterpipe ... [it] was an order from a company just like I've got all my other orders. ... For me this was not like: 'Well and here I'm going to use my roots, and now I finally can show who I am'.

> My father is Palestinian, my mother was Belgian, and yes, that influences you ... because you've got the two cultures.... [But] I don't think that what I'm doing now ... is caused by me being raised with two cultures.... Still I get many comments like: 'Well, your work is very feminine, and very oriental' ... I don't think anyone can see that in my work.

Similar to Onat, Saida also claims to excel in quality and originality, referring to the established creative norms in her majority-dominated professional field. Drawing upon her symbolic capital, she defines her creative field as one of flatware designers, an international subfield made up of only a few. This enables her to stand out against the larger mass of designers. She portrays her work as original and unique, mentioning to keep the bond with silversmithing, yet making products with 'a wink' or 'a twist'.

To fit in, Saida deploys her institutionalised cultural capital in her reference to the award of 'designer of the year', an acknowledgement of her work by media and peers in her creative field, and how it opened up the Belgian market for her. She also mentions the established large firms Hermès and Puiforcat for which she has worked in the past. These references, as well as stating that she is generally working on command, indicate that she not only understands the dynamics of her field, but she is also part of a larger network of important majority stakeholders within it.

Saida also draws upon her objectified cultural capital in constructing her work as functional. By doing so, she disassociates herself with aesthetics-for-aesthetics, fitting into the designing industry where functionality needs to be balanced with form. Significantly, she argues that her ethnic minority background is irrelevant to her production. She does so by explicitly rejecting being pinned down in categories such as 'feminine' and 'oriental'. Stressing that there are no elements of her background in her work helps her to construct herself and her products as fitting into the majority-dominated creative field. Finally, Saida enacts her embodied cultural capital by constructing herself as a designer, making use of craft and tradition, yet brought to an industrial process. In Saida's field of flatware designing there is often no other way to distribute work than to cooperate with larger firms. By doing so, she constructs herself as a creative entrepreneur fitting into the design industry.

Conclusion

Taking a subject-centred approach to ethnic minority entrepreneurship, following critical entrepreneurship studies, yet taking this further by bringing back in individual agentic actions for entrepreneurial and business strategies, this chapter aims to understand how ethnic minority entrepreneurs in the creative industries deploy their identity to craft legitimacy. Our findings expose the current bias in the conceptualisation of ethnic minority entrepreneurs almost as non-subjects prevalent in most classical ethnic minority entrepreneurship research. In line with the emerging stream of ethnic entre-preneurship literature with a focus on the personal level (e.g. Brettell and Alstatt 2007; Essers and Benschop 2007; Kontos 2003; Pio 2007), this chapter calls into question the tendency of the extant literature to represent these entrepreneurs as mere representatives of a group which is deterministically 'caught' in multiple structural factors, obscuring their individual agency. Although this neglect is likely the effect of representations of the prototypical entrepreneur as a white man (Ogbor 2000) which makes it hard to reconcile ethnic minority entrepreneurs with the quintessential characteristics of entre-preneurs, our analysis shows that it is possible. Moreover, we demonstrate how an ethnic minority background can reflexively and agentically be deployed as a symbolic asset by individual entrepreneurs and form a quintes-sential element of the creative business.

Our study thus adds to the recent studies that 'give voice' and unveil the individuals behind the facades of only seemingly monolithic ethnic groups (e.g. Essers and Benschop 2007; Kontos 2003; Pio 2007). Focusing on the notion of legitimacy, we have attempted to embed these voices more tightly in the business-related processes that affect both ethnic minority entrepren-eurs' understanding of themselves and their business within the field. The major contribution of this study is to bring back the focus on the act of entre-preneurship when studying ethnic minority entrepreneurs. By doing so, we aim to understand the value of ethnic identity for ethnic minority business strategies, and to account for the full agency of ethnic minority entrepreneurs. To strategically navigate through fields shaped by multiple (often majority) actors and unequal power relations, they construct professional narratives balancing the conflicting needs to fit in and stand out in their field (cf. De Clercq and Voronov 2009; Deephouse 1999).

We see ethnic minority entrepreneurs in the creative industries – due to the 'call to action' of the double-opportunity structure they are in – to proac-tively construct legitimacy narratives, and to proactively incorporate, adapt, address or resist the discourses that are useful for doing so (e.g. Clarke *et al.* 2009). Comparing our four strategies, we note that the degree to which the ethnic minority background is discursively deployed varies greatly, warranting studies to focus on the individual level. This indicates that ethnic minority entrepreneurs maintain individual latitude in defining their professional selves as well as their creative work, which should be accounted for in research. A theoretical perspective highlighting ethnic minority entrepreneurs' agency allowed us to reveal the heterogeneity of ways in which ethnic minority backgrounds can be deployed by individuals, affecting their business strat-egies. Such heterogeneity has been explained before in terms of individuals' biographies (e.g. Brettell and Alstatt 2007; Kontos 2003) which fosters the development of a personal and professional 'sense of the self' in which one's ethnic minority background features in different degrees and distinct ways. However, we account with this study for the idea that this does not occur automatically or in a deterministic way. As our data show, ethnic minority entrepreneurs as agents self-reflect on themselves and the world around them and act accordingly, making a difference (Giddens 1982, 1984).

Finally, in reconnecting with the act of entrepreneurship, we are in this study able to show how ethnic minority entrepreneurs create for themselves an alternative subjectivity. By actively claiming their legitimacy, ethnic minority creatives also claim their full subject positions as proactive entrepreneurs, creating a renewed and reclaimed ethnic entrepreneurial identity. This means that ethnic minority entrepreneurs are not only able to construct legitimacy via their identity, but also vice versa. Indeed, it is not only identity that may be used as a discursive resource for business legitimacy; also, because the ethnic minority entrepreneurs in this study construct themselves as legitimate, they are able to use this legitimacy as the basis for a reclaimed full identity position as being an entrepreneur. By doing so, they are able to reject the potential excluding ethnocentrism of the environment, often stigmatising minorities as subordinate 'others' (Prasad 2006; Said 1978). This shows the worth of both identity and legitimacy as a discursive resource, and again warrants our perspective on individual experiences as well as bringing in the business strategies of ethnic minority entrepreneurs.

Taking stock of these insights, we believe that future research could gain from approaching ethnic minority entrepreneurs in the first place as individual entrepreneurs and acknowledging that they as agents do make a difference in their businesses, by letting the role of their identity and position in society emerge from the empirical analysis of their entrepreneurial actions.

References

Aldrich, H.E. and Fiol, C.M. (1994), Fools rush in? The institutional context of industry creation. *Academy of Management Review*, **19**(4), pp. 645–670.

Aldrich, H.E., Cater, J., Jones, T., McEvoy, D. and Velleman, P. (1985), Ethnic residential concentration and the protected market hypothesis. *Social Forces*, **63**(4), pp. 996–1009.

Bagwell, S. (2008), Transnational family networks and ethnic minority business development. The case of Vietnamese nail-shops in the UK. *International Journal of Entrepreneurial Behaviour and Research*, **14**(6), pp. 377–394.

Basu, A. and Altinay, E. (2002), The interaction between culture and entrepreneurship in London's immigrant business. *International Small Business Journal*, **20**(4), p. 371.

Basu, D. and Werbner, P. (2001), Bootstrap capitalism and the culture industries: A critique of invidious comparisons in the study of ethnic entrepreneurship. *Ethnic and Racial Studies*, **24**(2), pp. 236–262.

Baumann, S. (2007), A general theory of artistic legitimation: How art worlds are like social movements. *Poetics*, **35**, pp. 47–65.

Blair, H. (2001), You're only as good as your last job: The labour process and labour market in the British film industry. *Work Employment & Society*, **15**(1), pp. 149–169.

Bourdieu, P. (1986), The forms of capital. In J.G. Richardson (ed.), *Handbook of Theory and Research for the Sociology of Education*, New York: Greenwood Press, pp. 241–258.

Boyd, R.L. (1998), The storefront church ministry in African American communities of the urban north during the great migration: The making of an ethnic niche. *The Social Science Journal*, **35**, pp. 319–332.

Brandellero, A. (2011), *The Art of being Different: Exploring Diversity in the Cultural Industries*, Faculty of Social and Behavioural Sciences, Department of Sociology and Antropology, University of Amsterdam, Amsterdam.

Brettell, C. and Alstatt, K. (2007), The agency of ethnic minority entrepreneurs. Biographies of the self-employed in ethnic and occupational niches of the urban labor market. *Journal of Antropological Research*, **63**, pp. 383–397.

Brown, A.D. (2006), A narrative approach to collective identities. *Journal of Management Studies*, **43**, pp. 731–753.

Brown, A.D. and Coupland, C. (2005), Sounds of silence: Graduate trainees, hegemony and resistance. *Organization Studies*, **26**(7), pp. 1049–1069.

Chaganti, R. and Greene, P.G. (2002), Who are ethnic entrepreneurs? A study of entrepreneurs' ethnic involvement and business characteristics. *Journal of Small Business Management*, **40**(2), pp. 126–143.

Clarke, C., Brown, A. and Hope-Hailey, V. (2009), Working identities? Antagonistic discursive resources and mangerial identity. *Human Relations*, **62**(3), pp. 323–352.

De Clercq, D. and Voronov, M. (2009), The role of cultural and symbolic capital in entrepreneurs' ability to meet expectations about conformity and innovation. *Journal of Small Business Management*, **47**(3), pp. 398–420.

DCMS (2001), *Creative Industries Mapping Document 2001*, 2nd edn, London: Department of Culture, Media and Sport.

Deephouse, D.L. (1999), To be different, or to be the same? It's a question (and theory) of strategi balance. *Strategic Management Journal*, **20**, pp. 147–166.

Delmestri, G., Montanari, F. and Usai, A. (2005), Reputation and strength of ties in predicting commercial success and artistic merit of independents in the Italian feature film industry. *Journal of Management Studies*, **42**(5), pp. 975–1002.

Essers, C. and Benschop, Y. (2007), Enterprising identities: Female entrepreneurs of Moroccan or Turkish origin in the Netherlands. *Organization Studies*, **28**(1), pp. 49–69.

Essers, C. and Benschop, Y. (2009), Muslim businesswomen doing boundary work. The negotiation of Islam, gender and ethnicity within entrepreneurial contexts. *Human Relations*, **62**(3), pp. 403–423.

Essers, C., Doorewaard, H. and Benschop, Y. (2013), Family ties: Migrant business women doing identity work on the public–private divide. *Human Relations*, **16**(12), pp. 1645–1665.

Faulkner, R. and Anderson, A. (1987), Short-term projects and emergent careers: Evidence from Hollywood. *American Journal of Sociology*, **92**, pp. 879–909.

Florida, R. (2002), *The Rise of the Creative Class, and How It's Transforming Work, Leisure, Community and Everyday Life*, New York: Basic Books.

Florida, R. (2005a), *Cities and the Creative Class*, London: Routledge.

Florida, R. (2005b), *The Flight of the Creative Class: The New Global Competition for Talent*, New York: HarperCollins.

Giddens, A. (1982), *Profiles of Critiques in Social Theory*, London: Macmillan.

Giddens, A. (1984), *The Constitution of Society*, Cambridge/Malden, MA: Polity Press.

Hytti, U. (2003), *Stories of Entrepreneurs: Narrative Construction of Identities*, Turku: Turku School of Economics and Business Administration, Small Business Institute.

Johnson, C., Dowd, T.J. and Ridgeway, C.L. (2006), Legitimacy as a social process. *Annual Review of Sociology*, **32**(1), pp. 53–78.

Jones, C. (2002), Signalling expertise: How signals shape careers in creative industries. In M. Perperl, M. Arthur and N. Anand (eds), *Career Creativity. Explorations in the Remaking of Work*, Mahwah, NJ/New York: Lawrence Erlbaum Associates, pp. 195–204.

Jones, G.R. and Butler, J.E. (1992), Managing internal corporate entrepreneurship. An agency theory perspective. *Journal of Management*, **18**(4), pp. 733–749.

Knight, F.H. (1921), *Risk, Uncertainty and Profit*, Boston, MA: Houghton Mifflin.

Kontos, M. (2003), Considering the concept of entrepreneurial resources in ethnic business: Motivation as a biographical resource? *International Review of Sociology*, **13**(1), pp. 183–204.

Light, I.H. (1972), *Ethnic Enterprise in America: Business and Welfare Among Chinese, Japanese and Blacks*, Berkeley: University of California Press.

Light, I.H. and Bonacich, E. (1988), *Immigrant Entrepreneurs: Koreans in Los Angeles*, Los Angeles: University of California Press.

Lounsbury, M. and Glynn, M.A. (2001), Cultural entrepreneurship: Stories, legitimacy and the acquisition of resources. *Strategic Management Journal*, **22**(6/7), pp. 545–564.

Mavrommatis, G. (2006), The new 'creative' Brick Lane: A narrative study of local multicultural encounters. *Ethnicities*, **6**(4), pp. 498–517.

Menger, P.M. (1999), Artistic labor markets and careers. *Annual Review of Sociology*, **25**, pp. 541–574.

Minahan, S. (2005), The organizational legitimacy of the Bauhaus. *The Journal of Arts Management, Law, and Society*, **35**(2), pp. 133–145.

NESTA (2006), *Creating Growth: How the UK Can Develop World Class Creative Businesses*, London: NESTA.

Nicholson, L. and Anderson, A. (2005), News and nuances of the entrepreneurial myth and metaphor: Linguistic games in entrepreneurial sense-making and sense-giving. *Entrepreneurship Theory and Practice*, **29**, pp. 153–172.

Nwankwo, S. (2005), Characterisation of Black African entrepreneurship in the UK: A pilot study. *Journal of Small Business and Enterprise Development*, **12**(1), pp. 120–136.

Ogbor, J.O. (2000), Mythicizing and reification in entrepreneurial discourse: Ideology-critique of entrepreneurial studies. *Journal of Management Studies*, **37**(5), pp. 605–635.

Pio, E. (2005), Knotted strands: Working lives of Indian women migrants in New Zealand. *Human Relations*, **58**(10), pp. 1277–1300.

Pio, E. (2007), Ethnic entrepreneurship among Indian women in New Zealand: A bittersweet process. *Gender, Work and Organization*, **14**(5), pp. 409–432.

Prasad, A. (2006), The jewel in the crown: Postcolonial theory and workplace diversity. In A.M. Konrad, P. Prasad and J.K. Pringle, *Handbook of Workplace Diversity*, Thousand Oaks, CA: Sage, pp. 121–144.

Raghuram, P. and Hardill, I. (1998), Negotiating a market: A case study of an Asian woman in business. *Women's Studies International Forum*, 215, pp. 475–483.

Ram, M. (1992), Coping with racism: Asian employers in the inner-city. *Work Employment and Society*, **6**(4), pp. 601–618.

Ram, M. and Deakins, D. (1996), African-Carribeans in business. *Journal of Ethnic and Migration Studies*, **22**(1), pp. 67–84.

Ram, M., Smallbone, D., Deakins, D. and Jones, T. (2003), Banking on 'break-out': Finance and the development of ethnic minority businesses. *Journal of Ethnic and Migration Studies*, **29**(4), pp. 663–681.

Riessman, C.K. (1993), *Narrative Analysis*, edited by Judith L. Hunter, *Qualitative Research Method Series*, Thousand Oaks, CA/London: Sage.

Said, E.W. (1978), *Orientalism*, New York: Pantheon Books.

Schumpeter, J.A. (1934), *The Theory of Economic Development: An Inquiry into Profits, Capital, Credit, Interest, and the Business Cycle*, London: Oxford University Press.

Smallbone, D., Bertotti, M. and Ekanem, I. (2005), Diversification in ethnic minority business. The case of Asians in London's creative industries. *Journal of Small Business and Enterprise Development*, **12**(1), pp. 41–56.

Smallbone, D., Kitching, J. and Athayde, R. (2010), Ethnic diversity, entrepreneurship and competitiveness in a global city. *International Small Business Journal*, **28**(2), pp. 174–190.

Suchman, M.C. (1995), Managing legitimacy: Strategic and institutional approaches. *Academy of Management Review*, **20**(3), pp. 571–610.

Towse, R. (2003), Cultural industries. In R. Towse, *A Handbook of Cultural Economics*, Cheltenham: Elgar, pp. 170–177.

Waldinger, R., Aldrich, H.E. and Ward, R. (1990), *Ethnic Entrepreneurs. Immigrant Business in Industrial Societies, Sage Series on Race and Ethnic Relations*, Newbury Park, CA/London: Sage.

Werbner, P. (1999), What colour 'success'? Distorting value in studies of ethnic entrepreneurship. *Sociological Review*, **47**(3), pp. 548–579.

Wilson, N. and Stokes, D. (2004), Laments and serenades: Relationship marketing and legitimation strategies for the cultural entrepreneur. *Qualitative Market Research: An International Journal*, **7**(3), pp. 218–227.

Zhou, M. (2004), Revisiting ethnic entrepreneurship: Convergencies, controversies, and conceptual advancements. *International Migration Review*, **38**(3), pp. 1040–1074.

10 A critical reflection on female migrant entrepreneurship in the Netherlands

Karen Verduyn and Caroline Essers

Introduction

Western governmental discourse on entrepreneurship contains a structural grand narrative of entrepreneurs who are seen to play an important role in the machine of the economy, an implicit responsibility to deliver economic results, and to provide a steady basis for growth so that the national economy can progress (cf. Perren and Jennings 2005). This hegemonic discourse on the important function of entrepreneurship is powerful, as it calls upon the wider taken-for-granted ideology of rational economic behaviour and enterprise (ibid.). It romanticises entrepreneurship as having the supremacy to create wealth for everyone and to liberate and elevate people who occupy marginalised positions, as a key driver in both economic and personal growth. Accordingly, Western governments have sought to advance a vision of a society in which the values of enterprise, resourcefulness and self-reliance can be appropriated by everyone, whatever their background (Karnani 2009). However, although mostly presented otherwise, entrepreneurship is not a neutral discourse. Entrepreneurship indeed may have positive aspects but it also destabilises societal and economic power relations, and it involves various categories of in- and exclusion: groups of people who allegedly can and cannot be termed 'entrepreneurs' (Jones and Spicer 2009). Moreover, the consistent attribution of positive value to entrepreneurship simultaneously marginalises other economic actors. Therefore, 'instead of seeing enterprise as a magic cure to the problems of late modernity, critics talk of entrepreneurship as politically charged' (Jones and Spicer 2009, p. 40).

In this chapter we question the presupposed view, and its accompanying entrepreneurship discourse, which regards entrepreneurship as something 'good' and worth being stimulated. By bringing into play the stories of female ethnic entrepreneurs with Dutch institutional stories, we aim to exemplify how these institutions view these women and their entrepreneurial efforts, and how these women relate to their entrepreneurial practices and the role of Dutch institutions. The rationale behind choosing this particular group of women is that they are usually and typically marginalised within the dominant entrepreneurship discourse which in itself is gendered and ethnocentrically biased (Ogbor 2000; Bruni *et al.* 2004; Essers and Benschop 2007, 2009; Essers *et al.* 2010). Studying the stories of female migrant entrepreneurs in a wider Dutch institutional context, we examine what happens when entrepreneurship is being applied to 'elevate' this group. Since the dynamics of centre–margin positionalities are central to our investigations we turn to deconstruction analysis as an inspirational source for our analysis. In the next section we will first shed light on the dominant entrepreneurship discourse that seems to sustain this ideologised tale of optimism as well as some of the upcoming stories of scepticism that have started to co-create a critical theory of entrepreneurship.

The gendered and ethnicised politics of entrepreneurship

In line with the overall scope of this book, our chapter counters the standing entrepreneurship discourse and entrepreneurship literature which argues that the success of an entrepreneur is an isolated, non-contextual process (Schumpeter 1976; McClelland 1987; Chell 2001) as well as the image of the successful entrepreneur as romanticised by the media, governments and scientists, an image laden with myth (Smith and Anderson 2004, p. 136). Mainstream entrepreneurship literature implicitly prescribes masculinity and Western-ness for successful entrepreneurship versus femininity and non-Western-ness, a binary and hierarchical way of reifying and normalising existing power positions (Wekker and Lutz 2001, p. 27). This may create problematic effects, as it may result in discriminatory practices by practitioners and politicians, while at the same time urging businesspeople to construct their entrepreneurial selves in relation to this archetypical entrepreneur and thus adjust their behaviour and identities accordingly (Ogbor 2000; Bruni *et al.* 2004; Essers and Benschop 2007).

We write this chapter within the context of a Western society which is highly polarised with regard to Muslim/non-Muslim relations, i.e. the Netherlands. Turks and Moroccans comprise, respectively, the first and third largest groups of, mostly Muslim, migrants in the Netherlands. Because they share a similar migration history as so-called guest workers in the 1960s and 1970s, and their religion and socio-economic position is alike, their sociopolitical situation is to some extent comparable. Family reunification, supported by the Dutch government, stimulated their final stay. The original governmental approach to have these migrants retain their own identities was criticised from the 1990s onward by several politicians, as this allegedly contributed to the isolation and socially and economically lower status of immigrants. Later, migrants became the targets of attack in discourse on the multicultural society, and right-wing politicians, in particular, even stereotyped migrants as uneducated and therefore dumb, uncivilised, criminal and dangerous (Ghorashi 2003). It is generally being purported that migrants have to assimilate into Dutch culture or leave, resulting in an Us/Them dichotomy in Dutch society and a negative image, specifically for people of Moroccan and Turkish descent (Gijsberts and Dagevos 2004). Many politicians and policy makers have used 'the migrant woman as victim' analogy to construct this binary ethnic division and to prove the undesirability of Islamic components in Dutch society (Lutz 1991; Van Nieuwkerk 2003). In particular, Muslimas' (female Muslims) femininity serves symbolically to represent the 'Other', such as the headscarf which is considered oppressive and incompatible with the Dutch self-image as an emancipated society (Van Nieuwkerk 2003).

Yet, in contrast to this image of the oppressed Muslima, the labour market participation among Turkish and Moroccan women has strongly increased: the labour participation of Moroccan women doubled between 1995 and 2009 to 36 per cent, and the labour participation of Turkish women increased from 17 per cent to 41 per cent in the Netherlands (statline.cbs.nl). Some of these migrant women start(ed) their own businesses. Of all entrepreneurs of Moroccan and Turkish origin (respectively 5,500 and 13,700), 14.5 per cent and 17.5 per cent are women, whereas 31 per cent of all 899,000 entrepreneurs of native Dutch origin are women (statline.cbs.nl).

The Dutch government has endeavoured to elevate the alleged oppressed position of female Muslim migrants through programmes launched by the Ministry of Social Affairs, such as the so-called 'Thousand and one power' programme (inspired by the *One Thousand and One Nights*), to upgrade these women's Dutch language skills and provide them with (voluntary) work experience. Entrepreneurship is being brought to the fore through programmes and research projects, particularly by the Ministry of Housing, Communities and Integration (the Ministry of Economic Affairs is contemplating a target group policy) as a solution to be/come equal or to create equality – and hence to stimulate integration – because of its (assumed) emancipatory powers. Accordingly, many local government organisations and institutes such as the Chamber of Commerce try to stimulate these women's entrepreneurial activities in order to get them out of welfare by letting them start up a company while initially continuing their welfare.

Methodological approach

The aim of this chapter is a critical reflection of female ethnic entrepreneurship in the Netherlands, a 'category' of entrepreneurs which is usually and typically excluded, not only in popular discourse but also in mainstream entrepreneurship literature. We set out to question what tends to go unquestioned: the optimistic stance taken towards entrepreneurship, and its associated ideological constructs. We want to scrutinise what 'happens' around them. Our analysis has been inspired by deconstruction, originally stemming from the work of Derrida (1977, 1982), who introduced the concept of 'différance', literally referring to the (systematic) play of differences underlying any (social) system (Derrida 1982). Deconstruction offers an analytical strategy (or mode of reading) that exposes multiple ways of telling, reading and interpreting a story (Martin 1990); it 'is able to reveal ideological assumptions' (ibid., p. 340). What deconstruction does is bring to the fore the interplay between what is usually being presented as true, or as desirable, versus what is consequently being overshadowed, rejected or hidden. Deconstruction is about the interplay between such binaries: one central (dominant, preferred, superior), the other marginal; a hierarchical relation between a centre and its periphery. Obvious examples of oppositions in relation to the entrepreneurship phenomenon are: male–female and white–ethnic (see above). Deconstruction makes it possible to bring such oppositions, as well as the assumptions upon which they rely, to the surface, and to show how they are connected rather than opposed.

For the purpose of our research aim, we believe that applying such ideas of deconstruction is highly relevant. After all, the studied female entrepreneurs may be regarded as 'emancipatees', in the sense of a group to be emancipated from a marginal position towards a more 'central' (included) position in Dutch society. Assuming that the emancipat*ed* is the 'superior' category, we need to see how this centre–margin interplay manifests itself, and if and how the emancipatee indeed moves towards a centre and leaves a marginal position.

Deconstruction has been adopted and employed as a research strategy in a manifold of research domains, and also within organisation studies (Martin 1990; Boje 1995, 2001; Chia 1994, 1996). In line with such contributions, we have performed a number of 'steps' in our analysis. The first step was to filter out the dominant assumptions from our data. We did so by considering what was being presented as opposites (cf. us vs. them). Sometimes this was stated explicitly, sometimes it was not (nevertheless, such a term as 'them' (see also Milay, quoted below) evidently already implies an 'us'). We have sought to scrutinise such dichotomies (marking the poles, for example, 'assimilation is good' vs. 'assimilation is bad'), and discussed which of the two poles we found to be privileged (conceived of as more true, more valuable, more important, more universal), and by whom. The pole being privileged may be considered the 'centred' pole, in deconstructive terms; the other is considered the exception, peripheral, marginal, derivative, overlooked and/or suppressed. Evidently, what is being presented as a centred view potentially differs depending on whose point of view we depart from: the 'officials' or the women.

Subsequently deconstructing the opposites implies 'destabilising' them, by drawing out/pointing towards the infinitude of possible readings/versions of any story, or text. The 'result' then is a revelation of blind spots (explication of what is overlooked), not in order to close the story down again (replace one centre with another), but to disrupt taken-for-granted-ness, and to reveal ambiguity and contradiction.

We present and analyse three out of a total of 15 collected narratives of originally Moroccan and Turkish entrepreneurs and connect these with five stories of employees of Dutch official institutions related to entrepreneurship. These particular stories have been selected because we consider them to be most distinctive and revealing with regard to this chapter's theme. Evidently, we cannot guarantee that there were no biases when selecting (and analysing) these cases, but we believe that being 'objective' is virtually impossible (Essers 2009a), nor even a 'requirement' in doing research of this kind. If we take Derrida seriously, there cannot 'be' such a construct as objectivity. Nevertheless, when conducting and reporting on research projects related to multicultural issues which moreover stem from qualitative interviews, it is important to reflect on the possible effects the interviewer–interviewee dynamics have on the writing of the data (Alvesson and Sköldberg 2000). Since both authors are Dutch female academics and regard themselves as agnostic, it is a given that both authors' nationality and (cultural) background have affected the way they have analysed and interpreted the data (Essers 2009a). We have tried to reflect on this issue where we thought this was possible and relevant.

Interviews with the entrepreneurs and the officials have been recorded and transcribed (literally) by a research assistant. Subsequently, the transcripts were analysed by both authors using categorical content analysis (Lieblich *et al.* 1998). By coding the transcript texts we sought to filter out the most important topics, themes and common patterns. Applying a more holistic content analysis, the ambiguities within and among these narratives concerning these themes were sought. Subsequently, those parts of the narratives referring to these themes were analysed inspired by deconstruction, as explained above. Since we wanted to interpret these themes in the light of the content that emerged from the rest of these entrepreneurs' narratives we took an interpretative, in-depth approach and avoided generalisations. We present only the stories which we considered to be the most illustrative and contrasting ones in all the interviews with regard to the positive, emancipatory and elevating powers attributed to entrepreneurship. Our deconstructive analyses illustrate the underlying patterns and the diversity of this phenomenon. In the next section we present fragments of the stories and discuss them in light of the dominant assumptions they portray.

Presenting the stories

The institutional point of view

The Chamber of Commerce, originally having a predominantly administrative function, currently adopts an active role in stimulating entrepreneurship. When it comes to ethnic entrepreneurship, a Chamber of Commerce employee (Milay, originally Turkish) claims:

> I am also involved in ethnic minority entrepreneurship, together with a colleague. This is connected with the fact that we saw that these

customers did not approach us as often, of their own accord.... So we stimulate this target group, meaning the ethnic minority entrepreneurs, quantitatively, but especially qualitatively.... We want to know how this target group moves and where they can be found.

Yet she perceives the 'target group' as 'a difficult group to approach':

We initially thought the threshold was too high for this target group, and we have tried to lower the threshold in the municipality of N.... But that was not the problem.... You have to approach them differently, much more personally.

Something similar is voiced by Anne (originally Dutch), a civil servant with the Ministry of Economic Affairs:

If certain problems arise, problems that arise for many entrepreneurs, we do try to turn it into policy.... The idea behind it is that we'd create a lower threshold [meaning for them to become entrepreneurs; *authors*.... For me it remains a difficult group. Turkish and Moroccans. I do come across them, but not so often.

Both the Chamber of Commerce and the Ministry of Economic Affairs make a division between the 'higher thresholds' with ethnic minority entrepreneurs who are sometimes female, and the lower ones when it comes to Dutch entrepreneurs. To overcome this higher threshold, they feel they have to approach 'them' differently from the Dutch entrepreneurs, thus affirming the Us–Them dichotomy among entrepreneurs which we described earlier. Likewise, the employees from the institutions and other organisations surrounding these women's entrepreneurial efforts tend to often refer to 'problems' as perceived within this 'target group'. To address these problems, the municipality of N., for instance, has initiated research on ethnic entrepreneurs and has started up a project based on this research providing personal coaches. The municipality has subsidised enterprises at a particular location, mostly owned by migrants, stimulating them to improve their ventures. This project amounted to 400,000 euros. Furthermore, it is presupposed that ethnic female entrepreneurs would have limited access to resources (a notion that is supported by extant literature: ethnic minorities seem to favour access to resources through familial and other ties: Portes 1995; Kloosterman *et al.* 1999). One such resource is finance. It follows that these 'different' entrepreneurs – particularly women (ethnic minority) entrepreneurs – are considered financially less interesting for banks:

They go to banks for small loans. And banks do not find them interesting enough.

(Anne, civil servant, Ministry of Economic Affairs)

This is why micro-financing has been brought to life:

> We're a small bank for micro-finance. We try to reach a target group that is being excluded by the usual banks. We are being subsidised by a non-interest-bearing loan of 15 million euros from the Ministry of Economic Affairs. The exploitation costs are being brought in by four large banks.
>
> (Fenny, a Dutch female from the financial organisation Qredits)

Deconstructing these quotes yields something interesting: small loans are seen as less, not good enough, and therefore such an initiative as Qredits is set up especially to put the marginalised, 'excluded' target group usually being on the periphery in a more central position. However, when it comes to actually 'reaching' the target group, there is a certain arrogance:

> They should know about us. After all, everyone who starts a business has to go to the Chamber of Commerce. There they are informed about us.
>
> (Fenny)

Hence, we see an interesting contradiction: although recently set up, everyone, whatever their background, should know they are there. After all, the procedural steps taken after one has 'naturally' enrolled at the Chamber of Commerce should lead them there. Likewise, this attitude of such Dutch institutions coincides with the hegemonic idea of entrepreneurship and how 'the entrepreneur' should behave (see Ogbor 2000; Essers 2009b). The dominant general societal idea that entrepreneurship is something to be stimulated, as we have exemplified above, is very firmly sustained in these institutional stories:

> We are very much in favour of stimulating entrepreneurship for everyone. Where we can support this we like to do so. And if specific problems occur with particular target groups we see if we can do something about that.
>
> (Herma, a Dutch female employee at the Municipality of N.)

Explicitly, as well as implicitly, in all of the institutional stories, the idea that entrepreneurship should be stimulated, also for women of ethnic origin, is simply taken for granted, as a fact. None of the interviewed institutions questioned the idea that entrepreneurship should be stimulated. This resonates with the general idea of entrepreneurship being a positive economic activity under all circumstances. When asked why entrepreneurship should be stimulated, in general, and specifically for women of ethnic minority backgrounds, Milay answers:

> I think that labour, and entrepreneurship is a form of labour isn't it, with more risk involved evidently, but it is a means to get people to

participate. It creates self-assurance, and independence, thus providing the [minority] women with more space and self-acceptance.... It is a means to get a bit of respect.... In the current situation, these women are not able to show their talents.

Here, we see how entrepreneurship is indeed almost seen as an ideal to elevate and emancipate (female) minorities; it would increase minorities' participation, self-assurance and independence, and not stimulating entrepreneurship would decrease these women's agency, as also underlined by Malach Pines *et al.* (2010). The conviction that entrepreneurship is something good is so powerful that these Dutch institutions find themselves in a certified position, where they can unquestioningly 'pull' 'them' into entrepreneurship, where things are apparently good:

> I think we should go to the entrepreneur, don't wait till they eventually come to us. All from the starting point: this target group hás to move forward.
>
> (Milay)

From our deconstructionist stance, however well intended their efforts ('stimulate this target group'), these 'facilitators' may be seen to firmly depart from their own stance and conviction of what is the right way forward for these women ('centre'). What with all the trouble they take and the determination in their stories, the general talk of 'target groups', 'lowering thresholds' and 'the personal approach' indeed has a very strong Us–Them connotation: lowering thresholds so that the 'other' can become like 'us' and assimilate into a Western kind of entrepreneur (Calas *et al.* 2009; Essers 2009b; Ogbor 2000). A binary is being created between 'different' and 'same'. Dutch entrepreneurs are considered the centre, the norm ('did not approach us as often', implying 'as the "normal" ones do'). In particular, the wording 'lower/higher threshold' seems to imply a boundary, where on the one hand you're in and on the other you're not, a notion that is in itself already problematic because of its static and reifying nature (cf. Cooper 1986). Strikingly, Milay (of Turkish origin) inhabits the same centre, referring to 'these customers' and 'this target group'. Her institutionalised position seems to have pulled her across the boundary, now underwriting and executing general societal ideas. This not only applies to the different–same dichotomy, but also to how these institutions claim the minority entrepreneurs should go about their entrepreneurial practices, as we have seen above. We see the same kind of thing happening when it comes to networking. Next to all their other initiatives aimed at supporting entrepreneurship as outlined above, the municipality of N. has initiated an association for ethnic minority entrepreneurs:

> We stimulated this, initiated it, as a municipality, because we saw that the ethnic entrepreneurs do not unite in networks, and networks are

particularly effective for learning from one another. We have put enormous effort in this. Currently it is a bit slow with this association. It is a mystery to me. As European, Western entrepreneurs, we are very much directed towards networking. Maybe it is because of their culture, they tend to find one another more via their families.

(Herma, civil servant in the municipality of N.)

This quote seems to demonstrate a typically Western notion of the necessity to network in an organised, 'official' way in order to be entrepreneurially successful (see also Calas *et al.* 2009). Hence, just as it is being purported in the general popular entrepreneurship discourse, and the standing entrepreneurship literature, these institutions stipulate the necessity to network. This civil servant talks from her own Western perspective and constructs an ideological truth by building a dichotomy between 'the allochtonous' who do not network in the way they are perhaps 'supposed' to do, similar to European, Western entrepreneurs. Therefore, directed by this conviction, the municipality has even initiated a network for 'them'.

The ethnic minority, female entrepreneurs' point of view

The following excerpt from Mechan's story illustrates how she constructs a dichotomy between Us and Them, also emphasising the 'being different' versus 'becoming similar'/'the same':

Actually ever since I have worked for Osmose [a consultancy firm dealing with multicultural issues] I'm very conscious, have become even more conscious, that we are different, that we are Turkish. But: this is a mere fact and I think that some things should just be accepted. What I want most is to pack my things and go back to Turkey.

(Mechan, Turkish ethnic origin, owner of a nail studio)

Whereas the Dutch dominant discourse and the institutions seem to favour participation, Mechan firmly favours the other side. Where the favouring of the same implies striving for integration, assimilation and inclusion, Mechan wants to accept being different, thus resisting the idea of having to be the same, resisting the ideology of equality associated with integration and participation. Claiming to be 'fed up' with the integration requirement, she has distanced herself and started her own business, as she seems to feel that this will enable her to live 'her own life'. In that sense entrepreneuring seems to be a vehicle for her to emancipate (but notably not to integrate). By wanting to start a company in Turkey she seems to want to resist this dominant idea. She idealises Turkey as opposed to the Netherlands (even speaking of 'going *back*' while she was not born there). Hence, we observe here that not only Dutch institutions create dichotomies regarding integration and US/Them, but this female entrepreneur of Turkish origin does so as well, albeit with a different emphasis. She does not want to be 'pulled in' (see above) to the (Western) centre, but rejects it; a separating move rather than a connecting one.

Other than Mechan, we see Gül, a real estate agent of Turkish origin, finding agency in her being 'different' as an entrepreneur in the Netherlands:

> Being Turkish is really advantageous, with the language and everything, it is an enrichment. A colleague of mine, a top business, asked us to work with them, and we were brought into the deal precisely because we are Turkish. Why? Because we have a better understanding of this target group. Allochtonous people have a different mentality in doing business; much more based on trust. When they are with me they say much more. I can persuade them much better than a Dutch person. A Dutch agent won't succeed in this.

Gül asserts that in her business 'being different' is an advantage and should be encouraged. In this sense she goes further than Mechan; not only accepting being different but emphasising it; it is a 'unique selling point' for her, being a Turkish female entrepreneur. Here, the Us/Them dichotomy is deployed as an advantage; 'allochtonous' clients would apparently sooner trust her than a Dutch real estate agent. The apparent prejudices are turned against the tide and used to create a competitive advantage. Nevertheless, by doing so Gül also constructs a binary between the 'allochtonous' entrepreneur and the 'autochtonous' entrepreneur, the first being more capable of persuading clients from another ethnic background. However, when it comes to networking, Gül does want to be included and hence wants to reverse the dichotomy. As is the case here, her being Turkish, or 'different', seems disadvantageous:

> At network meetings, I come in, and then everyone stares at me. Cos, you know, a foreigner, not blond. It's a real man's world. They just watch, and then I think, just walk over to me. Be a man and come and present yourself. This is a network drink, so you are allowed to talk with me now!

When it comes to networking events Gül wants to integrate, but may be viewed as (too) different (too) 'exotic'. Likewise, when the successful Gül at one point goes to a bank (where she is even a member of the member's council), she is met with suspicion:

> I received a great project, real top! So I said I needed an overdraft facility, just in case I needed to do some pre-financing. Yet at a certain moment they said, we are not going to do this. I wanted 25.000 Euros, which is really only peanuts! So I asked, why, you have to tell me why, I can back everything up, I have a contract to prove the deal's OK. But they said: at

your age, in the real-estate business, living in a nice house, driving a nice car.... They found it suspicious. Really, I almost had to cry. So if you do well, it is also not OK!

Here as well, prejudice does not work to her benefit. Gül is excluded, this time from attaining short-term funding. She claims that the bank did not base its judgement on facts but on a hunch, perhaps due to the fact that the Dutch media often relate stories alleging that Turkish criminals are involved in whitewashing activities. She felt at the time that she was being judged on the basis of her Turkish ethnicity where apparently this particular bank could not imagine the combination of being young, being prosperous and of Turkish origin to result in honourable success. Apart from exposing a case of blatant partiality, Gül's story offers an apparent paradox, something which decon-struction in particular can bring to light. Whereas Mechan 'simply' reverses the dichotomy (resisting integration, wanting to be different rather than the same), Gül wants both: to stand out/be different and to be included. Con-sequently, she seems to experience directly how bipolar reasoning plays out. She wants to 'network' in the Western way, as is the advice of the institu-tional officers we have spoken with, but to no avail. She does want to obtain finance through a bank, but to no avail. With Gül, 'in' and 'out' are seen to become mutual; they are linked to each other, and are no longer 'strict' opposites.

We see the same binaries come into play in the stories of the female migrant entrepreneurs as in the institutional stories: us–them, inclusion–exclusion, equality–difference, integration–isolation. From an institutional point of view the first term evidently presents the optimistic, what is to be desired (the ideology even), and the second the negative, the less desired, or even that which should be eliminated. And as the allochtonous female entre-preneurs' stories place other emphases, and point towards a mutuality between the poles, we can begin to see the contours of ambiguity here. 'Out' is just as much 'in' as the reverse, and 'in' is merely relative. Likewise, entrepreneurship is not necessarily instrumental to integration, as we will see with Aida (of Moroccan origin, who has owned a shop selling wedding dresses).

Aida, initially unemployed, also went to a bank, in her case to get a loan to set up her business. A coach allocated to Aida by the unemployment agency approved her business plan and even went with her to a bank which also approved her business plan and granted her a loan. Yet, Aida seems to be ambiguous about her entrepreneurial motivation and competences:

As a girl I was raised to obey the men. I did administrative work for a long time. Then I became unemployed, got into welfare. There I received leaflets convincing me to become self-employed. It was sort of always in the back of my mind, that I would want something like that, that I'd like to be my own boss.

Out of caution, Aida wants to start small:

> I want to start from home, I said. But they [meaning the unemployment
> agency] said I couldn't start from home, and needed to have a 'real' shop.
> The first month went well, but soon it slowed down. This meant no
> income, but I had to go on using the loan to pay the rent and other fixed
> costs.

In the end, Aida's business initiative fails. She blames the employment
agency:

> I told the unemployment agency that it was not working, that business
> stayed slow. I talked to them again, said that in hindsight having my own
> business was perhaps not such a good idea. I wanted to stop, I kept trying
> to contact this coach until October when all my money was gone.

Aida even tried taking legal steps against them (to no avail). According to
Aida, the employment agency should have been more scrupulous in judging
her business plan, 'they' should have told her to wait, because of the ongoing
credit crisis; 'they' should have told her that people do not buy wedding
dresses between March and October, and so on. As far as her coach is concerned, he was apparently paid by the unemployment agency to guide her
during the first two years, but did not deliver and even 'disappeared'. Aida's
story exposes conflicts of interest, disruption, even discomfort: was it actually
in her best interests to start a business? The unemployment agency seems to
have imposed a 'traditional' Western entrepreneurship model upon Aida (see
also Calas *et al.* 2009), one that insists on operating from a real shop instead of
from her own home. Apparently there has been a gap between both parties'
idea(l)s and aims. The question arises: Who benefits? Who benefits from
stimulating ethnic minority women such as Aida to start up their own businesses? These critical questions resonate with Karnani (2009) who cynically
stated: 'Romanticizing the poor harms the poor.' It is the economy that
benefits here, not necessarily the starters, as with Aida's story. In Aida case the
institutional help seems only to have placed her in a more marginalised position, where the institution did not necessarily practise a socialisation strategy,
but one to get someone off their welfare benefits and thus to contribute to
the economy and society financially. The (hegemonic!) goal seems to be to
economise, not to socialise. Yet of course this story is Aida's version, not that
of the unemployment agency. In her story Aida puts herself in a victimised
position, claiming the agency could have known and should have done things
differently. Aida constructs a binary between an 'Omni-knowing' agency and
the 'poor, dependent, victimised (migrant) woman', thus placing herself in
the margins rather than in the stronger, emancipated centre.

Discussion and conclusion

Using insights of deconstruction to question dominant entrepreneurship assumptions, our analysis has demonstrated how both Dutch institutions and ethnic minority women construct dichotomies when it comes to ethnic minority women and their entrepreneurial endeavours. The institutions as well as the female ethnic entrepreneurs sustain the-us-versus-them dichotomy as found in general societal discourse and in the standing literature on migrant entrepreneurship and female entrepreneurship. The institutions firmly sustain the optimistic stance as is found in the standing literature on entrepreneurship. Accordingly, the institutions purport that 'they' should network like 'us', know about 'our' helpful institutions, and behave 'professionally' when it comes to location, finance, etc., just like 'normal' Dutch entrepreneurs. The ethnic female entrepreneurs, on the other hand, want to emphasise the fact that they are different from 'us', to absolve themselves from assimilation, and even to deploy this as a competitive advantage. With these women, inclusion seems to be a highly ambiguous construct. We have seen how Mechan's story lays bare the very assumption underlying integration: that there is indeed something different; and for her, to integrate is to reject difference. Rather than doing that, she suggests one should accept difference rather than deny or reject it, and try to 'adjust' it accordingly.

If we take a critical look at the consequences of the institutions' optimism and efforts at stimulating entrepreneurship we get a feel for the strength of the ideological obscuration. Assuming that these women indeed come from unequal, 'worse' places (the 'oppressed', victimised migrant women), entrepreneurship seems to be unquestioningly applied (imposed even, as in Aida's case) in order to emancipate and elevate them. Our analysis reveals what is being overlooked when simply pushing a one-size-fits-all idea (or ideal) of what is required for entrepreneurial success, 'treating' entrepreneurship as something uni-form to which these entrepreneurs have to conform, underwriting the ethnocentric and gendered subtext of entrepreneurship (Ogbor 2000; Essers *et al.* 2010).

It has become clear that there is more to 'us' versus 'them' and 'in' versus 'out' than their simply being opposites. As to the issue of whether and how entrepreneurial efforts indeed seem to 'elevate' (emancipate) individuals, our analysis has illustrated that this is also not unproblematic. When we look at these women, and how they deal with the ideological constructs that invade their entrepreneurial efforts, we can observe that Mechan is responding creatively to the limitations – and interference – she perceives in the institutional conditions that surround her. This has stimulated her to create her own space and life conditions and to go on doing so, by wishing to move to Turkey to grow and expand her business (as well as to avoid perceived problems within the Dutch context). The 'trap' she has been perceiving seems to be precisely the thing that has made her into a more autonomous, free agent. She has bent the stifling conditions to her advantage. Gül is also responding creatively to the institutional conditions she perceives – as well as the ideologies that accompany them – by using her ethnic background, including her knowledge of the Turkish language and other allochtonous cultures, to her advantage, as well as by deliberately networking actively with a variety of people from diverse backgrounds (in terms of ethnicity, gender and profession). She also seems to be bending the ideological trap, using it to her advantage, rather than abiding by it or being defeated by it. 'Even' with Aida we can say that she is creatively dealing with the circumstances: we can just as well portray her as someone constructing a highly creative and convincing narrative where it is not her fault but rather the unemployment agency's that her business did not work out. Rather than labelling her the 'sorry case' or the 'unfit entrepreneur', we may just as well argue that she is actually a very clever storyteller. She is bending her own misery to her advantage by putting the blame on UWV and her missing coach. So despite – or even precisely because of – the institutional conditions that surround them, these women portray (creative) potential, but not in the way intended by the officials, and other organisations surrounding their entrepreneurial activities and not because this is being *stimulated*. We feel that entrepreneuring itself is not 'the problem' here, but we suggest that it is the idea of stimulating entrepreneurship that seems to be problematic, together with the (unquestioned) ideology underlying the stimulating activities. Entrepreneuring may be emancipating when these entrepreneurs can make sense of it in their own (cultural) way, but not when they are 'stimulated' to adhere to some ideal. The ideal needs to be shaken up, to be accepted as something that is only temporarily stabilised, but is continuously in need of reconsideration. Deconstruction here literally suggests a 'play of differences'.

References

Alvesson, M. and Sköldberg, K. (2000), *Reflexive Methodology*, London: Sage.

Boje, D. (1995), Stories and the storytelling organization: A postmodern analysis of Disney as 'Tamara Land'. *Academy of Management Journal*, **38**(4), pp. 997–1035.

Boje, D. (2001), *Narrative Methods for Organizational and Communication Research*, London: Sage.

Bruni, A., Gherardi, S. and Poggio, B. (2004), Entrepreneur-mentality, gender and the study of women entrepreneurs. *Journal of Organizational Change Management*, **17**(3), pp. 256–268.

Calas, M., Smircich, L. and Bourne, K. (2009), Extending the boundaries: Reframing 'entrepreneurship as social change' through feminist perspectives. *Academy of Management Review*, **34**(3), pp. 552–569.

Chell, E. (2001), *Entrepreneurship: Globalization, Innovation and Development*, London: Thomson Learning.

Chia, R. (1994), The concept of decision: A deconstructive analysis. *Journal of Management Studies*, **31**(6), pp. 781–806.

Chia, R. (1996), *Organizational Analysis as Deconstructive Practice*, Berlin: Walter de Gruyter.

Cooper, J. (1986), Organization/disorganization. *Social Science Information*, **25**, pp. 299–335.

Derrida, J. (1977), *Of Grammatology*, Baltimore, MD: Johns Hopkins University Press.

Derrida, J. (1982), *Margins of Philosophy*, Hassocks: Harvester.

Essers, C. (2009a), Reflections on the narrative approach: Dilemmas of power, emotions and social location while constructing life-stories. *Organization*, **16**(2), pp. 163–181.

Essers, C. (2009b), *New Directions in Postheroic Entrepreneurship. Narratives of Gender and Ethnicity. Advances in Organization Studies*, Malmö: Liber.

Essers, C. and Benschop, Y. (2007), Enterprising identities: Female entrepreneurs of Moroccan and Turkish origin in the Netherlands. *Organization Studies*, **28**(1), pp. 49–69.

Essers, C. and Benschop, Y. (2009), Muslim businesswomen doing boundary work: The negotiation of Islam, gender and ethnicity within entrepreneurial contexts. *Human Relations*, **62**(3), pp. 403–424.

Essers, C., Benschop, Y. and Doorewaard, H. (2010), Female ethnicity: Understanding Muslim migrant businesswomen in the Netherlands. *Gender, Work and Organization*, **17**(3), pp. 320–340.

Ghorashi, H. (2003), Ayaan Hirsi Ali: Daring or dogmatic? Debates on multiculturalism and emancipation in the Netherlands. *Focaal, European Journal of Anthropology*, **42**, pp. 163–169.

Gijsberts, M. and Dagevos, J. (2004), Concentratie en wederzijdse beeldvorming tussen autochtonen en allochtonen. *Migrantenstudies*, **20**(3), pp. 145–168.

Jones, C. and Spicer, A. (2009), *Unmasking the Entrepreneur*, Cheltenham: Edward Elgar.

Karnani, A. (2009), Romanticizing the poor harms the poor. *Journal of International Development*, **21**(1), pp. 76–86.

Kloosterman, R., van der Leun, J. and Rath, J. (1999), Mixed embeddedness: (In)formal economic activities and immigrant businesses in the Netherlands. *International Journal of Urban and Regional Research*, **23**(2), pp. 252–266.

Lieblich, A., Tuval-Mashiach, R. and Zilber, T. (1998), *Narrative Research: Reading, Analysis and Interpretation*, London: Sage.

Lutz, H. (1991), *Migrant Women of 'Islamic Background': Images and Self-images*, Amsterdam: Stichting MERA, Middle East Research Associates.

Malach Pines, A., Lerner, M. and Schwartz, D. (2010), Gender differences in entrepreneurship: Equality, diversity and inclusion in times of global crisis. *Equality, Diversity, and Inclusion: An International Journal*, **29**(2), pp. 186–198.

Martin, J. (1990), Organizational taboos: The suppression of gender conflict in organizations. *Organization Science*, **1**(4), pp. 339–359.

McClelland, D. (1987), Characteristics of successful entrepreneurs. *Journal of Creative Behaviour*, **21**(3), pp. 219–233.

Ogbor, J. (2000), Mythicizing and reification in entrepreneurial discourse: Ideology-critique of entrepreneurial studies. *Journal of Management Studies*, **37**(5), pp. 605–635.

Perren, L. and Jennings, P. (2005), Government discourses on entrepreneurship: Issues of legitimization, subjugation, and power. *Entrepreneurship: Theory and Practice*, **29**(2), pp. 173–184.

Portes, A. (1995), *The Economic Sociology of Immigration: Essays on Networks, Ethnicity, and Entrepreneurship*, New York: Russell Sage Foundation.

Schumpeter, J. (1976), *History of Economic Analysis*, edited from manuscript by E. Boody Schumpeter, New York: Oxford University Press.

Smith, R. and Anderson, A. (2004), The devil is in the e-tale: Forms and structures in the entrepreneurial narratives. In D. Hjorth and C. Steyaert (eds), *Narrative and Discursive Approaches in Entrepreneurship*, Cheltenham: Edward Elgar, pp. 125–143.

Van Nieuwkerk, K. (2003), Multiculturaliteit, islam en gender. *Tijdschrift voor gender studies*, **6**(3), pp. 6–20.

Wekker, G. and Lutz, H. (2001), Een hoogvlakte met koude winden. De geschiedenis van het gender- en etniciteitsdenken in Nederland. In M. Botman, N. Jouwe and G. Wekker (eds), *Caleidoscopische visies. De zwarte, migranten en vluchtelingen-vrouwenbeweging in Nederland*, Amsterdam: KIT.

Part IV

Challenging the gendered subtext in entrepreneurship

11 Critically evaluating contemporary entrepreneurship from a feminist perspective

Susan Marlow and Haya Al-Dajani

Introduction

This chapter offers an overview of critical arguments which analyse and evaluate the influence of gender on women's entrepreneurial propensity and performance. In addition, we extend this increasingly well-rehearsed debate by adopting a contextualised critique which acknowledges intersectional influences on entrepreneurial activity. As such, we present a summary of foundational arguments regarding the relationship between gender, women and entrepreneurial activity while challenging the acontextual and universalistic assumptions embedded within this debate.

While one of the first acknowledged explorations of women's business ownership emerged in 1979 (Schwartz 1979), the recognition that gender might influence entrepreneurial activity was largely ignored until the 1990s (Henry *et al.* 2015). However, since that time, increasing attention has been afforded to how social constructions of gender impact upon women's propensity for and experiences of entrepreneurial activity (McAdam 2012). This analysis has undergone several iterations advancing from a descriptive focus upon gender as a variable to contemporary critiques embedded in feminist theorising (Ahl and Marlow 2012). Yet, one noticeable tendency within much of this debate has been a presumption of gender as generic, and women themselves are a homogeneous category whose gendered ascription generates universal experiences of subordination (for exceptions, see Essers and Benschop 2009; Essers *et al.* 2010).

Developing a somewhat generic debate to uncover the embedded biases within the ontological foundations of entrepreneurship has been revelatory in exposing the discriminatory presumptions that inform normative understandings of 'who or what' is an entrepreneur (Gartner 1988). It reveals that the ideal representation of the preferred entrepreneur is male, white and middle class (Ogbor 2000; Ahl 2006; Marlow 2014). This narrowed vision of how credibility as an entrepreneurial actor is achieved conceptually and empirically limits understanding of entrepreneurship and entrepreneurial behaviour. Accordingly, a focus on, and analysis of, the influence of gender on women's engagement with entrepreneurial activities has been of considerable importance in revealing the discriminatory and limiting ontology which has informed the dominant perspective upon entrepreneurship. Consequently, the analytical exposure of gendered biases shaping entrepreneurial activities has fuelled an academic debate which has grown in scope and complexity over recent years.

As this debate has evolved, however, it has led to new questions and challenges regarding the assumption of women as ciphers of the gendered subject, how context shapes the articulation of gendered behaviour in the realm of entrepreneurship and competing notions of intersectionality and positionality (Martinez-Dy et al. 2014). In effect, the need to move beyond a simple association between a universal gendered subject and her acontextual experiences of entrepreneurship is pressing. We adopt this view and draw upon an example of entrepreneurial activity by women who are seldom recognised in the entrepreneurship literature, and displaced by conflict from Iraq, Palestine, and Syria to Jordan. In doing so, we respond to the calls in the literature and use women, gender and entrepreneurship as a lens to recognise the importance of context, intersectionality and positionality. To develop these arguments, this chapter is structured as follows: first, there is an overview of contemporary theorising regarding gender and entrepreneurship and how this influences women's venturing. This is followed by the second section which explores the notion of context and how this influences the enactment of gender and women's entrepreneurial activity. The third section explores notions of intersectionality and positionality; we then provide an empirical example illustrating these constructs in action and conclude by reviewing the implications of our arguments.

Gender, women and entrepreneurship

Entrepreneurship has traditionally been presented as the pursuit of opportunities to generate new ventures which create a diverse range of wealth producing outcomes (Storey and Greene 2010). As entrepreneurship ostensibly has no formal entry barriers but rather, pivots upon the development and application of individualised effort, ambition, energy and creativity it has been positioned as the epitome of the neo-liberal turn which has emerged since the early 1980s (Mole and Ram 2012). Indeed, we might describe entrepreneurship as the 'poster boy' for neo-liberalism given the focus upon the role of individuality and agency as pathways to achievement (du Gay 1996; Giddens 1992). Yet, there is a paradox at the heart of this debate; whilst entrepreneurship has been presented as a meritocratic domain with no entry boundaries where potential can be realised, it is in fact, a highly conservative socioeconomic arena. As such, the greater the resource base available to prospective entrepreneurs, the more successful will be their ventures (Jayawarna et al. 2013) and in addition, social ascriptions, such as gender, critically impact upon entrepreneurial potential (Martinez-Dy et al. 2014). Thus, those with a rich resource base and who fit an entrepreneurial ideal type are more likely to attain legitimacy and success in this field.

Mapping this critique onto a gendered analysis reveals that the characteristics of the ideal entrepreneur – innovative, competitive, aggressive – fit very neatly into a masculinised profile (Ahl 2006). This effectively positions women outside this idealised template which, in turn, affects a biased understanding and evaluation of their entrepreneurial activities. This prejudicial ontology has been revealed and explored by those such as Mirchandani (1999), Ogbor (2000), Marlow (2002) and Ahl (2006), who argue that the mainstream debate within entrepreneurship has managed to be simultaneously gender blind and gender biased. The consequences of this unconscious bias have, on the one hand, rendered women invisible in that all entrepreneurs are universally coded male. On the other hand, women are 'othered' as, when their entrepreneurial efforts have been recognised, they have been assessed against a mythical stereotypical male. The culmination of this is a feminised entrepreneurial–deficit model.

Recent shifts in the analysis of women, gender and entrepreneurship which draw upon feminist perspectives have, however, increasingly disputed the notion of a female entrepreneurial deficit (Ahl and Marlow 2012). Rather, developing arguments focus on two broad challenges: first, a confusion between structure and agency. In effect, women have been perceived as deficient entrepreneurs due to a lack of *agentic* ability. Yet feminist analyses suggest that multiple *structural* constraints combined with stereotypical assumptions regarding poor legitimacy limit women's ability to accrue entrepreneurial resources (finance, networks, time, experience, knowledge) which negatively impacts upon start-up propensity and future firm performance (Marlow and McAdam 2013). Second, the extent of difference which can be afforded to owner/founder sex has been challenged. We know that when weighted for similarity, female-owned firms appear to perform slightly better on all measures than those of their male peers (Robb and Watson 2011), that women founders are equally motivated to maximise economic returns from their ventures (Saridakis *et al.* 2014) and that in a context of deprivation there are no differences in bootstrapping strategies (Jayawarna *et al.* 2015). Yet, given embedded gendered assumptions, the quest for difference persisted (and persists) with small variations exaggerated to satisfy social expectations of male dominance and female deficit (McAdam 2012; Henry *et al.* 2015).

While there has been considerable progress in the gendered critique of entrepreneurship, it is notable that denotations of gender remain a proxy for femininity (Kelan 2009). As such, women are primary gendered subjects within the entrepreneurial discourse (for rare exceptions, see Hamilton 2013; Smith 2010). Given the negative values associated with femininity, women are generically disadvantaged as gendered subject beings (Butler 1993). Thus, this disadvantage has been transposed to the context of entrepreneurship but has been hidden by assumptions of gender-neutral scientific enquiry, buttressed by a logic and rationality (Harding 1993). Only by rebalancing the current gender agenda to fully and separately acknowledge the assumptions fuelling masculinity as a default setting can we challenge these presumptions and, in so doing, analytically expose how both women and men 'do' gender and 'do' entrepreneurship.

As a more theoretically informed debate has emerged to challenge notions of entrepreneurship as a gender–neutral meritocracy and women as deficit actors, the issue of causality has also been considered regarding to what extent gender as a variable can be effectively identified as a definitive influence on entrepreneurial activity (Gill 2011). This debate introduces a context and intersectionality perspective. Reflecting upon these critiques, it has been taken for granted that the institutional context of the mature, developed economy is the normative setting for entrepreneurial activity (Bruton *et al.* 2008; Imas *et al.* 2012). This assumption not only excludes the majority of the global economy – particularly developing economies where entrepreneurial activity is often the only option for economic participation – it also reflects an incipient imperialism which pervades entrepreneurship research. While context is being increasingly recognised as critical in shaping entrepreneurial activity (Zahra *et al.* 2014), it is also acknowledged that individuals are highly heterogeneous and cannot be simply categorised by simplistic generic ascriptions, such as their gender or race. How diverse characteristics intersect to position individuals within a context must be interrogated if we are to advance knowledge of entrepreneurial propensity and performance. Consequently, unless gender theorising within entrepreneurship adopts a critical feminist perspective, refutes the dominance of gender as a category, questions universality and explores contextual influences, it is in danger of producing, at best, a blunt instrument which assumes that gender only applies to women and homogenises disadvantage. At worst, in making such assumptions, debate is in danger of reproducing the subordination it purports to critique by adopting a narrow, conservative perspective (Ahl and Marlow 2012).

To summarise these arguments, it is evident that the theoretical analyses and empirical evidence exploring the relationship between gender, women and entrepreneurship has developed considerably in regards to sophistication and substance since the early 1990s (McAdam 2012). There has been a welcome shift from a focus on the individual woman, her lack of entrepreneurial agency, small samples and atheoretical description (Carter and Shaw 2006) to far more complex debates. These focus on how the construct of gender constrains women's life chances and socio-economic participation which relatedly spill over into entrepreneurial activity (Henry *et al.* 2015). In turn, this debate has been increasingly informed by feminist theory to analyse and explain how women fit into the contemporary entrepreneurial turn while challenging the ontological and epistemological assumptions underpinning the entrepreneurship discourse (Marlow and Martinez-Dy 2015). However, how context and heterogeneity frame the enactment of entrepreneurship requires acknowledgement and explanation; thus we now turn to the notion of context and, in particular, the implication of this construct for analysing the influence of gender on women's entrepreneurial activities.

Context

As Wright (2012, p. 9) notes, 'context has received relatively little attention in the entrepreneurial literature [however] studying entrepreneurs in the context in which they find themselves is central to understanding the entrepreneurial process'. By context, we mean the diverse range of influences which shape, enable and constrain human behaviour. When applied to the field of entrepreneurship, Zahra *et al.* (2014) suggest that such influences may be broadly analysed as institutional, temporal, spatial and social. Each of these aspects will affect entrepreneurial propensity and experience at multiple and integrated dimensions both horizontally and vertically.

Within the institutional context, institutional theory is central to analysing firm performance given that it encompasses formal rules and regulations and informal norms, culture and values (Bruton *et al.* 2010). This, aspects such as formal regulatory constraints upon entrepreneurial activities, funding regimes, attitudes to failure and cultural perceptions of the value of entrepreneurship all contribute to specific institutional contexts which support or constrain entrepreneurial activity.

When considering the temporal context, timing has a critical effect on entrepreneurial venturing in terms of specific eras as well as in relation to the life cycle of the firm. Thus, in the current era, entrepreneurial activity is afforded considerable status and legitimacy as a desirable activity with the potential to offer a positive contribution to society by creating wealth and employment. However, looking back in time (for instance, the era between 1945 and 1980), entrepreneurship was dismissed as inconsequential given the focus on the corporate entity as the normative site of commercial activity (Marlow 2002). In addition, there is a temporal progression in the life of firms as they move from start-up to maturity and/or market exit. Depending on the particular stage, they will have differing forms, functions and processes; as such, the temporal context is critical to understanding issues of legitimacy, strategy and performance.

Zahra *et al.*'s (2014) third type of context is the spatial context. This denotes the physical environment where entrepreneurial activity occurs; thus, if there is a strong urban infrastructure, accessing markets for firms within cities is relatively straightforward when compared with, for example, entrepreneurs operating in rural areas in developing economies. In addition, where firms cluster in one area – such as the ubiquitous Silicon Valley – there are numerous advantages of proximity and mutual leverage arising from a contextual clustering (Welter 2011).

The last type of Zahra *et al.*'s (2014) context is social context. This refers to the availability of networks which enhance connections between a range of stakeholders – such as investors – vital for entrepreneurial success as well as support and advice networks which act to encourage entrepreneurial activity (Jayawarna *et al.* 2015).

Consequently, context is fundamental in terms of legitimating entrepreneurship at particular points in time, enabling or constraining access to critical entrepreneurial resources and as a broad external socio-economic framework for entrepreneurial activity. Such aspects of context clearly overlap and meld to generate a platform for entrepreneurial activity. Yet, to these encompassing domains, we would suggest that gender also acts as a contextual lens which shapes the development of entrepreneurial propensity and venture creation. Drawing upon the work of Welter and Smallbone (2008) and Welter (2011), we concur that gender also forms a facet of contextualised behaviour. Thus, how the institutional framework positions women in the socio-economic context and their ability to achieve mobility across contexts of space and time will impact upon entrepreneurial endeavours. Examples of how a gendered context channels women's entrepreneurial propensity are illustrated in the work of Klyver and colleagues (2013). When evaluating the relatively low levels of entrepreneurial participation of Swedish women, Klyver et al. (2013) argue that the institutional context ensures the availability of good-quality public sector employment with associated maternity benefits and childcare provision. Combined with a lower evaluation of the role and status of entrepreneurship given the stronger (if diminishing) welfare capitalism context of Scandinavia (Ahl and Nelson 2015), self-employment is a less likely choice for many women where better alternatives for economic participation are readily available. Welter and Smallbone (2008) explored the gender context of a transitional economy, Uzbekistan, to evaluate the ease with which women can develop their entrepreneurial potential; given the patriarchal context, they found women exploiting sexual stereotypes to navigate the regulatory regime. Thus, women emphasised their femininity and lack of understanding of corrupt systems they encountered when attempting to create a new firm which prompted men to help them negotiate these institutionalised challenges. Similarly, Al-Dajani and Marlow (2010) explored a context of displacement and patriarchy to analyse how Palestinian women, displaced to Amman in Jordan owing to conflict in the Middle East, established home-based enterprises in Amman in Jordan.

In effect, there are broad-based categories which comprise context and which, in turn, act as conduits for entrepreneurial activity. We suggest that such categories should also be translated through a gendered lens to assess their impact upon the entrepreneurial propensity and experiences of women – given that gender is in and of itself a dimension of context. Yet, how women are positioned within the overlapping cusp of various contextual dimensions and the implications of such to enact their entrepreneurial potential will depend on the resources they command and are able to invest in their ventures (Martinez-Dy et al. 2014). In effect, context will funnel perceptions of and possibilities for entrepreneurial activity; how individuals are able to exploit the opportunities within their operational context will depend on their ability to access a matrix of resources. This argument acknowledges heterogeneity in that while, for example, women are categorised by a universal gendered ascription which may then be used as a contextualised framework for their entrepreneurial activities, within that framework individuals will have more or less scope to negotiate the challenges they encounter (Marlow and Martinez-Dy 2015). This scope arises from positioning within an inter-sectional matrix of advantage and disadvantage where gender intersects with other socially derived categories to generate heterogeneity of opportunity and action (Crenshaw 1989). How such intersectionality positions women within the context of entrepreneurship is explored in the next section.

Intersectionality, positionality, gender and entrepreneurship

Intersectionality originated in black feminist thought but has emerged as a critical element of contemporary feminism (Hancock 2007). The construct acknowledges the intersection of social categories of difference; for example, race/ethnicity, gender, class and so on evaluating how they coalesce to shape life chances. As such, intersectionality offers a theoretical perspective to acknowledge the analysis of inter-categorical heterogeneity and related domains of oppression.

In terms of entrepreneurship, intersectionality has been used to study various combinations of intersections, such as race, class and gender (Gill 2011), gender, ethnicity and religion (Essers and Benschop 2009; Essers *et al.* 2010), and gender, ethnicity, national origin and national context (Verduijn and Essers 2013). As such, it is acknowledged that separate evaluations of, for example, women's entrepreneurship and immigrant/ethnic minority entre-preneurship fail to recognise how such constructs overlap and form an inter-secting matrix which informs diverse forms of oppression (Essers *et al.* 2010).

While intersectional analyses have advanced debate by acknowledging how categorical characterisations overlap and generate complex socio-economic hierarchies which then constrain access to and accrual of a range of resources, the debate has been subject to some critique. Primarily, it is argued that there is a rather static focus on disadvantage and constraint but little acknowledgement of how individuals can be advantaged through their position in intersectional categories (Van der Tuin and Geerts 2013; Nash 2008). Responding to such concerns, the work of Anthias (2001, 2006, 2008) extends this debate when recognising the concept of translocational positionality; she argues that intersectionality is a 'social process related to practices and arrangements' that gives rise to particular forms of positionality (2006, p. 27). The construct of positionality is two-fold: first, it combines social position, as outcome, with social positioning, a processual set of prac-tices, actions and meanings; second, it is conceptualised as comprising the space at the intersection of structure and agency. Importantly, positionality is said to be translocational, or, in other words, 'in terms of locations which are not fixed but are context, meaning and time related and which therefore, involve shifts and contradiction' (Anthias 2008, p. 5). As such, it moves away from the idea of given groups or categories, and towards broader social loca-tions and processes.

This debate is useful in exploring how positionality shapes entrepreneurial resource allocation and accrual. It is deemed axiomatic that those who have access to a diverse range of resources such as finance, human capital, social networks and so on to support their entrepreneurial ambitions will create more sustainable ventures (Jayawarna *et al.* 2014). Yet, while extant evidence acknowledges the importance of resource utilisation, rather less consideration is offered to the inequality which bounds access to appropriate resources. Thus, when applied to resource accrual, positionality theory interrogates the manner in which context positions individuals and groups within certain social hierarchies and its implications for unequal resource distribution. To focus specifically on women, it enables us to analyse how gender intersects with, for example, class and race to position individuals in a context of privilege or disadvantage (Martinez-Dy *et al.* 2014).

Thus, an intersectional approach recognising positionality offers an intriguing avenue to advance our understanding of the notion of context in entrepreneurship studies. Aspects of intersectionality can platform diversity between categories of women differentially positioned by specific constraints or privileges within their context such as class, disability, age and so on, and thus inform entrepreneurial resource mobilisation strategies. From these limited examples it is evident that intersectional and positional perspectives are able to offer conceptual shape to the variety of social conditions in which entrepreneurial activity is embedded, thereby intervening in and advancing existing theories of entrepreneurial context. We now demonstrate how these constructs are articulated through the lived experiences of women, using an empirical example of entrepreneurial activity within a context of displacement, patriarchy and poverty.

Displacement, gender and entrepreneurship

Although rarely visible within the mainstream entrepreneurship literature, displaced and refugee women in the Global South engage in a wide array of entrepreneurial ventures (Al-Dajani and Marlow 2014). Our research with displaced and refugee female entrepreneurs residing and operating in Jordan spans approximately 15 years and indicates trends that are similar to displaced women's entrepreneurship in other parts across the Middle East region. Through the enterprises they initiate and grow, displaced female entrepreneurs resourcefully navigate the subordinating patriarchal cultures of their own displaced communities as well as that of the Jordanian host nation, and the legal terms that deny them full citizenship (Al-Dajani and Marlow 2010). The prevalence and invisibility of their entrepreneurial ventures is largely embedded within their positionality, determined by their socio-political identity, ethnicity, gender, poverty and displacement (Al-Dajani and Marlow 2013).

To research this phenomenon and the diversity of women's experiences effectively, the adoption of a feminist research approach and methodology was axiomatic, since our ambition is to offer voice and visibility to these displaced women, as their experiences and opinions are largely ignored and excluded from the wider agenda. Thus, a qualitative, in-depth exploration based on interview conversations has been employed, and has focused on the displaced women's entrepreneurial journeys from start-up to the present, to reveal the 'everydayness of entrepreneurship' (Steyaert and Katz 2004), and to gain an understanding of how the displaced female entrepreneurs negotiated, interpreted and addressed the reality which confronted them in terms of their positionality within the Jordanian context.

Perhaps unsurprisingly, the majority of displaced female entrepreneurs participating in our research agreed that while wealth creation was a strong motive for business creation when starting up their enterprises, the stronger motivations were preserving their heritage and identity, and supporting their displaced ethnic communities. They achieved these aims by establishing enterprises that produced and celebrated their indigenous crafts, and contracted poor home-based female suppliers from their own displaced communities or other displaced communities in Jordan. In doing so, the displaced female entrepreneurs were able to (1) elevate their social positioning within their own displaced communities, (2) create substantial awareness of their heritage among their clientele which led to increased sales, profits and customer loyalty, (3) preserve craft production processes that were getting lost in their home nations, and, (4) support their communities which were neglected by local and international aid agencies.

As well as maintaining and promoting their own heritages and ethnicities, the majority of displaced female entrepreneurs repeatedly displayed their loyalty to their host nation, and voiced their readiness to be part of Jordanian society by supporting the three national campaigns of 'Jordan First', 'National Agenda' and 'We Are All Jordan' endorsed by the Jordanian government since 2003 to aid national political unity (Tobin 2011). They did this by integrating the slogans, symbols and logos of the campaigns into their displays, presentation and merchandise.

Although there is a context of continuous political volatility which engulfs the Middle East region and thus damages the survival and sustainability of many enterprises in Jordan, the vast majority of the small entrepreneurial ventures owned by the displaced women participating in our research showed remarkable longevity, suggesting a strong survival and resilience trend. Repeatedly, the majority of participating displaced female entrepreneurs acknowledged their unexpected significant business increases during the Israel–Lebanon war in 2006, and since 2011 when the Egyptian revolution and the Syrian conflict erupted. Not only did tourist numbers increase dramatically in Jordan as a result of these crises, but also businesses which had worked previously in those countries arrived in Amman looking for alternative contractors. Such business surges balanced the harmful effects when tourism decreased dramatically in Jordan, and when the nation's sociopolitical stability was affected; for example, during the 9/11 New York bombings in 2001, the start of the war on Iraq in 2003, the terrorist attacks

188   S. Marlow and H. Al-Dajani

on Amman in 2005, and, more recently, the economic crisis that consumed Dubai, and the ongoing repercussions of the Arab Spring.

Despite their persistence and insistence on contributing to the creation of a resilient and sustainable craft sector in the Jordanian market, these women's tireless efforts continue to be only visible to their clients. However, there has recently been a surge of young Jordanian women designers starting up trend-setting enterprises that fuse together traditional crafts and designs with modern ones, and that blend together elements from different Arab ethnicities and heritages, to create unique, modern products and items that can be Arab rather than uniquely Jordanian, Iraqi, Palestinian, or Syrian. Contrary to the displaced female entrepreneurs in our research, these young Jordanian female designers and their enterprises are receiving wide acclaim and recognition within Jordan and the Middle East region, and are celebrated as empowered female role models. The irony is that these young Jordanian women consider their own role models as those young Palestinian refugee women who originated Jordan's first traditional embroidery enterprises soon after they arrived in Jordan in 1967.

Conclusion

Within this chapter we have discussed the critical arguments which analyse and evaluate the influence of gender on women's entrepreneurial propensity and performance. We began with an overview of contemporary theorising regarding gender and entrepreneurship, and how this influences women's ventures. This was followed by an exploration of the notion of context and how it influences the enactment of gender and women's entrepreneurial activity, as well as the notions of intersectionality and positionality. To illustrate these constructs in action, we presented findings from our research on displaced women's entrepreneurship in Jordan.

While these findings acknowledged the diversity among the displaced women's positionality in their host nation – Jordan – they also illustrated a shared approach to how the displaced women challenge the institutional norms that subordinate them, by creating sustainable and successful enterprises that capitalise on aspects of their positionality. Their resilience demonstrated how they do gender, and how they do entrepreneurship, and how they used both to overcome the consequences of controlling structural constraints such as the denial of full citizenship and its benefits. Given the considerable numbers of women displaced throughout the Global South, there remains an urgent need for the recognition and understanding of their entrepreneurial ventures through feminist perspectives and analyses. Doing so will not only contribute to the gender and entrepreneurship field, but also to the wider entrepreneurship arena.

Finally, in conducting our research with displaced female entrepreneurs in Jordan, we concur that identifying and accessing invisible female entrepreneurs in a conservative patriarchal context is problematic, and a fundamental barrier to bridging the gap in entrepreneurship research. Thus, it is hardly surprising that relatively little is known about the entrepreneurial ventures of such women. To overcome such constraints, the participation of indigenous, experienced and credible researchers is vital, as their prospects of accessing invisible groups are greater due to their localised social and cultural capital. Thus, we have argued that entrepreneurship is a contextualised activity influenced by time, space, social influences and institutional norms. In addition, we suggest that gender is also a contextual perspective which, when utilised to analyse women's entrepreneurial activities, reveals the normative biases within the ontological framing of entrepreneurship. Using gender as a contextual lens has been critical in making women visible in contemporary debate; but to ensure that this critical analytical flow avoids becoming a dead-end through assumptions of generic universality we must now recognise intersectional influences to reveal how women are positioned within heterogeneous entrepreneurial contexts.

References

Ahl, H. (2006), Why research on women entrepreneurs needs new directions. *Entrepreneurship Theory and Practice*, **30**(5), pp. 595–623.

Ahl, H. and Marlow, S. (2012), Gender and entrepreneurship research: Employing feminist theory to escape the dead end. *Organization*, **19**(5), pp. 543–562.

Ahl, H. and Nelson, T. (2015), How policy positions women entrepreneurs: A comparative analysis of state discourse in Sweden and the United States. *Journal of Business Venturing*, **30**(2), pp. 273–291.

Al-Dajani, H. and Marlow, S. (2010), The impact of women's home-based enterprise on marriage dynamics: Evidence from Jordan. *International Small Business Journal*, **28**(5), pp. 470–487.

Al-Dajani, H. and Marlow, S. (2013), Empowerment and entrepreneurship: A theoretical framework. *International Journal of Entrepreneurial Behaviour Research*, **19**(5), pp. 503–524.

Al-Dajani, H. and Marlow, S. (2014), Empowerment, place and entrepreneurship. In F. Welter and T. Baker (eds), *The Routledge Companion to Entrepreneurship*, London: Routledge.

Anthias, F. (2001), New hybridities, old concepts: The limits of culture. *Ethnic and Racial Studies*, **24**(4), pp. 619–641.

Anthias, F. (2006), Belongings in a globalising and unequal world: Rethinking translocations. In N. Yuval-Davis, K. Kannabiran and U. Vieten (eds), *The Situated Politics of Belonging*, London: Sage.

Anthias, F. (2008), Thinking through the lens of translocational positionality: An intersectionality frame for understanding identity and belonging. *Translocations: Migration and Social Change*, **4**(1): pp. 5–20.

Bruton, G.D., Ahlstrom, D. and Obloj, K. (2008), Entrepreneurship in emerging economies: Where are we today and where should the research go in the future. *Entrepreneurship Theory and Practice*, **32**(1), pp. 1–15.

Bruton, G.D., Ahlstrom, D. and Li, H. (2010), Institutional theory and entrepreneurship: Where are we now and where do we need to move in the future? *Entrepreneurship, Theory and Practice*, **34**(3), pp. 421–440.

Butler, J. (1993), *Bodies That Matter: On the Discursive Limits of Sex*, New York: Routledge.

Carter, S. and Shaw, E. (2006), *Women's Business Ownership: Recent Research and Policy Developments*, report to the Small Business Service, London. Available at http://webarchive.nationalarchives.gov.uk/20090609003228/www.berr.gov.uk/files/file38330.pdf (accessed 31 May 2016).

Crenshaw, K. (1989), Demarginalizing the intersection of race and sex: A black feminist critique of antidiscrimination doctrine, feminist theory and antiracist politics. *University of Chicago Legal Forum*, pp. 139–167.

Du Gay, P. (1996), *Consumption and Identity at Work*, London: Sage.

Essers, C. and Benschop, Y. (2009), Muslim businesswomen doing boundary work: The negotiation Of Islam, gender and ethnicity within entrepreneurial contexts. *Human Relations*, **62**(3), pp. 403–423.

Essers, C., Benschop, Y. and Doorewaard, H. (2010), Female ethnicity: Understanding Muslim immigrant businesswomen in the Netherlands. *Gender, Work and Organization*, **17**(3), pp. 320–339.

Gartner, W. (1988), 'Who is an entrepreneur?' is the wrong question. *American Journal of Small Business*, **12**(4), pp. 11–23.

Giddens, A. (1992), *The Transformation of Intimacy*, Cambridge: Polity Press.

Gill, R. (2011), *Globalization and Intersectionality in US Discourses and Practices of Entrepreneurship*. Paper presented at the EGOS Symposium, June, Gothenburg, Sweden.

Hamilton, E. (2013), The discourse of entrepreneurial masculinities (and femininities). *Entrepreneurship and Regional Development*, **25**(1–2), pp. 90–99.

Hancock, A. (2007), When multiplication doesn't equal quick addition: Examining intersectionality as a research paradigm. *Perspectives on Politics*, **5**(1), pp. 63–79.

Harding, S. (1993), Rethinking standpoint epistemology: What is strong objectivity? In L. Alcoff and E. Potter (eds), *Feminist Epistemologies*, New York: Routledge.

Henry, C., Foss, L. and Ahl, H. (2015), Gender and entrepreneurship approaches: A methodological review. *International Small Business Journal*, **34**(3), pp. 217–241.

Imas, J.M., Wilson, N. and Weston, A. (2012), Barefoot entrepreneurs. *Organization*, **19**(5), pp. 563–585.

Jayawarna, D., Jones, O. and Macpherson, A. (2014), *Resourcing the Start-up Firm*, London: Routledge.

Jayawarna, D., Jones, O. and Marlow, S. (2015), Resourcing new business ventures: The influence of gender upon social networks. A Comparison of male–female social networks, *Scandinavian Journal of Management*, **31**(3), pp. 316–329.

Jayawarna, D., Rouse, J. and Kitching, J. (2013), Entrepreneur motivations and life course. *International Small Business Journal*, **31**(1), pp. 34–56.

Kelan, E.K. (2009), *Performing Gender at Work*, London: Palgrave Macmillan.

Klyver, K., Nielsen, M. and Evald, M. (2013), Women's self-employment: An act of institutional (dis)integration? A multilevel, cross-country study. *Journal of Business Venturing*, **28**(4), pp. 474–488.

Marlow, S. (2002), Female entrepreneurs: A part of or apart from feminist theory? *International Journal of Entrepreneurship and Innovation*, **2**(2), pp. 23–37.

Marlow, S. (2014), Exploring future research agendas in the field of gender and entrepreneurship. *International Journal of Gender and Entrepreneurship*, **6**(2), pp. 102–120.

Marlow, S. and McAdam, M. (2013), Advancing debate and challenging myths – Exploring the alleged case of the under-performing female entrepreneur. *International Journal of Entrepreneurial Behaviour and Research*, **19**(1), pp. 114–124.

Marlow, S. and Martinez-Dy, A. (forthcoming), Women entrepreneurs and their ventures. In C. Henry, T. Nelson and K. Lewis (eds), *The Routledge Companion to Global Female Entrepreneurship*, London: Edward Elgar.

Martinez-Dy, A., Martin, L. and Marlow, S. (2014), Developing a critical realist positional account of intersectionality theory. *Journal of Critical Realism*, **13**(5), pp. 447–464.

McAdam, M. (2012), *Female Entrepreneurship*, London, Routlege.

Mirchandani, K. (1999), Feminist insight on gendered work: New directions in research on women and entrepreneurship. *Gender, Work and Organization*, **6**(4), pp. 224–235.

Mole, K. and Ram, M. (2012), *Perspectives on Entrepreneurship*, London: Palgrave.

Nash, J. (2008), Re-thinking intersectionality. *Feminist Review*, **89**, pp. 1–15.

Ogbor, J.O. (2000), Mythicizing and reification in entrepreneurial discourse: ideology-critique of entrepreneurial studies. *Journal of Management Studies*, **37**(5), pp. 605–635.

Robb, A. and Watson, J. (2011), Gender differences in firm performance: Evidence from new ventures in the USA. *Journal of Business Venturing*, **27**(5), pp. 544–578.

Saridakis, G., Marlow, S. and Storey, D. (2014), Do different factors explain male and female self-employment rates? *Journal of Business Venturing*, **29**(3), pp. 345–362.

Schwartz, E.B. (1979), Entrepreneurship: A new female frontier. *Journal of Contemporary Business*, winter, pp. 47–76.

Smith, R. (2010), Masculinity, doxa and the institutionalisation of entrepreneurial identity in the novel *City Boy*. *The International Journal of Entrepreneurship and Gender*, **2**(1), pp. 27–48.

Steyaert, C. and Katz, J. (2004), Reclaiming the space of entrepreneurship in society: Geographical, discursive and social dimensions. *Entrepreneurship and Regional Development*, **16**, pp. 179–196.

Storey, D. and Greene, F. (2010), *Small Business and Entrepreneurship*, London: Pearson.

Tobin, S. (2011), *Jordan's Arab Spring: The Middle Class and Anti-revolution*, Washington, DC: Middle East Policy Council.

Van der Tuin, I. and Geerts, E. (2013), From intersectionality to interference: Feminist onto-epistemological reflections on the politics of representation. *Women's Studies International Forum*, **41**(3), pp. 171–178.

Verduijn, K. and Essers, C. (2013), Questioning dominant entrepreneurship assumptions: The case of female ethnic minority entrepreneurs. *Entrepreneurship and Regional Development*, **25**(7–8), pp. 612–630.

Welter, F. (2011), Contextualising entrepreneurship – Conceptual challenges and ways forward. *Entrepreneurship Theory and Practice*, **35**(1), pp. 165–178.

Welter, F. and Smallbone, D. (2008), Women's entrepreneurship from an institutional perspective: The case of Uzbekistan. *International Entrepreneurship and Management Journal*, **4**(4), pp. 505–520.

Wright, M. (2012), Entrepreneurial mobility, resource mobilisation and context. In F. Welter, D. Smallbone and A. Van Gils (eds), *Entrepreneurial Processes in a Changing Economy*, London: Edward Elgar, pp. 6–24.

Zahra, S., Wright, M. and Abdelgawad, S. (2014), Contextualisation and the advancement of entrepreneurship research. *International Small Business Journal*, **32**(5), pp. 479–501.

12 On entrepreneurship and empowerment

Postcolonial feminist interventions

Banu Özkazanç-Pan

Introduction

In recent decades, many non-Western nations that were once centrally planned or ruled by authoritarian governments have been slowly transitioning to market-based economies. In these transitions, existing institutional arrangements have started to become undone and are redone in different ways as states have begun divesting ownership of various organisations and in particular industries. State-run organisations and ownership structures are now being dismantled for the promise of rapid economic development under neoliberal regimes. Yet the adoption of market-based ideologies by governments and the promises of rapid economic growth have not been without criticism, particularly from those scholars adopting feminist and political economy lenses. In this chapter, I deploy feminist frameworks on postcoloniality and political economy to examine how such transitions are based on particular assumptions about the role of the state and women in nations by using the exemplar of Turkey. As a middle-income transition economy with a Muslim majority population, Turkey makes for an interesting case study in the intersections of neoliberal ideology, Islam and secularism, and economic development through entrepreneurship. In the next section I discuss the contributions of feminist scholarship in postcolonial work and political economy in order to lay the foundations for the analysis and critique of entrepreneurship and development in Turkey. Following this, I outline the historical and contemporary economic, socio-cultural and political context of Turkey to foreground the discussion on entrepreneurship as a national development tool/mantra. My focus is on the ways in which entrepreneurship is being heralded as a form of citizenship (Altan-Olcay 2014) and the gendered subtext and assumptions of this activity that ultimately do not alter existing institutional arrangements of gender inequality.

Feminist approaches to postcolonial and political economy scholarship

While contributions of feminist theorising to postcolonial and political economy scholarship are varied and substantial, in this chapter I focus on the role of the nation state with respect to the opportunities and challenges it represents for gender equality and women's empowerment vis-à-vis development through entrepreneurship. To this end, feminist scholarship within postcolonial studies, particularly those that adopt a materialist perspective, focuses on the structural and institutional arrangements that allowed colonialism to take shape in different contexts and nations (see Landry and MacLean 1993). Moreover, such analyses point out that questions over accumulation and 'value' are central to the ways in which coloniality formed and reformed relations in society, but also in the ways the nation state was involved in the process of value assignment and citizenship (Spivak 1985). On this point, Spivak further suggests that 'the complicity between cultural and economic-value systems is acted out in almost every decision we make' (1985, p. 83). Although not an explicitly feminist postcolonial scholar, Parry (2004) similarly calls attention to the ways in which many postcolonial scholars have decoupled the material from the cultural as if the entire colonial enterprise was textually accomplished. For Parry (2004), capitalistic forms of economic exchange enabled by the nation state paved the way for the possibility and eventual emergence of colonialism. Thus, contemporary forms of neoliberalism continue this value-assigning practice that enabled colonialism to emerge as a socio-cultural and material enterprise. To this end, feminist scholarship in political economy has called attention to the economic and political structural arrangements adopted by nation states in perpetuating gender inequality.

Within the feminist political economy literature, the seminal work and ideas of Ester Boserup (1970/2007) as well as Diane Elson and Ruth Pearson (1981, 1997/2011) highlight the gendered assumptions around women's roles in agricultural and factory production respectively. Guided by their ideas, a growing number of feminist researchers within this area have deployed gender analysis to critique the outcomes of structural adjustment policies (Elson 1995; Marchand and Runyan 2010) within the broader context of neoliberal economic development policies (Jackson and Pearson 2005; Pearson 2003; Rai and Waylen 2013; see also Visvanathan and Yoder 2011). Others have examined the intersections of work and families in the context of globalisation, given that women carry out the majority of unpaid social reproduction and care work globally (Barker 2005; Barker and Feiner 2004; Pearson 2013). More recently, feminist scholars have also critiqued the adoption of entrepreneurship as the new tool for neoliberal development with its attendant claims of gender equality and women's empowerment (Vossenberg 2014).

This is perhaps most acute in transition economies, whereby governments have started to adopt neoliberal adjustment policies to promote market-based relations among individuals as the norm while continuing to diminish social protection and welfare programmes. In this chapter, I focus on these ongoing trends in Turkey whereby a gendered neoliberal citizenship is emerging in the guise of empowered female entrepreneurs (Altan-Olcay 2014). I begin by discussing the historic context of Turkey with regard to religion, gender and development before moving on to examples of entrepreneurship programmes.

Historical context: Islam, secularism and the making of the modern Turkish nation state

As a Muslim-majority country, Turkey is situated geographically and culturally at the crossroads of multiple histories, nations and people, and is a republic built from the ruins of the Ottoman Empire. Historically within this context, Islam has played an important role in the production of laws and traditions under the Ottoman Empire (Zürcher 2004). In this sense, Islam is a way of life based on the religious texts of the Qur'an coupled with the hadith or teachings of the prophet Mohammed and occupies a central role in the daily lives of religious individuals. Simultaneous with the pivotal role of Islam in the Ottoman era, a series of economic and political reforms, the Tanzimat, were carried out between 1812 and 1914 which gave rise to scattered free-trade liberalism in the Ottoman lands (Quataert 1994). Towards the end of these reforms, the Young Turk revolution of 1908 coupled with the First World War eventually led to a 'national economy' model being adopted in favour of free trade (Quataert 1994, p. 763). The state emerged as the singular hegemonic apparatus determining the rights and obligations of its citizens with the rise of the secular Turkish republic in 1923 under Mustafa Kemal Ataturk.

Under Ataturk, Shari'a or using Islam to define state ideology, laws and policies was abolished with a strict adopted separation of religion (Islam) from state. In addition, Turkish women were granted many rights that few European women enjoyed at the time (White 2003). The modern Turkish republic was based on six themes: secularism (from the French *laïcité*), republicanism, statism, nationalism, populism and reformism (Warhola and Bezci 2010). During the early years of the republic, Western and European laws, customs and ideologies were imported into Turkey as part of state-led modernisation and development efforts (Zürcher 2004). Ultimately, Turkey adopted an 'active secularism' where the 'state itself actively embraced and fostered a nonreligious worldview in the public realms' (Warhola and Bezci 2010, p. 428) while relegating Islam and its practice to the private sphere (White 2012). Over time, this radical break with history, both intellectually and materially, gave rise to political Islam and Islamic political parties most prominently in the mid-1990s. With the election of Islamist parties into power, including the Refah Party (Welfare Party) and the current Adalet ve Kalkinma Partisi (AKP) or Justice and Development Party, tensions between religious and secular proponents in terms of the role of Islam in state ideolo-gies, laws and policies continue (Bonner 2004; Fuller 2008; Somer 2007).

Yet to assume a dichotomy between secular principles and Islam or between modernity and Shari'a is specious (Hashmi 2002), as the Turkish social, cultural, political and economic context demonstrates the complex, contradictory and relational aspects of these assumed–opposite ideologies. In effect, the 'clash of civilizations' (Lewis 1990; Huntington 1993) premise is constantly challenged as Islamic nations aim to adopt an 'Islamic approach to modernity' (McDaniel 2003) and foster economic development policies sens-itive to Islamic teaching and law (Mirakhor and Hamid 2009; Pramanik 2002). Already scholars have noted how Islamic principles of social justice and wealth distribution (*zakat*) and community (*ummah*) among other Qu'ranic teachings contribute to positive employment relations (Syed and Ali 2010) and economic prosperity (Kuran 1995) while also noting how par-ticular aspects of Islam with respect to usury and inheritance laws have led to economic underdevelopment (Kuran 2004).

To this end, Turkey is an interesting example in the study of the intersec-tions of Islam, ethics, and development programmes, as the policies and prac-tices espoused by the current ruling Islamist party follow many of the tenets of capitalist and market-based economies (Hale and Ozbudun 2010). Under conditions of globalisation, tensions between Islam, with its varied interpreta-tions and practices in politics and culture (see Moaddel 2002), and Western ideologies, can seem inevitable. This is particularly relevant when Western and US.-based neoliberal ideologies with respect to development are imported into a Muslim-majority nation that defines itself through the uneasy intersection and 'interdependence between Islam, secularism, and democrat-isation' (Gol 2009, p. 795). It is also particularly relevant when 'the Kemalist modernization program was copied from Europe and did not evolve from Turkey's Islamic tradition' (Malik 2003, p. 132). It is quite important to examine these questions in terms of understanding the ethics of development in Muslim-majority nations such as Turkey. The examination of these issues is not sufficient, however, to uncover concerns over gender relations and equality that take place through intersections of gendered Islamic, secularist and economic development discourses. The critical issue is how, in an era of globalisation, neoliberal development ideologies and practices that adopt entrepreneurship as the solution to unemployment may perpetuate gender inequality in Turkey.

To this end I first discuss entrepreneurship as the hegemonic mantra/dis-course of how nations can promote economic development, followed by a discussion of 'gender and development' discourses and programmes. I suggest that the entrepreneurship discourse, with its US.-based neoliberal assump-tions, is being imported into contemporary Turkey through the reforms of the current Islamist party as well as by the practices of certain women-focused business organisations. Within this context, entrepreneurship is seen as a solu-tion to women's unemployment 'problem' by the state and promoted as part of the political and social reforms necessary for European Union accession. Adopting a feminist perspective, I question whether this approach can result in gender equality in the context of Turkey.

Importing ideas and practices from the West

In the USA, the entrepreneur and entrepreneurship are heralded as hallmarks of a successful market economy and are considered vital to achieving US global competitiveness (i.e. Startup America Partnership). On the policy side, efforts have been made to offer ideas to promote and enable processes of entrepreneurship within the context of globalisation (Kelley *et al.* 2011). A similar focus on understanding and promoting entrepreneurship has taken shape in the academic business field as scholars have focused on understanding the drives and antecedents of entrepreneurship (Shane and Venkataraman 2000) based on the assumption that such activities are reproducible.

From this perspective, entrepreneurship is a strategy and a practice embarked upon by individuals and states in their attempts to become financially and economically 'successful' in an interdependent global economy. Understood within the contemporary context of a neoliberal logic dominating global economic restructuring and development policies, entrepreneurship can enable people and states to be differentiated in terms of the products or services they provide in globally dispersed production networks (see Levy 2008). These neoliberal concepts as well as approaches to entrepreneurship have also found resonance in Turkey and speak to the ongoing practice of importing and relying on Western ideas and practices.

Under the current Islamist government, there has been an acceleration in the adoption and promotion of neoliberal economic policies both as a way to foster economic growth (T.C. Ozellestirme Idaresi Baskanligi 2012) and to satisfy structural reforms required in the ongoing road to EU accession (Kutuk 2006). Along with several high-profile entrepreneurship summits, the current President Recep Tayyip Erdogan and his ruling party have spoken publicly about the need for entrepreneurship as a nationalistic duty in an era of competitive globalisation. Yet these efforts have not been without criticism. I expand upon them below.

Neoliberal economic policies: critics and Islamists

Despite the growing popularity of entrepreneurship, the movement towards neoliberal economic policy and its ensuing practices in organisations and enterprises can perpetuate historic structures of inequality among states and people (Hoogvelt 2001). Within this context, structural reforms that mimic Western institutional preferences, including EU accession reforms and IMF structural adjustments, as a means to 'join' the global economic order may provide a 'return on investment' for Western and other investors but not necessarily benefit all Turkish citizens (see Karatas and Uz 2009). Moreover, critical examination of privatisation in state-owned industries, such as petroleum and paper, suggests that Turkish national production will not keep up with demand and lead to more dependence on imports (Yeldan 2005). Consequently, opposition parties (i.e. Cumhuriyet Halk Partisi/Republican People's Party), labour unions, NGOs and civic organisations among others have voiced concerns over wages, job losses, workers' rights, and Turkish national sovereignty and solidarity within the context of ongoing privatisation efforts by the AKP (Onis 2011). Others have suggested more radically that the AKP represents the hegemony and extension of American interests in the Middle East and have called it 'Turkey's brand of Islamized Americanization' (Tugal 2007, p. 34).

Simultaneously, economic liberalisation reforms initiated under Prime Minister Ozal in the 1980s and accelerated under the AKP's tenure have allowed groups marginalised under secular state ideology to emerge as politically and economically powerful in the form of a religious entrepreneurial class (Tavernise 2007, 2008) with its own conservative elite (Sayari and Hasanov 2008; Yilmaz 2009). Partly in response to the state's rigid secular ideology, this emerging class has interpreted neoliberal approaches to commerce and enterprise through an Islamic sensibility and produced locally grounded forms of Islamic capitalism (Nasr 2010).

While these critiques and Islamist interpretations of neoliberal economic policies are quite relevant to modernity and development projects in Turkey, they are not sufficient to address gender equality and human rights within the context of globalisation. That is, while Turkey as a whole has seen GDP growth near 7 per cent and the rise of a new Islamist middle class, women's involvement in the public sphere trails that of other comparable middle-income countries, particularly in terms of women's parliamentary members, literacy rates and wage employment in the non-agricultural sector (UNDP 2015). Consequently, liberalisation policies have not provided the return on investment with regard to gender equality. This trend is noted by the UN Conference on Trade and Development (UNCTD) secretariat as posing a 'moral challenge' and being potentially a 'source of economic instability' (UNCTD 2012, p. 1). In many ways, social and legal reforms coupled with liberalisation efforts have had mixed results in terms of gender equality and opportunities for women in the MENA region (Middle East North Africa) (Moghadam 2005). Next I examine this issue in the context of Turkey.

Entrepreneurship to solve Turkish women's unemployment 'problem'

In recent decades, centrally planned economies have begun promoting entrepreneurship as one of the ways in which they are adopting market-oriented growth policies. Coupled with the promise of entrepreneurship in job creation and economic growth and wealth is the claim that it can allow women the opportunity to enter the formal labour market, become empowered and pave the way for gender equality. In Turkey, women's unemployment and low rates of participation in the economy (Ecevit 2007; Soysal 2010; World Bank and DPT 2009) and rates of labour force participation that continue to be around half that of men across different regions (OECD 2006) have set the stage for the promotion of entrepreneurship as the solution (Ecevit 2007). With its high scores on the human development index (high human development) and low scores on gender equality (UNDP 2011), Turkey ranks 124 out of 135 nations for gender equality. It scores even lower – 129 out of 135 – for women's economic participation and opportunity (Hausman et al. 2012).

According to various statistical analyses, Turkish women constitute between 2 and 7 per cent of all entrepreneurs in Turkey (OECD 2015; Global Entrepreneurship Monitor 2011). Existing female entrepreneurs tend to be clustered in stereotypically feminine fields such as sewing, catering and crafts, prompting Ozar (2007) to observe that these activities reflect an extension of domestic work in the public sphere. Like many other nations, these low rates of entrepreneurship among women are based on reduced access to financial capital (Ozar 2007), lack of human capital (Cetindamar et al. 2012), and structural and cultural barriers, such as patriarchal gender norms and stereotypes (Altan-Olcay 2014; Ince 2010; Karatas-Ozkan et al. 2010). Moreover, efforts to promote women's entrepreneurship have been mixed at best, suffering from a proliferation of agencies, lack of coordination, and different motivations of funders, organisers and participants (Ecevit 2007; Ozar 2007).

On this very point, scholars have suggested that individually focused enterprise activities may not necessarily lead to long-term changes necessary for gender equality given the socio-political nature of economic activities (Al-Dajani and Marlow 2013) and the lack of gender awareness in macroeconomic policy (Razavi 2011). These observations extend earlier critical perspectives on entrepreneurship (Tedmanson et al. 2012; Verduijn et al. 2014), including feminist ones (Calas et al. 2009) which raise concerns over the possibility of gender equality arising from women's involvement in enterprises. Extending my own work in this area (Özkazanç-Pan 2015) which deployed Islamic and secular feminist lenses to examine this issue in Turkey, my analysis in this chapter relies on feminist frameworks in the postcolonial and political economy to question whether the Turkish government's provisioning and resourcing of entrepreneurship as a form of economic development can result in gender equality.

Entrepreneurship as women's empowerment: (im)possibilities?

In the Turkish context, it is important to note the historic economic and political dependencies between Turkey and supranational development and finance agencies, such as the World Bank and the International Monetary Fund, in terms of financial obligations. The Turkish government has relied on these institutions for financing many social and economic projects over four decades. These loans have come with structural adjustment programmes guided by neoliberal economic ideologies and have led to micro-economic policy shifts in Turkey, resulting in new forms of gendered governance, citizenship and relations among people (Altan-Olcay 2014). For example, development projects emanating from the World Bank aimed at fostering economic stability and independence do so based on a neoliberal economic interpretation of entrepreneurship. Specifically, World Bank programmes in partnership with the Turkish government believe that 'empowering more women entrepreneurs to participate in business will unleash significant growth potential and further develop the Turkish private sector' (World Bank 2015, p. 50). Yet such (Western) aid policies end up reproducing patriarchy in their aims to 'help' Third World women as they reinforce existing gender stereotypes around women's roles in the labour market (Gunduz-Hosgor and Smits 2008). For example, while secular and Islamic women's groups each have different entrepreneurship programmes in place in Turkey, these programmes do not change structural arrangements that produced gendered social stratification in the first place (Özkazanç-Pan 2015).

In effect, state-approved development policies that promote entrepreneurship produce a gendered subject, namely the Turkish female entrepreneur, whose enterprise activities are seen as successful in their ability to fulfil traditional gender roles (i.e. wife) rather than enabling the full participation of women in society. This gendered interpretation of business success exists in the Turkish patriarchal context where state-run business development institutions such as KOSGEB offer varying amounts of grants to male versus female or disabled entrepreneurs (KOSGEB 2010). The result is the equating of female entrepreneurs being 'in need of' the benevolent patriarchal state as reflected in the lending practices of KOSGEB. Arat (2009) suggests that these practices reflect broader and ingrained patriarchal attitudes towards women in the Turkish context (Arat 2009). As such, the gendered entrepreneurship discourse of the West perpetuates gendered neoliberal ideologies globally and reinforces existing Indigenous forms of patriarchy. On this very point, Moghadam (2005) suggests that liberalisation policies can reinforce 'patriarchal gender contracts' in the MENA regions whereby men are assumed to be the breadwinners and financially responsible for women, who are wives, mothers and caregivers (p. 117). In light of these critiques, can state-promoted entrepreneurship provide a form of empowerment or potentially become the pathway to gender equality in the spirit of CEDAW (Convention on the Elimination of all forms of Discrimination against Women), which was adopted by Turkey in 1985 (Kardam 2005)?

Feminist praxis requires a commitment to dismantling gendered power relations in society and in effect represents an ethico-political act (see Hesse-Biber 2007). As Barker and Feiner suggest, 'feminist, egalitarian principles of inclusion call for the restructuring of society's political-economic system to create conditions in which everyone can participate in the production of goods and services we need for our daily lives' (2004, p. 132). Based on this, embarking upon entrepreneurship is not only an economic endeavour but an ethical and political feat in asserting one's democratic right to participate in the economy as an equal member of society. In the Turkish context, this notion is particularly relevant, as both secularist and Islamic actors have excluded women from power while simultaneously relying on women to further gendered nationalist secular and Islamic political agendas (Turam 2007). Thus, is there any potential for gender equality and women's empowerment in the heralding of entrepreneurship, particularly in the Turkish context?

If we consider entrepreneurship as a form of social change (Steyaert and Hjorth 2007; Steyeart and Katz 2004), the bureaucratic apparatus responsible for provisioning, resourcing and supporting economic growth needs to be aligned with gender equality in both macro-economic and micro-economic policy. Beyond this, sections of government responsible for economic growth cannot be separated from those that are considered to be the realm of the private sphere. In the Turkish context, the Ministry of Family and Social Policy is responsible for all policies related to families, women and children, while the Ministry of Development is responsible for policies related to economic development. In many ways, this bifurcation in government reflects assumptions on the separation of the private/home sphere from the public sphere whereby women, reproductive work and caregiving are not considered integral to economic growth. This is true not only in the Turkish context but in many other nation states whereby women's labour in the home and in reproductive work are not calculated or accounted for in the formal economy (Barker 2005).

While nation states that are democracies claim to represent the voices of all participating citizens, the onus for fostering gender equality cannot be passed on to women through entrepreneurship activities. Furthermore, simply associating *women's* entrepreneurship with gender equality rather than considering how men undertake entrepreneurship may perpetuate gender norms in society is unacceptable and unfruitful as a means for social change. In light of these observations, democratic nation states still occupy an important position in the allocation of resources and in supporting civil society. The erosion of centrally planned economies and the adoption of market-based policies in many nations has resulted in an awkward space for possibilities of gender equality. In Turkey, old patriarchal bargains (Kandiyoti 1988) are being renegotiated by a cadre of religious and secular female entrepreneurs whose goals of economic independence and empowerment are both realised and simultaneously challenged by their own government and by society. To this end, the possibilities of entrepreneurship as a form of social change remain at large in a pendulum society between Islam and secularism.

References

Al-Dajani, H. and Marlow, S. (2013), Empowerment and entrepreneurship: A theoretical framework. *International Journal of Entrepreneurial Behavior and Research*, **19**(5), pp. 503–524.

Altan-Olcay, O. (2014), Entrepreneurial subjectivities and gendered complexities: Neoliberal citizenship in Turkey. *Feminist Economics*, **20**(4), pp. 235–259.

Arat, Y. (2009), Religion, politics and gender equality in Turkey: Implications of a democratic paradox. *Third World Quarterly*, **31**(6), pp. 869–884.

Barker, D.K. (2005), Beyond women and economics: Rereading 'women's work'. *Signs*, **30**(4), pp. 2189–2209.

Barker, D.K. and Feiner, S.F. (2004), *Liberating Economics: Feminist Perspectives on Families, Work, and Globalization*, Ann Arbor, MI: The University of Michigan Press.

Bonner, A. (2004), An Islamic reformation in Turkey. *Middle East Policy*, **11**(1), pp. 84–97.

Boserup, E. (1970/2007), *Woman's Role in Economic Development*, London: Earthscan.

Calas, M.B., Smircich, L. and Bourne, K.A. (2009), Extending the boundaries: Reframing 'entrepreneurship as social change' through feminist perspectives. *Academy of Management Review*, **34**(4), pp. 552–569.

Cetindamar, D., Gupta, V.K., Karadeniz, E.E. and Egrican, N. (2012), What the numbers tell: The impact of human, family and financial capital on women and men's entry into entrepreneurship in Turkey. *Entrepreneurship and Regional Development*, **24**(1/2), pp. 29–51.

Ecevit, Y. (2007), *Turkiye'de kadin girisimciligine elestirel bir yaklasim*, International Labour Organization. Available at http://staging.ilo.org/public/libdoc/ilo/2007/107B09_140_turk.pdf (accessed 7 June 2016).

Elson, D. (1995), Gender awareness in modeling structural adjustment. *World Development*, **23**(11), pp. 1851–1868.

Elson, D. and Pearson, R. (1981), Nimble fingers make cheap workers: An analysis of women's employment in third world export manufacturing. *Feminist Review*, **7**(1), pp. 87–107.

Elson, D. and Pearson, R. (1997/2011), The subordination of women and the internationalization of factory production. In N. Visvanathan, L. Duggan, N. Wiegersma and L. Nisonoff (eds), *The Women, Gender, and Development Reader*, 2nd edn, New York: Zed Books, pp. 212–224.

Fuller, G.E. (2008), *The New Turkish republic: Turkey as a Pivotal State in the Muslim World*, Washington, DC:United States Institute of Peace Press.

Global Entrepreneurship Monitor (2011), *GEM Turkey Report 2010*. Available at www.gemconsortium.org/report/48353 (accessed 7 June 2016).

Gol, A. (2009), The identity of Turkey: Muslim and secular. *Third World Quarterly*, **30**(4), pp. 795–811.

Gunduz-Hosgor, A. and Smits, J. (2008), Variation in labor market participation of married women in Turkey. *Women's Studies International Forum*, **31**, pp. 104–117.

Hale, W. and Ozbudun, E. (2010), *Islamism, Democracy, and Liberalism in Turkey*, New York: Routledge.

Hashmi, S.H. (ed.) (2002), *Islamic Political Ethics, Civil Society, Pluralism, and Conflict*, Princeton, NJ: Princeton University Press.

Hausman, R., Tyson, L.D. and Zahidi, S. (2012), *The Global Gender Gap Report 2012*, World Economic Forum. Available at http://www3.weforum.org/docs/WEF_GenderGap_Report_2012.pdf (accessed 31 May 2016).

Hesse-Biber, S.N. (2007), Feminist research: Exploring the interconnections of epistemology, methodology, and method. In S.N. Hesse-Biber (ed.), *Handbook of Feminist Research: Theory and Praxis*, Thousand Oaks, CA: Sage, pp. 1–26.

Hoogvelt, A. (2001), *Globalization and the Postcolonial World: The New Political Economy of Development*, 2nd edn, Baltimore, MD: Johns Hopkins University Press.

Huntington, S.P. (1993), The clash of civilizations? *Foreign Affairs*, **72**(3), pp. 22–49.

Ince, M. (2010), Women in the Turkish firms in the globalization process. *Business and Economics Research Journal/İşletme ve Ekonomi Araştırmaları Dergisi*, **1**(1), pp. 55–68.

Jackson, C. and Pearson, R. (eds) (2005), *Feminist Visions of Development: Gender Analysis and Policy*, 2nd edn, London: Routledge.

Kandiyoti, D. (1988), Bargaining with patriarchy. *Gender and Society*, **2**(3), pp. 274–290.

Karatas, C. and Uz, I. (2009), Turkey's accession to the European Union and the macroeconomic dynamics of the Turkish economy. *Turkish Studies*, **10**(4), pp. 539–557.

Karatas-Ozkan, M., Inal, G. and Ozbilgin, M. (2010), Turkish women entrepreneurs: Opportunities and challenges. In S. Fielden (ed.), *International Research Handbook on Successful Women Entrepreneurs*, Thousand Oaks, CA: Sage, pp. 175–188.

Kardam, N. (2005), *Turkey's Engagement with Global Women's Human Rights*, Burlington, VT: Ashgate.

Kelley, D.J., Bosma, N. and Amoros, J.E. (2011), *Global Entrepreneurship Monitor – 2010 Global Report*, Babson College and Universidad del Desarrollo. Available at www.gemconsortium.org/report/47109 (accessed 31 May 2016).

KOSGEB (2010), Küçük ve orta ölçekli işletmeleri geliştirme ve destekleme idaresi başkanliği, Girişimcilik destek programi. Available at www.kosgeb.gov.tr/Pages/UI/Destekler.aspx?ref=8 (accessed 31 May 2016).

Kuran, T. (1995), Islamic economics and the Islamic subeconomy. *The Journal of Economic Perspectives*, **9**(4), pp. 155–173.

Kuran, T. (2004), Why the Middle East is economically underdeveloped: Historical mechanisms of institutional stagnation. *Journal of Economic Perspectives*, **18**(3), pp. 71–90.

Kutuk, Z. (2006), Turkey and the European Union: The simple complexity. *Turkish Studies*, **7**(2), pp. 275–292.

Landry, D.E. and MacLean, G. (1993), *Materialist Feminisms*, Oxford: Blackwell.

Levy, D.L. (2008), Political contestation in global production networks. *Academy of Management Review*, **33**(4), pp. 943–962.

Lewis, B. (1990), The roots of Muslim rage. *The Atlantic*, **266**(3), pp. 47–60.

Malik, M. (2003), Islam's missing link to the West. *Middle East Policy*, **10**(1), pp. 121–134.

Marchand, M.H. and Runyan, A.S. (eds) (2010), *Gender and Global Restructuring: Sightings, Sites and Resistances*, New York: Routledge.

McDaniel, C. (2003), Islam and the global society: A religious approach to modernity. *Brigham Young University Law Review*, **2**, pp. 507–540.

Mirakhor, A. and Hamid, I.S. (2009), *Islam and Development: The Institutional Framework*, New York: Global Scholarly Publications.

Moaddel, M. (2002), The study of Islamic culture and politics: An overview and assessment. *Annual Review of Sociology*, **28**, pp. 359–386.

Moghadam, V.M. (2005), Women's economic participation in the Middle East: What difference has the neoliberal policy turn made? *Journal of Middle East Women's Studies*, **1**(1), pp. 110–146.

Nasr, V. (2010), *The Rise of Islamic Capitalism*, New York: Free Press.

OECD (Organization for Economic Cooperation and Development) (2006), *Difference between the Female and the Male Participation Rate; TL3 Regions, France, Portugal and Turkey TL2 Regions*. Available at doi:10.1787/reg_glance-2009-graph19_6-en (accessed 7 June 2016).

OECD (Organization for Economic Cooperation and Development) (2015), *Entrepreneurship at a Glance*. Available at doi:10.1787/entrepreneur_aag-2015-en (accessed 7 June 2016).

Onis, Z. (2011), Power, interests and coalitions: The political economy of mass privatisation in Turkey. *Third World Quarterly*, **32**(4), pp. 707–724.

Ozar, S. (2007), Women entrepreneurs in Turkey: Obstacles, potentials and future projects. Available at https://www.researchgate.net/publication/265204331_Women_Entrepreneurs_in_Turkey_Obstacles_Potentials_and_Future_Prospects (accessed 31 May 2016).

Özkazanç-Pan, B. (2015), Secular and Islamic feminist entrepreneurship in Turkey. *International Journal of Gender and Entrepreneurship*, **7**(1), pp. 45–65.

Parry, B. (2004), *Postcolonial Studies: A Materialist Critique*, New York: Routledge.

Pearson, R. (2003), Feminist responses to economic globalisation: Some examples of past and future practice. *Gender and Development*, **11**(1), pp. 25–34.

Pearson, R. (2013), Gender, globalization and the reproduction of labor: Bringing the state back in. In S.M. Rai and G. Waylen (eds), *New Frontiers in Feminist Political Economy*, New York: Routledge, pp. 19–42.

Pramanik, A.H. (2002), Islam and development revisited with evidences from Malaysia. *Islamic Economic Studies*, **10**(1), pp. 39–74.

Quataert, D. (1994), Part IV: The age of reforms. In H. Inalcik and D. Quataert (eds), *An Economic and Social History of the Ottoman Empire, Volume 2: 1600–1914*, Cambridge: Cambridge University Press, pp. 759–944.

Rai, S.M. and Waylen, G. (2013), *New Frontiers in Feminist Political Economy*, London: Routledge.

Razavi, S. (2011), *World Development Report 2012: Gender Equality and Development*: An Opportunity Both Welcome and Missed (An Extended Commentary), United Nations Research Institute for Social Development (UNRISD). Available at http://networkideas.org/featart/oct2011/Shahra_Razavi.pdf (accessed 31 May 2016).

Sayari, S. and Hasanov, A. (2008), The 2007 elections and parliamentary elites in Turkey: The emergence of a new political class? *Turkish Studies*, **9**(2), pp. 345–361.

Shane, S. and Venkataraman, S. (2000), The promise of entrepreneurship as a field of research. *Academy of Management Review*, **25**, pp. 217–226.

Somer, M. (2007), Moderate Islam and secularist opposition in Turkey: Implications for the world, Muslims and secular democracy. *Third World Quarterly*, **28**(7), pp. 1271–1289.

Soysal, A. (2010), Turkiye'de kadin girisimciler: Engeller ve firsatlar baglaminda bir degerlendirme. *SBF Dergisi*, **65**(1), pp. 83–114.

Spivak, G.C. (1985), Scattered speculations on the question of value. *Diacritics*, **15**(4), pp. 73–93.

Steyaert, C. and Hjorth, D. (2007), *Entrepreneurship as Social Change*, Cheltenham: Edward Elgar.

Steyaert, C. and Katz, J. (2004), Reclaiming the space of entrepreneurship in society: Geographical, discursive and social dimensions. *Entrepreneurship and Regional Development*, **16**(3), pp. 179–196.

Syed, J. and Ali, A.J. (2010), Principles of employment relations in Islam: A normative view. *Employee Relations*, **32**(5), pp. 454–469.

Tavernise, S. (2007), In Turkey, a sign of a rising Islamic middle class. *New York Times*, 25 April. Available at www.nytimes.com/2007/04/25/world/europe/25iht-25turkey.5431051.html (accessed 31 May 2016).

Tavernise, S. (2008), Newfound riches come with spiritual costs for Turkey's religious merchants. *New York Times*, 28 December. Available at www.nytimes.com/2008/12/26/world/europe/26wealth.html (accessed 31 May 2016).

T.C. Ozellestirme Idaresi Baskanligi (2012), Available at www.oib.gov.tr/index.htm (accessed 31 May 2016).

Tedmanson, D., Verduyn, K., Essers, C. and Gartner, W.B. (2012), Critical perspectives in entrepreneurship research. *Organization*, **19**(5), pp. 531–541.

Tugal, C. (2007), NATO's Islamists. *New Left Review*, **44**, pp. 5–34.

Turam, B. (2007), *Between Islam and the State: The Politics of Engagement*, Stanford, CA: Stanford University Press.

UNCTD (United Nations Conference on Trade and Development) (2012), *Inclusive and Gender-sensitive Development Paths*, Doha Conference, Qatar, 21–26 April. Available at http://unctad.org/meetings/en/SessionalDocuments/td456_en.pdf (accessed 31 May 2016).

UNDP (United Nations Development Program) (2011), *Human Development Report 2011 – Sustainability and Equity: A Better Future For All*. Available at www.undp.org/content/dam/undp/library/corporate/HDR/2011%20Global%20HDR/English/HDR_2011_EN_Complete.pdf (accessed 31 May 2016).

UNDP (United Nations Development Program) (2015), *UNDP Turkey Human Development*. Available at www.tr.undp.org/content/turkey/en/home/library/human_development/human-development-report-2015.html (accessed 7 June 2016).

Verduijn, K., Dey, P., Tedmanson, D. and Essers, C. (2014), Emancipation and/or oppression? Conceptualizing dimensions of criticality in entrepreneurship studies. *International Journal of Entrepreneurial Behavior and Research*, **20**(2), pp. 98–107.

Visvanathan, N. and Yoder, K. (2011), Women and microcredit: A critical introduction. In N. Visvanathan, L. Duggan, N. Wiegersma and L. Nisonoff (eds), *The Women, Gender and Development Reader*, London: Zed Books, pp. 47–54.

Vossenberg, S. (2014), Beyond the critique: How feminist perspectives can feed entrepreneurship promotion in developing countries, Maastricht School of Management Working Paper #14. Available at https://www.msm.nl/resources/uploads/2014/05/MSM-WP2014-14.pdf (accessed 31 May 2016).

Warhola, J.W. and Bezci, E.G. (2010), Religion and state in contemporary Turkey: Recent developments in 'laiklik'. *Journal of Church and State*, **52**(3), pp. 427–453.

White, J.B. (2003), State feminism, modernization, and the Turkish republican woman. *Feminist Formations*, **15**(3), pp. 145–159.

White, J.B. (2012), *Muslim Nationalism and the New Turks*, Princeton, NJ: Princeton University Press.

World Bank (2015), *World Bank Group – Turkey Partnership: Country Program Snapshot*. Available at www.worldbank.org/content/dam/Worldbank/document/eca/Turkey-Snapshot.pdf (accessed 7 June 2016).

World Bank and DPT (Devlet Planlama Teskilati), (2009), *Female Labor Force Participation in Turkey: Trends, Determinants and Policy Framework*, report no. 48508-TR. Available at http://siteresources.worldbank.org/TURKEYEXTN/Resources/361 711-1268839345767/Female_LFP-en.pdf (accessed 31 May 2016).

Yeldan, A.E. (2005), *Assessing the Privatization Experience in Turkey: Implementation, Politics and Performance Results*, Washington, DC: Economic Policy Institute. Available at http://yeldane.bilkent.edu.tr/EPI_Report2005_Yeldan.pdf (accessed 31 May 2016).

Yilmaz, K. (2009), The emergence and rise of conservative elite in Turkey. *Insight Turkey*, **11**(2), pp. 113–136.

Zürcher, E.J. (2004), *Turkey: A Modern History*, New York: I.B. Tauris.

13 Bridging the gap between resistance and power through agency

An empirical analysis of struggle by immigrant women entrepreneurs

Huriye Yeröz Aygören

Introduction

There is an increasing focus on the complex and dynamic relationship between power and resistance in the organisation and management fields (Fleming and Spicer 2008; Martí and Fernández 2013; Mumby 2005). Scholars argue against the widely established dichotomist approach towards the power/resistance relationship which provides a strict and narrow description for the contrast between the 'diabolic world of power' and the 'liberated world of resistance' (Fleming and Spicer 2007, 2008). Instead, they suggest that resistance and power are 'transversal, iterative and adaptive responses to each other' (Hardy and Thomas 2014) and they are manifested in the form of overt or subtle actions (Fleming and Sewell 2002). Mumby (2005, p. 23) opens up the possibility of discussing agency by defining resistance as

> an effort to engage in some form of praxis – individual or collective, routine or organized actions in the context of established social patterns and structures (including mechanisms of control), such that these patterns and structures are, at some level, de-reified and their identity logic interrogated.

The main tenet of this chapter is to understand the complexity of the relationship between power and resistance by employing the definition of agency as a 'socio-culturally mediated capacity to act' (Ahearn 2001). In other words, agency is approached from both the power and the meaning perspectives.

A micro-level approach is used while examining a group of immigrant woman entrepreneurs (IWE) where the effects of power are most evident (Thomas and Davies 2005). Following the important insight that the 'articulations of selfhood' have been central in woman entrepreneurs' engagements with power in entrepreneurship discourse (Essers and Benschop 2007), this chapter contributes to critical perspectives in management and entrepreneurship literature with an ethnographical understanding of the native's point of view (Ortner 2001; Watson 2011) which shows how the issues of power and resistance are interpreted in understanding cultural construction of agency in the context of entrepreneurship (Kondo 1990).

The concept of 'struggle' is adopted to scrutinise and explain the dialectical power–resistance relationship among the IWE and the established orders in which they are embedded (Fleming and Spicer 2008). Adopting the similar notion of struggle in examining the persistent presence of gender inequality, MacLeod (1992, p. 534) demonstrates a more complex and ambiguous style of struggle in which women 'accept, accommodate, ignore, resist, or protest'. This chapter furthers such discussion through a mind-stretching approach to how IWE find themselves in social complexity with forces coming from gender, ethnicity, class and entrepreneurship (power), and how they empower themselves and others in reworking these relations (resistance and agency).

A social constructionist lens has been used to explain the links and connectedness between self, project and their socio-cultural context in the entrepreneurship literature (Anderson *et al.* 2012; Downing 2005; Fletcher 2006). I seek to follow the same path, taking an exclusive focus on the ordinary daily practices of entrepreneurs. The findings of this research contribute to this perspective by bringing forward the everyday struggle of the IWE as a more obvious element of entrepreneurship than their private practices (Bourne and Calás 2012; García and Welter 2013). As a result, I demonstrate that meaning has superseded issues of power in itself for all the IWE examined, mainly because the purpose and meaning are especially significant in entrepreneurial opportunity enactment processes (Clarke and Holt 2010).

I also extend this conversation with a critical lens where entrepreneurship translates into an ethico-political field of power (Ahl 2006; Calás *et al.* 2009) and resistance (Essers *et al.* 2013; Lewis 2006) without emphasising either dominating (Bruni *et al.* 2004) or liberating (Scott *et al.* 2012) processes and effects of entrepreneurship. Interrogating the dualistic approach, critical accounts demonstrate how issues of meaning are central to the power–resistance relationship (Pio and Essers 2014). Yet, this relationship is exclusively framed in terms of discursive engagements and practices, and the literature has not approached the theorisation of identity and difference from an embodied perspective (Kenny and Fotaki 2015).

Respectively, I pose the question 'How do entrepreneurs struggle with difference[s] given the discursive and material resources available to them?' as the overarching research question in this study. I delve into the contextualisation of entrepreneurship, power and resistance. As the findings of this research reveal, entrepreneurship is part of an everyday tactic on the public scene much more than private activity. Thus, it becomes obvious that entrepreneurship can make a difference for entrepreneurs by reconnecting and repositioning themselves through different forms of agency in their struggles.

The first part of this chapter focuses on setting up the theoretical framework, which not only unpacks relevant entrepreneurship literature but also situates its content vis-à-vis ethnographic and organisational accounts on power, resistance and agency. This is followed by an introduction to the methodological approach and tools used for material generation and analysis. These sections pave the way for a discussion on the IWE's specific encounters with 'struggle', 'tactics' and 'agency' in relation to power. The chapter concludes with theoretical contributions.

Power, resistance and forms of agency in entrepreneurship

Understanding the individual, the project (Bruyat and Julien 2001) and the social context (Spedale and Watson 2014) as well as the link between them (Anderson *et al.* 2012) is the major prerequisite in discussing how entrepreneurial action emerges. However, constructionist accounts have paid little attention to the nature of this connection. A greater clarity is necessary in thinking through this connection, as growing evidence points out how experiences of entrepreneurship differ in relation to the position of entrepreneurs within the ranks of social hierarchies (Ainsworth and Hardy 2008; Verduijn and Essers 2013).

I focus upon examining the points of encounter between the enterprise discourse with certain connotations and individuals with specific embodied histories and resources. This way, the chapter aims to articulate diverse practices where discursive and material are inextricably associated (Hardy and Thomas 2014). It is very important to explain resistance and power dynamics within the concept of agency in entrepreneurship (Goss *et al.* 2011). The agency the IWE deploy to fit themselves into established normative hierarchies provides a greater understanding of cultural/symbolic contexts of power and resistance relations as closely associated with entrepreneurs' own desires (Fenwick 2002), life orientations (Spedale and Watson 2014) and embodied individual histories (Aygören and Wilinska 2013).

Ethnographic accounts are drawn upon, specifically Sherry Ortner's (1995, 1997, 2001) studies on agency construction within relations of power and culture, to explain how the IWE became part of a 'struggle' on the basis of the two forms of agency: agency of power and agency of intentions. Agency of power enables people to act on their own, influence others and retain some sense of control in their lives. It is relevant for both resistance and domination. This view is especially useful for attributing an agency to the supposedly weak, as their struggle involves neither surrendering to power nor resisting it (Fleming and Spicer 2008; Mumby 2005), but finding ways to both recognise its force and form it to suit their own purposes (De Certeau 1998; Kondo 1990).

Agency of intention, on the other hand, contrasts agency of power by articulating projects, purposes and desires based on culture and orientations taken towards different others (i.e. culturally constituted desires and projects fulfilling meaning and purpose in life). This way, agency of intention emerges from cohabited and relational space, including what Kenny and Fotaki (2015) term 'compassionate borderspaces', where subjects relate to others in openness, care and compassion, and affect precedes instrumental and rational dispositions.

De Certeau's two distinctive concepts – 'tactics' and 'strategies' – help further operationalise relatively broad and intriguing concepts such as agency, and to make those concepts easily amenable to our research inquiry. This enables a combination of the issues of power and resistance in understanding the cultural construction of agency.

Methodological approach

My analysis uses the notion of lived experience and personal narratives as major analytical tools in generating, making sense of and examining the life stories of IWE. I adopt an intersectional approach towards the notion of experience, suggesting that women's experiences are gendered as much as embodied in class, race/ethnicity while it assumes a contextual construct (Brah and Phoenix 2004; Holvino 2010).The empirical material was generated through listening to life stories of IWE who migrated from Turkey to Sweden for different reasons. I searched IWE via ethnic and nusiness association networks operating nationwide. This search yielded 17 candidates with whom I carried out life story interviews between November 2011 and December 2012 at the women's workplaces or homes. The interviews were conducted in Turkish being the native language of the interviewees and then transcribed into English by myself. Life story materials were combined with non-participant observations of entrepreneurship practices in several of these women's businesses. I also attended by-invitation-only networking and special events organised by the women during this period.

IWE included in my research are summarised in Table 13.1.

To analyse the life stories of these 17 IWE, I first conducted a positioning analysis. A study of positioning allows the observation of different social locations of individuals and resources. As the first step, I attended particular events both prior to as well as following opportunity recognition and enterprising activities recognising the constitutive aspect of time and space for narratives (Baynham 2003). I was able to discern emerging patterns around particular individual biographies pertaining to distinct perspectives in relation to certain shared perspectives founded upon similar historical experience of material and socio-cultural contexts prior to and following the migration experience. Closer reading of rich material revealed the significance of gender, ethnicity, class and entrepreneurship for IWE albeit in varying degrees and ways (Yuval-Davis 2006). Through constructing, reading as well as examining the text, I assumed my role as a co-narrator from the beginning. The generated text altogether made me conclude that having the same ethnic and gender origin had an unforeseen effect on how the women formalised their life stories, as many reflections ended with phrases such as 'as you already know' (Essers 2009).

However, I took great care not to equate social categories with social grouping (Yuval-Davis 2010), as I recognised the potential effect of intersecting

Table 13.1 Summary of 17 immigrant women entrepreneurs (IWE) included in the life stories research project

Life story narrator	Migration history	Age at the time of migration (the year of migration)	Education: occupation prior to starting up	Starting up	Area of entrepreneurship
Leyla	Labour	2 (1968)	University: university student and elderly care	1988	Human resource consultancy
Ceren	Lifestyle	2 (1968)	High school: financial accountant and elderly caretaker	2006	Elderly care
Ayla	Political	28 (1983)	University: dentist	1995	Dentistry
Senay	Labour	0 (born: 1981, migration: 1974)	High school: beautician and elderly caretaker	2011	Beauty and personal care
Guler	Political	26 (1973)	University: psychologist and TV programme producer	2004	Educational consultancy
Merve	Labour	2 (1973)	High school: hairdressing	1990	Hairdresser
Nalan	Lifestyle	6 (1973)	High school: cook	2007	Knitware shop
Ramize	Political	23 (1982)	University: nurse	1996	Translation
Nejla	labour	0 (born: 1979, migration: 1977)	High school: nurse and elderly caretaker	2004	Beauty and personal care
Mine	Political	28 (1980)	University: dentistry	1996	Health and personal care
Nurten	Labour	0 (1966)	University: social services	2010	Wine trading
Zeynep	Labour	0 (born: 1989, migration: 1966	University student	2009	Event organising
Selin	Lifestyle	22 (2002)	High school: dancer	2008	Restaurant–café–bar
Sema	Labour	3 (1963)	High school: public service	1991	Restaurant–café–bar
Muge	Lifestyle	32 (2010)	University: marketing consultancy	2010	Marketing consultancy
Hatis	Labour	0 (born: 1983 migration: 1999)	High school: housekeeping	2005	Restaurant–café–bar
Aysen	Labour	2 (1963)	Secondary school: housekeeping	1993	Restaurant–café–bar

power hierarchies which shape individuals' life chances differently and in turn have a bearing upon qualitatively different experiences (Holvino 2010; Skeggs 2004); situated imaginations (Haraway 1988; Stoetzler & Yuval-Davis 2002) and in relating to others (Skeggs 2014). I then went on to examine what makes some women entrepreneurs under certain conditions identify or not with certain identity/social positionings (Brah and Phoenix 2004) as well as with certain ethical stances and practices (Kenny and Fotaki 2015) through mechanisms of 'identification' and 'dis-identification' (Sveningsson and Alvesson 2003). Wherever possible, I tried to present the most illustrative quotes by the same participants to provide a sense of sequential biographical order.

Introducing immigrant women entrepreneurs

My analysis yielded three socio-culturally differentiated groups of IWE on the basis of identification and dis-identification: namely 'migrant women', 'women migrants' and 'hybrid women'.

Migrant women

These political refugee women come from established families with urban backgrounds. Before migrating to Sweden in the early 1980s following the military coup in Turkey, most of them had already completed higher education and worked as professionals. They are the product of modernisation projects in Turkey in which women were positioned as equal to men both in the private and public domains (White 2004). Although migration disrupted some of the resources they had acquired before the coup, they had higher economic, social and cultural resources compared to women with working-class backgrounds. Therefore, in Sweden, they had more resources to act on and define themselves.

Women migrants

These women come from working- or lower class families which had usually migrated from rural areas or small towns in Turkey to Sweden in the 1970s as a labour force. In these families, the women's lives are organised on the basis of patriarchal cultural codes which would limit women's movements between the private and public spheres (Kandiyoti 1977). Their essential place is with the family and they are primarily socialised first as daughters and then as wives and mothers (Erman 2001). The women in this study have always worked following their middle education in Sweden. Nevertheless, protecting family honour and their sexuality remained essential in order to have a respectable life and to be respectful women (Baştuğ 2002).

Hybrid women

Like woman migrants, hybrid women came to Sweden in the early 1970s at very early ages to join their fathers or brothers as workers. They are migrants from small towns and their migration rationale does not necessarily follow the familiar immigrant narrative of breadwinning. Like migrant women, they come from families where the woman's position is not subordinate and the economic wealth of the family is steady and established. Nevertheless, their families are not highly educated as migrant women and, upon their arrival at very early ages, some have pursued higher education routes while others have not.

Immigrant women entrepreneurs struggling with social complexity of power and bridging the gap through agency

In order to trace which tactics of agency are used by IWE in order to overcome the dominating forces, I believe that it is important to look first at how gender and ethnicity connotations differ among women vis-à-vis their shared and contextualised perspectives founded on particular collective histories. Below Three main tactics used by IWE are examined below.

Struggling with gender and class

The narratives of the women show that they enter entrepreneurship primarily in an effort to resist Indigenous patriarchy and class inequalities. Woman migrants feel an urge to resist their prevailing conditions to achieve a change in their social status. They are realistic and aware of the available opportunities for them as women coming from working-class families (Skeggs 1997). They knew from the beginning that they would be working as beauticians, hairdressers or similar. They had not even imagined attending a university. Merve says:

> Since hairdressing fits me very well I have never considered higher education. Here in order to be a hairdresser you do not need to attend a university.

For these entrepreneurs participating in competence development programmes this was a common tactic. They recounted how important it was to have the relevant certificate in legitimising their skills in a given field:

> A certificate is necessary because otherwise you may burn people's skin, or in case you do burn their skin, you will know how to handle the situation. It was to assure my customers that I knew what I was doing because I had a certificate.

> (Nese)

Nese recognises the necessity and reacts by acquiring a licence to comply with what the market demands. In other words, by not resisting the market force she aims to secure her business. Woman migrants developed distinct strategies in relation to economic resources, as such economic freedom meant securing their independence, especially from the patriarchal structures they suffered.

> I did not need any help, neither did I ask anyone for help. Why would I do that? Otherwise people would claim some sense of ownership on what I have been trying to do, on my achievement!
>
> (Nese)

It was observed that this woman used her savings as economic capital and built up a tplan to establish a business to sever her sense of financial dependency on her ex-husband or father. Entrepreneurship was an important instrument where they could tell the world that they could make something meaningful, something which would fulfil the purpose of their life.

Struggling with ethnicity and class

The narratives of the women in this group show that practising entrepreneurship is an effort for them to produce in a social world where majority and minority ethnics are equally valuable. Education as an allocative mechanism in legitimating and defining the class position of migrant women was set as a prerequisite not only for paid or highly qualified jobs, but in almost any field where the woman entrepreneurs started up their own businesses. They try to accumulate cultural capital regardless of the existence of market pressure on that front.

> I worked in Turkey too as a dentist.... But my degree was not accepted here. For that reason, I have been here in the Karolinska Institute for three years.
>
> (Ayla)

Ayla does not problematise the requirements posed by the Swedish authorities and the long-term educational investment attached to such requirements, and instead prefers instead to adjust to those requirements.

For Mine, however, the issue was more complicated because the requirements simply cast too many questions on her sense of self. She mobilised exactly the same resources to fight conditions that, according to her, were unjust.

> Why study the same thing, the same science just in a different language ... I took that as an insult, right?

Resisting acquiring dental education in Sweden, Mine became a shareholder in a private clinic run by dentists of Turkish origin. They were able to positively differentiate themselves from others given some of the embodied skills reflected through familiar cultural settings and language skills, such as their common ethnicity, particular disposition towards health and so on. Eschewing the dominance of the Swedish language on the job market, some use transnational business as a tactic to overcome their disadvantaged positioning. For example, Leyla set up her first company while she was studying computer sciences at the university. This initiative was mainly due to her reflexive awareness of her limited occupational choices as a migrant when she and several other students with immigrant backgrounds discovered that they could not find an internship which was obligatory to complete their education. In order to carry on, she set up an IT company and hired those students from her class who could not find an internship opportunity.

> Recently I sent a group of unemployed Swedish engineers of Iraqi origin to work in Iraq for a Swedish multinational company, and I just found an Indian company for a woman who cannot speak Swedish properly but she can live with her Indian language.
>
> (Leyla)

Their struggle was mainly about compensating for their disadvantage arising from their ethno-cultural positioning by trying to enhance their class positions through practising certain tactics in enterpreneuring.

Struggling with capitalist work ethics and practices

For this group of women entrepreneurship is an effort to resist unethical market forces. Hybrid women entrepreneurs' narratives revealed a strong reflexive awareness of how the moral aspects of work could have been suppressed by instrumental orientations and practices. This understanding led them to pursue certain tactics to encounter such suppression while starting up their businesses, as revealed in Ceren's story below.

> I used to work at Siemens as a purchasing specialist for 20 years and later I had to take some extra jobs at elderly care prior to my venturing. I believed in something. I wanted the elderly whom I took care of to be happy. That became my philosophy.

While starting up her own business, Sema says:

> Birgit [the former owner of the business] used to work here for 35 years. Then she had health problems and she decided to sell her business. The night before the transfer I could not sleep as I imagined the abyss she could fall down.... Next day, when she took the key and just as she was

handing it over to me, I held her hand and said that 'this key should stay at your disposal until the day we sell this place; when this happens we can together leave the keys'.

By acting in this way, Sema relates to Birgit in prioritising ethical values over a more individualistic approach.

Discussion

The concept of struggle is used to explain the power–resistance relationship between the sampled IWE and where they come from and where they found themselves. While such orders cause these women to resist and break free in the first place by founding their own businesses, they then tend to pursue their own paths in compliance with their own specific (individual) biographies constituted through collective life trajectories and histories. My research revealed that IWE manage the complex and interactive relationship between power and resistance through agency. They combine different variants of power and resistance in a dynamic interface to determine their strategies and tactics in their entrepreneurial experience.

IWE in the study exhibited agency of power and agency of intention in reconnecting and repositioning themselves in the face of particular struggles concerning their positioning in social hierarchies and their ethical concerns. For instance, while some women capitalised on their own ethnicity by positively differentiating themselves from others given some of the embodied skills such as cultural similarity and language skills, some did not. Their migration and entrepreneurial experiences were strongly shaped by women's socioculturally constructed class locations prior to migration. Their stories differed greatly on how they voiced their dissenting concerns (Huault, Perret & Spicer 2012). While the 'women migrants' and 'migrant women' have sought meaning through the agency of power, that is, by trying to exert influence on others and taking control of their lives through relaxing social hierarchies, 'hybrid women' have primarily sought meaning around the agency of intention by going over to capitalist work practices which suppresses the 'ethics of difference' on the basis of relating to others pre-reflectively (Kenny and Fotaki 2015).

The women migrants' stories show how entrepreneurship provided a shelter in the absence of male supremacy. Accordingly, they claim to be seen as subjects who develop their own capital towards fulfilling their aims detached from the men's expectations (Lovell 2000).

For the migrant women, it was about autonomy and recognition coming with professional practice as they arrived in Sweden with heavy cultural baggage, including higher education, professional experience and communicative knowledge. For hybrid women, the suppression of moral aspects of their work under instrumental orientations proved to be repressive so that they all wanted to be a part of the solution along with their specific individual histories. Although these women usually came from working-class families, some were able to tap into higher education possibilities and, if not, they were able to tap into the two cultural reservoirs of Swedish and Turkish contexts. Being positioned in the middle of the strata, they showed greater variety in responding to their circumstances and a wide array of resources on their identity.

In examining the categories of IWE, I observed significantly that emancipation is the driving force for most of them to start up their own business. Many of these women state that they feel or would like to see themselves elevated through the activity of entrepreneurship. Yet, the notion of emancipation is not solely circumscribed by the power exercised within social hierarchies; for example, as a vehicle for social integration (Abbasian and Bildt 2009) or economic (Scott *et al.* 2012) and social improvement (Datta and Gailey 2012) that impacts upon an entrepreneur's own empowerment, as studies on empowerment usually conclude, but also concerns the open orientation taken towards the unknown others with care and compassion (Kenny and Fotaki 2015). The study thus supports such a concept of emancipation where entrepreneurship is regarded as a means of 'new openings for more liberating forms of individual and collective existence' (Verduijn *et al.* 2014).

Implications and conclusions

In this research, I sought new insights into the ways in which IWE responded to the available representations of entrepreneurship, gender, ethnicity and class. IWE from different backgrounds, social positioning and life trajectories applied different agency roles or tactics to respond to the pressures of the established power. An ethnographic perspective with its emphasis on meaning enabled an analysis where agency and resistance acted as a socio-cultural enactment beyond individualistic approaches (Watson 2011). In other words, such an approach helped articulate the agency and resistance as part of cultural constructs.

Thus this study contributes to the entrepreneurship literature first by displaying how the investigation of ordinary life experience can expose entrepreneurship as part of a social scene beyond the individual tactics employed to attain economic gain (Steyaert and Katz 2004). This is especially significant for women's entrepreneurship research where the constructionist approaches pay less attention to the individual (Hughes *et al.* 2012) in examining the relationship between context and entrepreneurship. This study contributes to this by approaching the individuals not only as embedded within socio-cultural contexts but also embodying them. This way, the study further explicates the nature of a connection between individual, organisation and socio-cultural contexts (Fletcher 2006; Spedale and Watson 2014).

Accordingly, I have shown that even if in many classical accounts of entrepreneurship entrepreneurs act as figureheads of capitalism (Williams and Nadin 2013), and even if entrepreneurship is a powerful and even a totalising discourse, these entrepreneurs find ways to rearrange established relations beyond the discursive frames of entrepreneurship (Cohen and Musson 2000). Despite being exposed to different dominant structures, gender, ethnicity, class and entrepreneurship, the women found something in entrepreneurship to make their own; i.e. to provide purpose and meaning in their lives (Essers *et al.* 2013). This analysis demonstrates close affinities with studies that examined the discursive construction of professional identities of IWE. I extend such insights on the nature of tactics which is primarily defined around discursive resources where I add the material dimension involved in discursive struggles.

Such an approach draws me to the conclusion that there is a continuous intertwined relationship between power and resistance, which also entails a continuous mutual tension affecting the IWE as both the subject and object of this relationship from time to time. Thus, the study provides an empirical analysis on the dimension of criticality in entrepreneurship, showing that appreciating entrepreneurship as a source of emancipation (Scott *et al.* 2012) or seeing it as a source of domination (Bruni *et al.* 2004) would undercut its complexity and entrepreneurs' joys and struggles in navigating within the different (b) orders. I contribute by elaborating upon the under-discussed concept of 'struggle' in order to explain the dialectical power resistance relationship and the established orders in which they are embedded (Fleming and Spicer 2008).

The study also counteracts the tendency towards demarcating the undertakings within the field of entrepreneurship as predominantly drawing upon economic exchange. I rather suggest paying greater attention to the flows and connections between this and other fields of practices such as education, and the domestic and public spheres, etc. over the biographies of IWE. For instance, care as a practice presupposes a different mode of relating to others with compassion and attentiveness (Skeggs and Loveday 2012). Care invokes different experiences and extends into multiple contexts and relations of power beyond the instrumental logic of the exchange of capital (Kenny and Fotaki 2015).

Indeed, IWE manage the complex and intertwined relationship between power and resistance. Yet their strategy and acts of agency sailing through the deep sea of power and resistance differ in compliance with the cultural, social and economic resources available to them. While some struggle more around identity, others struggle around activity (Fleming and Spicer 2008). Some accept, some adjust, and some try to make a change in the future. They all struggle to construct an environment in which they feel at home and happy.

Future studies may open up the nature and forms of struggles involving different aspects of power such as age, sexuality and disability in order to shed further light on the complexity of entrepreneurship experiences by diverse groups. Further research might examine the different and more ambivalent forms of struggles of entrepreneurs by adopting nuanced analytical processes of positioning such as passing, improvement or dissimulation beyond the poles of (dis)identification I adopted in this study.

References

Abbasian, S. and Bildt, C. (2009), Empowerment through entrepreneurship: A tool for integration among immigrant women? *IUP Journal of Entrepreneurship Development*, **6**(3/4), p. 7.

Ahearn, L.M. (2001), Language and agency. *Annual Review of Anthropology*, **30**, pp. 109–137.

Ahl, H. (2006), Why research on women entrepreneurs needs new directions. *Entrepreneurship Theory and Practice*, **30**(5), pp. 595–621.

Ainsworth, S. and Hardy, C. (2008), The enterprising self: An unsuitable job for an older worker. *Organization*, **15**(3), pp. 389–405.

Anderson, A.R., Dodd, S.D. and Jack, S.L. (2012), Entrepreneurship as connecting: Some implications for theorising and practice. *Management Decision*, **50**(5), pp. 958–971.

Aygören, H. and Wilinska, M. (2013), 'People Like Us': Experiencing difference in the working life of immigrant women. *Equality, Diversity and Inclusion*, **32**(5–6).

Baştuğ, S. (2002), The household and family in Turkey: An historical perspective. In İçinde R. Liljeström and R. Özdalga (eds), *Autonomy and Dependence in the Family: Turkey and Sweden in Critical Perspective*, İstanbul: Swedish Research Institute, pp. 99–115.

Baynham, M. (2003), Narratives in space and time: Beyond 'backdrop' accounts of narrative orientation. *Narrative Inquiry*, **13**(2), pp. 347–366.

Bourne, K. and Calás, M. (2012), Becoming 'real' entrepreneurs: Women and the gendered normalization of 'work'. *Gender, Work & Organization*, **20**(4), pp. 425–438.

Brah, A. and Phoenix, A. (2004), Ain't I a woman? Revisiting intersectionality. *Journal of International Women's Studies*, **5**(3), pp. 75–86.

Bruni, A., Gherardi, S. and Poggio, B. (2004), Entrepreneur-mentality, gender and the study of women entrepreneurs. *Journal of Organizational Change Management*, **17**(3), pp. 256–268.

Bruyat, C. and Julien, P.A. (2001), Defining the field of research in entrepreneurship. *Journal of Business Venturing*, **16**(2), pp. 165–180.

Calás, M., Smircich, L. and Bourne, K. (2009), Extending the boundaries: Reframing 'entrepreneurship as social change' through feminist perspectives. *Academy of Management Review*, **34**(3), pp. 552–569.

Clarke, J. and Holt, R. (2010), The mature entrepreneur: A narrative approach to entrepreneurial goals. *Journal of Management Inquiry*, **19**(1), pp. 69–83.

Cohen, L. and Musson, G. (2000), Entrepreneurial identities: Reflections from two case studies. *Organization*, **7**(1), pp. 31–48.

Datta, P. and Gailey, R. (2012), Empowering women through social entrepreneurship: Case study of a women's cooperative in India. *Entrepreneurship Theory and Practice*, **36**(3), pp. 569–587.

De Certeau, M. (1998), *The Practice of Everyday Life: Living and Cooking. Volume 2*, Minneapolis: University of Minnesota Press.

Downing, S. (2005), The social construction of entrepreneurship: Narrative and dramatic processes in the coproduction of organizations and identities. *Entrepreneurship Theory and Practice*, **29**(2), pp. 185–204.

Erman, T. (2001), Rural migrants and patriarchy in Turkish cities. *International Journal of Urban and Regional Research*, **25**(1), pp. 118–133.

Essers, C. (2009), Reflections on the narrative approach: Dilemmas of power, emotions and social location while constructing life-stories. *Organization*, **16**(2), pp. 163–181.

Essers, C. and Benschop, Y. (2007), Enterprising identities: Female entrepreneurs of Moroccan or Turkish origin in the Netherlands. *Organization Studies*, **28**(1), pp. 49–69.

Essers, C., Doorewaard, H. and Benschop, Y. (2013), Family ties: Migrant female business owners doing identity work on the public–private divide. *Human Relations*, **66**(12), pp. 1645–1665.

Fenwick, T.J. (2002), Transgressive desires: New enterprising selves in the new capitalism. *Work, Employment & Society*, **16**(4), pp. 703–723.

Fleming, P. and Sewell, G. (2002), Looking for the good soldier, Švejk alternative modalities of resistance in the contemporary workplace. *Sociology*, **36**(4), pp. 857–873.

Fleming, P. and Spicer, A. (2007), *Contesting the Corporation: Struggle, Power and Resistance in Organizations*, Cambridge: Cambridge University Press.

Fleming, P. and Spicer, A. (2008), Beyond power and resistance New approaches to organizational politics. *Management Communication Quarterly*, **21**(3), pp. 301–309.

Fletcher, D.E. (2006), Entrepreneurial processes and the social construction of opportunity. *Entrepreneurship and Regional Development*, **18**(5), pp. 421–440.

García, M.-C.D. and Welter, F. (2013), Gender identities and practices: Interpreting women entrepreneurs' narratives. *International Small Business Journal*, **31**(4), pp. 384–404.

Goss, D., Jones, R., Betta, M. and Latham, J. (2011), Power as practice: A microsociological analysis of the dynamics of emancipatory entrepreneurship. *Organization Studies*, **32**(2), pp. 211–229.

Haraway, D. (1988), Situated knowledges: The science question in feminism and the privilege of partial perspective. *Feminist Studies*, **14**(3), pp. 575–599.

Hardy, C. and Thomas, R. (2014), Strategy, discourse and practice: The intensification of power. *Journal of Management Studies*, **51**(2), pp. 320–348.

Holvino, E. (2010), Intersections: The simultaneity of race, gender and class in organization studies. *Gender, Work & Organization*, **17**(3), pp. 248–277.

Huault, I., Perret, V. and Spicer, A. (2012), Beyond macro- and micro-emancipation: Rethinking emancipation in organization studies. *Organization*, **21**(1), pp. 22–45.

Hughes, K.D., Jennings, J.E., Brush, C., Carter, S. and Welter, F. (2012), Extending women's entrepreneurship research in new directions. *Entrepreneurship Theory and Practice*, **36**(3), pp. 429–442.

Kandiyoti, D. (1977), Sex roles and social change: A comparative appraisal of Turkey's women. *Signs*, **3**(1), pp. 57–73.

Kenny, K. and Fotaki, M. (2015), From gendered organizations to compassionate borderspaces: Reading corporeal ethics with Bracha Ettinger. *Organization*, **22**(2), pp. 183–199.

Kondo, D.K. (1990), *Crafting Selves: Power, Gender, and Discourses of Identity in a Japanese Workplace*, Chicago, IL: University of Chicago Press.

Lewis, P. (2006), The quest for invisibility: Female entrepreneurs and the masculine norm of entrepreneurship. *Gender, Work & Organization*, **13**(5), pp. 453–469.

Lovell, T. (2000), Thinking feminism with and against Bourdieu. *Feminist Theory*, **1**(1), pp. 11–32.

MacLeod, A.E. (1992), Hegemonic relations and gender resistance: The new veiling as accommodating protest in Cairo. *Signs*, **17**(3), pp. 533–557.

Martí, I. and Fernández, P. (2013), The institutional work of oppression and resistance: Learning from the Holocaust. *Organization Studies*, **34**(8), pp. 1195–1223.

Mumby, D.K. (2005), Theorizing resistance in organization studies: A dialectical approach. *Management Communication Quarterly*, **19**(1), pp. 19–44.

Ortner, S.B. (1995), Resistance and the problem of ethnographic refusal. *Comparative Studies in Society and History*, **37**(1), pp. 173–193.

Ortner, S.B. (1997), Thick resistance: Death and the cultural construction of agency in Himalayan mountaineering. *Representations*, pp. 135–162.

Ortner, S.B. (2001), Specifying agency: The Comaroffs and their critics. *Interventions*, **3**(1), pp. 76–84.

Pio, E. and Essers, C. (2014), Professional migrant women decentring otherness: A transnational perspective. *British Journal of Management*, **25**(2), pp. 252–265.

Scott, L., Dolan, C., Johnstone-Louis, M., Sugden, K. and Wu, M. (2012), Enterprise and inequality: A study of Avon in South Africa. *Entrepreneurship Theory and Practice*, **36**(3), pp. 543–568.

Skeggs, B. (1997), *Formations of Class and Gender: Becoming Respectable*, London: Sage.

Skeggs, B. (2004), Context and background: Pierre Bourdieu's analysis of class, gender and sexuality. *The Sociological Review*, **52**(2), pp. 19–33.

Skeggs, B. (2014), Values beyond value? Is anything beyond the logic of capital? *The British Journal of Sociology*, **65**(1), pp. 1–20.

Skeggs, B. and Loveday, V. (2012), Struggles for value: Value practices, injustice, judgment, affect and the idea of class. *The British Journal of Sociology*, **63**(3), pp. 472–490.

Spedale, S. and Watson, T.J. (2014), The emergence of entrepreneurial action: At the crossroads between institutional logics and individual life-orientation. *International Small Business Journal*, **32**(7), pp. 759–776.

Steyaert, C. and Katz, J. (2004), Reclaiming the space of entrepreneurship in society: Geographical, discursive and social dimensions. *Entrepreneurship & Regional Development*, **16**(3), pp. 179–196.

Stoetzler, M. and Yuval-Davis, N. (2002), Standpoint theory, situated knowledge and the situated imagination. *Feminist Theory*, **3**(3), pp. 315–333.

Sveningsson, S. and Alvesson, M. (2003), Managing managerial identities: Organizational fragmentation, discourse and identity struggle. *Human Relations*, **56**(10), pp. 1163–1193.

Thomas, R. and Davies, A. (2005), What have the feminists done for us? Feminist theory and organizational resistance. *Organization*, **12**(5), pp. 711–740.

Verduijn, K. and Essers, C. (2013), Questioning dominant entrepreneurship assumptions: The case of female ethnic minority entrepreneurs. *Entrepreneurship & Regional Development*, **25**(7–8), pp. 612–630.

Verduijn, K., Dey, P., Tedmanson, D. and Essers, C. (2014), Emancipation and/or oppression? Conceptualizing dimensions of criticality in entrepreneurship studies. *International Journal of Entrepreneurial Behaviour & Research*, **20**(2), pp. 98–107.

Watson, T.J. (2011), Ethnography, reality, and truth: The vital need for studies of 'how things work' in organizations and management. *Journal of Management Studies*, **48**(1), pp. 202–217.

White, J.B. (2004), State feminism, modernization, and the Turkish republican woman. *NWSA Journal*, **15**(3), pp. 145–159.

Williams, C.C. and Nadin, S.J. (2013), Beyond the entrepreneur as a heroic figure-head of capitalism: Re-representing the lived practices of entrepreneurs. *Entrepreneurship & Regional Development*, **25**(7–8), pp. 552–568.

Yuval-Davis, N. (2006), Belonging and the politics of belonging. *Patterns of Prejudice*, **40**(3), pp. 197–214.

Yuval-Davis, N. (2010), Theorizing identity: Beyond the 'us' and 'them' dichotomy. *Patterns of Prejudice*, **44**(3), pp. 261–280.

Part V

Deconstructing entrepreneurship

14 The governance of welfare and the expropriation of the common

Polish tales of entrepreneurship

Dorota Marsh and Pete Thomas

Introduction

Over 20 years ago Poland commenced the transformation from a communist to a neoliberal economy. The introduction of economic 'shock therapy' in 1989 signified a first wave of neoliberalism in Poland, which established foundations for the whole transformation and more importantly the subsequent neoliberal orientation of successive Polish governments. The core of the shock therapy was based on Reaganomics and Thatcherism, with a particularly strong emphasis on privatisation and the liberalisation of markets, accompanied by the withdrawal of the state from its role as regulator of economic processes (Shields 2007, 2012; Kabaj 2010; Balcerowicz 2004; Kowalik 2009, 2012). After 50 years of the state guaranteeing full employment and full social assistance, the sudden shock of unemployment and poverty affected those who in the former system had been proud citizens (predominantly members of the working class) but who, after 1989, found themselves unable to maintain an adequate standard of living in the new economic reality (Bauman 2006).

Contrary to the feelings of millions of Poles (86 per cent of the population), who link the economic situation to a negative impact upon their own lives (Rogulska 2012), international commentators presented Polish transformation as a success story, and the Polish government proudly 'on behalf of all Poles pronounce[d] Polish success' (Tusk 2011), and continues to do so (Komorowski 2012). As the only European Union member state not to experience an economic contraction since the start of the financial crisis (Rae 2012), enthusiastic assessments of the successes of the Polish economy have appeared regularly in the international press; for example: 'Poland is an exception in a world brought to its knees by financial crisis' (Sheets 2013); 'Poland has been one of the world's great development success stories of the past two decades' (Economist 2012); 'Poland, the star performer of the region – an economic powerhouse in Europe' (The Warsaw Voice 2012).

Part of this transition to apparent neoliberal success lies in the development of entrepreneurship as a motor of economic development. A discourse of enterprise has been fostered and promoted in Poland, and is seen as a necessary step away from the past and its planned economy and state intervention. In this chapter we explore how the discourses of *homo sovieticus* and *homo entrepreneurus* have been deployed as discursive resources by the proponents of change. In particular, we examine how these discursive resources have played a part, not only in concealing the social cost of neoliberal transformation, but also in naturalising and legitimising policies resulting in a growing number of the 'working poor' employed on 'junk contracts'; unemployment; large-scale poverty; and the deterioration of living conditions for many in Poland (Rae 2012; Kowalik 2009). We forgo the simplistic idea of transition and challenge the view that the 'triumph' of a market economy and neoliberalism is a simple outcome of a naturally evolving social process, 'as the very expression of the eternal nature of human societies' (Bermúdez 2012, p. 1). Instead, we believe that it is important to examine the process in a more nuanced way to uncover the mechanisms used in creating the new regime, with specific attention paid to the role and power of economic elites in the process (Harvey 2005), and in this case the role they play in the establishment of an entrepreneurial discourse.

In our approach to transformation we understand it not as a purely objective process that automatically produces a particular outcome, but as 'a strategy for achieving and stabilising a new "fix" between a regime of capital accumulation and a regime of political regulation' (Jessop 2004, cited in Fairclough 2007, p. 52). This strategy includes material transformation but also a discursive dimension (Jessop 2004). Jessop (2004) notes that during periods of major social restructuring a proliferation of interpretations is possible, since the discursive space is open for different forces to propose new visions and policies. As social life is characterised by antagonism and never-ending struggles over the creation of meaning (Laclau and Mouffe 1985), the 'fix' achieved is never more than temporary.

Not wishing to overstate the contingency of social practices, we use Chouliaraki and Fairclough's (1999) version of Laclau and Mouffe's (1985) framework of hegemony, in which articulation brings together shifting elements of social practice and stabilises them into more or less relative permanence. It is this relative permanency of the articulation of social elements that constitutes hegemony in which social forms can temporarily assume a definite shape. Fairclough (2007) adds that some of those ways of representing or imagining (the future) may be less effective in securing support for their strategies, while others become a plausible imaginary for a new political-economic fix, potentially securing a hegemonic social order. In order for discourse to operationalise and actualise a new political-economic order, the discourse has to be of a particular kind, what Laclau and Mouffe (1985) would term 'a nodal discourse'. Nodal discourses are materially grounded and promoted to achieve a high level of adequacy in operationalising imaginaries into realties (Fairclough 2013). Thus, only those imaginaries that correspond with material processes and forces will become hegemonic (Jessop 2004). The most influential are economic imaginaries, which can address economic strategies 'providing a means to integrate private, institutional and wider public narratives about past experiences, present difficulties, and future prospects' (Jessop 2004, p. 27).

Fairclough (2005) has argued that discourse plays an important role in processes of transition and has stressed the potential of critical discourse analysis in examining the transition economies of Eastern Europe. In particular he draws attention to the shift of nodal discourses, from 'construals', representations or imaginaries to operationalised new ways of acting. Thus, in our case, the discourse of neoliberalism may be seen as a nodal discourse, but such nodal discourses are often articulated together with other nodal discourses in attempts to move beyond mere representation. In the context of Poland's transition there are several prior discourses that stem from the history and experience of the Polish people, but in this chapter we focus on the nodal discourses of *homo sovieticus* and *homo entrepreneurus*, and explore how these discourses have been articulated with neoliberalism in the process of change.

We have selected sources which we found helpful in addressing the ideological use of both discourses in facilitating a particular model of social change; however, this selection is by no means exhaustive, and should be treated as exclusively illustrative. In our selection of sources we focused on their contribution to the process of meaning making (Fairclough 2003) to enable us to assess the social effects of the meanings of those texts. Following this approach we concentrated our analysis on those sources which we considered to be particularly influential in disseminating the narratives of *homo sovieticus* due to their extensive distribution, namely the most-read Polish newspapers such as *Tygodnik Powszechny*, *Gazeta Wyborcza*, *Wprost*, *Rzeczpospolita* and *Nasz Dziennik*. These sources were, however, less suitable in the process of tracing the intensification of the discourse of *homo entrepreneurus*. For that reason our selection of sources was based on the criterion of the extent to which these sources were incorporated into other texts, as per Fairclough's (2003) notion of analytical intertextuality. As the discourse of *homo entrepreneurus* was predominantly present in official, political documents, we based our analysis on the key political texts, including the writings of Balcerowicz (the author of Polish shock therapy), manifestos of Platforma Obywatelska (the leading Polish neoliberal party) as well as official press releases issued by the current Polish government and president. These sources, initially disseminated on a smaller scale, became rapidly popularised by the public media and subsequently commonly incorporated into other texts.

In analysing the process of transition, we acknowledge a distinction between the actual process of transformation (set of changes) and the discourse of transformation (or, more precisely, the discursive character of strategies for transformation), and more importantly we analyse the relationship between both, following Fairclough's example (2007). Discourses contribute to and shape the processes of change, and the boundaries between discourses and other elements of social life are fluid. This dialectical relationship (Fairclough 2007) is particularly important in our analysis, as we are aiming to uncover how the ways of representing are transformed into material realities, but also into other moments of social practice such as power, social relations and institutions (Harvey 1996). We acknowledge that discourse is not privileged in this dialectical view of social practice and that each moment of social practice contains the others in ways that are not separable, but for the sake of our analysis here we focus on the moment of discourse as of particular interest.

The 'importation' of Western neoliberalism into Poland cannot be seen as a simple transition, nor can the movement of the discourse of neoliberalism be seen as a straightforward migration of ideas. As discourses move across boundaries they are recontextualised; that is, they are modified to suit the new context into which they move (Fairclough 2005). This recontextualisation means that the discourses can be enacted to varying degrees and in a variety of ways. In this analysis we consider the recontextualisation of the neoliberalist discourse as an imaginary, which is then enacted as it is articulated together with prior discourses and social practices. The role of agency in this process should not be underplayed. Van Dijk (2006) sees manipulation as one of the discursive social practices of dominant groups geared towards the reproduction of their power, so our analysis should attend to the ways in which discourse is used by powerful agents in the 'transition' of Poland.

In short, our analytical framework deploys three key elements: the conceptualisation of transition in terms of moments of social practice; the recontextualisation of neoliberalist discourse into the Polish context; and the articulation of this nodal discourse alongside prior discourses, and specifically that of *homo sovieticus* and *homo entrepreneurus*. This way of interpreting the process of transformation allows us to break with the tradition of continuity, and the assumption that there exists some homogeneous and linear teleology. Projects and policies that are materialised in particular spaces, despite being driven by the same ideology, may differ in their translation into practice. These local peculiarities are important for understanding how the neoliberal 'ideational project' gains its momentum and hegemonic status (Mirowski 2013).

The discourse of neoliberalism and *homo sovieticus*

Elsewhere, we have attributed the growing enthusiasm for Western neoliberal thinking in Poland to its 'postcolonial legacy', with Thompson's (2008) notion of the surrogate hegemon explaining how Poland has recoiled from Soviet colonisation and fallen into the arms of its 'adored' West (Marsh and Thomas 2010). Poland has in effect rebounded from an unwilling relationship with one ideology into an enthusiastic relationship with another; from communism to neoliberalism. Thus, what warrant scrutiny are the methods the elite have used to justify and promote the introduction of neoliberalism.

Despite the optimistic promises made by the architects of the Polish neoliberal project that 'communism would be replaced by a competitive system – a stable capitalism, whose mechanisms have been known for a hundred years.

We were safe and poor, we were supposed to become safe and rich' (Sikorska 2004, pp. 20–21), the new reality could not be further from these promises. As the economic situation of large numbers of Poles deteriorated, the increase in social differentiation became one of the most frequently described phenomena of transformation (Smith and Lee 2011). Kowalik (2009) describes the neoliberal system as an elitist model of wealth distribution due to its consequences, mainly a 'higher level of social inequalities (growing polarisation of society), mass unemployment and a large scale of poverty' (Kowalik 2009, p. 215). Polish public discourse, however, rarely acknowledges these unsightly consequences of transformation, and occasional attention given to the unemployed and poor is presented as 'collateral damage'. These collateral victims are 'dismissed as not important enough to justify the cost of their prevention, or simply "unexpected" because the planers did not consider them worthy of inclusion among the objects of preparatory reconnoitring' (Bauman 2011, p. 8). We would argue that in order to deal with the negative impact of transformation, the Polish government has deployed discursive resources to maintain political stability and to legitimise policies aimed at minimising the welfare state. In particular, it has deployed the notion of *homo sovieticus* as a reminder of 'the bad old days'.

The term *homo sovieticus* (originally introduced by Russian writer and philosopher Aleksander Zinowiew in 1980s) was popularised in Polish public discourse by Tischner in the 1990s and became one of the most frequently used terms to describe the condition of societies going through the process of transformation (Tyszka 2009). The term describes the primitive individual, a 'client of the communist system defined by acceptance of the totalitarian system; a human who is intellectually enslaved, deprived of dignity and driven by opportunism'. Tischner (2005) elaborated on the negative traits of *homo sovieticus*, a one-dimensional human terrorised by the system and concentrating on the most basic needs. *Homo sovieticus* is, on the one hand, enslaved by the totalitarian system, and on the other, by using the advantages of the generous welfare state, accepts the disadvantages of that system and develops a survival strategy to benefit from it (Wnuk-Lipiński 2008). Blachnicki (2011) adds that *homo sovieticus* is predominantly a collective being for whom collective values are more important than the individual sense of responsibility.

The narratives of *homo sovieticus* were particularly popular during the first years of transformation (marked by the highest level of unemployment), when those on the receiving end of the shock therapy who dared to complain were quickly labelled as passive, apathetic individuals unable to control their own destiny and take responsibility for their own fate. Despite the lack of any valid underpinning, the category of *homo sovieticus* became a very handy instrument used to stigmatise those individuals, who were labelled as the 'losers' of transformation as opposed to the 'winners', rewarded by the market for their talents and hard work. Polish public discourse (predominantly represented by neoliberal-oriented newspapers such as *Gazeta Wyborcza* and *Wprost*) was littered with articles fuelling hostility towards the unemployed and poor, and disseminating a simplistic explanation of poverty. *Gazeta Wyborcza* (Gadomski 2004) claimed that poor, marginalised individuals suffer from various 'deficits' of skills and mental instability, and are reluctant to take the risk of liberating themselves from the margins of 'normal' society. *Wprost* (Leśniewski and Zieliński 2001) went even further, stating that more than half of the Polish unemployed were not good enough to be given jobs as they were plagued by certain 'sub-syndromes' of *homo sovieticus*: 'the unemployed illiterate syndrome', 'Arizona syndrome' (unemployed alcoholics and drunks), 'unemployment hereditary syndrome' (entire families without work) and 'Snail Syndrome' (unemployed and immobile).

The way of summarising a socialist mentality as a specific syndrome of attitudes of large groups of Polish society, who happened to live and work under the communist regime, became particularly useful in official explanations of the cultural and mental barriers of those who struggled to adapt to the new social reality. Referring to those who were affected by *homo sovieticus* syndrome stigmatised certain behaviours, which resemble behavioural patterns from the communist period, predominantly the inability of people to make the sudden leap from the totalitarian mentality to new, market-driven, proactive attitudes (Willemans 2010). As Marody (2011, p. 89) notes, the term *homo sovieticus* 'became an equivalent of adjectives' used during the communist era 'such us "unadjusted", "unmodernized" and conservative'.

This pathologisation of those who found the new reality of neoliberal capitalism difficult served the neoliberal government as a justification and legitimisation of the structural problems of Polish neoliberal capitalism. The neoliberal elite attributed the failures of the system to the civilisationally incompetent masses, inhibited by the syndrome of *homo sovietiucs*. Simultaneously, the demeaning way of describing the poor and the unemployed was used as the sole explanation of the 'incidental' problems of transformation presented as related to the relics of the previous system, which promotes a mentality that prevents them from accepting new social and economic realities (Sutowski 2009). Engaging in a blame game provided the neoliberal elite with an effective technology for addressing the problems of transformation. Instead of challenging the foundations underlying the new system, the discourse of *homo sovieticus* was used to reinforce the neoliberal agenda and prepare 'the stage' for 'solutions', which did not address the causes rooted in political and economic domination of the neoliberal social order (Sum 2012).

This ideological diagnosis of what constitutes the general source of 'troubles' engendered by transformation allows the subsequent operationalisation of the economic solutions based on the withdrawal of the state. The neoliberal legends associating poverty with social pathologies are translated into material reality by disseminating an ideological assumption that 'social interventionism' creates permanent dependence on benefits and consequently demotivates people. Based on this, neoliberal reasoning explains that the instruments of social assistance offered by the state restrict the entrepreneurial activity of society. Consequently, economic growth becomes impossible, as demotivated people are not willing to contribute to society (Balcerowicz 2004). Following this logic, Balcerowicz (2004) concludes that the unemployed can only be protected by a lack of state intervention, as any form of assistance increases the number of unemployed. This way of reclassifying unemployment and poverty becomes politically very useful, as it helps propagate the view of social inequalities as a natural and inevitable element of every society, with any attempts to minimise it perceived as immoral and creating immoral behaviours (Wozniak 2012). If poverty is assumed to be a fault of individuals suffering from various deficits (communist mentality, various sub-syndromes of *homo sovieticus*, etc.) then the welfare state supporting these 'relics of communism' can be presented as a continuing element of the totalitarian state that must be removed.

The neoliberal elite enthusiastically advocates scaling down any form of social assistance as, according to the ideologically driven reasoning, helping those people requiring social assistance results in approving their demanding attitude (*homo sovieticus*), which consequently inhibits economic growth. Thus, poverty is not seen as a political problem and is not associated with the failure of the neoliberal government to create jobs; this after all is the role of private enterprise. By reducing poverty to the idea of an underclass living in 'Polish favelas' (Jedrzejko 2008), the exoticisation of poverty helps neoliberal elites distance themselves and their programmes from any responsibility for the social cost of the operationalisation of the neoliberal vision. Thus, the understanding of unemployment as a natural and beneficial element of the new economic reality means that the naturalisation of poverty becomes easier, particularly when the discourse of *homo sovieticus* is deployed to blame 'the poor for being poor'. Consequently, helping the poor at the expense of others is not only seen as ineffective but is often described as 'socialist theft' (Wojciechowski 2002). Analogies are even drawn between the welfare state and a concentration camp (Cukiernik 2012), with social assistance captivating people's minds, enslaving them by not only minimising their freedom but, more importantly, by building the dependence of the individual on the state. This understanding of the welfare state demonises it as an intervention instrument used by the state to limit an individual's freedom and initiative (Jaroszyński 2012).

This discursive offensive, aimed at shaping cultures through the rhetorical management of representation, known as 'cultural governance' (Fairclough 2000), has been a powerful tool in legitimising economic changes. By changing the public perception of unemployment and poverty as deriving from individuals' deficits, syndromes or pathologies (Tarkowska 2008), the neoliberal government obtains public acceptance for the policies disadvantaging an 'underclass' through a 'social relation of difference' (Harvey 2010, p. 104). The use of deliberately constructed distinctions within the social division not only helps sustain control but also prevents any potential for commonality or solidarity. Fragmented social relations are perpetuated by the ongoing binary representation of good and evil that Poles use to describe the socialist versus capitalist values and attitudes (Swader 2010). Further, Polish neoliberals have successfully convinced their citizens that each individual is responsible for his or her own destiny, and those who do not succeed have only themselves to blame. Seduced by narratives resembling 'the American dream', Poles support the rich and successful and accept the uneven redistribution of wealth and social inequalities, and the Polish media propagate this 'rags-to-riches' mantra, which is presented as available to everyone. Within this context the discourse of enterprise and entrepreneurship assumes great significance.

The discourse of neoliberalism and *homo entrepreneurus*

The enterprise discourse in Poland

If the deployment of the *homo sovieticus* discourse facilitated the legitimisation of the reduction of the role of the state and the minimisation of welfare, the *homo entrepreneurus* discourse similarly produces and reproduces the neoliberal model of economy, and also reshapes how people think and act. The discourses are interrelated, though not necessarily articulated together. The term *homo sovieticus* was explicitly popularised predominantly in the academic and public sphere via various genres (academic articles, interviews with sociologists and philosophers) and was very rarely present in official, political documents; one can imagine politicians wanting to avoid alienating large numbers of the electorate. Nevertheless, the discourse provided justification for political initiatives that moved the country away from its communist past. The discourse of *homo entrepreneurus*, however, has dominated the neoliberal party manifestos and became rapidly popularised by the public media. The discourses have a mutually reinforcing relationship not only between the arguments used but also more importantly on the basis of common neoliberal ideology.

The neoliberal solutions to the problems of poverty and unemployment emphasise the need for a change of attitudes, values and behaviours of those who are 'guilty' of being the losers in transition. The government restricts the role of the state, and disciplines the poor and unemployed by withdrawing its assistance in line with the postulated motto of 'take matters into one's own hands' (*weź los w swoje ręce*), which is seen as a natural solution to any individual problem, including unemployment. Since the withdrawal of the state from various functions means that the regulatory competence of the state is shifted on to individuals, this form of neoliberal moralisation (Brown 2006) acts as a regulative mechanism of constant segregation for economically useful and useless individuals. In the public discourse of the past 20 years the dominant voices have been those of the privileged beneficiaries of the neoliberal economy, while the voices of losers are silent, neglected or simply branded as the marginal complaints of those who do not understand the new system (Golka 2009).

This cultural governance (Fairclough 2005), governing by shaping and changing the culture of dependency (and moral deficiency), aims to produce the 'entrepreneurial self' (Peters 2001). Indeed, the moral regulation known from many Western states including the United Kingdom during the 1980s (Keat and Abercrombie 1991; Ray 1991) is being adopted in Poland with the same ideological aim of shaping social relations based on the principles of competition, individualisation of society and the creation of 'responsible' individuals. There are some obvious similarities in the mechanisms of this cultural reconstruction (Peters 2001), including the aforementioned reshaping of social policy in order to discipline individuals through the reduction of social assistance, legitimised by the stigmatisation and pathologisation of poverty and unemployment. Similar to Western states, the Polish government reinforces views attributing individual success to an entrepreneurial attitude and resourcefulness (Skora 2011); however, we see this process not only as a tool of neoliberal governance of welfare, but in the case of Poland as a deliberate way of orchestrating the expropriation of the common, a point we will return to shortly.

Entrepreneurship is typically presented as beneficial for societies, as entrepreneurs are believed to perform socially beneficial roles and contribute to prosperity and economic development. The entrepreneur, it is noted in the literature, makes a fundamental contribution to economic growth by establishing firms and offering innovative technology (Baumol *et al.* 2007). This connection between entrepreneurship and economic growth is seen as essential (Spulber 2011) and for this reason governments should make it easy for entrepreneurs to form and run businesses by introducing policies focusing on 'unleashing entrepreneurship' (Baumol *et al.* 2007). Evoking Schumpeter's ideas of entrepreneurship as a fundamental phenomenon of economic development (Schumpeter 1934), most of the literature on entrepreneurship depicts entrepreneurs in a positive manner, as people who are superior and extraordinary (Berglund and Johansson 2007). The typical representation of the entrepreneur is as the hero of capitalism (Burch 1986; Gilder 1981) or economic life (Gilder 1984). This way of portraying entrepreneurs as 'an ideal type or object of desire' (Williams 2012), built on the image of the (male) hero with super-normal qualities (Ogbor 2000; Bill *et al.* 2010) is constantly reproduced. As Berglund and Wigren (2012, p. 10) note, 'it seems hard to escape the grand narrative of entrepreneurship, constantly emphasizing the heroic, profit-making entrepreneur, and the creation of fast growing firms that can play powerful games in a market-driven society'.

These ideological narratives have been evident in Polish public discourse since the early stages of transformation; however, they have become particularly intense since 2001, with the foundation of the neoliberally oriented political party the Civic Platform (Platforma Obywatelska: PO), and its subsequent growing importance on the Polish political scene. In the 2001 election PO was the largest opposition party, remained the second largest party at the 2005 election and in 2007 and 2011 PO won the parliamentary elections. The 2001 political manifesto of the Civic Platform was summarised by the slogan 'To free the energy of all Poles' (Platforma Obywatelska 2001). The primary concern of the Civic Platform, clearly emphasised in their political promises, was to free the entrepreneurial spirit via the ongoing liberalisation of the Polish economy. Solutions proposed by the Civic Platform included lowering taxes, the marketisation of public services, or in more general terms a shift in the balance between the rights of entrepreneurs and businesses, which would be restored through a flexible labour market. From this perspective there are no other solutions for creating jobs and limiting unemployment other than the neoliberal panacea known from Western narratives: entrepreneurial activity. Helping entrepreneurs and facilitating an entrepreneurial climate is presented as the only way of creating economic growth, which, as neoliberal politicians claim, automatically increases the standard of living of the whole society and minimises poverty. Interestingly, the problem of the poor and unemployed was not seen as worth a separate chapter in the official election programme; instead the authors demonstrated their concern with public spending, presenting it in negative terms as *marnotrawione pieniadze* ('wasted money') (Platforma Obywatelska 2001, p. 11). This familiar reasoning evokes the narratives linking entrepreneurship with positive outcomes for the whole society and it is expressed in enthusiastic statements such as: 'In today's economy, the "growth hormone" of labour demand is the development of entrepreneurship. If we want it to happen in Poland, we need "to help Polish entrepreneurs, stimulate the natural resourcefulness of Poles"' (Platforma Obywatelska 2001, p. 6). Most of this logic was repeated in the subsequent election programmes in 2005, 2007 and 2011, with the emphasis on the stimulation of economic growth via the facilitation of entrepreneurship by limiting the intervention of the state in the economy, limiting the control and inspection of businesses, the reduction of taxes and the reduction of labour costs (Rokita and Kawalec 2005).

The recontextualisation of the Western discourse of *homo entrepreneurus*, which has occurred predominantly through political texts emphasising the importance of entrepreneurship, is also accompanied by the introduction and dissemination of the entrepreneurial myth in academic contexts. Polish academics have enthusiastically promoted and glorified entrepreneurship, since it is perceived as the fundamentally important activity that stimulates the economy, through technological and organisational innovations, investment and capital growth, minimisation of unemployment and improvement of social and technological infrastructure (Adamczyk 1995). The education of Polish society on the importance of entrepreneurship goes further than in any other European country, exemplified by the fact that in 2009 the government introduced entrepreneurship as a compulsory subject in all secondary schools (Kołodziejska 2012). The younger Polish generation learns about entrepreneurship from academic texts accentuating individual material gains above any other benefits of enterprise. Entrepreneurship is defined as:

[A] specific human attitude towards surrounding people and environment, expressed in creative and active efforts to improve the existing state of things, ready to take on new activities or expanding existing ones, and strive to achieve complex – usually increased – material benefits that lead to a noticeable growth in achieved profits (income) and the improvement of living and working conditions.

(Piecuch 2010, p. 38)

Additional references to Schumpeter (1962) conveniently emphasise entrepreneurship as an activity of reorganising already existing means of production (rather than creating anything new). Clearly the Polish hero–entrepreneur is the one who, driven by rent seeking, accumulates capital through dispossession and actively seeks out opportunities for the extraction of rents from the common. This discourse has had significant effects on Polish society and on the material well-being of many Poles, to which we now turn.

The effects of the entrepreneurship discourse: 'petty entrepreneurs' and the economic elite

Official narratives present a glorious impression of Polish entrepreneurship referring to the high number of newly established businesses as a miracle; the statistics from 2012 record a large increase in the number of new entrepreneurs, and this is attributed to the successful governmental policy of stimulating entrepreneurship (Jedliński 2013). Others point out that a large number of new entrepreneurs have been forced into self-employment through job loss or a lack of other opportunities. These necessity 'entrepreneurs' responded to the growing deregulation and flexibilisation of the labour market by becoming subcontractors in order to retain their jobs (often providing services for their former employers), with the pension contribution and the cost of employment shifted to them. The neoliberal media has conveniently not provided any comparison between the growth of entrepreneurship and the high number of job losses recorded in 2011 and 2012 (Kolany 2012), an easy process, as 30 per cent of employees are employed on short-term 'junk contracts'.

Funds from the European Union have contributed to the number of newly established businesses, and during the past five years 125,000 microenterprises have been created; however, only 20 per cent stay in business for more than a year (Dąbrowski 2012), and in some cases the European Union grants were used for consumption and pension contributions rather than investment. According to Eurostat (MSP 2012), Polish small enterprises have the lowest level of innovation (technological and non-technological) in Europe, which indicates that most of these petty enterprises represent a survival strategy for those who were forced into self-employment rather than the claimed flourishing of entrepreneurial spirit. Fragmented, individualised social relations, weakening any forms of socialisation, result in the unmaking of the Polish working class, replacing any form of collectivity with autonomous entrepreneurs. As Tabb (2002, p. 29) notes, 'the aim of neoliberalism is to put into question all collective structures capable of obstructing the logic of the pure market'.

It would seem that a large number of 'entrepreneurs' lack positive motivation to develop their enterprises and have simply been left with no other options in a state that has decimated social welfare and collective activity. These 'losers', however, represent only one side of the story. In the Polish case the analysis of the operationalisation of the nodal discourse *homo entrepreneurus* needs to go beyond the problem of the dissemination of the importance of entrepreneurship as a tool for disciplining individuals. The mechanism of Polish transformation from the communist system to capitalism differs from the Western transition from feudalism to capitalism (and the consolidation of the capitalist rule). The economic imaginary of *homo entrepreneurus* has played a particularly important role in the process of transition 'not from plan to market, but from plan to clan' (Stark 1990), or what Staniszkis (1991) labels 'political capitalism'. As Frane and Tomšič (2012) note, the nature of post-communist society is influenced by the political elites, who exert control over the transition process. In our analysis we make an attempt to examine the role of the *homo entrepreneurus* discourse as one of the key discursive resources (along with *homo sovieticus*) used to legitimise the self-reproduction of the ruling class.

This ruling class does not necessarily resemble the class of private proprietors, who claimed economic power through primitive accumulation during the period of transition that led to the emergence of capitalism. In Poland (and other Eastern European transition economies) the new *grande bourgeoisie* (Szelényi and Szelényi 1995) is made up of the communist nomenclature (Staniszkis 1991), which has established itself as a new economic elite in the absence of a substantial class of private proprietors. We agree with Zybertowicz (2006) that it is virtually impossible to fully comprehend today's economic and social 'reality' of Poland without understanding the largely unrecognised (or deliberately neglected) mechanisms of post-communist transformation, which have seen a transition 'from good communists to even better capitalists' (Stoica 2004), and a largely fictitious portrayal of post-socialist entrepreneurship.

Scattered attempts to uncover how the old (communist) power structure was reproduced in the neoliberal state indicate that cadres rather than capitalist entrepreneurs have been the main beneficiaries of transformation, as the former communist elite (nomenclature) have successfully converted their political power into economic ownership. The magnitude of this process (begun in the late 1980s) intensified during the process of privatisation of the public sector in the 1990s. As Stark (1990, p. 351) notes, 'rather than simply stimulating the expansion of the traditional private sector, policy makers began designing variety of measures for the privatization of the public sector itself'. The political bourgeoisie, made up of members of the old communist elite, successfully enhanced and consolidated its role in economic life and emerged as one of the key groups of the new entrepreneurial class. Staniszkis

(1991, p. 129) describes the reallocation of state assets into the hands of the former communist elite as 'making owners of the nomenklatura'. Accompanied by economic frauds, organised crime, rampant corruption and non-accountability, these 'dirty phenomena' (Zybertowicz 2006, 2008) are at the very core of transformation rather than incidental pathologies, as the mainstream literature on transformation suggests (Wnuk-Lipiński and Ziółkowski 2001, cited in Zybertowicz 2006). Lü (2000, p. 234) adds that in almost all the former communist countries, public officials 'had been transformed from revolutionary cadres to "feudal nobles" enjoying a "legitimized corruption" of privileges. They were soon to become "new-age entrepreneurs", empowered with pre-transition connections and privileges.' Those members of the communist elites, who managed to convert their political capital into economic wealth, took advantage of the myriad systemic flaws of transformation and, more specifically, the preconditions they actively created.

Hanley (1999, p. 143) refers to transformation in Poland as 'the surreptitious seizure of state-owned property by communist-era officials', the 'propertisation' of the nomenclature resulting in the enriching of the former cadres at the expense of society. This process of siphoning off resources from the state initiated more than 20 years ago still prevails in the current Polish economic 'reality', signifying a large-scale expropriation of the common. We refer here to Harvey's (2003) 'accumulation by dispossession' deliberately engineered by elites, of which the privatisation of public assets results from both internal motivation and external pressure (for example, in return for financial assistance). In Harvey's sense, accumulation by dispossession is an alternative to Marx's primitive accumulation and includes the processes of appropriation of wealth by capital, without creating value in production, as the neoliberal policies are characterised by the redistribution of wealth and income rather than by growth generation (Harvey 2005).

Accumulation by dispossession can take many forms. The Polish context differs from the violent process of expropriation, in that, through mass scale social engineering the process happens in society voluntarily and is successfully incorporated into the capitalist logic. The Polish state apparatus has facilitated conditions for capital accumulation and accumulation by dispossession to occur simultaneously, and in an interconnected way through the intense dissemination of the narratives of *homo entrepreneurus*. When, through the discursive strategies the heroic image of the entrepreneurs becomes naturalised, material dimensions fostering the climate of entrepreneurship can be created without any contestation.

The consequences of the *homo entrepreurus* discourse are two-fold. On the one hand, the Polish state apparatus uses the discourse similarly to Western governments to stigmatise poverty via narratives of a culture of dependency (Fairclough 2000), and to legitimise dismantling the welfare state, shifting responsibilities for poverty from state to individuals (Graff 2012). On the other hand, it is used to facilitate conditions for the ongoing expropriation of the common. We refer here to what Jones and Murtola (2012a) describe as the 'open secret of entrepreneurship' – dispossession of value produced in common. In the context of the Polish neoliberal project we could argue that this expropriation of the common, which takes place when the entrepreneur excludes others (involved in cooperative effort) from the value they created and becomes the only beneficiary of this value, has even more extended meaning. Clearly the appropriation of the production from the common is captured by the entrepreneur (via branding, intellectual property rights, etc.), but in the case of Poland, the common appropriated by the 'entrepreneurs' includes not just the productive capacity and former public goods but rather a mass scale appropriation of the nation's whole productive property by the new capitalist class (Kowalik 2012). Instead of dividing the wealth created by the common with the common, Tittenbrun (1995) and Poznański (2000, 2001) demonstrate how over the period of transformation neoliberal policies reduced almost 9,000 state-owned enterprises to 70 (Żaryn 2013) via legal and illegal means, facilitating accumulation by dispossession and consolidating the power of a new class of 'entrepreneurs'. This theft from the public (selling state companies at depressed values) has created a class of private capitalists made up of an emerging 'entrepreneurial' group of the former communist political elite, foreign investors and a new petty bourgeoisie (small business owners). Labelling the elite as 'entrepreneurs' enables them to maintain their economic power, elevates their status to the heroes of Polish economy and reinforces neoliberal 'political capitalism'. As Harvey (2005, p. 40) notes, the open project resulting in 'the restoration of economic power of a small elite would probably not gain much support'; thus the neoliberal discursive smokescreen articulating entrepreneurship as something that everyone can engage with and benefit becomes a useful tool in gaining social legitimacy for capital accumulation.

Conclusion

This chapter seeks to build on the body of literature that develops a critical understanding of entrepreneurship (see e.g. Ogbor 2000; Armstrong 2005; Hjorth and Steyaert 2009; Steyaert and Hjorth 2007; Jones and Spicer 2009; Kenny and Scriver 2012; Tedmanson *et al.* 2012) which not only challenges the notion of entrepreneurship as an exclusively positive and desirable activity, but more importantly highlights the hegemonic effects of ideologically driven entrepreneurialism (Verduijn *et al.* 2014). Typically, the majority of academic critique of entrepreneurship focuses on the contestation of entrepreneurship, but rarely engages in debates on the more fundamentally important issue of the 'gross inequities of what is done under cover of "entrepreneurship"' (Jones and Murtola 2012b, p. 117). Thus, we contribute to those limited accounts classified as the dystopian perspective on entrepreneurship (Verduijn *et al.* 2014), which provides an insight into how entrepreneurship deployed as an ideological discourse supports the reproduction of capital (Costa and Saraiva 2012). Similar to Costa and Saraiva (2012), we noted that the promotion of entrepreneurship (in our case in an academic context as well as in the public domain) contributes ideologically to 'the raising of the contemporary capitalist enterprise as the only possible model for the generation of wealth in society' (Costa and Saraiva 2012, p. 590). However, our contribution goes further with regard to uncovering the way in which entrepreneurialism serves to provide ideological support for the expropriation of the common. In this sense, we agree with Jones and Murtola (2012a, p. 647) when they say that 'a recognition of the other side, of the expropriation of the common, is hardly discernible'; and that highlighting the mechanisms of how entrepreneurship captures and expropriates the common is indeed 'one of the greatest contributions of critical understandings of entrepreneurship' (Verduijn *et al.* 2014, p. 99). Our account of how entrepreneurship can be deployed as an ideological solution to crisis, but also how dispossession and expropriation of the common 'produces particular forms of inequality and domination' (Jones and Murtola 2012b, p. 133), further illustrates the profound necessity of exposing entrepreneurship to public examination.

Specifically, we have argued that the linear modernist frameworks used to conceptualise profound social changes, such as those of transformation in Poland, tend to neglect not only the historical context of particular countries, but more importantly ignore the role and power of economic and political elites in the process. In our view, the way in which neoliberalism has unfolded in Poland has involved the recontextualisation of a Western discourse into the Polish context, with its material operationalisation being influenced by key discursive features of the existing Polish context. We have argued that during periods of major social change articulated discursive resources are deployed, and their plausibility is particularly important for their further dissemination, appropriation and translation into material practice.

In proposing this approach, we explored how certain discoursal and non-discoursal 'moments' of social life (Fairclough 2013) affected the emergence, selection, implementation and retention of the Polish neoliberal discourse via the key polarised, nodal discourses of the 'demons' of the communist past and the 'new' entrepreneurial future. We demonstrated how the edited and re-edited discourse of *homo sovieticus* was used as a tool to stigmatise (certain behaviours), but more importantly how this nodal discourse was operationalised. The demeaning way of describing the poor and the unemployed was used as the sole explanation for the 'incidental' problems of transformation, providing the neoliberal elite with an effective technology for reinforcing their agenda. Thus, we believe, the constitutive effects of the discourse of *homo sovieticus* modified the institutional materiality leading to the retreat of the state. We have argued that instead of addressing the causes of problems of transformation rooted in the political and economic domination of the neoliberal social order, the government deployed the ideological discourse of entrepreneurship as the sole route out of these problems. Similar to Western states, the Polish government used the discourse of entrepreneurship as the tool of the neoliberal governance of welfare, but also as a deliberate way of orchestrating the expropriation of the common. We demonstrated how, by engineering the privatisation of public assets, the Polish government facilitated accumulation by dispossession, and how by labelling the elite as 'entrepreneurs', and using a discursive smokescreen of entrepreneurship, the restoration and consolidation of a new class of 'entrepreneurs' was legitimised.

References

Adamczyk, W. (1995), Przedsiębiorczość. *Przegląd Organizacji*, **11**, pp. 12–15.

Armstrong, P. (2005), *Critique of Entrepreneurship: People and Policy*, Basingstoke: Palgrave Macmillan.

Balcerowicz, L. (2004), *Wkierunku ograniczonego państwa*, Pruszkow: Oficyna Wydawnicza Rewasz.

Bauman, Z. (2006), *Praca, konsumpcjonizm i ubodzy*, Krakow: WAM.

Bauman, Z. (2011), *Collateral Damage: Social Inequalities in a Global Age*, Oxford: Polity Press.

Baumol, W., Litan, R. and Schramm, C. (2007), *Good Capitalism, Bad Capitalism, and the Economics of Growth and Prosperity*, New Haven, CT: Yale University Press.

Berglund, K. and Johansson, A. (2007), The entrepreneurship discourse – outlined from diverse constructions of entrepreneurship on the academic scene. *Journal of Enterprising Communities: People and Places in the Global Economy*, **1**(1), pp. 77–102.

Berglund, K. and Wigren C. (2012), Soci(et)al entrepreneurship: The shaping of a different story of entrepreneurship. *Tamara – Journal for Critical Organization Inquiry*, **10**(1), pp. 9–22.

Bermúdez J.M. (2012), *The Neoliberal Pattern of Domination: Capital's Reign in Decline*, Leiden: Brill.

Bill, F., Bjerke, B. and Johansson A.W. (2010), *(De)mobilizing the Entrepreneurship Discourse: Exploring Entrepreneurial Thinking and Action* (ebook), Cheltenham: Edward Elgar.

Blachnicki, B. (2011), Obywatele na scenie życia politycznego-ewolucja czy rewolucja. In A. Walecka-Rynduch (ed.), *Współczesna przestrzeń polityczna*, Kraków: Oficyna Wydawnicza AFM, pp. 25–39.

Brown, W. (2006), *Edgework: Critical Essays on Knowledge and Politics*, Princeton, NJ: Princeton University Press.

Burch, J.G. (1986), *Entrepreneurship*, New York: John Wiley & Sons.

Chouliaraki, I. and Fairclough, N. (1999), *Discourse in Late Modernity*, Edinburgh: Edinburgh University Press.

Costa, A.S.M. and Saraiva, L.A.S. (2012), Hegemonic discourses on entrepreneurship as an ideological mechanism for the reproduction of capital. *Organization*, **19**(5), pp. 587–614.

Cukiernik, T. (2012), Państwo opiekuńcze jest tyranem! *Opcja na Prawo*, **6**.

Dąbrowski, P. (2012), Hodujemy pokolenie leniwych biznesmenów. *Dziennik Gazeta Prawna*.

Fairclough, N. (2000), *New Labour, New Language?* London: Routledge.

Fairclough, N. (2003), *Analyzing Discourse*, London: Routledge.

Fairclough, N. (2005), Critical discourse analysis in transdisciplinary research. In R. Wodak and P. Chilton (eds), *A New Agenda in (Critical) Discourse Analysis:*

Theory, Methodology and Interdisciplinarity, Amsterdam: John Benjamins Publishing, pp. 53–70.

Fairclough, N. (2007), Discursive transition in Central and Eastern Europe. In Shi-Xu (ed.), *Discourse as Cultural Struggle*, Hong Kong: Hong Kong University Press, pp. 49–73.

Fairclough, N. (2013), *Critical Discourse Analysis: The Critical Study of Language*, London: Routledge.

Frane, A. and Tomšič, M. (2012), The dynamics of elites and the type of capitalism: Slovenian exceptionalism? *Historical Social Research*, **37**(2), pp. 53–70.

Gadomski, W. (2004), Jak walczyć z biedą. *Gazeta Wyborcza*, **244**, pp. 12–13.

Gilder, G. (1981), *Wealth and Poverty*, New York: Bantam Books.

Gilder, G. (1984), *The Spirit of Enterprise*, New York: Simon and Schuster.

Golka, M. (2009), Polska transformacja w perspektywie postkolonialnej. *Ruch Prawniczy, Ekonomiczny i Socjologiczny*, **2**, pp. 439–456.

Graff, A. (2012), Więcej niż równy kawałek tortu. *Gazeta Wyborcza*.

Hanley, E. (1999), Cadre capitalism in Hungary and Poland: Property accumulation among communist-era elites. *East European Politics and Societies*, **14**(1), pp. 143–178.

Harvey, D. (1996), *Justice, Nature and the Geography of Difference*, Malden, MA: Blackwell.

Harvey, D. (2003), *The New Imperialism*, Oxford: Oxford University Press.

Harvey, D. (2005), *A Brief History of Neoliberalism*, Oxford: Oxford University Press.

Harvey, D. (2010), *The Enigma of Capital: And the Crises of Capitalism*, London: Profile Books.

Hjorth, D. and Steyaert, C. (eds) (2009), *The Politics and Aesthetics of Entrepreneurship. A Fourth Movements in Entrepreneurship Book*, Cheltenham: Edward Elgar.

Jaroszyński, P. (2012), Pulapki państwa opiekuńczego. *Nasz Dziennik*.

Jedliński, K. (2013), Rekord polskiej przedsiębiorczości. *Puls Biznesu*.

Jędrzejko, M. (2008), Fawele po polsku. *Gazeta Wyborcza*.

Jessop, B. (2004), Critical semiotic analysis and cultural political economy. *Critical Discourse Studies*, **1**(1), pp. 1–16.

Jones, C. and Murtola, A-M. (2012a), Entrepreneurship and expropriation. *Organization*, **19**(5), pp. 635–655.

Jones, C. and Murtola, A-M. (2012b), Entrepreneurship, crisis, critique. In D. Hjorth (ed.), *Handbook on Organisational Entrepreneurship*, Cheltenham: Edward Elgar, pp. 116–133.

Jones, C. and Spicer, A. (2009), *Unmasking the Entrepreneur*, London: Edward Elgar.

Kabaj, M. (2010), Bezrobocie – mity i rzeczywistość. Available at www.lewica. pl/?id=23009 (accessed 5 May 2013).

Keat, R. and Abercrombie, N. (eds) (1991), *Enterprise Culture*, London: Routledge.

Kenny, K. and Scriver, S. (2012), Dangerously empty? Hegemony and the construction of the Irish entrepreneur. *Organization: The Critical Journal of Organization, Theory and Society*, **19**(5), pp. 615–633.

Kolany, K. (2012), Polski rynek pracy jak w Hiszpani i Portugalii. Available at www. bankier.pl/wiadomosc/Polski-rynek-pracy-jak-w-Hiszpanii-i-Portugalii-2702413. html (accessed 5 May 2013).

Kołodziejska, A. (2012), Można, czy nie można nauczyć przedsiębiorczości w szkole? Available at http://bezrobocie.org.pl/wiadomosc/764239.html (accessed 18 April 2012).

Komorowski, B. (2012), The opening speech at the 22nd Economic Forum in Krynica-Zdrój, 4–6 September. Available at www.forum-ekonomiczne.pl/xxii-economic-forum-2012/?lang=en#.Ucrgd7RY7lI (accessed 5 May 2013).

Kowalik, T. (2009), *Polska Transformacja*, Warszawa: Muza SA.

Kowalik, T. (2012), *From Solidarity to Sellout. The Restoration of Capitalism in Poland*, New York: Monthly Review Press.

Laclau, E. and Mouffe, C. (1985), *Hegemony and Socialist Strategy*, London: Verso.

Leśniewski, B. and Zieliński, M. (2001), Bezrobocie: Polityczne rękodzieło. *Wprost*, **952**(8).

Lü, X. (2000), *Cadres and Corruption: The Organizational Involution of the Chinese Communist Party*, Stanford, CA: Stanford University Press.

Marody, M. (2011), Homo sovieticus and the change of values. In H. Best and A. Wenninger (eds), *Landmark 1989: Central and Eastern European Societies Twenty Years After the System Change*, Berlin: Lit Verlag, pp. 80–90.

Marsh, D. and Thomas, P. (2010), Poland, postcolonialism and the neoliberal project. Paper presented at the Critical Management Studies Conference, Naples, 21–24 July.

Mirowski, P. (2013), *Never Let a Serious Crisis go to Waste: How Neoliberalism Survived the Financial Meltdown*, London: Verso.

MSP (2012), Wiadomości Gospodarcze. Ministerstwo Skarbu Państwa. Available at http://inwestor.msp.gov.pl/portal/si/338/25869/Obecny_stan_aktywnosci_innowacyjnej_polskich_przedsiebiorstw.html (accessed 15 June 2013).

Ogbor, J.O. (2000), Mythicizing and reification in entrepreneurial discourse: Ideology-critique of entrepreneurial studies. *Journal of Management Studies*, **37**, pp. 605–635.

Peters, M. (2001), Education, enterprise culture and the entrepreneurial self: A Foucauldian perspective. *Journal of Educational Enquiry*, **2**(2), pp. 58–71.

Piecuch, T. (2010), *Przedsiębiorczość. Podstawy teoretyczne*, Warszawa: Wydawnictwo C.H. Beck.

Platforma Obywatelska (2001), *Program Platformy Obywatelskiej*, Warszawa. Available at www.platforma.org (accessed 5 May 2013).

Poznański, K. (2000), *Wielki przekręt. Klęska polskich reform*, Warszawa: Towarzystwo Wydawnicze i Literackie.

Poznański, K. (2001), *Obłęd reform: Wyprzedaż Polski*, Warszawa: Ludowa Spółdzielnia Wydawnicza.

Rae, G. (2012), *Austerity Policies in Europe: The Case of Poland*, Berlin: Freidrich Ebert Foundation Central and Eastern Europe.

Ray, L. (1991), A Thatcher export phenomena? The entreprise culture in Eastern Europe. In R. Keat and N. Abercrombie (eds), *Enterprise Culture*, London: Routledge.

Rogulska, B. (2012), Czy Polacy boja się kryzysu?, Warszawa: CBOS. Available at www.cbos.pl/PL/wydarzenia/20_konferencja/Czy%20Polacy%20boja%20sie%20kryzysu_BR.pdf (accessed 15 June 2013).

Rokita, J. and Kawalec, S. (2005), *Państwo dla obywateli. Plan rządzenia 2005–2009*, Warszawa: Instytut Pastwa i Administracji.

Schumpeter, J.A. (1934), *The Theory of Economic Development*, Cambridge, MA: Harvard University Press.

Schumpeter, J.A. (1962), *Teoria rozwoju gospodarczego*, Warszawa: PWN.

Sheets, C.A. (2013), The East European miracle: How did Poland avoid the global recession? *International Business Times*, 17 May.

Shields, S. (2007), From socialist solidarity to neo-populist neoliberalisation? The paradoxes of Poland's post-communist transition. *Capital and Class*, **31**(3), pp. 159–178.

Shields S. (2012), Opposing neoliberalism? Poland's renewed populism and post-communist transition. *Third World Quarterly*, **33**(2), pp. 359–381.

Sikorska, M. (2004), Changes in the attitudes of Poles towards work: Self-fulfilment and fear of unemployment. In A. Jasińska-Kania and M. Marody (eds), *Poles among Europeans*, Warsaw: Wydawnictwo Naukowe, pp. 20–41.

Skora, M. (2011), Transformacja jako czynnik konstuujacy nowe grupy zagrożone ubóstwem w kontekście twz. trudnych rynków pracy. In M. Popow, P. Kowzan, M. Zielińska, M. Prusinowska and M. Chruściel (eds), *Oblicza biedy we współczesnej Polsce*, Gdańsk: Doktoranckie Koło Naukowe 'Na Styku' Uniwersytet Gdański, pp. 19–34.

Smith, D. and Lee, R. (2011), *Geographies and Moralities: International Perspectives on Development, Justice and Place*, Wiley-Blackwell ebook.

Spulber, D. (2011), The role of the entrepreneur in economic growth. In R. Litan (ed.), *Handbook on Law, Innovation and Growth*, Cheltenham: Edward Elgar, pp. 11–45.

Staniszkis, J. (1991), *The Dynamics of the Breakthrough in Eastern Europe: The Polish Experience*, Berkeley: University of California Press.

Stark, D. (1990), Privatization in Hungary: From plan to market or from plan to clan? *East European Politics and Societies*, **4**(3), pp. 351–392.

Steyaert, C. and Hjorth, D. (2007), *Entrepreneurship as Social Change*, Cheltenham: Edward Elgar.

Stoica, C.A. (2004), From good communists to even better capitalists? Entrepreneurial pathways in post-socialist Romania. *East European Politics and Society*, **18**(2), pp. 236–277.

Sum, N. (2012), Towards a cultural political economy: Discourses, material power and (counter-)hegemony. *CPERC Working Paper 2012–01*.

Sutowski, M. (2009), Słownik transformacyjny: homo sovieticus. *Krytyka Polityczna*, 21 June. Available at www.krytykapolityczna.pl/Transformacja-20-lat-po/Slownik-transformacyjny-Homo-sovieticus/menu-id-227.html (accessed 5 May 2013).

Swader, C. (2010), Homo sovieticus in interpersonal relationships before and after the collapse of communism. In H. Best and A. Wenninger (eds), *Landmark 1989: Central and Eastern European Societies Twenty Years After the System Change*, Munster: LIT Verlag, pp. 62–79.

Szelényi, I. and Szelényi, S. (1995), Circulation or reproduction of elites during the postcommunist transformation of Eastern Europe. *Theory and Society*, **24**(5), pp. 615–638.

Tabb, W. (2002), *Unequal Partners: A Primer on Globalization*, New York: The New Press.

Tarkowska, E. (2008), Extreme poverty in Poland: Insufficient knowledge, paternalistic attitudes, negative stereotypes. Paper presented at the International Conference on Exclusion, a Challenge to Democracy. How Relevant is Joseph Wresinski's Thinking? held at the Paris Institute of Political Studies – ATD Fourth World, AFSP, CEVIPOF, 17–19 December.

Tedmanson, D., Verduijn, K., Essers, C. and Gartner, W.B. (2012), Critical perspectives in entrepreneurship research. *Organization*, **19**(5), pp. 531–541.

The Economist (2012), Don't forget Poland, 18 December. Available at www.economist.com/blogs/freeexchange/2012/12/learning-abroad (accessed 12 May 2013).

The Warsaw Voice (2012), Poland: An economic powerhouse in Europe. Available at www.warsawvoice.pl/WVpage/pages/article.php/25210/article (accessed 13 June 2013).

Thompson, E. (2008), Postkolonialne refleksje. Na marginesie pracy zbiorowej "From Sovietology to Postcoloniality: Poland and Ukraine from a Postcolonial Perspective" pod redakcją Janusza Korka. Porównania, **5**, pp. 113–125.

Tischner, J. (1990), Homo sovieticus – pomiędzy Wawelem a Jasna Góra. Tygodnik Powszechny, 24 April.

Tischner, J. (2005), Etyka Solidarności oraz homo sovieticus, Kraków: Znak.

Tittenbrun, J. (1995), The managerial revolution revisited: The case of privatisation on Poland. Capital and Class, **19**(1), pp. 21–32.

Tusk, D. (2011), Kancelaria Premiera (official information channel of The Office of the Polish Prime Minister. Available at www.youtube.com/watch?feature=player_embeddedandv=ScdrhIMFs_w#.

Tyszka, K. (2009), Homo sovieticus. Two decades later. Polish Sociological Review, **168**, pp. 507–522.

Van Dijk, T. (2006), Discourse and manipulation. Discourse and Society, **17**(2), pp. 359–383.

Verduijn, K., Dey, P., Tedmanson, D. and Essers, C. (2014), Emancipation and/or oppression? Conceptualizing dimensions of criticality in entrepreneurship studies. International Journal of Entrepreneurial Behavior and Research, **20**(2), pp. 98–107.

Willemans, D. (2010), The Homo Sovieticus Mentality. The Failure of Socialism and its Consequences, Krakow: Uniwersytet Jagielloński.

Williams, C. (2012), The hidden enterprise culture. In A. Southern (ed.), Enterprise, Deprivation and Social Exclusion: The Role of Small Business in Addressing Social and Economic Inequalities (ebook), Abingdon: Routledge.

Wnuk-Lipiński, E. (2008), Długie pożegnania. Tygodnik Powszechny, 13 January.

Wnuk-Lipiński, E. and Ziółkowski, M. (2001), Pierwsza dekada niepodległości. Próba socjologicznej syntezy, Warszawa: ISP PAN.

Wojciechowski, M. (2002), Socjalizm to kradzież. Rzeczpospolita, 25–26 May.

Wozniak, W. (2012), Nierówności społeczne w programach partyjnych i prezydenckich, Warszawa: Wydawnictwo Naukowe Scholar.

Żaryn, S. (2013), Zwijanie przemysłu. Gazeta Bankowa, 16 June.

Zybertowicz, A. (2006), Hidden actors, overlooked dimensions and blind intellectuals. Nine paradoxes that account for institutionally entrenched ignorance. In S. Eliaeson (ed.), Building Democracy and Civil Society East of the Elbe: Essays in Honour of Edmund Mokrzycki, London: Routledge, pp. 226–237.

Zybertowicz, A. (2008), Przemoc Układu: O peerelowskich korzeniach sieci biznesowej Zygmunta. In R. Sojak and A. Zybertowicz (eds), Transformacja podszyta przemocą: O nieformalnych mechanizmach przemian, Toruń: Wydawnictwo Naukowe Uniwersytetu Mikolaja Kopernika, pp. 187–266.

15 Deconstructing ecopreneurship

Annika Skoglund

[T]he transition to sustainable development will need ecopreneurship on a grand scale.

(Pastakia 1998, p. 157)

Indeed, there may be social ecopreneurial capacities latent in all of us just waiting to be given an opportunity to bring this sense of sustainable community to worldly fruition.

(Isaak 2002, p. 88)

Introduction

Ecopreneurship has been constructed as a latent salvation to the negative effects of entrepreneurship. Entrepreneurship relies on and supports a market system, and is unable 'to deal with the negative environmental externalities' that the market brings with it, Pastakia argues (1998, p. 157). This leads to a depletion of biodiversity, eco-systems imbalance and a loss of resilience, which puts our life-support systems at stake (ibid.). By changing the prefix to 'eco', on the other hand, efforts have been made to embed entrepreneurship in the socio-ecological system. Ecopreneurship seeks to 're-define the way business is conducted' and offers 'some hope for retrieving the situation' (ibid., p. 157). It even 'embodies prophylactic action', Pastakia insists (ibid., p. 172). Ecopreneurship can be commercial or social, and according to Isaak (2002), some ecopreneurships are more ideal than others. Pastakia seems to agree, writing about 'ecopreneurship of the highest order' (Pastakia 2002, p. 97). First-rate ecopreneurship, Isaak elaborates, is 'an existential form of business behaviour committed to sustainability' that is 'transformative for self, society and economic sector' (ibid., p. 81). Ecopreneurship thus shares some purifying capabilities with ecology, a concept that has become a 'new metaphor for cleansing ourselves of all mental pollution' (Wali 1995:107).

Several scholars contend that ecopreneurs are different from entrepreneurs. Ecopreneurs are 'a new breed of eco-conscious change agents' (Pastakia 1998, p. 157) who 'radically transform the economic sector' (Isaak 2002, p. 81) with a 'life-long commitment to sustainability in everything that is said and done' (ibid., p. 82). Furthermore, ecopreneurs can be more or less 'radical' (Tilley and Young 2009) and find 'spiritual fulfilment' (Isaak 2002, p. 84) in protecting and restoring 'the wellbeing of the natural environment' (Tilley and Young 2009). With the help of creative strategies, they should even seek to diffuse their ideas 'to the largest possible clientele in the shortest possible time' (Pastakia 1998, p. 158).

As the foregoing examples from academic literature attest, texts about ecopreneurship shape the ecopreneur at the intersection of discourses of enterprise and ecology in a variety of ways. Academic literature on ecopreneurship, however, is united in the idea that ecopreneurship is a positive activity that should increasingly replace traditional forms of entrepreneurship. While scholars have criticised entrepreneurship literature for how it supports a masculine hero entrepreneur (for a summary see Berglund and Johansson 2007; Tedmanson *et al.* 2012), who expropriates the common (Jones and Murtola 2012), often with a religious face (Sorensen 2008), the ecopreneur has unquestionably been left to flourish in a taken-for-granted goodness of creativity and self-transcendence (see e.g. Aydin 2013).

This chapter will, first, trace the dissemination of prevailing assumptions about ecopreneurship, and second, examine with some scepticism the 'truths' generated. The bulk of the empirical material for the analysis comprises various texts drawn from academic literature, policy and social media. By merging Derridean deconstruction with category analysis, I will analyse ecopreneurship to decipher the omitted and unsaid that underpin the truth about the goodness of the ecopreneur. That is, I will critically interrogate what sort of figure the ecopreneur is becoming with a focus on the potential it offers, the practices it is described to pursue, and the promises it is supposed to deliver. If we deconstruct this category of entrepreneur, we will learn what qualities he or she is required to possess to fall within the category. In addition, we will learn 'who' is included in, or excluded from, ecopreneurship discourse (cf. Jones and Spicer 2009, p. 85). The chapter ends by exploring the consequences of the accentuating knowledge production about ecopreneurship and its correlating attraction: the ecopreneur.

The chapter is organised as follows. I begin by introducing the reader to Derridean deconstruction and poststructuralist 'readings' of text via intertextual category analysis. I then turn to the texts to trace which potentials, practices and promises the category of ecopreneur comprises. I discuss the findings by summing up the main characteristics of the ecopreneur, to unearth common polarisations as well as the unsaid and obscured. To conclude, I offer the reader membership in the category of ecopreneur to provoke reflection about such a refinement of one's potential.

Deconstruction, intertextuality and category analysis

A text not only produces but presupposes who we are and what we should do, letter for letter, word for word. In this sense, Derridean deconstruction follows in the footsteps of Saussure, who argued that 'the signified and the signifier are the two sides of one and the same production'; they are inseparable (Derrida 1981, p. 18). There is no language that provides us with virgin meanings; rather, we should embrace an awareness of the transformations that occur when texts unfold. There is 'no simple element that will be *present* in and of itself, referring only to itself' but we have a formal play of differences, or traces, that do not fit with 'structure' (ibid., pp. 26–27, italics in original). Derrida speaks about 'differance' with an 'a', which should be understood as something unstable, a 'movement of differences' (Newman 2001, p. 9). 'Differences are effects of transformations', and meanings are only created in relation to past and future elements of language 'in an economy of traces' (Derrida 1981, pp. 27–29). However, we seldom think actively about the differences and 'opposite other' that make up meaning; we rather 'imagine an essential ontology attached to the language we use' (Calás 1993, p. 307). Essentialist representations may thus be found in descriptions of both objects and practices, which are analysed as if they were ex-nihilo observations. From a Derridean poststructuralist perspective, however, the text is never written on a blank sheet; it is underlaid by other texts and multiple sources (Hartman 1992). A text is not envisaged as a single document with a sole voice, but is constituted by polyphonic authors and readers in a dialogic context. To understand a text intertextually is thus to rearticulate traces of the author, the reader and the context. Following these steps, the researcher can pursue a deconstructive reading by questioning 'the way in which texts try to portray the truthfulness of what they are saying by noticing' what is left out and unsaid in the construction of truth effects (Calás 1993, p. 307). The impossibility of providing exact descriptions opens the way to a deconstruction that turns 'concepts against their presuppositions, to reinscribe them in other chains' and 'produce new configurations' (Derrida 1981, p. 24). Moreover, Derrida wished to bring forth the historical paths of metaphysics, i.e. to unearth the fixed, unquestioned legacies within philosophical perspectives (see e.g. Derrida 1995), to be able to unravel their current effects and 'critique [of] oppositional and binary thinking' (Newman 2001, p. 2). A Derridean deconstruction can thus afford to explore a 'radical exteriority' that does not reinvigorate the authority or structures that are sought to be overthrown (ibid.). Rather, Derrida warns us against radical political theory that is indebted to metaphysical structures, i.e. that still incorporates the potential for domination, Newman (2001) contends.

Even if there is an apparent distance between Derridean deconstruction and ethnomethodology, I aim to bridge this distance a little and unsettle truths with the help of category analytical tools. Via 'category analysis' it is possible to look at the details of how texts reproduce truth by how the categories, seen as collections of associated characteristics and features (cf. Antaki and Widdicomb 1998), omit 'the other' and create differences in repetitive ways. A category analysis can, for example, pinpoint which qualities, activities and expectations belong to a certain category, and discuss these in relation to other categories as well as to social norms (Börjesson and Palmblad 2008). In the case of ecopreneurship, we may thus analyse how the category 'ecopreneur' is constructed, somehow, by how academics, policy makers and ecopreneurs themselves speak about the members of this category. Hence, this merger of Derridean deconstruction and category analysis opens up for an analysis that may include a set of texts, to acknowledge a broader play of differences. While Derridean deconstructionists often focus on one individual text to unearth in detail the obscured and unsaid in a specific play of differences, my choice of many texts opens up for an acknowledgement of a richer variety of differences and their intertextuality. Undoubtedly, this deconstructionist manoeuvre requires an additional analytical tool to be able to systematically handle the articulate richness that construes ecopreneurship. That is why a category analysis becomes a vital complement to the Derridean deconstruction of authority.

Regarding the choice of texts, the texts analysed have chosen the researcher, rather than the other way around. This reversal of methodological thinking is fundamentally a decontructionist exercise inspired by Derrida (2008, p. 48ff.) by which the researcher lets him/herself be led from one conceptualisation of ecopreneurship to another. To be able to start somewhere, I searched on Google Scholar to find those works on ecopreneurship that have been mostly cited. Upon reading some of these articles, I found a group of scholars who discussed the topic among themselves, and I let their internal citation practice lead me onward. I proceeded with the analysis of these interrelated articles with a focus on 'who' the ecopreneur became in the terminology of these key ecopreneurship scholars. I repeated the exercise of a normal Google search to find policy texts in line with my research curiosity. Finally, I repeated this exercise to find descriptions of practising ecopreneurs. These two latter empirical sources did not show the same degree of direct interrelatedness as in the case of the scholarly genre, and thus represent a more arbitrary choice of empirical material, i.e. I used what I arbitrarily found on the internet. To simplify, using Derrida, who considers that there is no centre of contexts, and hence no 'absolute anchoring' to rely on (Wood 2009) but that '[t]he subject is a fable' (Derrida 1995, p. 102), my reading focused on what qualities the category of ecopreneur was given in the literature. To merge the analytical approaches of deconstruction and category analysis is thus fruitful for a general exploration of the unintended consequences, or effects, of absent others as well as bystanders, in the construction of the ecopreneur.

Analysing the construction of this somehow special category of entrepreneur can unearth how belonging to this category is textually negotiated and legitimately obtained, what explanatory power such membership gives and what the limits of membership are (Börjesson and Palmblad 2008, p. 29). Derrida considers categories and distinctions as 'acts of violence', since they establish meaning (Frazer and Hutchings 2011, p. 9). Membership in one category may open up certain possibilities for us, while membership in another category may direct our path differently. To exemplify, in comparison to the category of 'young criminal', a 'young entrepreneur' will be coupled to a more prosperous future, in less need of social support (Börjesson and Palmblad 2008). Conclusively, classification of characteristics and qualities into categories not only seeks to fixate knowledge, but is unavoidably a moral activity that spreads from one text to another, often with wide distribution socially (ibid., p. 50). Texts produced by experts, for instance, 'slide over into the social space' (Calás 1993, p. 310). It can therefore be helpful to deconstruct ecopreneurship by analysing the categorisation efforts that are repeated between academic literature and policy texts, as well as self-portraits by those who categorise themselves as ecopreneurs. I therefore focus on the category of ecopreneur by focusing in turn on the nuances of the potentials (i.e. qualities), practices (i.e. what the ecopreneur does) and the promises (i.e. what ecopreneurship is to bring about). After an illustration of the nuances that construe the category of ecopreneur, I show how the texts analysed polarise the category of ecopreneur to the category of the conventional entrepreneur. In comparison to Harvey Sacks' category analysis with a focus on 'occasionedness' (Antaki and Widdicomb 1998, p. 3), a Derridean deconstruction of categories, however, needs a reading of category construction intertextually. This means that the analysis needs to bring in the reformed context and effects of transformations, to unravel the repetitively unsaid. Having stated this, what Sacks and Derrida share is that neither neglect that 'an authentic story draws on the same resources as a subversive alternative that pretends to authenticity' (Potter 1996, p. 3). This is important to remember, as the analysis aims to uncover how others seek to establish truth, without questioning if their construction is true or not, but questioning the effects of their truth-assembling.

Just an ecopreneur – or an ideal green–green ecopreneur?

Commercial ecopreneurs, as Schuyler (1998) stated, ensure that environmental problems are addressed at the same time as profits are made. These commercial types of ecopreneurs, moreover, mainly seek 'to maximise personal (organisational in the case of a corporation) gains by identifying green business opportunities' (Pastakia 1998, p. 159). They take a lead role and demonstrate 'the economic benefits that come from being greener', Schaper (2002, p. 27) adds. They have 'entrepreneurial flair' and provide a 'missionary zeal' for the organisation, Dixon and Clifford (2007, p. 327) suggest. They define the ecopreneur as an individual or an organisation that merges an economically viable business with environmental and social values (Dixon and Clifford 2007). Hence, ecopreneurs are those who manage to secure that 'sound business practice' is 'genuinely consistent with idealism and environmental best practice' (ibid., p. 327). Furthermore, the ecopreneur is sometimes constructed as a mission-driven middle hand between large corporations engaged in corporate social responsbility (CSR), small communities with environmental needs and governmental agencies. According to Schaper (2002, p. 27), however, they are not subject to government regulations, stakeholders and lobby groups, but act as proactive push factors.

They make environmental 'progress in their core business' and 'generate new products, services, techniques and organizational modes that substantially reduce environmental impacts and increase the quality of life' (Schaltegger 2002, p. 46). Ecopreneurs, then, differ from 'conventional entrepreneurs' in that they 'build bridges between environmental progress and market success' (ibid.). One specific ecopreneur is used as an example, portrayed to 'embody the combination of strong environmental and social values with an energetic entrepreneurial attitude' (ibid., p. 47). The ecopreneur is conclusively constructed by Schaltegger (ibid., p. 47) as someone who shows 'personal mastery' and 'consider[s] their professional life as a creative act'.

At the same time as the ecopreneur is established academically to be a very special individual, Isaak (2002, p. 88) proposes that 'there may be social ecopreneurial capacities latent in all of us'. On the other hand, some scholars outspokenly strengthen the emphasis that the 'ecopreneur' is a man: 'The ecopreneur is driven by the desire to protect the environment while achieving his [sic] entrepreneurial vision' (Ndedi 2011). Isaak extends his definition of ecopreneur and considers there to be an 'ideal type of ecopreneur' and outlines ecopreneurs who are more or less green (Isaak 2002, p. 81). In fact, he concludes that first-rate ecopreneurs create more than green businesses, they create 'green-green businesses' and seek to 'radically transform the economic sector' (ibid., p. 81). Isaak continues to aggressively accuse conventional entrepreneurship and mainstream management for a lack of consideration of the Earth as a 'home'. Globalised managers are too mobile, leaving their roots behind, or even cutting them off, he insists. The 'corporate headquarters', furthermore, is left in 'organisational chaos' in the chase of 'freedom from' rather than 'freedom to' (ibid., p. 82). The globalised manager even 'leaves a mess – environmental waste … and a disintegrated family where he or she is rarely to be seen' (ibid., p. 82). When an ecopreneurial start-up grows into a business to maintain, it is thus better if the ecopreneur leaves and starts up a new green-green business, Isaak contends.

Turning to ecopreneurship in developing countries, an even stronger spiritual quality is added. In India, Isaak exemplifies, social ecopreneurship builds on 'deep spirituality' and is fundamentally 'an existential choice' (ibid., p. 84). The basis for entrepreneurship is not personal 'material rewards', but 'spiritual fulfilment' and 'worldly success in the long term' (ibid.). Grassroots ecopreneurs are likened to 'change agents' and one of them has even been called an 'agricultural saint' (Pastakia 1998, p. 164). Moreover, these ecopreneurs often target niche markets (Pastakia 2002) and direct their efforts to villages and small communities to stimulate self-reliance (Pastakia 1998). There are also expectations of ecopreneurs to stimulate change in others. They should, for example, educate users about non-sustainability and create a demand for alternatives (Pastakia 1998).

They should even meet consumer resistance, which could reach a maximum 'when the change implies embracing a new philosophy or outlook to life since this could mean drastically modifying consumption patterns and lifestyles', Pastakia concludes (1998, p. 165).

Even though academics have spoken about prospective ecopreneurship policies (Moghimi and Alambeigi 2012), few hard-core ecopreneurship policy texts can be found through a Google search. The United Nations Environment Program (UNEP) briefly mentions ecopreneurship in a report on eco-labelling. The report asks if ecopreneurs think differently, and outlines differences between the entrepreneur and ecopreneur. Ecopreneurs are assigned similar potentials, practices and promises as reflected in the academic literature. They are 'highly concerned', feel 'personal obligations', take on 'high responsibility', think about consequences for their children and grand-children, are 'open-minded', and seek positive change. Another report, which reviews academic literature in the perimeter of green entrepreneurship, pro-poses that Master's students should be provided with more knowledge to 'allow them to effectively operate their ecopreneurial ventures' (Melay and Kraus 2012).

Thus far, then, there seem to be few policy texts that specifically speak about ecopreneurship. The organisation Ecopreneurship.eu primarily addresses the transition to more sustainable energy systems (Ecopreneur.eu 2014). Green entrepreneurship may thus be a more common concept for policy makers, as the report and review by Melay and Kraus (2012) illustrates. Another concept that also builds on ideas on how communities can support biospheric life is the literature on 'eco-cultures', where more blueprints may be found (see e.g. Böhm *et al.* 2015).

There is a richer variety of ecopreneurial adventures to explore on the internet, from how you can become a 'Green Wedding and Event Planner' (Triple Pundit 2010) or a Pakistani ecopreneur within farmer communities, to tips and tricks offered by a Swedish 'ecomum' who '#justlovessustaina-bilitycommunication' for the sake of her children (Ekomorsan 2014, author translation). Academic literature is sometimes discussed as a back-drop to examples of what eco-ideas people are pursuing in their daily lives. Several blogs and Facebook groups repeat the now familiar potentials, practices and promises of ecopreneurship (see Table 15.1). Both the green ecopreneur and the green-green ecopreneur are common forms. An eco-preneur can, for example, be quite businesslike and help others to 'strate-gise, launch, get funded and drive the business through digital marketing' (Ecopreneur 2014). Or, as an ecopreneur based in Asia describes himself (Merrin 2009):

> I connect businesses with nature conservation projects so that conserva-tion projects have the funds to continue their awesome projects and busi-ness owners have the opportunity to experience how they can improve the world that they live in with their staff.

Table 15.1 Summary of findings: ecopreneurial potentials, practices and promises

Potentials	Practices	Promises
Personal commitment, highly concerned and deeply responsible	Planning for long-term consequences	Sound business merged with environmental and social values
Open-minded	Generating innovations Reducing environmental impact	Positive change
Idealistic	Combining environmental concerns with economic development Providing holistic vision	Translation of idealism into business
Energetic	Taking initiative	New start-ups
Relational being	Networking Forming symbiotic relationships Fostering coexistence	Merging corporations, communities and state agencies, community-level entrepreneurship
Radical	Securing true environmental compliance Meeting consumer resistance to philosophical change	First-rate ecopreneurship Green-green business, modified consumption patterns and lifestyles
Spiritual	Missioning Shouldering our hopes for a better future Harnessing energy of religious movement Self-transcending	Professional life as creative act
Proactive	Pushing frontiers and leading change	Environmental progress
Green leader	Shaping the face of the company	Green brand
Enterprising	Bridging economy, environment and society	Increased quality of life
Commercial	Pulling the whole market towards more environmental progress Using business tools Maximising personal gains	Capitalisation on environmental opportunities
Social	Restoring the planet	Self-reliance
Creative	Deploying creative strategies Educating users about non-sustainability	Diffusion of ecopreneurship

Potentials	Practices	Promises
Intentional	Securing equal respect of all living beings	No one deprived of anything
Mindful	Considering the whole system	Create a movement
Masculine	Protecting the vulnerable nature	Security
Feminine	Protecting coming generations	Sustainability

Even if many descriptions of the ecopreneur promote the commercial type, we are told that ecopreneurs must defend themselves against accusations of greenwashing. The reason is that '95% of eco-friendly products on the market today are greenwashed' (CEO blog nation 2014). It is accordingly important to measure one's greenness, and ensure that all suppliers are as green (CEO blog nation 2014). But it is not only instrumental measurement that is needed. An ecopreneur must take on a personal commitment and concern 'about the whole of humanity'. It is a person or an organisation that is 'not only to make profits, but to serve the humanity and to ensure that the world's resources are available for the new generations' (Quicklogo Blog 2011):

> He [sic] may not be a person or entity only involved in products like solar powered cells, water conservation system or compostable packaging. In fact, an ecopreneur is anyone who ranks environment more than or equally to profits as his [sic] most effective criteria as a business owner.
>
> (Quicklogo Blog 2011, citing Reuters 2007)

The differences between the ecopreneur and the entrepreneur are strengthened in other examples. The intentionality of the ecopreneur is emphasised and polarised to the accidental conventional entrepreneurs (Quicklogo Blog 2011). Entrepreneurs are described as motivated by greed and capital accumulation. They seek to become millionaires, while ecopreneurs are constructed as provident and focused problem solvers. Ecopreneurs even redefine wealth: the Quicklogo Blog continues by referring to John Ivanko, co-author of a book about ECOpreneuring. Their redefinition of wealth embraces 'life's tangibles: health, wellness, meaningful work, vibrant community life and family' (Quicklogo Blog 2011). Besides, the ecopreneur becomes a category attached to an increased life expectancy, since this category values life, in comparison to its dark side other. Ecopreneurs even become a category which secures 'that every living being' is equally respected. An ecological account of respect for all life (i.e. not only human life) is thus added to the practices linked to the ecopreneur as category. Ecopreneurship, furthermore, comes 'with the promise' that no one should be deprived of anything. (Quicklogo Blog 2011) Ecopreneurs should even empower their customers and stakeholders, we are enthusiastically told at another website (Homegrown 2013).

> There is an emphasis on one word here: relationships. We all know that we are in an interconnected world. We live and operate in a system of relationships that affect each other. Therefore ecopreneurs are those entrepreneurs who are conscious that their enterprises are systems operating within a larger system: our society and natural environment. To be aware of this makes one deliberate in building businesses that respect the natural environment – not exploiting it, and ensuring that we diminish the negative impact we do.
>
> (Homegrown 2013)

On this website key steps are provided to facilitate ecopreneurship. These steps include that one should consider the whole system, be passionate, purpose-driven and be conscious and mindful. A true ecopreneur should not 'just create an enterprise' but 'Create a Movement'. Finally, to be an ecopreneur is to be 'more than "environmentally conscious"'; it is 'really an *awareness* of how you relate to the bigger picture' that is needed. This means, the text continues, that 'it is a lifestyle that *you* yourself as the entrepreneur must live out' (Homegrown 2013, italics in original).

Ecopreneurial potentials, practices and promises

In comparison to entrepreneurship discourse, where the individual is predominantly taught to self-manage as a human resource (Rose 1998), in relation to the market and the specific company within which that person works (Costa and Saraiva 2012; see also Du Gay 1996), the first-rate ecopreneur is mainly constituted in opposition to such a work–life identity. Evidently, ecopreneurship thrives on various forms of resistance, from visions of subtle reformations to the direct transformation of structures (cf. Berglund and Gaddefors 2010). While the entrepreneur has been categorised as self-interested (Jones and Spicer 2009), the above counter-narrative about ecopreneurial qualities construes relationality and concern for others as a basic quality and potential for the ecopreneurial self. The neoliberal mass phenomenon of entrepreneurship for everyone, to foster an enterprising self to collectively defend society from a lack of self-management and self-reliance (Berglund and Skoglund 2016), is remoulded in the case of ecopreneurship. Ecopreneurship fosters an individual who is critical of entrepreneurship, to facilitate self-regulation with the help of basic assumptions within ecology to defend the environment from the impacts of conventional entrepreneurship. By transforming what scholars understand as ancient ecological practices – often found far away – into ecopreneurial ones, there is a hope that the human being could better adapt to an ecological understanding of the world in which we all live. This adaptation builds on the concept that we all live off nature, understood as providing us with ecological services via ecopreneurs, who are moulded with great eco-specificity. Table 15.2 summarises as 'potentials, practices and promises' the characteristics found to be paramount in becoming an ecopreneur.

Notably, a similar 'psychologising rhetoric' that surrounded the 'charismatic leader' (Calás 1993, p. 313) appears in the summary of the ecopreneur in Figure 15.1. There is a personalisation of the ecopreneur, who is constructed with the help of extraordinariness and an orientation towards non-physical faith, a constant inclusion of the Divine or personal values, so-called 'spirituality at work' (cf. Kauanui *et al.* 2010, p. 53), but importantly, complemented with an underdog position (cf. Skoglund 2015). This spiritual face of the ecopreneur has a family resemblance with entrepreneurship policies and academic literature that constantly hunt for our 'creativity' (Sorensen 2008). In talk about entrepreneurship, '[c]reativity comes to signify an ongoing and never completed transition, life as always being on the way to somewhere else, a perpetual change of mind, an inspiration of the Spiritus Sanctus of a new millennium' (Sorensen 2008, p. 91). The entrepreneur becomes an 'economic savior' (ibid., p. 91), while the ecopreneur thrives on becoming an ecological saviour, renewing all economic relations. To be able to deliver this alternative form of entrepreneurship, a more or less stark difference is

Table 15.2 How ecopreneurship literature polarises between the two categories

Ecopreneur	Entrepreneur
Ecological	Market-oriented
Problem solver	Problem creator
Responsible	Irresponsible
Spiritual	Rational
Alternative	Mainstream
Rooted	Rootless
Ordered	Chaotic
Integrated	Disintegrated
Creative	Repetitive
Self-transcendent	Self-obsessive
Relational	Selfish
Collaborative	Competitive
Moderate	Excessive
Radical	Robotic
Open-minded	Narrow-minded
Informative	Secretive
Intentional	Strategic
Transformative	Degrading
Positive	Blank
Long-term thinker	Short-term thinker
Self-reliant	Capital-reliant
Provident	Greedy

CCN Ecopreneurs make an effort to empower people that they know, members of their community, and work towards engaging others globally to contribute financially towards conservation based projects.

A CCN Ecopreneur embodies the key elements of a social entrepreneur, by finding ways to help solve social problems in our society. Like social entrepreneurs, Ecopreneurs don't leave it up to governments or the business sector to solve social issues. They find what is not working and solve the problem by changing the system, spreading the solution and persuading people to get involved in making the change.

At CCN we have identified that governments and businesses are not acting fast enough to stop the destruction of our world's forests. This is a global problem that has an impact on everyone, and we have created a solution that allows everyone to make a difference by funding forest conservation projects. Through social marketing initiatives, CCN is able to create a global network of "Green Minded" individuals and businesses to contribute to saving our world's forests.

CCN offers people a career path within our unique business system. To learn more about the benefits of becoming an eCo-Entrepreneur and the type of rewards you can receive, read our section on "**How You Can Earn**" and **Join us today**!

Figure 15.1 'Entrepreneurial hero' repeated with ecological touch. CCN (Conservation Central Network) promotes ecopreneurship to stop the destruction of forests.

Source: Network (2015).

made up between the two categories of entrepreneurs: the ecological and the conventional. Since my deconstruction was based on the foregoing ecopreneurship literature, policy texts and ecopreneurial endeavours described on various websites, the summary in Table 15.2 comprises the polarisation these texts made of the ecopreneur in relation to the conventional entrepreneur. Since conventional entrepreneurship is often strongly criticised from the position of the ecopreneur, Table 15.2 illustrates a polarisation between the two categories.

How can we then, as critical entrepreneurship scholars, problematise the taken-for-granted goodness of ecopreneurship? Apart from criticising ecopreneurship for how it moulds a specific type of underdog heroism (Skoglund 2015), it can also be problematised in relation to how 'natural resources have been brought into the cycle of capital' (Jones and Murtola 2012, p. 641). Jones and Murtola explore where conventional entrepreneurship is placed in contemporary class struggle, i.e. a struggle situated on the terrain of control of the public domain. They conclude that entrepreneurship is production in and of the common, and expropriation of the common. However, there is a difference between the conventional entrepreneur they describe, who is to be in control of flows, and the ecopreneur, who is to insert him/herself into the socio-ecological flow to accomplish self-reliance by missioning, bridging and hopefully restoring the common. The ecopreneur is thus still the 'locus of creation', but may have changed how and where cooperation and production of the common is achieved (Jones and Murtola 2012, p. 649). Moreover, while entrepreneurship is production in and of the common, as well as expropriating the common (Jones and Murtola 2012), ecopreneurship openly problematises the latter and thrives on that problematisation.

'What is the absent other then?' one must ask in a deconstruction. Even if the category analysis has shown how texts produce truth by mobilising differences, it is still unclear what the nuances in the texts and their intertextualities have obscured. There are at least two unsaid issues that play an important role in ecopreneurship. The first issue refers to humans and the second issue refers to nature. I am here particularly interested in those humans who are members of neither category but who serve to support the truth of the saviours of our time. I am also curious about how the strong critique of expropriation of the common within ecopreneurship is served by a silence about nature. In the constitution of ecopreneurship as authentically spiritual, radical, alternative and environmentally progressive, 'ordinary' humans and nature are left on the sidelines. They figure as mere bystanders, underpinning the story about the creative ecologically concerned class. Non-active and non-creative humans who do not fulfil the social norm of being active eco- or entrepreneurs silently function as consumers who passively receive until they are converted. Nature, which supposedly is to be protected, is 'creatively' turned into a good or service. As David Harvey notes for the creation of ecosystems in general, these come about to mirror 'the social systems that gave rise to them' (Harvey 1996, p. 185). Ecopreneurial projects have understudied effects on wealth distribution, and by extension, unknown social consequences. In a different way than we are used to within entrepreneurship, the above-mentioned textual bystanders, namely non-entrepreneurial humans and nature, secure the potentialities, practices and promises of the ecopreneur at the same time as this bystanding resurrects its enemy: expropriation of the common. That is, even first-rate, green-green, ideal ecopreneurship that thrives on this contemporary class struggle transforms nature and human beings into logistical units that are to be spiritually processed. Even the truth of first-rate ecopreneurship builds on conventional classifications and separations, of use for continued accumulation by some. Furthermore, the basic presumption in many ecopreneurial projects is that some people living alternatively, or just far away from countries defined as 'developed', are somehow also 'closer to nature' (Harvey 1996, p. 188). Thus, if we acknowledge that ecopreneurship is a Western construction, indebted to 'the romantic reaction to modern industrialism', it is also easier to understand why Indigenous groups are unsentimental about their ecological practices (Harvey 1996, p. 187). This unsentimental mode of pre-capitalist being leads to other forms of social-ecological transformations and unintended consequences that the ecopreneurial literature neglects. Tellingly, the creation of the ecopreneur also destroys (Schaltegger 2010, p. 76) in unpredictable ways. Scholars in entrepreneurship studies broadly speaking have nonetheless neglected 'what is destructed' (Berglund and Gaddefors

2010, p. 143), due largely to their will to positive prophesies. Thus, future research on ecopreneurship initiatives could advance both theory and practice by unpacking the link between sustainable development and entrepreneurship more thoroughly. For instance, it may be illuminating to analyse the destruction involved when risks are outsourced from the state to the people in the making of poor communities into adaptable self-reliant ones (Duffield 2007, p. 69).

Reflection

After reading this chapter about the masculine and spiritually empowered category of ecopreneurs, some readers may actually be tempted to belong to it. According to Isaak (2002, p. 88), ecopreneurial qualities may after all be latent in all of us. If you subject yourself to the possibility of becoming an ecopreneur, you should start by releasing your slumbering abilities to value life and humanity more than money, even if you aim to become a so-called commercial ecopreneur. If you aspire to become a category member of the most charming ideal green-green ecopreneur, however, you will have to prepare for deeper enhancements of personhood. You will be expected to intentionally, creatively and passionately contribute to solutions for survival to deliver a higher life expectancy, environmental progress and self-reliance. At the same time as you toil to further this missionary process, you will be required to express either spirituality or radicalness. You will henceforth be qualified as ecopreneur if you manage to express that you have turned inward, gone beyond awareness and pursued self-transcendence (Aydin 2013, pp. 35–37). In addition, you will have to live your life as a creative act in support of ecological co-existence. Furthermore, you will have to excel in open-mindedness, socially embracing other humans as the holistic relational being that you are, at any time ready to convert them with full-frontal attack, from unsustainable killers to supporters of sustainable life. Inseparable from a counter-movement, you will refine your own potentials, practices and promises in opposition to the selfish and greedy characters that occupy the pernicious category of entrepreneur and its promise of the premature death of all. You will emerge having a problematic relationship to the ordinary and be inextricably entrenched in creating something new. You will end up as an underdog hero, moderately and providently pushing frontiers. But let us neither be fooled by the ideal charming ecopreneur, nor mired in its credible complacency and secluded accumulation, utility and logistical life that support its truth. Instead, let us ask and never finally answer: What life is possible for the absent other?

Conclusion

This chapter has traced the dissemination of prevailing assumptions about ecopreneurship and problematised the taken-for-granted goodness of ecopreneurship by merging Derridean deconstruction with category analysis. With the help of this method, the nuances of the ecopreneurial potentials, practices and promises have been unearthed and the polarisation of the two categories – the ecopreneur and the entrepreneur – has been exposed. The results of this uncovering of the basic assumptions of what ecopreneurship and its correlating subject consist of show that ecopreneurship thrives on a criticism of conventional entrepreneurship, specifically its ecological impacts, and awards the ecopreneur the role of the underdog hero. I found both feminine and masculine forms of underdog heroism. One Swedish 'ecomum' spoke about care of future (human) generations, while a more masculine securitisation was offered by ripping up the shirt of a man to release the wildness of the greens growing from his fertile chest. In comparison to a quantitative study about stereotypical gender roles in social entrepreneurship and ecopreneurship, which concludes that 'females are more likely to engage in social and environmental entrepreneurial activity than males' (Hechavarria *et al.* 2012, p. 144), the category analysis pursued in this study shows that a masculine conventional entrepreneurial figure is remoulded into a masculine ecopreneurial one. This softer version, maybe even non-stereotypical, but indeed paternal category of entrepreneur, will probably be affirmed, lived out and enjoyed by both sexes. Ecopreneurship literature, policy texts and ecopreneurial companies alike could thus afford to pay more attention to the effects their fables have on social relations, especially when it comes to a transformation of gender issues and, by extension, repositioned hegemonies. The chapter also unearthed that an odd mix of pre-capitalist practices and conventional entrepreneurial practices constitute ecopreneurship. Such an exoticist interest in pre-capitalist, sometimes spiritualist, ways of living has understudied effects and unknown social consequences that the ecopreneurship literature would need to acknowledge if it is to be taken seriously as more than a predetermined dissemination of a Western legacy. The obscured destructive element of ecopreneurship hides most insidiously behind the face of the first-rate, green-green ideal ecopreneur, who in good faith responds to the outsourcing of risks and seeks to protect some life ecopreneurially.

References

Antaki, C. and Widdicomb, S. (1998), Identity as an achievement and as a tool. In C. Antaki and S. Widdicomb (eds), *Identities in Talk*, London: Sage, pp. 2–15.

Aydin, E. (2013), *The Effect of Individual Creativity on Ecopreneurship: Creativity*, Saarbrücken: Lambert Academic Publishing.

Berglund, K. and Gaddefors, J. (2010), Entrepreneurship requires resistance to be mobilized. In F. Bill, B. Bjerke and W.A. Johansson (eds), *(De)Mobilizing the Entrepreneurship Discourse: Exploring Entrepreneurial Thinking in Action*, Cheltenham: Edward Elgar.

Berglund, K. and Johansson, W.A. (2007), Constructions of entrepreneurship: A discourse analysis of academic publications. *Journal of Enterprising Communities: People and Places in the Global Economy*, **1**(1), pp. 77–102.

Berglund, K. and Skoglund, A. (2016), Social entrepreneurship: To defend society from itself. In A. Fayolle and P. Riot (eds), *Rethinking Entrepreneurship Debating Research Orientations*, London/New York: Routledge, pp. 57–77.

Böhm, S., Pervez Bharucha, Z. and Pretty, J. (eds) (2015), *Ecocultures: Blueprints for Sustainable Communities*, New York: Routledge.

Börjesson, M. and Palmblad, E. (2008), *Strultjejer, arbetssökande och samarbetsvilliga, Kategoriseringar och samhällsmoral i socialt arbete*, Malmö: Liber.

Calás, B.M. (1993), Deconstructing charismatic leadership: Re-reading Weber from the darker side. *The Leadership Quarterly*, **4**(3–4), pp. 305–328.

CEO blog nation (2014), *Being an Ecopreneur: Lily Tran and BoxUp*. Available at http://ceoblognation.com/2014/07/ecopreneur-lily-tran-boxup/ (accessed 2 April 2015).

Costa, A. and Saraiva, L. (2012), Hegemonic discourses on entrepreneurship as an ideological mechanism for the reproduction of capita. *Organization*, **19**(5), pp. 587–614.

Derrida, J. (1981), *Positions*, Chicago, IL: University of Chicago Press.

Derrida, J. (1995), Eating well, or the calculation of the subject. In E. Weber (ed.), *Points … Interviews 1974–1994*, Stanford, CA: Stanford University Press, pp. 255–287.

Derrida, J. (2008), *The Animal That Therefore I Am*, New York: Fordham University Press.

Dixon, S. and Clifford, A. (2007), Ecopreneurship – A new approach to managing the triple bottom line. *Journal of Organizational Change Management*, **20**(3), pp. 326–345.

Du Gay, P. (1996), *Consumption and Identity at Work*, London: Sage.

Duffield, M. (2007), *Development, Security and Unending War, Governing the World of Peoples*, Cambridge: Polity Press.

Ecopreneur (2014), *Business Opportunities*. Available at www.ecopreneur.co.za/green-business-opportunities/ (accessed 16 February 2015).

Ecopreneur.eu (2014), *Memorandum of Understanding and Positions on European Policy*.

Ekomorsan (2014), *Jobbar för en giftfri skola*. Available at http://ekomorsan.com (accessed 2 April 2015).

Frazer, E. and Hutchings, K. (2011), Avowing violence: Foucault and Derrida on politics, discourse and meaning. *Philosophy and Social Criticism*, **37**(1), pp. 3–23.

Hartman, D. (1992), Intertextuality and reading: The text, the reader, the author, and the context. *Linguistics and Education*, **4**, pp. 295–311.

Harvey, D. (1996), *Justice, Nature and the Geography of Difference*, Oxford: Blackwell.

Hechavarria, M.D., Ingram, A., Justo, R. and Terjesen, S. (2012), Are women more likely to pursue social and environmental entrepreneurship? In D.K. Hughes and E.J. Jennings (eds), *Global Women's Entrepreneurship Research: Diverse Settings, Questions and Approaches*, Cheltenham: Edward Elgar, pp. 135–151.

Homegrown (2013), *Ecopreneurs: Creating Mindful, Passionate, Purpose-Driven Movements*, Vol. 2015.

Isaak, R. (2002), The making of the entrepreneur. *Greener Management International*, **38**, pp. 81–91.

Jones, C. and Murtola, A-M. (2012), Entrepreneurship and expropriation. *Organization*, **19**(5), pp. 635–655.

Jones, C. and Spicer, A. (2009), *Unmasking the Entrepreneur*, Cheltenham: Edward Elgar.

Kauanui, S., Thomas, K., Sherman, C., Waters, G. and Gilea, M. (2010), An exploration of entrepreneurship and play. *Journal of Organizational Change Management*, **23**(1), pp. 51–70.

Melay, I. and Kraus, S. (2012), Green entrepreneurship: Definitions of related concepts. *International Journal of Strategic Management*, **12**(2), p. 1.

Merrin, P. (2009), *Asia Ecopreneur, Linking Ecopreneurs from around Asia*. Available at http://asia-ecopreneur.blogspot.se/2009_10_01_archive.html (accessed 2 April 2015).

Moghimi, S.M. and Alambeigi, A. (2012), Government facilitator roles and ecopreneurship in environmental NGOs. *International Journal of Environmental Responsibility*, **6**(3), pp. 635–644.

Ndedi, A. (2011), *The Development of Ecopreneurship Education in South African Universities Curriculum* (30 March 2011).

Network, C.C. (2015), *Be a CCN Ecopreneur*. Available at https://conservation centralnetwork.com/quick-links/how-we-do-it/be-a-ccn-ecopreneur/ (accessed 2 April 2015).

Newman, S. (2001), Derrida's deconstruction of authority. *Philosophy and Social Criticism*, **27**(3), pp. 1–20.

Pastakia, A. (1998), Grassroots ecopreneurs: Change agents for a sustainable society. *Journal of Organizational Change Management*, **11**(2), p. 157.

Pastakia, A. (2002), Assessing ecopreneurship in the context of a developing country – The case of India. *Greener Management International*, pp. 93–108.

Potter, J. (1996), *Representing Reality – Discourse, Rhetoric and Social Construction*, London: Sage.

Quicklogo Blog (2011), *Ecopreneurship – Entrepreneurs and Ecology*. Available at www. quicklogodesign.com/blog/ecopreneurship-entrepreneurs-and-ecology–.VOMe NsYyCll (accessed 16 February 2015).

Rose, N. (1998), *Inventing Ourselves, Psychology, Power and Personhood*, Cambridge: Cambridge University Press.

Schaltegger, S. (2002), A framework for ecopreneurship – Leading bioneers and environmental managers to ecopreneurship. *Greener Management International*, pp. 45–58.

Schaltegger, S. (2010), A framework and typology of ecopreneurship: Leading bioneers and environmental managers to ecopreneurship. In T.M. Schaper (ed.), *Making Ecopreneurs: Developing Sustainable Entrepreneurship*, Farnham, Surrey: Gower Publishing, pp. 75–94.

Schaper, M. (2002), The essence of ecopreneurship. *Greener Management International*, pp. 26–30.

Schuyler, G. (1998), Merging economic and environmental concerns through ecopreneurship. *Digest*, **98**(8), pp. 1–6.

Skoglund, A. (2015), Climate Social Science – Any future for 'blue-sky research' in management studies. *Scandinavian Journal of Management*, **31**(1), pp. 147–157.

Sorensen, M.B. (2008), 'Behold, I am making all things new': The entrepreneur as savior in the age of creativity. *Scandinavian Journal of Management*, **24**, pp. 85–93.

Tedmanson, D., Verduyn, K., Essers, C. and Gartner, B.W. (2012), Critical perspectives in entrepreneurship research. *Organization*, **19**(5), pp. 531–541.

Tilley, F. and Young, W. (2009), Sustainability entrepreneurs – Could they be the true wealth generators of the future? *Greener Management International*, **55**, pp. 79–92.

Triple Pundit, people, planet, profit (2010), *Ecopreneurship Opportunity: Green Wedding and Event Planner*. Available at www.triplepundit.com/2010/09/ecopreneurship-opportunity-green-wedding-and-event-planner/ (accessed 2 April 2015).

UNEP (2009), Training Handbook – Ecolabelling – DTIE, Enabling developing countries to seize eco-label opportunities – Capacity building and technical assistance for industries and governments in developing economies. *Programme*, U.N.E. (ed.).

Wali, K.M. (1995), ecoVocabulary: A glossary of our times. *Bulletin of the Ecological Society of America*, **76**(2), pp. 106–111.

Wood, S. (2009), *Derrida's 'Writing and Difference': A Reader's Guide*, London/New York: Continuum International Publishing Group.

Index

Page numbers in *italics* denote tables, those in **bold** denote figures.

Taylor & Francis eBooks

Helping you to choose the right eBooks for your Library

Add Routledge titles to your library's digital collection today. Taylor and Francis ebooks contains over 50,000 titles in the Humanities, Social Sciences, Behavioural Sciences, Built Environment and Law.

Choose from a range of subject packages or create your own!

Benefits for you
>> Free MARC records
>> COUNTER-compliant usage statistics
>> Flexible purchase and pricing options
>> All titles DRM-free.

Benefits for your user
>> Off-site, anytime access via Athens or referring URL
>> Print or copy pages or chapters
>> Full content search
>> Bookmark, highlight and annotate text
>> Access to thousands of pages of quality research at the click of a button.

REQUEST YOUR **FREE** INSTITUTIONAL TRIAL TODAY

Free Trials Available
We offer free trials to qualifying academic, corporate and government customers.

eCollections – Choose from over 30 subject eCollections, including:

Archaeology	Language Learning
Architecture	Law
Asian Studies	Literature
Business & Management	Media & Communication
Classical Studies	Middle East Studies
Construction	Music
Creative & Media Arts	Philosophy
Criminology & Criminal Justice	Planning
Economics	Politics
Education	Psychology & Mental Health
Energy	Religion
Engineering	Security
English Language & Linguistics	Social Work
Environment & Sustainability	Sociology
Geography	Sport
Health Studies	Theatre & Performance
History	Tourism, Hospitality & Events

For more information, pricing enquiries or to order a free trial, please contact your local sales team: www.tandfebooks.com/page/sales

Routledge
Taylor & Francis Group

The home of
Routledge books

www.tandfebooks.com

For Product Safety Concerns and Information please contact our EU
representative GPSR@taylorandfrancis.com
Taylor & Francis Verlag GmbH, Kaufingerstraße 24, 80331 München, Germany

www.ingramcontent.com/pod-product-compliance
Ingram Content Group UK Ltd.
Pitfield, Milton Keynes, MK11 3LW, UK
UKHW021011180425
457613UK00020B/897